CAPITALISM
MAGIC
THAILAND

The **ISEAS – Yusof Ishak Institute** (formerly Institute of Southeast Asian Studies) is an autonomous organization established in 1968. It is a regional centre dedicated to the study of socio-political, security, and economic trends and developments in Southeast Asia and its wider geostrategic and economic environment. The Institute's research programmes are grouped under Regional Economic Studies (RES), Regional Strategic and Political Studies (RSPS), and Regional Social and Cultural Studies (RSCS). The Institute is also home to the ASEAN Studies Centre (ASC), the Singapore APEC Study Centre, and the Temasek History Research Centre (THRC).

ISEAS Publishing, an established academic press, has issued more than 2,000 books and journals. It is the largest scholarly publisher of research about Southeast Asia from within the region. ISEAS Publishing works with many other academic and trade publishers and distributors to disseminate important research and analyses from and about Southeast Asia to the rest of the world.

CAPITALISM
MAGIC
THAILAND

MODERNITY WITH ENCHANTMENT

PETER A. JACKSON

 YUSOF ISHAK INSTITUTE

First published in Singapore in 2022 by
ISEAS Publishing
30 Heng Mui Keng Terrace
Singapore 119614

Email: publish@iseas.edu.sg
Website: bookshop.iseas.edu.sg

The responsibility for facts and opinions in this publication rests exclusively with the author and his interpretations do not necessarily reflect the views or the policy of the publisher or its supporters.

ISEAS Library Cataloguing-in-Publication Data

Name(s): Jackson, Peter A., author.
Title: Capitalism magic Thailand : modernity with enchantment / by
   Peter A. Jackson.
Description: Singapore : ISEAS - Yusof Ishak Institute, 2022. | Includes
   bibliographical references and index.
Identifiers: ISBN 9789814951098 (soft cover) | ISBN 9789814951975
   (pdf) | ISBN 9789814951982 (epub)
Subjects: LCSH: Magic—Economic aspects—Thailand. | Wealth—
   Thailand—Religious aspects. | Cults—Thailand.
Classification: LCC BF1623 F55J12

Typeset by ISEAS Publishing
Printed in Singapore by Markono Print Media Pte Ltd

Contents

Part Three • How Modernity Makes Magic

Conclusion

Images

Note on Transliteration, Referencing and Honorific Titles

There is no generally agreed system of representing Thai in roman script, and all systems have some limitations because the twenty-six letters of the roman alphabet are not sufficient to represent all the consonants, vowels, diphthongs and tones of Thai. In this book I adopt a modified version of the Thai Royal Institute system of romanizing Thai. This system makes no distinction between long and short vowel forms, and tones are not represented. I differ from the Royal Institute system in using "j" for the Thai "jor jan", not "ch", except in accepted spellings of royal titles and personal names. Hyphens are used to separate units of compound expressions that are translated as a single term in English, such as *latthi-phithi*—"cult". Where a cited author uses a different system of transcribing Thai, that spelling is retained in quotations.

I follow the Thai norm of referring to authors by given names, not surnames, and all citations by Thai authors are alphabetized in the bibliography and elsewhere by given names. I follow authors' preferred spellings of their names in English when this is known rather than following the transliteration system used elsewhere in this book.

Thai has a large number of honorific titles that are used before the names of respected persons and revered deities, spirits and religious figures. In this book honorific titles are italicized, such as *Luang Phor Ngoen*, for "Reverend Father Ngoen". Some of the most commonly used titles in this book and their translations are:

Ajan — A title for a respected Buddhist monk or lay specialist regarded to be a teacher, religious instructor or adept in ritual lore.

Jao — Lord.

Jao Mae — Lord Mother.

Luang Phor — Reverend Father.

Luang Pu — Reverend Grandfather.

Phra — An honorific for a Buddhist monk, Buddha image, deity or royal figure.

Somdet — A royal-conferred title for senior monks in the administration of the Buddhist sangha or monkhood. Also a title for senior members of the royal family.

Thao — Lord.

Introduction

Modern Magic and Prosperity in Thailand

> When Asia's major religious traditions are commodified, they do
> not lose their symbolic power and efficacy. They intimately embrace
> the ... forces of the market. (Pattana Kitiarsa 2008a, p. 8)

Growing numbers of anthropologists and religious studies scholars
have detailed the rise of diverse new forms of both fundamentalist and
magical religiosity in Southeast Asia over recent decades.[1] They have
also outlined the ways that these phenomena fundamentally challenge
the predictions of Weberian sociology—still influential in fields such
as history and politics—that modernity is a process of ineluctable
rationalization and a condition of unavoidable disenchantment.[2]
But these empirically based critical studies have not yet presented
integrated accounts of how modernity produces new modalities of enchantment. While we have excellent critiques of Weberian sociology,
we have comparatively few positive accounts that theorize the productive relationship of modernity to magic and enchantment. In this
study I argue that since the end of the Cold War the performatively
productive role of ritual practice operating in the specific conditions of
neoliberal capitalism, new visual technologies and digital media have
been engines of modern religious enchantment in Thailand and across
mainland Southeast Asia. The performative effects of ritual practice
(Tambiah 1977, 1981, 1985) provide a frame for bringing separate accounts of the enchantments of neoliberalism (Comaroff and Comaroff
2000) and the auraticizing effects of new media (Morris 2000a), as
well as the retreat of rationalizing state power from the religious field

(Hefner 2010), into a fuller account of how modernity makes new forms of magic.

My analysis is built upon a study of cults of wealth centred on a range of Buddhist, Hindu, Chinese and Thai spirits and deities that have become prominent features of the religious landscape in Thailand since the 1980s. While having diverse origins, these cults are not isolated instances of ritual innovation but rather form a richly intersecting symbolic complex that is now central to national religious life, including monastic Buddhism. Emerging from multiple religious and cultural origins, I detail the many similarities among the cults of wealth, their close relationship with cults of amulets and professional spirit mediumship, and I trace how these prosperity cults intersect symbolically in a wide range of settings and ritual products. I explore how movements that began as expressions of popular devotion outside of official Buddhism have moved from the sociological margins to the mainstream of Thai religious life.

An important aim of this book is to bring the significant trans-formations of ritual magic into the history of modern Thailand. I do not argue for the objective reality of magic. But I do argue for the sociological, economic and political reality of magic as a core dimension of modern Thai society and political economy. I present an alternative history of Thai modernity, arguing that neoliberal capital-ism and new media operating across a religious field that is primarily oriented towards ritual practice are together actively producing new forms of enchantment. I focus on prominent instances of modern Thai magic—the symbolic complex of cults of wealth, amulet cults and professional spirit mediumship—as case studies of the processes that have produced new modalities of enchantment at the apexes of the Thai economy and political system over the past four decades.

Understanding the importance of the symbolic complex of cults of wealth requires rethinking the place of Buddhism in the Thai religious field and fashioning an expanded analytical vocabulary that enables us to appreciate the interpenetration, and also the tensions, between these cults and Buddhism. I propose several contributions to the col-laborative endeavour of developing a body of concepts that does full justice to the distinctiveness and expanding diversity of Thai religious life.

The Thai cults of wealth, together with their material expression in cults of amulets and associated rituals of spirit possession, are examples of much broader phenomena of efflorescing religious enchantment across mainland Southeast Asia and beyond. While drawing empirically from Thailand, the arguments presented here speak to religious developments across Asia. In recent times, much academic and media attention has been directed to the growth of fundamentalisms in different religious traditions. A parallel and equally significant expansion of magical cults has also been taking place. Over the past several decades, religious modernity has trended in two apparently opposing directions, with fundamentalisms and magical cults both being equally contemporary phenomena that together reflect inherent divisions and tensions within the modern condition.

The two analyses presented here—the symbolic complex of Thai cults of wealth and the production of magic in global modernity—are intimately interrelated. By studying Thai prosperity cults, I explore the conditions under which capitalist modernity produces novel forms of enchantment, not only in Southeast Asia but more generally across the globe. The symbolic and ritual intersections of the multiple cults of wealth in Thailand provide a basis for understanding how new forms of enchantment have emerged in a wide number of societies. While drawing on an analysis of post–Cold War cults of wealth in Thailand, this study presents broader conclusions that are relevant beyond Southeast Asia and that provide insights into processes of neoliberal mediatized enchantment at the global level. And while methodologically based within anthropology and cultural studies, the results of this study also have significant implications for all fields of the humanities and social sciences.

To appreciate the central importance of the prosperity cults in Thailand's contemporary religious field requires a theoretical frame based on an understanding of the radical modernity of these ritual enchantments of the market and media. The cults of wealth have at times been misunderstood as residues of premodern "superstitions" and they have been critiqued by doctrinal Buddhists as perverse commodifications that debase Thai religion. These views, which position doctrinal Buddhism as an ideal religious form, hinder the development of a balanced appreciation of how the cults of wealth have emerged and the important roles they play in the religious lives of large numbers of Thais from all social strata across all regions of the country. Accounts that dismiss the cults as premodern residues and religious perversions also prevent us from appreciating the importance of these phenomena beyond Thailand in understanding the production of magical enchantments within global modernity.

Many critiques of the cults of wealth are based on implicit if not explicit assumptions that modernity has a direction that is necessarily rational. These views are so strong in some fields that they have not been overturned even in the face of decades of research demonstrating that they are not valid. By itself, the accumulation of empirical findings of modern magical enchantment—based on several decades of research by dozens of scholars from around the world and published in volumes of monographs and journal articles—has not been sufficient to overturn the teleology of rationalist modernity. It is also necessary to challenge the theoretical foundations of the assumption that modernity has a necessarily rational direction for the results of anthropological research to be taken seriously and to have their full due influence. The critical task is both empirical and theoretical. Theoretical frameworks are needed by which the accumulated empirical evidence of modern enchantment can achieve the force that it warrants.

Furthermore, just as a theoretical frame is needed to give valence to the empirical findings of the international expansion of novel religious forms of enchantment, so too we need a conceptual context to appreciate the full import of the cults of wealth within the Thai religious field. There are two interlocking theoretical projects in this book. One is to present a set of concepts that enable us to appreciate the place of the cults of wealth within the Thai religious field and in relation to Buddhism. I describe the hierarchical dominance of Buddhism in a ritual-centred amalgam composed of multiple, contextually distinct cultic forms that are drawn from diverse cultural sources and which, while cohering into an overarching religious field, do not merge according to current models of hybridity or syncretism. My aim is to provide a set of concepts to better appreciate a religious system that is founded upon irreducible, and expanding, diversity rather than a unitary cosmology or notions of doctrinal orthodoxy. The second theoretical task is then to understand how these diverse cults instantiate processes of modern enchantment at the global level.

Drawing on Bruno Latour (1993), I understand modernity to be a dual condition of ideological rationalization alongside, and in parallel with, practices of ritual-based enchantment. Weber's sociology provides an account of one half of the "world historical process" of modernity; namely, the rationalization of social processes and the disenchantment of world views. What Weber's sociology did not do, and which remains to done, is to fully understand the other half of the world historical process, which has seen the proliferation of multiple alternative modernities based on magical practices and rituals of enchantment. While overlooked, devalued and disparaged in accounts that mistake rationalization for the totality of modernity, processes of modern enchantment are just as globally significant as the rise of new forms of religious doctrinalism and fundamentalism.

To present my intersecting arguments I bring several fields of research into conversation: anthropology, religious studies, history and political studies. I am keenly aware of the risks involved in writing a book that develops two broad sets of arguments that, although related, draw on different disciplinary fields and emerge from distinctive intellectual histories. The real world, however, rarely stays within the safe bounds of the issues and methods of a single academic discipline. While there are risks involved in multidisciplinary research, cross-fertilization between fields of inquiry also has the potential to open up perspectives that remain beyond sight in single-discipline studies.

To make the steps that I have followed across disciplinary boundaries clear I at times summarize past studies. For some readers this might seem that I am covering familiar ground that has already been reported elsewhere. Scholars in different fields, however, do not always read the work of colleagues in other disciplines or appreciate the significance of findings in other fields for their own work. For example, in Chapter One I revisit critiques of Weberian sociology of religion presented by anthropologists of religion because their world-level importance has not yet been fully appreciated in some other disciplines. Much social research continues to operate on the assumption that disenchantment is the inevitable end point of modern processes, if only we are patient to wait long enough.

The chapters in this book are arranged into three sections, which respectively focus on the broader comparative setting and conclusions and the specific case studies of the Thai cults of wealth, amulets and spirit possession. Part One—"Why Religious Modernity Trends in Two Opposing Directions"—outlines critiques of Weberian sociology of religion and Bruno Latour's account of the "modern constitution" as a condition fractured between rationalizing purification and hybridizing practice. In the second chapter of Part One I detail how this fractured modern constitution underpinned the expansion of Western colonial power in Southeast Asia and created lasting divisions within the Thai religious field. Part Two—"Thailand's Cults of Wealth"—is the empirical core of this study, bringing together detailed studies of the cults of wealth as well as outlining conceptual frames to analyse the character of these ritual forms, their amalgamation into a symbolic complex and their close relationships with the cult of amulets and professional spirit mediumship, two other emergent forms of modern enchantment in Thailand. Part Three—"How Modernity Makes

Magic"—presents my conclusions on the imbricated set of forces that are actively producing and remaking new forms of magical enchantment within global modernity.

In this book I further develop some of my earlier work in relation to insights gained from more recent study and from productive conversations with scholars working on religion in Thailand and across the region. I relate my earlier work on Thai religion and forms of power to other studies of Thai magical ritual and place it within a broader narrative of the multiple transformations of religion wrought by global modernity. In several chapters I refer to the doctoral studies of Erick White and Benjamin Baumann, members of a new generation of scholars of urban and rural religiosity in Thailand whose work, at the time of writing, is in the process of being published and is bound to have transformative influences in the years ahead. The work of Bénédicte Brac de la Perrière on spirit cults in Burma and collaborations with networks of scholars researching the efflorescence of spirit mediumship across mainland Southeast Asia have also led me to see the close association of the cults of wealth with possession rituals. I have collaborated with Bénédicte Brac de la Perrière in comparing the rise of new spirit medium cults across the Buddhist societies of mainland Southeast Asia (see Brac de la Perrière and Jackson 2022). And Benjamin Baumann and I have detailed dramatic changes in the gendering of spirit possession rituals in Thailand and Myanmar, where gay and transgender ritual specialists are increasingly assuming roles traditionally held by women (see Jackson and Baumann 2021). Conversations and collaborations with these and other colleagues have helped me see connections I had previously overlooked and have guided me in addressing omissions in my previous studies.

After first reporting the emergence of new cults of wealth during Thailand's decade-long economic boom from the mid-1980s until the onset of the Asian economic crisis in 1997 (Jackson 1999a, 1999b), I waited some years to see if these cults might decline or disappear in the aftermath of the economic turmoil of the late 1990s. I also waited to see whether, as predicted by modernization theory, they might be overcome by forces of rationalizing disenchantment in the face of the transnational supremacy of neoliberal capitalism and globalizing media in the early twenty-first century. However, over two decades after first writing about the cults of wealth, they remain just as important, if not more so, to Thai religious life. It is clearly time to take the cults of wealth seriously and to acknowledge their significance both within Thailand and internationally.

This book does not present the full story of Thailand's cults of wealth or of modern magic within global modernity. By and large, I have bracketed out the role of politics on the efflorescence of the cults. The place of prosperity cults within Thai politics and their relation to state power are such significant questions that they deserve a full separate study. The political roles of the cults also became more visible in the period after 2000, while this present study focuses predominantly, but not exclusively, on the sociological transformations of the Thai religious field in the final decades of the twentieth century. There is a historical sequencing as well as a methodological focus to this book, which concentrates on the impacts of markets and media on ritual within Thai vernacular religion while leaving the politics of the cults to a separate study to follow. In that related study I aim to detail how the cults of wealth were appropriated to an increasing range of state projects after the turn of the twenty-first century.

The Dualities of Religious Modernity

In terms of theories of religion and modernity dominant through most of the twentieth century, the period since the end of the Cold War has produced a spectrum of counter-intuitive results. The international efflorescence of diverse forms of magical religiosity and the spread of doctrinalist fundamentalism in a number of religious traditions not only challenge the secularization thesis. The simultaneous flourishing of spirit mediumship, faith healing, and magic also challenges the view that a disenchantment of the world is the end point of rational modernity. As Niels Mulder wrote towards the end of Thailand's economic boom decade in the 1990s:

> We find fundamentalism, reform, new sects and new interpretations, religious reflection of all sorts; but also a resurgence of magic, mediumship, faith healing, esotericism. All are flourishing and vying with each other to attract the devotee in Southeast Asia at present. (Mulder 1996, p. 25)

The rise of magical movements is perhaps the most unexpected aspect of the post–Cold War worldwide resurgence of religiosity. According to Weberian sociology, modernity leads to a rationalization of social life and the disenchantment of magical views of the world. As Antônio Flávio Pierucci writes:

> For Weber, the disenchantment of the world (*Entzauberung der Welt*) takes place precisely in more religious societies, and it is an *essentially religious process*, because it is the ethical religions that provide the elimination of magic as a means of salvation.... Which

is why Weber more than once adds the adjective *religious*: '*religious* disenchantment of the world [*die* religiöse *Entzauberung der Welt*]'. (Pierucci 2000, p. 136; emphases in original)

According to this account, the doctrinalism that we see in many contemporary fundamentalist movements should be leading to an even greater elimination of magic from the modern world. Yet in fact we see the opposite. At least in parts of Mainland Southeast Asia such as Myanmar, Thailand, Cambodia and Vietnam, we are seeing the rise both of doctrinal reformism (see Jackson 2003) as well as new forms of magical ritual. Since the 1970s, anthropologists have pointed out that late modernity has been associated with a higher degree of magical ritual expression in Thailand. Anatole-Roger Peltier (1977), Niels Mulder (1979, pp. 51–52) and Stanley Tambiah (1984, p. 374) were among the first to note the growth of supernatural rituals among a wide range of groups in Thailand. In 1979, Mulder argued that sociological modernization in Thailand was producing more "animism", not less:

> The … Animist concept of power, such as it is comprehended in the Thai world view, can only be strengthened by [the] changes towards modernity…. The world of modernity is a world of increasingly rapid change filled with self-seeking impersonal power and the experience of powerlessness for most. No wonder that the old Animist perceptions of power are strongly revitalised, not only in Thailand but worldwide…. According to the research of Peltier (1977), the number of magically gifted *Luang Phor* monks who are famous for their protective amulets has spectacularly increased over the past fifteen to twenty years…. Certain shrines, such as the Brahma at the Erawan Hotel, enjoy a steadily increasing popularity in this time of modernity that erodes the expectations of stability…. The concept of power has not changed and is strengthened by the experience of disorder and insecurity…. Thai Animistic perceptions are strengthened and validated by the experience of 'modernity' and are very timely indeed. (Mulder 1979, pp. 51–52)

In the early 1980s, Tambiah wrote of the relations between capitalism and the expansion of the cult of amulets, describing how in October 1978 the Bangkok Bank of Commerce sponsored a *kathin* robes offering ceremony at the mountain monastery of the magic monk *Ajan* Chuan in Northeast Thailand. Tambiah argued that a metropolitan Thai bank's sponsorship of a religious ritual in a regional area of the country represented a novel situation in which Buddhism and "high finance come together in a direct partnership in which the banks do well by doing good" (Tambiah 1984, p. 274). Tambiah also reported that in 1978, at the instigation of a businessman who supervised the Bangkok Bank of Commerce's branches in five north-eastern provinces, the bank sponsored the minting of "a large quantity of amulets with *Ajan* Chuan's head on one side and the bank's insignia on the other" (Tambiah 1984, p. 274). Tambiah went on to argue that "[m]odernization theorists should contemplate this new conjunction between religion and commerce in the context of the spread of capitalism in the Third World" (Tambiah 1984, p. 274).

The triumph of Asian capitalism since the end of the Cold War has not been associated with a rationalizing demythologization or disenchantment of social life. Rather, we have seen an integration of religiosity and economic practice within an expanding field of magical ritual. Why should magical forms of religion have proved so popular in an increasingly marketized world? Why has Thailand's cultural production in recent decades been filled with growing numbers of supernaturalist prosperity movements that glorify consumerism, and not with "Protestant ethic" Buddhist movements that emphasize reason, order and self-control? Thailand has no paucity of ascetic Buddhist reform movements (e.g., Santi Asoke; see McCargo 1993, 1997 and MacKenzie 2007) or of doctrinalist philosopher monks (e.g., Buddhadasa; see Jackson 2003). In recent decades, however, their influence and impact on Thai religious life has considerably declined.

In looking for answers to the questions posed by the rise of the Thai cults of wealth an important starting point is the observation that they are not unique. Irene Stengs argues that "the effervescence of the Thai religious realm should be understood in the wider context of the global proliferation of religious movements that characterized the final decades of the twentieth century" (Stengs 2009, p. 24). Charles Keyes et al. (1994, p. 9) observe that a number of "new religions" have emerged in various parts of Asia in the context of rapid economic growth. Indeed, the Thai prosperity cults bear many similarities to what James H. Foard (n.d.) has called Japanese endemic religion, which emerged in the context of that country's rapid industrialization in the 1960s and 1970s. Summarizing Foard, Keyes et al. describe Japanese endemic religion as

> a kind of minimal religious practice that absolutely every Japanese participates in to some degree and which helps bind the Japanese together.... Japanese endemic religion is nurtured by mass media and an elaborate commercialisation of ritual goods and services.... Endemic religion derives its authority from its practice, which generates 'tradition' as an ongoing process. Because endemic religion is pervasive, representatives of the state may manipulate its rich associations to bolster national identity. At the same time, the

diffuse authority of endemic religion can be invoked by a variety of different interests and used to generate new meanings, including ones that run counter to those promoted by the state. (Keyes et al. 1994, pp. 10–11)

Like Japanese endemic religion, Thailand's cults of wealth have contributed to social cohesion, involve the commodification of religious products, are based more on ritual practice than doctrine or teachings, are nurtured by the press and mass media, and have also become intimately linked with the state. Comparative research across Asia suggests that prosperity religions are associated with periods of rapid economic growth in capitalist Theravada and Mahayana Buddhist societies that have a relatively unfettered press and electronic media. Robert Weller identifies several factors behind the religious efflorescence in capitalist Asian societies. He regards one of the most important trends related to market-oriented modernity almost everywhere in Asia as being "the decline of state-supported religious monopolies" (Weller 2008, p. 22), arguing that we "see the most pluralisation where institutional control over religion is relatively weak" (Weller 2008, p. 22). He also observes that "religious celebration of market amorality … is most likely in periods that combine rapid economic transformation, opportunity and frustration" (Weller 2008, p. 23). All these factors were present in Thailand in the 1980s and 1990s, with a retreat of the Thai state from its historical role in managing religious culture at the same time that the market economy boomed, rapidly expanding wealth in highly uneven ways across the population. The Thai cults of wealth are religious expressions of the impact of new economic arrangements and communications technologies upon a highly complex Buddhist culture and reflect shifting notions of cultural and national identity as large numbers of people in Thailand have reimagined their society's position within global networks over a very short period.

Introducing Thailand's Cults of Wealth

Until the onset of the Asian financial crisis in July 1997, Thailand experienced a decade-long economic boom when average annual GDP growth rates at times exceeded ten per cent. This explosion of wealth and commercial opportunities was unprecedented in the country's history and created a euphoric mood of national confidence that influenced social and cultural as well as religious life. Writing at the height of Thailand's boom years, Jean Comaroff noted the relationship between economic and symbolic productivity in this period, describing Thailand as a society "where the dynamism of capitalist production is rivalled only by the drive of diverse forms of ritual creativity, both within and outside Buddhism" (Comaroff 1994, p. 301). One of the most prominent aspects of this ritual creativity was the development of a wide range of what Richard Roberts (1995, p. 2) has called "prosperity religions"—popular movements that emphasize wealth acquisition as much as, if not more than, salvation.

New forms of magical ritual associated with a diverse range of divine personalities—who are also at the centre of efflorescing forms of professional spirit mediumship and are represented on sacralized magically powerful amulets—are linked to prosperity and wealth and have become significant features of the Thai religious landscape in recent decades. Wealth constitutes the basis, the practice and the objective of these religious movements, and as they rose rapidly to prominence in parallel with Thailand's economic boom decade they accentuated established patterns of symbolic blending and prosperity-enhancing ritual by drawing from the Thai, Chinese and Indian religious traditions.

The most prominent prosperity movements in Thailand are the worship of the spirit of King Chulalongkorn (Rama V; r. 1868–1910) and, more generally, the Thai monarchy; devotion to the Chinese Mahayana Buddhist bodhisattva Guan Yin, called Kuan Im in Thailand; cults of Hindu deities such as Brahma, Ganesh and Rahu; and movements surrounding Theravada Buddhist monks called *keji ajan*, or "magic monks", who are believed to possess the ability to magically empower wealth-enhancing amulets. The spirits whose blessings are sought in the cults of wealth are viewed as repositories of potency and special knowledge about the modern world. They are believed to have privileged access to esoteric knowledge of lucky numbers in lotteries, how to succeed in business, and auspicious days and times to conduct economic and political affairs, including when to stage military coups. The meanings of the new movements are not found in any explicitly presented statement of doctrine. There is no prophet for the cults of wealth, although there is much financial profit associated with them. Rather, the meanings of these movements develop from informal information flows, from conversations amongst the faithful and, most importantly, from the symbolic representation of the cults in mass media, including the national press and digital communication technologies. These trends by no means exhaust the phenomenon of commercially oriented religiosity in modern Thailand. The controversial Wat Phra Dhammakaya movement, widely criticized for adopting a direct marketing approach based on the Amway model to promote

IMAGE 1. Ritual Products Advertised in 7-Eleven Mail Order Catalogue
"Belief" (*khwam-cheua*) page from the December 2017 mail order catalogue of the 7-Eleven convenience store chain advertising ritual products of the Oom Maharuai ("aum super-rich") Company associated with cults of wealth. Images of seven magic monks believed to possess the power to sacralize amulets appear above the company name. **Top:** locket of the magic monk *Luang Phor* Ngoen ("Reverend Father Money"); **middle:** watch of the Hindu monkey deity Hanuman holding a "flag of magical power" (*thong song rit*); **bottom:** lip gloss cream magically empowered (*pluk sek*) by nationally famous tattoo master *Ajan* Nu Kanphai to be spread on the lips to "call in money, good luck and wealth" (*riak sap chok lap*). 7-Eleven is Thailand's largest chain of convenience stores and it markets ritual products from its thousands of stores across the country.

its teachings among Bangkok's middle classes, is another prominent Thai prosperity religion.[3]

In 1973, Tambiah wrote that in terms of then-current theories of modernization, laissez-faire capitalism and the accumulation of goods by individuals for their own benefit could not be expected to become a universally acceptable activity in Buddhist societies such as Sri Lanka, Burma and Thailand (1973, p. 16). This is no longer the case in Thailand. Wealth accumulation has come to the fore, and magical ritual has proved to be a highly amenable symbolic system for unfettered capitalism in a neoliberal economic setting centred on consumerism. Thai capitalism has broken free of the religious restraints that Weber, Tambiah and others believed constrained it. Christine Gray argues that religion in Thailand played "an active if not dominant role in the promotion of capitalism" in the 1960s and 1970s (Gray 1986, p. 62). This has remained the case in subsequent decades. In contrast to earlier views of the incompatibility of Buddhism with capitalist development, Jovan Maud observes that the relationships among magic, religion and the marketplace that are so visible in Thailand today reflect "the fact that capitalist modernity has produced a proliferation of enchantments" and that "neoliberal economies, supposedly characterised by 'economic rationalism', have produced novel forms of 'irrationality'" (Maud 2007, p. 11). Pattana Kitiarsa notes, in contrast to Thomas Kirsch's (1977) prediction in the 1970s that Thai religiosity was trending in the direction of "Buddha-isation", that twenty-first-century religious observance is defined by a "fragmented worship of various popular icons and cults" (Pattana 2012, p. 112). Seeking supernatural intervention to achieve success, wealth and power, the Thai cults of wealth have continued to grow in popularity despite the setback of the 1997 Asian economic crisis and the intense political conflicts that have destabilized Thai society in recent decades. Furthermore, these cults have moved rapidly from the sociocultural margins to the centre of national religious life, being incorporated within state projects as well as being brought within the orbit of state-sponsored monastic Buddhism.

From the Margins to Mainstream: Magical Cults among Thailand's Middle Classes and Power Elites

A central argument of this book is that Thailand's cults of wealth are not marginal phenomena but rather have become central elements of twenty-first-century religious life that, in many ways, are as sociologically and religiously significant as institutional Buddhism. Significantly, some of the key constituents of the complex of prosperity cults, such as the movements centred on the worship of Kuan Im and the spirit of King Chulalongkorn, did not emerge from Theravada Buddhism. Indeed, many of the prosperity cults began outside the Buddhist sangha hierarchy, although since the boom years of the 1990s many Buddhist monks and monasteries have participated as one arm of these popular wealth-oriented movements. Nidhi Eeoseewong argues that the cults of wealth began moving from being heterodox and marginal to mainstream phenomena in the mid-1990s:

> They have arisen and developed outside the monastery [i.e., outside Buddhism] and also tend to be followed outside the monastery. Nevertheless, even though the cults of King Chulalongkorn and *Jao-mae* Kuan Im arose outside the monastery, they have very quickly spread extensively within the monastery, which makes these two middle-class cults so exceptionally interesting. (Nidhi 1994, p. 106)

In 1994, Nidhi predicted that despite their non-Buddhist origins the King Chulalongkorn and Kuan Im movements would ultimately be incorporated within "official" (*thang-kan*)—that is, state-sponsored—Thai religion (Nidhi 1994, p. 79). Nidhi's prediction had in fact come to pass by the time of the onset of the economic crash in July 1997.

From the late nineteenth century, modernist state projects in Thailand based on essentialist constructs of "Thai culture", "Thai religion", "the Thai nation" and "the Thai people" were invoked to suppress local identities, cultures and languages as well as to critique magical religiosity. Within these modernizing projects, folk religion was often labelled as "superstition" (*khwam-ngom-ngai*) or "black magic" (*saiya-sat*) and was devalued in the name of promoting reformist versions of Theravada Buddhism (see Jackson 1989, 2003). Since the 1980s, however, so-called "superstition" has reasserted its presence in the centres of Thai cultural life and political power in the form of cults of magically empowered amulets (Tambiah 1984; Jackson 1999a), a growing prominence of Chinese and Indian religious ritual in the lives of ethnic Thais (Nidhi 1994; Jackson 1999b), an efflorescence of spirit mediumship (Morris 2000a; White 2014), and cults of revered kings and related historical figures (Jackson 1999b; Stengs 2009).

In his study of Christianity in the postmodern West, David Lyon argues that while institutional religiosity is "in pretty poor shape ... the religious *realm*, including faith and spirituality, is far from dormant, let alone dead" (Lyon 2000, p. ix; emphasis in original). Lyon relates an Australian Aboriginal legend that tells of a mighty river that once flowed across the land:

> Many generations living on its banks were sustained by the river, until gradually it ceased to flow. The people watched aghast as the symbol of their security dried up and disappeared. Some waited for it to return while others went to find out what had happened. It turned out that the river still flowed, but had changed course upstream, creating a billabong on the curve where the Aboriginals still sat.... In the Australian story, the river still ran, but elsewhere. (Lyon 2000, pp. 20–21)[4]

Indeed, the river of religiosity still flows strongly through modern societies such as Thailand. But it now often takes novel forms that might not be easily recognized in terms of established definitions of what constitutes religion. Research and scholarship need to go where the river of Thai religion now flows, which is often far removed from temples and monasteries and may be found in marketplaces and department stores as well as in diverse forms of new mass media and digital internet platforms.

While, as detailed in the following section, reformist Buddhists have often critiqued the cults of wealth as *phuttha phanit*—commodifications of Thai Buddhism—I take a converse perspective and regard Thailand's prosperity movements as an expansion of religious symbolisms to envelop the market. The prosperity cults integrated Thailand's newly marketized social formation within religious symbolisms and became the productive core of a new highly popular expression of Thai religio-cultural symbolism and ritual. This analysis also presents a corrective to the dominance of Buddhism in many histories and political studies of modern Thailand. For several decades, anthropologists have detailed the importance of non-institutional ritual and belief for all strata of Thai society, rich and poor, urban and rural. But when historians and political scientists address questions of religion they tend to focus on institutional Buddhism and overlook or dismiss ritual as "premodern residues" of "superstition" and "mysticism".

The elision of non-institutional religiosity from narratives of modern Thai history reflects a much broader problem affecting understandings of the direction of religious change in contemporary societies, and indeed of what constitutes modernity itself. Appreciating the significance of Thailand's new cults of wealth involves overturning misconceptions about the place of ritual and spirit possession in modern religious life. Even more importantly it requires critically reassessing theories of the place of religion in modernity that dominated social and political analysis for much of the twentieth century. As Keyes et al. point out, "Western theories of modernisation ... presupposed the liberation of people from superstition and time-consuming and expensive rituals so that they could participate in a new rationalised order oriented toward the attainment of self-sustaining economic growth" (Keyes et al. 1994, p. 4). In a dramatic repudiation of these theories of modernization, in the 1980s and 1990s Thailand achieved historically unprecedented economic growth at the same time that more time and money was spent on magical rituals than in previous periods of the modern era.

In Southeast Asian religious studies, magical ritual has tended to be studied as a form of religious expression located outside the state and national bureaucracy, whether in rural villages or, more recently, as emerging from and practised in the spaces of the expanding market economy and mediatized popular culture. Supernatural cults and magical ritual have often been seen as being in opposition to the religious forms of Southeast Asia's ruling elites and official expressions of national religious culture, with many studies representing them as expressions of popular devotion among rural peasants and urban underclasses regarded as being politically disenfranchised and economically dispossessed by capitalist expansion. These studies follow accounts from Southeast Asia (e.g., Ong 1988), Latin America (e.g., Taussig 2003) and South Africa (e.g., Comaroff and Comaroff 2002) that describe how those marginalized by global capitalism have turned to the supernatural to adapt to the challenging economic conditions confronting them.

Indeed, one group of scholars argues that prosperity religions have emerged among underclasses in times of crisis in capitalism. These analysts describe market-induced religious resurgence as a response to the precaritization of life under neoliberalism among those dispossessed by the commodification of ever more domains of social life (see for example Comaroff and Comaroff 1999, 2000). Alan Klima has studied gamblers, spirit mediums and informal moneylenders in Thailand, who, he states, collectively engage in "seemingly irrational, superstitious, and corrupt practices of money" (Klima 2006, p. 35). Drawing on Comaroff and Comaroff (1999, 2000), Klima labels these groups "a fractured international underclass trying desperately to make sense of, and gain access to, the mesmerizing exchange of money" (Klima 2006, p. 36). In a comparative study of religious change across modern Asia, Thomas Reuter and Alexander Horstmann emphasize religion as responding to "displacement and insecurity", "disenfranchisement", "cultural crisis and fragmentation" (Reuter and Horstmann 2013, pp. 1–2). They regard "religious revitalisation" in modern Asia as aiming at "remedying certain aspects of a changed life situation that are considered undesirable" and as arising when people have "a sense of being under threat or having … suffered a great loss" (2013, p. 2).

Another group of analysts contends, however, that new magical cults of wealth emerge during economic booms among the beneficiaries of capitalism (e.g., Keyes 2006, p. 6). These accounts have studied gospels of prosperity (e.g., Lyon 2000) among rising middle classes and the new rich in economies undergoing rapid growth, especially but by no means exclusively in East and Southeast Asia. In these accounts, new forms of religious expression are seen as responses to the experience of success among the winners, rather than the losers, from neoliberal capitalism. In contemporary Thailand an opposition between an ostensibly elite, national form of Buddhism, on the one hand, and non-state, subaltern magical cults, on the other, is inaccurate. The Thai cults of wealth are followed not only by those from lower socio-economic strata but are also central to the religious lives of many members of Thailand's economic, social and political elites. In Thailand (see Pattana 2005b) and elsewhere in East Asia (see Weller 1994), the middle classes as well as business and political elites are conspicuous in seeking supernatural assistance. In his research in Thailand in the 1970s, Tambiah observed that the cult of magical amulets and related supernatural aspects of Thai Buddhism were central to the lives of the country's ruling elites, although a superficial performance of secular or Buddhist modernity may have obscured a reliance on magic:

> The cult of amulets is no mere 'superstition' or 'idolatry' of the poor or unlettered. If you confronted a prosperous man in the streets of Bangkok—well dressed in suit and tie, or imposing in military uniform—and asked him to open his shirt collar, you would see a number of amulets encased in gold, silver, or bronze hanging on his gold necklace. (Tambiah 1984, p. 197)

While Pattana and some other scholars have been interested in "the question of how marginalised individuals use popular religion to strategically empower themselves" (Pattana 2005b, p. 221), in this study I am primarily concerned with how Thailand's middle classes and elites draw on popular religion to empower and enrich themselves. I study religious change not as a response to threat or loss but rather as the deployment of ritual technologies to take advantage and to make the most of the opportunities provided by the modern social order. Oscar Salemink points out that in contrast to accounts that interpret spirit mediumship as compensating for the vagaries of the market and the risks of life, in Vietnam the importance of new cults of wealth lies not so much in warding off harm as in their positive role: spirits are actively sought out because they are believed to help in commercial ventures (Salemink 2008a, p. 167). While spirit mediums and magic monks may come from lower socio-economic backgrounds and use their ritual skills as a means of social enhancement, their clients are often members of wealthy elites. As Pattana observes,

> magic monks and mediums are well aware that possessing money is the most crucial factor determining to which social class one belongs. Their desirous will to have rich clients and a large sum of donations is strongly felt in their ritual performances and conversations with clients or disciples. (Pattana 2005b, p. 222)

The often middle-class and elite backgrounds of the followers of the cults of wealth parallels the interest of these same sections of the Thai population in astrology. In her study of Thai astrology, Nerida Cook notes that the professional astrology associations in Bangkok "cater mainly to a middle-class section of the community, the portion of the Thai population which is most interested in astrology and fortune-telling in general" (Cook 1989, p. 36). Thailand's professional astrology associations participate in the annual Red Cross fair in Bangkok, which is under royal sponsorship (p. 38n6). Cook argues that astrology continues to play an important role in Thailand because it is "an intrinsic aspect of a world-view concerned with auspiciousness, power and legitimacy. This is an inheritance from Thai astrology's elite background" (p. x). Historically, astrology was maintained as part of the educated tradition centred on the royal court and ruling elite (p. 40). While in the past astrology was part of the exercise of royal power, since the end of the absolute monarchy in Siam in 1932, this form of divination has been increasingly accessed by the middle classes.[5] Cook contends that astrology has come to be part of the sociopolitical worldview of middle classes that "seek to justify their new aspirations by reference to past precedent, and to ally themselves with the former ideologies of political legitimacy" (p. 318).

In a survey conducted in 1979, Suntaree Komin and Snit Smuckarn found that it was Thais with the highest incomes who were most likely to consult fortune tellers and astrologers, with the incidence of visiting astrologers and fortune tellers also increasing as the level of education rose (Suntaree and Snit 1979, p. 327, cited in Cook 1989, p. 207). Cook observes that the sections of Thai society that draw most upon astrology are those "who are most engaged in the optimization of different qualities of time", who are "most tied into the capitalist sector of the economy, and most tied into the notion of specific career paths, i.e. involving optimal development or progress over time" (Cook 1989, p. 319). In other words, it is businesspeople and professionals who are the major clients of fortune tellers and astrologers in Thailand.

Kornrawee Panyasuppakun details the continuing importance of astrology and magical cults of fortune telling in the lives of Thailand's business elites today. She reports that in Thailand in 2018, 35 per cent of all Thai babies were born by caesarean section. A key reason for the unusually high rate of surgical births in the country is because large numbers of parents wish to time the birth of their child to take place on an auspicious date, especially "a date that will help their business".[6] One mother interviewed recalled how they "'went to a venerated abbot and had him pick a date'.... Her son was born on December 5, the birthday of the late King Rama IX." A nurse at a Bangkok hospital whom Kornrawee interviewed told her that "[t]he obstetrician himself

IMAGE 2. "I Like Cash": The Magic Monks Chorp, Ngoen and Sot
A devotional poster of three *keji ajan* magic monks: *Luang Pu* Chorp of Wat Pa Sammanusorn in Loei Province; *Luang Phor* Ngoen of Wat Hiranyaram in Phichit Province; and *Luang Phor* Sot of Wat Pak-nam Phasi Charoen in Thonburi. The names of the three monks printed in large letters spell out the Thai sentence "[I] Like Cash (*chorp ngoen sot*)", followed by the sentence "[With the presence of these monks] this home is rich". (Source: Jattujak Weekend Market, Bangkok, 1997. From the author's collection.)

picked the date for me. It was the 6th day of the 6th month in the year 61. He said number 6 was lucky".[7] Her son was born on 6 June 2018, or BE 2561. Kornrawee notes that

> [t]he belief that a person's birthday determines the course of their life is prevalent in Thai society, especially among well-to-do people and celebrities who can afford to cover the cost of a C-section. Chompoo Araya Hargate, a top Thai celebrity and her billionaire husband, for instance, had renowned *feng shui* master Grienggrai Boontaganon set the delivery date for her.

Famous fortune-teller Arunwich Wongjatupat said nine out of 10 parents look for dates that will yield either prosperity or leadership qualities for their soon-to-be born child.[8]

While previous studies linking Thailand's modernizing elites, both royal and commoner, to institutional Buddhism (see C. Reynolds 1972; Ishii 1986; Somboon 1982; Jackson 1989) are not necessarily inaccurate, they have tended to overlook the participation of these modernizers in forms of ritual outside of institutional Buddhism. Gray notes that while "men of prowess" in Thailand build spiritual potency through acts of world renunciation, "[i]f they perceive these acts at all, Western diplomats and political analysts tend to view them as irrelevant to the 'hard facts' of political and economic life or merely as social irritants" (Gray 1995, p. 225). In contrast, in this study I consider forms of ritual that, to borrow the idiom of Tambiah's observation noted above, have often been hidden behind an apparent façade of rationalist modernity epitomized by Thai businessmen wearing Western-style suits and military officers wearing imposing uniforms.

Reformist Buddhist Critiques of the Cults of Wealth

While the cults of wealth are followed by large numbers of Thais from all social strata, they have at times been the object of trenchant criticism by reformist Buddhists. While reflecting the views of a minority in Thailand, intense critiques of the cults are nonetheless prominent among more doctrinal Buddhists. Some of the most vocal critics of the cults have been journalists and Buddhist intellectuals, who have access to the media and publications to disseminate their views. While reformist Buddhists are vociferous critics of the cults of wealth, they are not politically violent and their criticisms in publications and the media have not been transferred into practical interventions in prosperity-oriented rituals or cultic forms.

Critiques of "ignorant blind faith" (*khwam-ngom-ngai*) in the supernatural are widespread in Thailand's print media. The intensity of the opposition to spirit cults in some quarters is evident in the hybrid English-Thai title of one recent paperback, "*Fuck Ghost: samakhom tor-tan sing ngom-ngai*", whose Thai subtitle translates as "The society against ignorant blind faith". Written by an author using the English pen name of "Fuck Ghost" (2016), this text lambasted a diverse range of spirit cults for being in conflict with Buddhist teachings, and upon its release it was prominently displayed among new titles at major bookstores across Thailand.

Followers of the influential twentieth-century Theravada Buddhist philosopher monk Buddhadasa (see Jackson 2003; Ito 2012) are especially vocal critics of popular supernaturalism. They denounce these ritual forms as *phuttha phanit* ("Buddha-commerce"), an expression that describes the commodification of what the followers of Buddhadasa understand as true Buddhist teachings (Jackson 1999b, pp. 309ff.) and which they often regard as reflecting "superstitious" residues from Thailand's premodern past. According to Buddhadasa, arguably the most important reformist Buddhist thinker in twentieth-century Thailand, magical ritual or *saiyasat* is the "science of sleeping people" (*Photjananukrom Khorng Than Phutthathat* [2004?], p. 300). In contrast, Buddhist teachings, which Buddhadasa calls "the Buddhist science" (*phutthasat*), is the science of awakened people, uses reason and teaches self-reliance. These views are frequently expressed by lay journalists and Buddhist monks in the press and media.

In 1997, the renowned scholar monk *Phra* Dhammapitaka (Prayuth Payuttho), one of the intellectual mainstays of doctrinal Buddhism, published a book titled *If We Want to Overcome the Crisis We Must Abandon Our Attachment to Superstition (Saiyasat)*. In this text he isolated the widespread popularity of *saiyasat*—which he glosses variously in English as "animism", "supernaturalism", "superstition", "magic" and "black magic"—as being at the core of the problems that led to the late-1990s economic crisis in Thailand. *Phra* Dhammapitaka noted that Buddhist teachings do not call for the wholesale rejection of *saiyasat*, but he nonetheless makes it clear that he regards *saiyasat* to be a distinctly inferior religious form. He claims that over-reliance on *saiyasat* means that the Thai people have not developed mentally to a sufficient extent to deal with the complexities of the contemporary world, and that Buddhist meditative practice (*patipat tham*, "*dhamma* practice") would help develop the mental acuity, moral stamina and self-reliance that he argued the country needed to overcome its national economic problems at the height of the Asian economic crisis.

In the aftermath of the economic crash, *Phra* Panyananda—a prominent reformist monk and a well-known follower of Buddhadasa—emphasized the need for correct belief as the basis of Thai Buddhism:

'What is in crisis is the beliefs of Buddhists, not the religion', the monk [*Phra* Panyananda] told a recent seminar organised by the Princess Maha Chakri Sirindhorn Anthropology Centre. Most Thais have mixed an element of black magic [*saiyasat*] into their Buddhist beliefs, he said, and many famous monks are now known for their 'magical powers' instead of their teaching of *dharma* (Buddhist principles). The media, in addition to monks and politicians, are to blame for promoting these misbeliefs, leading to what he described as 'religious consumerism' [*phuttha phanit*].[9]

The strength of opposition to cults of wealth and magical *saiyasat* rituals in some quarters in Thailand is reflected in the fact that some media, such as *The Nation* daily newspaper, present critiques of these forms of religious enchantment as matters of editorial policy. On 5 February 2015, *The Nation* published an editorial titled "Protecting Thai Buddhism from TWISTED Teachings", in which the word "twisted" was printed in capital letters. In part, this editorial stated:

Thailand is routinely described as a Buddhist country.... However, in reality, our Buddhist identity often goes little further than what's written on our ID cards and house-registration documents. Many of us stick to animistic beliefs and superstitions.... The ignorance is exacerbated at many Buddhist temples, where monks take advantage of lay people's superstitious nature by selling amulets and services. Exorcisms, protective spells and trinkets are readily available at a price, and have become a lucrative trade for some monks.[10]

In a similar vein, in 2018, prominent progressive journalist Pravit Rojanaphruk published a column in the *Khao Sod English* newspaper titled "Let Thai Buddhism be Reborn", in which he wrote: "Many Thais are Buddhists only in name, attached to the rituals, superstitions and a sense of Buddhist chauvinism.... Superstition, attachment to various supposedly magical amulets ... these are but some of the troubling aspects of Thai Buddhism."[11] Despite their vociferous intensity, it is important to emphasize that the critiques of magical cults of wealth have not been matched by practical or legal interventions. Most followers of the cults have ignored the criticisms published in books and newspapers, focusing their attention on ritual practice rather than arguments over doctrine or correct belief.

Key Arguments: The Modernity of Magic and the Primacy of Ritual

Magic is Modern

Tambiah (1990) has deconstructed the history of the opposition of reason and science to magic. He argues that it was during the Enlightenment that a fundamental divide between prayer and spell was established, the former coming to be seen as characteristic of religion and the latter of magic (Tambiah 1990, p. 19). He points out that before the Reformation, Christians believed in the reality and efficacy of magic but condemned it as pagan fetishism. It was during the Reformation that Protestant reformers went a step further and not only declared magic to be false religion but also inefficacious action: "It is essentially in the modern period, since the Enlightenment, that a particular conception of religion that emphasises its cognitive, intellectual, doctrinal and dogmatic aspects, gained prominence" (Tambiah 1990, p. 4). Tambiah points to the imbrication of magical forms of inquiry in the origins of modern science, with luminaries regarded as the founders of modern rational science, such as Newton and Copernicus, having been deeply involved in magical inquiries. He also draws on the anthropological literature to argue that we cannot categorically define modern Western societies as having expelled magic, pointing to Bronislaw Malinowski's (1935) account of the magic of advertising for beauty products and its parallels with love magic among Trobriand Islanders.

Despite claims by some of their followers that contemporary religious movements represent a return to ancient tradition, efflorescing supernaturalism and new reformist and fundamentalist movements both emerge from, and are intimately part of, the modern world of market-based, commodified scientific technologies. The dynamism of the diversifying forms of spirit cults and magical ritual in Thailand and across Southeast Asia, and their emergence from the context of market-based, mediatized "global modernity" (Dirlik 2005), indicates that these religious forms are not residues of premodern tradition but rather represent highly contemporary phenomena.

In light of the efflorescence of magical ritual and spirit cults in Thailand and elsewhere in mainland Southeast Asia, we need to take Tambiah's deconstructive project forward. We need to view the sociological forces of modernity as not merely providing spaces for the survival of residues of magic among those excluded and disenfranchised by capitalism but as also actively producing magic anew among the wealthy and winners from global modernity. In this I follow studies of the modernity of contemporary forms of magical ritual. In his study "The Magic of Modernity", Bruce Kapferer summarizes studies of magical ritual that "powerfully insist that these practices are thoroughly modern" (Kapferer 2002, p. 16). Kapferer emphasizes that

> [t]he crucial argument regarding modern magical practices concerns their disjunction from pasts (histories and cosmologies prior to modern periods … before the imperial expansions of the West) and the radical reconfiguration of ideas and practices of the past in terms of the circumstances of the present. This position represents a major corrective to those orientations that see magical practices as survivals of tradition and refuse to attend to the import of their current reformulations in the political and social contexts of their use. (Kapferer 2002, p. 19)

Contemporary Thai magic such as the cults of wealth and amulets as well as new forms of professional spirit mediumship cannot be dismissed as premodern residues that have managed to hang on into the era of global capitalism. The forms of magical ritual studied in this book are not ancient. Modernity is making new forms of magic in Thailand, just as it has also engendered new forms of reformist doctrinal Buddhism. While there are continuities with practices, rituals and beliefs from the past, the alternative modernity of economically neoliberal, digitally mediatized, military dominated and monarchist Thailand is reproducing magic anew, with the forms of enchantment that are sociologically and economically significant and politically relevant in Thailand today coming into being out of significant transformations of premodern forms. As detailed in Chapter Two, Thai magical ritual, like monastic Buddhism, has not emerged unchanged from the successive historical vortices of European and American imperialism, Western discourses of civilization and rationality, new scientific technologies and globalizing capitalism.

As Kapferer observes, anthropologists have been especially interested in contemporary forms of magic because of their significance in revealing "the fabulations and transmutations of capital in globalizing circumstances, and the magical character of nationalist discourses of the modern and postcolonial state" (Kapferer 2002, p. 2). Magic, or what Erick White calls the ritual arts of efficacy in Buddhist societies, displays "creativity, innovation and adaptability" (White 2016, p. 17), and he notes that as Asian societies have modernized "the ritual arts of efficacy have sometimes experienced a frequently underappreciated transformation in their social organization, transmission and consumption" (p. 16). White also contends that the increasing dominance of capitalist modes of production, the expansion of a culture of consumerism, the rise of cultural heritage industries and the spread of ideologies of democratic governance have all "provided new models for how knowledge and practice within the ritual arts of efficacy can be organized, distributed and consumed" (p. 16).

An especially significant development in recent decades has been the professionalization of divination and spirit mediumship. By selling ritual services, diviners and spirit mediums have increasingly become full-time professionals. Edoardo Siani argues that because of the impact of the market and the professionalization of magical ritual, each ritual specialist "needs to differentiate him or herself in order to define the specificity and difference of their services and skills in a highly competitive market for divination services" (Siani 2018, p. 424). Siani contends that the consequent triumph of individuality over a previous standardization of belief and practice constitutes "a rupture from the past, when authenticity and adherence to a supposedly original knowledge was highly prized" (p. 423). In contrast to the previous conformity to tradition in Thai magical and divinatory rituals, "the contemporary Bangkok divination scene takes pride in its diversity" (p. 423).

The Empirical and Theoretical Primacy of Ritual Practice in Modern Enchantment

Another linking theme across the sections and chapters of this study is the priority of ritual and practice over doctrine and belief in the making of modern magic. In Chapter One I summarize Bruno Latour's account of modernity as a fractured condition divided between purifying processes of ideological rationalization and hybridizing practice. This account provides a framing analysis for understanding how religious modernity produces both purificatory doctrinalism and fundamentalist movements at the same time that new modalities of ritual magic also emerge. The Thai cults of wealth inhabit the hybridizing spaces of modern ritual practice, constituting an excluded other of both doctrinal religious and rationalist secular versions of modernity.

The emphasis on ritual practice over doctrine is a defining feature of new magical phenomena across mainland Southeast Asia. Summarizing the situation in Burma, Bénédicte Brac de la Perrière observes: "The spirit cult exists primarily in practice whereas Buddhism relies mainly on the transmission of a textual corpus for which the religious specialists (monks) are held responsible" (Brac de la Perrière 2009, p. 195). In her account of *len dong* spirit possession in the cult of the Mother Goddess in Northern Vietnam, Andrea Lauser notes that "there is no codified set of religious texts, and there is to date no overarching institutionalized organization that makes decisions concerning religious practice or doctrine" (Lauser 2018, p. 7). The emphasis on ritual practice in Thai religious life has a deep history. Peter Skilling argues that the complexities of religious life in pre-modern Siam demonstrate the inadequacy of describing the society as "Theravadin" (Skilling 2009, p. 183). He notes that the complex nature of Siamese religion in the middle ages was reflected in the phrase *samana-chi-phram* (Pali: *samaṇa jī brāhmaṇa*), which denoted diverse ritual specialists, including Buddhist mendicants, renunciants and brahmins, whose distinctions were not made in terms of religion, creed or faith "but rather in terms of ritual and function" (p. 184).

In Chapter Three I argue that the limitations of older theories of religion, and their failure to provide adequate frames to appreciate emergent phenomena such as the Thai cults of wealth, stem from their focus on belief and teachings and their neglect of ritual practice. In that chapter I also argue that the emphasis on ritual in Thai vernacular religion is a pragmatic response to the need to build a coherent religious field from multiple, doctrinally incompatible cultic forms. In Chapter Seven I argue that the productive, performative effects of ritual in mediatized neoliberal societies is key to the processes that bring modern enchantment into being. The performative effect of ritual underpins modern magic in Thailand, while at the global level modern enchantment emerges in the field of hybrid practice that Latour describes as the denied and excluded other of rationalizing modernist ideologies.

Interdisciplinary Method

Because Thai magical ritual exists in domains that Latour describes as non-rationalized practice-based hybridity, we will not be able to appreciate its significance in the country's modern history by methodologies that draw solely on analyses of religious texts, discourses and doctrines. The cults of wealth exist in a religious field that is structured more by ritual practice than by doctrine. The methods of this study consequently need to describe what people do as much as what they say or write. It is not legal statutes, administrative orders, doctrines or exegetical texts that we should look to in understanding magic in modern Thailand, but rather the ritual practices of the general public, businesspeople and state officials.

Religious studies approaches often focus on spaces and sites traditionally understood as religious, such as Buddhist monasteries, spirit medium shrines and religious icons and texts. The spaces of prosperity-oriented Thai ritual studied here, however, have expanded far beyond the conventional bounds of monasteries and shrines. Pattana Kitiarsa observes that the boundaries of Thai popular Buddhism "expand as far as its commercial influence spreads" (Pattana 2012, p. 2). Indeed, to study the cults of wealth we must also look outside monasteries to department stores, shopping malls and marketplaces, for it is in these locations that many contemporary forms of Thai religiosity are now most visibly expressed and where popular Thai religion is commodified, packaged, marketed and consumed. Sacredness and the supernatural have now colonized the commodified spaces of neoliberal capitalism and often take highly developed forms outside traditional religious locales. Because religiosity and magic have colonized the marketplace and media, the approaches of media studies and cultural studies—whose fields of expertise are the new worlds of consumerism and mass media—also provide valuable insights that have escaped some established approaches to the study of religion.

Jean Comaroff proposes that we need to regard Asian forms of capitalism as "signifying systems" and contemporary forms of religion in East and Southeast Asia as "evidence of the symbolic richness of the modern mind ... in response to an explosion of market commodities" (Comaroff 1994, pp. 303–4). It is iconic of the wealth-oriented focus of the prosperity cults that one is just as likely to find their ritual objects in commercial spaces as in traditional sacred localities such as monasteries. For these reasons, in this book I adopt an interdisciplinary approach that draws on anthropology, religious studies and history as well as cultural and media studies to understand how modernity in Thailand has produced new forms of commercially inflected enchantment. This approach takes us beyond an analysis in which religion, economy, media and popular culture are conceived as discrete constructs, enabling us to see these fields as interrelating semiotic domains marked by hierarchy and contestation. A semiotic analysis also helps us rethink the religion-capitalism relationship and leads us beyond an emphasis on the Thai cults of wealth as a commercialization of Buddhism to instead view them from an alternative perspective as a spiritualization of the market.

The modern structure of knowledge assumes that there has been an organizational divide between religion, society, politics, economics, art and culture. Furthermore, it is assumed that because of these sociological divides it is possible to establish epistemologically distinct disciplines of knowledge, which respectively take one of these several fields as their specialized object of inquiry. But if there is no clear separation of the socio-economic, religio-political and aesthetic-cultural fields, then the intellectual project of separating domains of disciplinary knowledge as being based upon ostensibly discrete objects of inquiry collapses. My method is necessarily cross-disciplinary because the phenomena studied here are not contained within any one field of modern knowledge, or indeed of modern social organization. Lauser makes this point with regard to *len dong* spirit mediumship in modern Vietnam, which, she states, "combines spiritual, social, political, economic, cultural and aesthetic dimensions, and … connects the different contexts it is manifested in, and it is affected by all of these contexts" (Lauser 2018, p. 13). This study is conducted at the multidisciplinary intersection of what Latour describes as "imbroglios of science, politics, economy, law, religion, technology, fiction" (Latour 1993, p. 2).

Disciplinary Boundaries and the Omission of Magic from Modern Thai History

If, as argued here, magical cults of wealth are culturally and, indeed, politically important in modern Thailand, why have they not figured prominently in most histories or political analyses of the country? There are several reasons why magical ritual has often been overlooked. First, the non-institutional dimensions of Thai ritual life are often undervalued, if not devalued, in studies that have drawn on older formulations of religious studies. From its inception, religious studies prioritized study of the texts and doctrines of monotheistic religions that place expressions of faith at the centre of their conception of the religious life. Within this understanding, forms of religious life that centre on ritual practice and which lack a canonical religious text or an institutional clergy have often fallen outside the scope of inquiry. Religious studies still struggles to arrive at a coherent account of Asian polytheisms that are founded more upon ritual practices than upon professions of faith in the revelations recorded in sacred texts.

The modern academy's failure, or rather inability, to view magic as a genuine force in the world of globalizing capitalism also emerges from the blinkering of perspectives and the silo-effects upon knowledge that are produced by the boundaries that separate different disciplines. While anthropology has treated modern magical rituals as phenomena worthy of study, this has not been taken up in mainstream historiography or political studies, or for that matter in cultural or media studies, all of which often remain under misapprehensions engendered by rationalist secular ideologies. The interdisciplinary approach adopted here aims to break through some of the barriers to conversation and analysis that are set up by structural divides between the disciplines in the modern university.

The "Invisibility" of Thailand's Ritual Economy

While this study focuses on cults that are oriented to the worship of quantitative increases in wealth and prosperity, my analysis of the empirical setting and local discourses of Thai religious practice is limited to qualitative approaches. Observations suggest that large amounts of money are involved in the rituals and cultic objects associated with the prosperity movements. The commodification of religion is a contentious issue in Thailand, however, and there are no reliable studies of the actual size of Thailand's ritual economy or the amounts of money that flow through the cults of wealth. Despite a plethora of statistical studies of the performance of different sectors of the Thai economy, we have no accurate measure of how much money has been spent in temple construction, merit-making donations or speculative investment in amulets and other ritual objects over recent decades.

Gray observes that a practical barrier to studying Thailand's ritual economy is the fact that money directed into monasteries and the purchase of objects such as magical amulets is defined in religious terms as "making merit". As Gray observes, "once wealth is channeled into the Sangha, into merit-making activities, it is no longer spoken of as wealth or money (*ngoen*), it becomes 'merit' (*bun*)" (Gray 1986, p. 52). As an example, Gray notes an expression used by one of her informants: "*Mi sattha 20 baht nai wat nan*". While literally translating as a person "had faith of 20 baht in that monastery" (p. 667n18), this statement in fact means that the person in question donated twenty baht to the monastery. The language of financial transfers to monasteries and spirit medium shrines, and of money used to purchase ritual objects related to the cults of wealth, in which "capitalist ideologies are portrayed as ideologies of merit" (p. 849), obscures the amount of funds involved in these transactions. As Gray laments: "Unfortunately, for the anthropologist as for the Buddhist layman, as soon as 'cash' enters the temple door, it disappears from analytic sight" (p. 77).

The Chapters

Part 1: Why Religious Modernity Trends in Two Opposing Directions

Chapter One: The Contradictions of Religious Modernity

Viewed at the global level, and in particular from the perspective of modern Thailand, not only is religion becoming more important, religious change is also taking place in two directions that earlier theories of modernity defined as being opposed, if not mutually exclusive. In contemporary Southeast Asia we find a parallel efflorescence of ritual-based magic and spirit mediumship in some localities, while anti-supernatural doctrinal accounts of Buddhism and Islam are influential in other settings. In Thailand we find movements to rationalize religious life on the basis of a purified text-based and doctrine-centred view of "true" original Buddhism at the same time that we also find other movements—which are now sociologically more numerous and more pervasive across the Thai religious field—that are based on ritual practices that invoke magical and enchanted imaginaries. Both of these contrasting trends—rationalizing doctrine-based and magical ritual-focused religiosities—have developed from the same matrix of mediatized techno-scientific capitalism. Yet, theories of modernity based on Enlightenment ideas that opposed magic to both rational science and "true" religion contend that we should be seeing a decline of magic in both secular and religious life. The fact that reformist Buddhism now exists alongside novel forms of enchantment suggests that, at least in the fields of religion and ritual, the very notion of modernity has been misconceived. It is not possible to imagine modernity as being equally productive of both rationalized doctrinal Buddhism and new forms of magical ritual without radically reassessing what modernity itself may be.

In Chapter One I argue that Bruno Latour's (1993) account of the modern world as one divided between a public discursive and ideological level of purificatory rationalization, on the one hand, and a practical level of hybrid non-rationalized practice, on the other, provides insights into how modernity is producing both doctrinalist reform movements and magical cults. In Thailand, some aspects of Buddhism have been reconstructed in accordance with notions of rational scientific modernity, while magical ritual has also flourished in what Latour describes as the non-rationalized field of hybrid practice. Drawing on Latour, we can also see that the divide between reformist

Buddhism and modern magic in Thailand is far from unique. Rather, it is one manifestation of the structural divide between rationalized discourse and non-rationalized practice that, drawing on his ethnography of scientific practice in the West, Latour contends is the character of social life in all parts of the world that now call themselves modern. I extend Latour's model to religion to argue that the modern Thai religious field is structured by discourses of rational secularization and disenchantment that overlay lived domains of enchanted ritual practice, which are exemplified by the cults of wealth. Drawing on Latour, I argue that magic is not only given new life by modernity; magic is produced *de nouveau* by one of the contradictory moments of modernity, which we need to understand as the coexistence of both rationalizing and enchanting processes.

Chapter Two: Semicolonial Modernity and Transformations of the Thai Religious Field

Even though the ideology of modernity as disenchanted is an inaccurate account of contemporary social conditions, it has nonetheless had real impacts on Thai intellectual and political cultures. In Chapter One I argue that the view of modernity as a world historical process of rationalization and disenchantment is an ideological project. In Chapter Two I detail how this ideology was linked with imperialism and discourses of European civilizational superiority and subsequently has had dramatic impacts across the world. In Thailand, as in some other Buddhist societies in Asia, it has resulted in a categorical distinction between "religion" (as disenchanted) and "belief" (as enchanted), as well as a regime of representation that positions religion or Buddhism (*sasana*) as dominant while often obscuring magical ritual and practice. In Chapter Two I describe how the impact of Western power has seen the creation of what I call the Thai regime of images, and which Christine Gray (1986) describes as Janus rituals, which at times has obscured the full range of Thai ritual activity from Western observers.

In response to Western influences, the self-modernizing semi-colonial Siamese state brought the institution of Buddhism under increasing bureaucratic and administrative regulation while relegating non-institutional ritual practices to a more private domain largely beyond the gaze of critical Western observers. Practised outside contexts that came to be defined as modern and public, magical ritual was permitted relatively free reign, continuing to be elaborated in innovative ways within popular culture in parallel with the modernizing transformations of institutional Buddhism effected by the state.

In this chapter I also present an alternative narrative of modern Thai history through the lens of magic, which has never been dispelled but rather was repositioned within the Thai polity and refashioned in its forms and character in response to Western influences and the local instituting of the regime of images.

Part Two: Thailand's Cults of Wealth

Chapter Three: Theorizing the Total Thai Religious Field

Western religious studies has at times taken the colonial-era construct of Buddhism as being equivalent to Thai religion as a sociological fact rather than a discursive construct, and as a result has not been able to integrate magic and ritual into a total picture of Thai religiosity. An expanded conceptual frame is needed to appreciate the distinctiveness and significance of the Thai cults of wealth. The form of complexity that characterizes Thai popular Buddhism—which is an open, expanding and dynamically evolving complex of cults—lies in the way that multiple ritual forms exist in parallel and share some common features but do not merge into a single hybridized unity. White captures the complexity and multiplicity of Thai popular Buddhism, and alludes to the analytical challenges this complex presents, when he writes that this religious field

> is too foundationally inchoate as an empirical reality to conform to any single, homogeneous, coherent or totalising model or representation. As an historical, social and cultural reality, Thai Buddhism is protean in its axiomatic diversity, ambiguity and contradictions. (White 2014, p. 134)

White summarizes the difficulties scholars face in accounting for the broader picture of the Thai religious field when he observes that

> [the] highly differentiated and pluralistic landscape of Thai Buddhist religiosity reveals a sociocultural environment in which multiple forms of Buddhism and multiple forms of spirit possession and mediumship are in conversation with multiple forms of Buddhist-inspired devotion and esoteric popular religiosity. (White 2014, p. 436)

As White also observes, "during the efflorescence of popular religiosity in the 1980s and 1990s, an already existing diversity increased even further" (White 2014, p. 257). Justin McDaniel describes the diversity of spiritual figures in modern Thai belief and practice as forming a "pantheon of famous monks, 'Hindu' deities, and Buddhas" (McDaniel

2011, p. 4), while Nidhi Eeoseewong argues that the Thai belief system "is able to increase the number of spirits and gods indefinitely" (Nidhi 1994, p. 90). Hans-Dieter Evers and Sharon Siddique (1993, p. 9) have remarked upon the fragmentation of the study of religion in Southeast Asia, which they see as a consequence of the "sheer religious diversity" between and within countries in the region. It is in part because of this empirical diversity and the analytical fragmentation of research that the interdisciplinary field of religion, society and politics in Southeast Asia is poorly conceptualized.

We need a range of new concepts to analyse forms of religious expression that have developed in polytheistic societies that were already culturally diverse and which have been further transformed by globalizing capitalism and new communications media. In Chapter Three I propose contributions to the conversation on developing an analytical vocabulary that appreciates the diversity and scope of the Thai religious field as a whole and the complex of cults of wealth in particular. I outline:

- Polyontologism as a non-blended mixing of religious forms;
- The *kala-thesa* "time and space" contextualized separation of culturally diverse ritual forms and a general tolerance of ambiguity, incommensurability and contradiction;
- The hierarchical dominance of Buddhism in structural and symbolic terms; and
- An emphasis on ritual practice over doctrinal harmonization.

Chapter Four: Royal Spirits, Magic Monks, Chinese and Indian Deities

This study does not consider a single religious movement or one deity or focus of devotional sentiment and ritual. It deals with a complex of multiple, intersecting movements, each of which has its own distinct object of devotion, its own rituals and often its own holy sites and places of worship and pilgrimage. What unites the Thai cults of wealth is not any common deity but rather their collective focus on wealth and prosperity, their recent development and historical novelty, as well as their symbolic contiguity and co-location in a range of domains and spaces from the shrines of professional spirit mediums to commercially produced ritual objects such as magically empowered amulets. In Chapter Four I summarize the most important cults of wealth that have become prominent over the past four decades. These include worship of the divine spirit of King Chulalongkorn; the Chinese Mahayana bodhisattva Kuan Im; Hindu deities such as Brahma, Ganesh and Rahu; and Buddhist monks regarded to possess supernatural powers to bless and magically empower amulets.

Chapter Five: Empowered Amulets and Spirit Possession

Thailand's cults of wealth lie at the intersection of two other major phenomena that are also distinctive emergent features of the Thai religious field and which reflect novel modalities of ritual enchantment; namely, the cult of amulets sacralized by magic monks and professional spirit mediumship. One of the most widespread and popular ways of demonstrating attachment to a deity, or to request a spirit's helping presence, is to own or wear an amulet bearing an image of the god. The faithful can also seek to communicate directly with a deity associated with a cult of wealth in a spirit possession ritual mediated by a professional spirit medium who channels that god. The cults of wealth, the cult of amulets and professional spirit mediumship are three distinct but also intersecting phenomena that have all emerged as novel expressions of Thai popular Buddhism since the middle of the twentieth century and which represent autonomous expressions of ritual and material religious practice. In Chapter Five I describe the material dimensions of the cults of wealth in the closely allied cult of amulets and the central place of spirit possession in the rituals associated with the cults. This chapter details how followers of the cults of wealth express their faith in the deities and spirits of prosperity and seek to communicate with these beings to request their help and support.

Chapter Six: The Symbolic Complex of Thai Cults of Wealth

In Chapter Six I present a synoptic perspective and argue that the Thai cults of wealth form a symbolic complex that draws upon religious, economic, political and other sources to create systems of meaning. Some of the cults considered in this book have been the focus of detailed study by specialist researchers, and I rely on the work of these scholars in summarizing the key features of each movement. My goal in Chapter Six is to weave the growing number of focused studies of Thai popular religion into a synoptic picture of a broader phenomenon that only becomes visible, and whose significance only becomes fully apparent, when the detailed accounts are brought together in conversation.

Part Three: How Modernity Makes Magic

Chapter Seven: Capitalism, Media and Ritual in Modern Enchantment

While critiques of Weberian accounts of modernity are well developed, positive accounts of the production of enchantment in modern societies are fragmented and partial. Jean and John Comaroff argue that new forms of magical ritual parallel the cultural logic of neoliberalism, while Rosalind Morris contends that mediatization produces forms of auraticization and a spectralization of social life in which the supernatural finds new spaces in which to flourish. Stanley Tambiah has described the performative character of ritual as constituting the enchanted fields of religious life. These separate accounts of processes of modern enchantment, however, do not yet speak to each other. In Chapter Seven I outline how the several partial accounts of modern enchantment can be woven together as the basis for a general model of the making of new modes of magic. I argue that the performative force of ritual explains why neoliberal capitalism and new media have been exceptionally active sources of enchantment in religious cultures that value ritual practice above doctrine and teaching.

Key Terms

Before beginning my accounts and analyses in the chapters that follow, in the next section I outline how I understand some of the key descriptive and conceptual terms used in this study. These terms are the focus of considerable discussion and debate and often take definitions that reflect the different theoretical frames of analysis within which they are deployed. I outline the background to some of these debates and how I position this study in relation to the at times divergent and contrasting settings within which the terms are used.

Notes

1. For example, see Brac de la Perrière 2011; Brac de la Perrière et al. 2014; Brac de la Perrière and Gaillard 2019; Endres and Lauser 2011; Irvine 1984; Johnson 2014; Keyes et al. 1994; Klima 2002; Lauser 2018; McDaniel 2011; Maud 2007; Morris 2000a; Mulder 1979, 1985; Nidhi 1993, 1994; Pattana 2012; Salemink 2007, 2008a; Siani 2017, 2018; Sorrentino, forthcoming; Stengs 2009; Tambiah 1984; Taylor 2004; Visisya 2018; and White 2014, 2017.

2. For example, see Comaroff 1994; Comaroff and Comaroff 1999, 2000; Gottowik 2014; Gray 1986; Hefner 2010, 2017; Jenkins 2000; Kapferer

2002; Lee 2020; Lee and Ackerman 2018; Lyon 2000; Saler 2006; and Tambiah 1985, 1990.

3. Wat Phra Dhammakaya was at the centre of a series of controversies about improper proselytizing methods, financial irregularities and heterodox teachings from the late 1980s. See Edwin Zehner 1990 and Rory Mackenzie 2007.

4. Lyon here cites Peter and Sue Kaldor (*Where the River Flows* [Homebush West: Anzea, 1988]), who in turn are quoted in Alister McGrath (*The Renewal of Anglicanism* [Harrisburg, PA: Morehouse, 1993], pp. 7–8).

5. The country was named Siam until 1939, after which the official name was changed to Thailand.

6. Kornrawee Panyasuppakun, "An 'Auspicious' Beginning?", *The Nation Weekend*, 29–30 September 2018, p. 1.

7. Ibid.

8 Ibid.

9. Mukdawan Sakboon, "Top Monk Sees Crisis in Beliefs Not Buddhism", *The Nation* (online), 14 January 1998 (accessed 20 January 1998).

10. Editorial, *The Nation*, 5 February 2015, p. 9A.

11. Pravit Rojanaphruk, "Let Thai Buddhism be Reborn", *Khao Sod English*, 24 February 2018, http://www.khaosodenglish.com/opinion/2018/02/24 (accessed 25 February 2018).

Key Terms: Debates, Theories and Contexts

Modernity

Understanding the full diversity of contemporary Thai religious life requires several paradigm shifts in our thinking, most importantly in what we understand by "modernity", as well as the assumptions underpinning academic disciplines such as sociology and political science, which have often taken this notion as their self-defining object of study. Indeed, the parallel development of both rationalizing religious fundamentalisms and magical cults—which respectively challenge accounts of modernity as a process of both secularization and disenchantment—have led some to question the value of the term modernity. Yet, the need to acknowledge, describe and account for the character and scale of the dramatic transformations of recent centuries continually forces us back to some notion of modernity as both a sociological and an epistemological condition that has developed within interweaving processes of economic, social, cultural, intellectual, political and religious change. Notions of modernity are repeatedly critiqued and challenged, yet they nonetheless refuse to die and continually reappear, often in new guises, after each new assault on their value and validity. Bruno Latour observes,

> Modernity comes in as many versions as there are thinkers or journalists, yet all its definitions point, in one way or another, to the passage of time. The adjective 'modern' designates a new regime, an acceleration, a rupture, a revolution in time. When the word 'modern', 'modernisation', or 'modernity' appears, we are defining by contrast, an archaic and stable past. Furthermore, the word is

always being thrown into the middle of a fight, in a quarrel where there are winners and losers, Ancients and Moderns. (Latour 1993, p. 10)

Given the multiplicity of forms of modern life, Michael Saler's extended descriptive definition, which sets the scene for his critique of accounts of the modern world as disenchanted detailed in Chapter One, provides an apt frame for the analyses in this book:

> In broad outline, modernity has come to signify a mixture of political, social, intellectual, economic, technological and psychological factors, several of which can be traced to earlier centuries and other cultures, which merged synergistically in the West between the sixteenth and nineteenth centuries. These factors include (but are not exhausted by) the emergence of the autonomous and rational subject; the differentiation of cultural spheres; the rise of liberal and democratic states; the turn to psychologism and self-reflexivity; the dominance of secularism, nationalism, capitalism, industrialism, urbanism, consumerism, and scientism. Different accounts of modernity may stress diverse combinations or accentuate some factors more than others. There is one characteristic of modernity, however, that has been emphasised fairly consistently by intellectuals since the eighteenth century: that modernity is 'disenchanted'. (Saler 2006, p. 694)

I address accounts of the multiplicity of modernities and detail Bruno Latour's account of modernity as a fractured condition of rationalization with hybrid practice in Chapter One.

Disenchantment and Enchantment

While many accounts of modernity represent it as a disenchanted condition, the notion of disenchantment itself is in fact poorly theorized. Indeed, the literature on modernity has focused much more pointedly on processes of rationalization and secularization, with accounts of disenchantment operating almost as an afterthought. Michael Saler and Richard Jenkins number among the few scholars to have addressed this gap. Saler sets the context of his account of modern enchantment, which I detail in Chapter One, by observing that by the disenchantment of the world Max Weber meant

> the loss of the overarching meanings, animistic connections, magical expectations, and spiritual explanations that had characterised the traditional world, as results of ongoing 'modern' processes of rationalisation, secularisation, and bureaucratisation. (Saler 2006, p. 695)

Jenkins describes Weber's notion of disenchantment as

> [t]he historical process by which the natural world and all areas of human experience become experienced and understood as less mysterious; defined, at least in principle, as knowable, predictable and manipulable by humans; conquered and incorporated into the interpretative schema of science and rational government. (Jenkins 2000, p. 12)

Jenkins makes the important point that secularization and disenchantment are not the same, although they are often confused and conflated (Jenkins 2000, p. 19). David Lyons observes that secularization originally described the transfer to the state of properties once owned by organized religion. In modernization theory, this historical loss of religious influence in Western Europe "was generalised into a theory that viewed societies as increasingly marked by a mutual exclusion of religion and modernity" (Lyon 2000, p. 22). Anthony Giddens reflects this view of secularization when he argues that "most of the situations of modern social life are manifestly incompatible with religion as a pervasive influence on day-to-day life" (Giddens 1990, p. 109, cited in Lyon 2000, p. 22). The categorical difference between secularization and disenchantment is highlighted by the fact that the two poles of the modern, ostensibly secularized world—namely, organized religion and non-religious secularism—are both equally critical of magical forms of enchantment. While secularist critics represent supernatural ritual as a superstitious residue of premodernity that holds society back from attaining rational scientific modernity, religious doctrinalists often see it as a form of heresy that needs to be expunged to attain pure and true religious insight.

Raymond Lee and Susan Ackerman propose that re-enchantment, which they relate to notions of charisma, emerges from an exhaustion of the project of rationalizing modernity in combination with romanticist challenges to processes of disenchantment: "[W]e conceptualise religious change in the new millennium as the reversibility of disenchantment" (Lee and Ackerman 2018, p. vii). However, Lee and Ackerman conflate the rise of magical cults, New Age shamanism and fundamentalist movements as all representing forms of re-enchantment. In this, they confuse two significantly different trends in modern religious change. It is important to differentiate the rise of anti-secularist, anti-magical forms of doctrinalism that emphasize scriptural sources of faith and aim to "purify" religion, on the one hand, from cults centred on magical ritual, on the other. In this study I restrict the notion of enchantment to the latter trend. Doctrinalism is anti-secularist, but in its emphasis on the primacy of correct belief and uprooting both heresy and ritualism it cannot be characterized as reflecting a form of enchantment or re-enchantment. In contrast to Lee and Ackerman, I also argue that enchantment is produced out of the conditions of late modernity and is not an anti-modernist reaction.

I should also emphasize that this book is not a study of "re-enchantment" in Thailand. Modern Thai ritual life has never been secularized or disenchanted. Enchantment has never been purged or eliminated even from official practices. Rather, as detailed in Chapter Two, in the process of modernization following the influences of the imperial and neo-imperial West, magical rituals were often relegated to an informal or inferior sector of social life where they were overlooked or ignored by much past academic research. This study is of the further effervescence of magical enchantments in Thailand as a consequence of late-modern economic, media and other influences.

Jenkins astutely points out that while the claim that the modern world is increasingly disenchanted is a central tenet of Weberian sociology of religion, what enchantment in fact denotes as a category of sociological analysis is rarely if ever defined. This is perhaps because most sociologists have assumed that modernity has expunged enchantment from the contemporary world and hence it is not in need of being considered in detail. In this gap, Jenkins provides the following definition:

> Enchantment conjures up, and is rooted in, understandings and experiences of the world in which there is more to life than the material, the visible or the explainable; in which the philosophies and principles of Reason or rationality cannot by definition dream of the totality of life; in which the quotidian norms and routines of linear time and space are only part of the story; and in which the collective sum of sociability and belonging is elusively greater than its individual parts. (Jenkins 2000, p. 29)

Saler's definition of the disenchantment of modernity, cited above, also provides a basis for a counterpoint definition of modern enchantment as "the production of overarching meanings, animistic connections, magical expectations, and spiritual explanations" out of the sociological conditions and processes of modernity. Erick White (2014) argues that in Thailand the expansion of the market and urbanization have fostered novel religious movements based on new forms of charismatic authority. He offers what can be regarded as a practical definition of the production of modern enchantment in Thailand when he states that these new movements reflect "an efflorescence of diverse and innovative models of religious personhood, devotional expression, esoteric mastery, and sacralising technique" (White 2014, p. 433).

Religion and Cults

As will be discussed in Chapter Two, as a result of Western influence in the region, Southeast Asian proponents of both secular and religious forms of modernity now maintain categorical distinctions between "magic", "supernaturalism" and "belief", on the one hand, and state-sanctioned and state-sponsored forms of "religion", on the other. In Thailand there is now a distinct set of discursive categories—*sasana, saiyasat, khwam-cheua, sattha, latthi, latthi-phithi*—that provide focuses for different sets of ideas and attitudes, and which also carry political and bureaucratic valence. Bénédicte Brac de la Perrière observes that many aspects of the ritual landscapes of mainland Southeast Asian societies remain under-examined because of a Buddhist-studies bias in the academy that emerged from the "contrast between religion and ritual that was historically produced in early modern Europe by the progressive differentiation of a properly religious field…. According to this view, actions that are not truly 'religious' in a given society are termed 'ritual'" (Brac de le Perrière 2017, p. 65).

Official and academic discourses in Thailand now distinguish between "magic" or the "supernatural", *saiyasat*, and "religion", *sasana*. *Saiyasat* involves the ritualistic invocation of supernatural power and includes magical rituals and practices. This broad term covers everything from protective amulets and tattoos to spirit mediumship, love potions and the worship of spirits inhabiting trees, mountains, termite mounds and freaks of nature, often believed able to predict lucky lottery numbers. Tambiah describes *saiyasat* as a "technology" (Tambiah 1977, p. 119), in the sense that it is a collective name for the instrumental knowledge of ritual. *Saiyasat* is often glossed as "animism" or "supernaturalism" by Western authors and is typically disparaged as "superstition", "mysticism" or "black magic" by both secular and religious critics in Thailand. Thai secularists critique *saiyasat* as being the opposite of scientific rational modernity, describing it as a "premodern residue" of "superstition" that they maintain holds Thailand back from becoming a fully modern society and polity. For their part, reformist Buddhists see *saiyasat* forms of supernaturalism as a perversion of orthodox religion, labelling it as a heretical or a superstitious "accretion" to true Buddhism. In summary, *saiyasat* is now the maligned other of both secular and religious expressions of modernity in Thailand.[1] Nonetheless, Craig Reynolds (2019, p. 152) makes the important point that the technologies of *saiyasat* are not only available to subaltern groups and marginalized classes but also to state institutions. Despite being an object of critique, *saiyasat* is widely accessed by all social strata and is a central component of vernacular Buddhism accessed by elites as well as the general public.

A distinction between formally recognized institutional "religion" (*sasana*), on the one hand, and popular or "cultic ritual" (*latthi-phithi*), expressions of "belief" (*khwam-cheua*) and "faith" (*sattha*), on the other, is now also established in the discourses of the Thai academy and national bureaucracy. Buddhist monasteries and the Buddhist monkhood, as well as Islamic mosques and other places of worship, which collectively fall under the umbrella of the term *sasana* or "religion", are administered within the civilian bureaucracy by the Department of Religious Affairs (*krom kan-sasana*), which is located within the Ministry of Culture. In contrast, the Ministry of the Interior is responsible for the oversight of Chinese Taoist temples, Brahmanical shrines, and sites of ritual practice that are described as expressions of "belief" (*khwam-cheua*) and "faith" (*sattha*) rather than as forms of "religion" or *sasana*. That is, the discursive divide between religion and ritual is institutionalized within the bureaucratic structures of the modern Thai state.

Eugénie Mérieau (2018) notes that the term *latthi*, which she translates as "cult", appeared in a contradistinctive relation with *sasana* ("religion") in the first Thai constitution promulgated in the aftermath of the June 1932 revolution that overthrew the absolute monarchy and instituted a constitutional monarchy form of government. Article 13 of this constitution stated that "a person shall enjoy full liberty to profess a religion (*sasana*) or cult (*latthi*), and shall enjoy liberty to perform rites (*phithi*) according to his own belief, provided that it is not against the duty of Thai citizens or contrary to public order or good morals of the people" (Mérieau 2018, p. 12).[2] In his studies of the cults of wealth of King Chulalongkorn and Kuan Im, which I detail in Chapter Four, Nidhi Eeoseewong (1993, 1994) describes these movements with the neologism *latthi-phithi* ("doctrine-ritual"), which he glosses in English as "cult". Nidhi defines *latthi-phithi* as "a ritually rich religious doctrine which is not a part of the 'principles' (*lak-kan*) or orthodoxy of the dominant religion (*sasana*) adhered to by the majority of people" (Nidhi 1993, p. 11n). While "cult" at times has negative connotations in English, I use this term to describe the prosperity movements because it is the now preferred translation of *latthi-phithi* in Thai academic discourse. In contrast to Nidhi's characterization of *latthi-phithi* as minority phenomena, however, I detail how the cults of wealth have moved from being unorthodox marginal ritual forms to become part of Thailand's cultural and religious mainstream. It should be noted, nonetheless, that *latthi-phithi* is used with negative connotations by some reformist Buddhists such as the clerical author *Phra* Phaisan Visalo, a well-known follower of the teachings of the philosopher monk Buddhadasa. In a book detailing what he sees as a series of crises confronting Thai Buddhism, *Phra* Phaisan laments that "cults" (*latthi-phithi*) are spreading like wildfire while "mainstream Buddhism is contracting and in decline" ([*Phra*] Phaisan 2003, p. 185). In his critique of the cults of wealth, *Phra* Phaisan observes,

> What is noteworthy about these cults (which tend to have laypersons as leaders) is that if they are not explicitly spirit medium cults then they have developed from such cults.... These cults have become widely popular because they are able to respond to the diverse desires of the middle class, which in general are desires for worldly success. ([*Phra*] Phaisan 2003, p. 185)

The Religious Field

In this study I draw on Pierre Bourdieu's notion of the religious field in characterizing the complexity of Buddhist and non-Buddhist teachings, ritual observances and material objects that constitute the totality of Thai religiosity. As White observes, Bourdieu conceptualized social and religious fields as "hierarchically structured arenas defined by social struggle over symbolic capital within a pluralistic field of associated competitors" (White 2014, p. 18). In his account of the religious field, however, Bourdieu argued that "most authors tend to accord to magic the characteristics of systems of practices and representations belonging to the least economically developed social formations or to the most disadvantaged social classes of class-divided societies" (Bourdieu 1991, p. 13). Bourdieu also continued to describe magic as a "survival" from the past (p. 13). The cults of wealth studied here present two significant contrasts to Bourdieu's account. First, I study modern magic among Thailand's elites and, second, I argue that magic is not a mere survival but rather is actively produced out of the conditions of modernity. I concur with White in distancing myself from a number of Bourdieu's assumptions, in particular "that religion is of declining importance in modernity,... that religion's principle social function is to naturalise inequality and differential power, and ... that religion's main appeal to elites is to legitimate dominance and its pleasures [while] its main appeal to non-elites is to compensate for domination and its suffering" (White 2014, p. 17n6).

Vernacular, Popular and Reformist Buddhism

This study focuses on aspects of the Thai religious amalgam that are often described as "popular Buddhism". This expression was coined by Anuman Rajadhon to denote religious forms in which animism and Buddhism together with elements of Brahmanism and Hinduism "have become intermingled in an inextricable degree" (Anuman 1968, p. 33, cited in Terwiel 2012, p. 2). Benjamin Baumann rephrases Stanley Tambiah's operative definition of Buddhism as "religious action in which monks officiate and participate" (Tambiah 1968, p. 43) to define Thai popular Buddhism as "religious practices in which monks are not the main incumbents—although they may be present" (Baumann 2017, p. 19). White regards Thai popular Buddhism as "a plural and contested relational milieu of competing religious authorities, actors, practices, ideologies and experiences" (White 2014, p. 357). He also observes that the modern efflorescence of religious phenomena outside the boundaries of the sangha or Buddhist monkhood "is diverse and far exceeds any simple designation of Thai popular Buddhism as centred on the magical, the supernatural, the apotropaic or the cultic" (White 2014, p. 294).

While earlier generations of scholars used terms such as "folk Buddhism" and "folk religion" to describe the Thai religious complex, it is now more common to use notions of "popular Buddhism" and "popular religion" because they link religion with popular culture as a form of everyday practice integrally related to the market and media. Pattana Kitiarsa (2012) notes that there is no Thai term equivalent to "popular Buddhism", although the expression *phuttha phanit* ("commodified Buddhism" or "commerce in Buddhism") is used, typically in a derogatory sense, to refer to the commercialization of Buddhism. The cults of wealth studied here fall within the scope of both the English expression "popular Buddhism" and the Thai notion of *phuttha phanit*, and in this study I use "popular" to also refer to non-state culture in marketized, mediatized settings. This contrasts with the term "folk", which tends to imply cultural forms in rural settings, and "official", which denotes cultural expressions that are promoted or supported by state actors and agencies.

Nonetheless, Bénédicte Brac de la Perrière (2009, p. 192) warns that the term "popular religion" in the context of Theravada Buddhism in Southeast Asia may at times be misleading because some rituals overlap with royal and elite religious practice and are not restricted to those from lower socio-economic strata. Indeed, as detailed in the following chapters, the participation of Thai elites, as well as ordinary people from all walks of life, is a notable feature of the cross-class appeal of the cults of wealth. Furthermore, many of the structural features of the cults of wealth are also characteristic of royal religious practice in Thailand. Given this, I use "popular" to denote the mass religion of the marketplace, while I use "vernacular" to refer to the totality of the Thai religious field, including folk (rural), popular (urban) and official (royal) forms of religious observance that include magical rituals conducted by monks as well as those that are practised outside Buddhist monasteries and conducted by non-monastic religious specialists. This use of "vernacular" draws from and engages White's (2022) use of the expression "vernacular religiosity" in Southeast Asia.

Popular and vernacular Buddhism are here also contrasted with "reform Buddhism" or "reformist Buddhism". Heinz Bechert (1994) also calls reformist Buddhism "Buddhist Modernism", which involves a demythologization of Buddhist teachings, the view that Buddhism is a philosophy that makes it compatible with modern science, and an expanding role of the laity in Buddhist affairs (cited in Preedee 2018, p. 224). Bechert defines the demythologization of Buddhism as the use of early scriptural sources "combined with a modernisation of concepts of cosmology and a symbolic interpretation of traditional myths which were customarily associated with Buddhism" (Bechert 1994, pp. 254–56, cited in Preedee 2018, p. 249n66). Clifford Geertz described the modern rationalization of religion as involving the systematization of doctrine, the intensification of religious concern and the expansion of formal religious organizations (Geertz 1973, p. 187, cited in Gottowik 2014, p. 17). In contrast to reformist and rationalized forms of Buddhism, this study considers the modern enchantment of Thai religiosity in the absence of a systematic doctrine and without formal religious organizations.

Magic

There is no general agreement on what "religion" and "magic" respectively constitute as either sociological phenomena or analytical categories. Indeed, some anthropologists and religious studies scholars have debated whether the Western distinctions between "religion", the "supernatural" and "magic" are valid in understanding the complex forms of religious expression and ritual found in Southeast Asia. White observes that the notion of "magic" is often a negative remainder category for phenomena that fall outside of religion or science, being used to describe "an intellectual wastebasket filled with logically unrelated leftovers sharing little collective substantive or definitional similarity" (White 2016, p. 3). What comes to be labelled as magic is "heterogeneous, diverse, and unstable", made evident by the "repeated inability to conceptually distinguish between religion and magic in a clear, convincing, or consistent manner" (p. 3). Furthermore, the term magic often operates as "a polemical weapon of rhetorical disparagement in the service of context-specific claims to power, control, authority, and legitimacy" (p. 3). Bourdieu similarly argues that magic came to be used as a derogatory term to describe older religious forms in settings of hierarchy and contestation:

> [A] system of practices and beliefs is made to appear as *magic* or *sorcery*, an inferior religion, whenever it occupies a dominated position in the structure of relations of symbolic power.... Thus, the appearance of a religious ideology relegates ancient myths to the state of magic or sorcery. As Weber notes, it is the suppression of one religion, under the influence of a political or ecclesiastical power, to the advantage of another religion, reducing the ancient gods to the rank of demons, that usually gave birth to the opposition between religion and magic. (Bourdieu 1991, p. 12; emphases in original)

White observes that in Buddhist studies both scholars and practitioners commonly use the term magic to refer to "spells and charms, amulets and talismans, potions and fumigants, numerology and divination, astrology and alchemy, the conjuring and expelling of evil spirits, necromancy and communication with deities, and sorcery and witchcraft" (White 2016, p. 4). As detailed above, in Thailand these diverse ritual forms are collectively called *saiyasat*, which I translate as "magic" in this study. What magical ritual arts share is forms of stylized action "designed to produce desired extraordinary consequences" (p. 5) in the world. Indeed, magical ritual action is designed "to access, channel, control, and manipulate otherwise hidden extraordinary potencies and powers" in the service of often pragmatic and mundane goals (p. 5). Stanley Tambiah describes magic as ritual action that is held to be automatically effective: "Magical acts in their ideal forms are thought to have an intrinsic and automatic efficacy" (Tambiah 1990, p. 7). Raymond Lee similarly defines magic as "the ritualistic means of world mastery" (Lee 2010, p. 182).

White urges us to avoid the term magic because of its use as a marker of otherness in modernist discourses, contending that it is more appropriate to call these diverse phenomena "ritual arts of efficacy centered on mundane, worldly concerns" (White 2016, p. 4). Nonetheless, White also observes that in an increasing number of studies magic has been relocated from the ambiguous margins of Buddhism to the substantive heart of the religion and that the conceptual vocabulary drawn upon in studying magic has "shifted to discussions of enchantment, the miraculous, ritual potency and other less pejorative interpretive frames" (pp. 12–13). While recognizing the pejorative connotations of magic in many modernist theoretical settings, I nevertheless use this term in this study precisely because of its capacity to challenge and unsettle views of modernity as a disenchanted condition. I use magic as a central term in the critiques developed here to argue that in many contemporary settings modernity is actively producing new magical imaginaries and rituals. As Bruce Kapferer (2002) observes, in the context of critiques of modernization theory, there has been a rehabilitation of magic in some fields of anthropology and religious studies. In summarizing the growing number of studies of modern magic, he notes that magic is increasingly viewed as a "hybrid form par excellence" that works in liminal spaces "at the boundaries and margins" (Kapferer 2002, p. 22). The rituals of modern magic "are frequently an amalgam of different forms" and are based on processes "of fusing or crossing different registers of meaning and reasoning. Such observations are problematic to a rationalizing approach" (p. 22). I draw extensively on this critical framing of modern magic in this study as well as Kapferer's contention that magic is a form of reason that appears in the modern world "in those spaces where other modes of reasoning have failed" (p. 8).

Ritual

While ritual, or ritualism, is disparaged as an inadequate or illegitimate form of observance in doctrine-centred views of religious modernity, I view ritual practice in positive terms in this book. Oscar Salemink observes,

> Ritual does not necessarily refer to religion in the narrow sense of the word, but to a formalization of behavior according to a particular script in a special time-space outside of the ordinary and everyday. In his classic work on ritual, Victor Turner focuses attention on this ritual time-space as liminal, that is, out of the ordinary, performative [*communitas*], governed by other rules of behavior than in everyday life (anti-structure), often mocking the everyday experience (inversion), and creating a sense of belonging for members of a particular group. In a context where ritual events

are no longer clearly linked with traditional rites of passage or religious events, Catherine Bell (1992), Felicia Hughes-Freeland and Mary Crain (1998) prefer to speak of the ritualization of behavior, practices, or processes. Ritual always refers to boundaries, categories, and groups and therefore is a social phenomenon that concerns questions of identity and identification—giving a partial answer to the question 'who are we?' (Salemink 2008, p. 267)

For practitioners, the central criterion in assessing ritual practice is not epistemological. It is not a matter of demonstrating, instantiating or validating doctrine or belief. Rather, the key criterion in ritual cultures is performative; that is, whether a practice is regarded as therapeutically effective in healing or ensuring prosperity and whether it is dramatically and performatively convincing in its aesthetic presentation. As Salemink notes, the compelling and central aspects of ritual are "efficacy and aesthetic pleasure" (Salemink 2007, p. 570). For ritual to be viewed as being convincing, it must conform to cultural expectations and norms of drama and performance as well as being viewed as therapeutically efficacious. Salemink further observes that "[c]ompleting the ritual engenders enhanced well-being and confidence in the future on the part of participants. In the eyes of the followers, then, the efficacy of the ritual lies in the effects in response to the wishes—whether they be well-being, health or wealth" (Salemink 2010, p. 275). This view of the performative efficacy of ritual practice is an important element of the account of the making of modern enchantment that I develop in Chapter Seven.

Spirit Possession and Spirit Mediumship

Kirsten Endres notes that some anthropologists distinguish between spirit mediumship as the expected possession of a ritual specialist by a spirit or deity in contrast to spirit possession as "an unexpected, unwanted intrusion of the supernatural in the lives of humans" (Endres 2011, p. 76). This distinction is sometimes made because in some Southeast Asian settings, as Andrea Lauser reports from Vietnam, "only a controlled medium is possessed by the spirits, whereas uncontrolled possession is the sign of a ghost obsession" (Lauser 2018, p. 21). Following Erick White (personal communication) and Bénédicte Brac de la Perrière (personal communication), however, in this study I use "spirit possession" to refer to all phenomena in which a nonhuman agency temporarily occupies and takes control of the body and agency of a human being. This may include both positive adorcistic forms of possession as well as negative forms of possession that the affected person, or those around them, seek to end through exorcism. Luc de Heusch (1962) coined the term "adorcism" to refer to ritual practices in which a possessed person placates, accommodates or invokes spiritual entities. It has a positive connotation and is contrasted with exorcism, which denotes the attempt to expel unwanted spirits from a possessed person. Jean-Michel Oughourlian (1991, p. 97) defines adorcism as "voluntary, desired, and curative possessions".

I use "spirit mediumship" to refer to forms of possession that are more frequent and regular, in which the identity of the possessing spirit is usually made clear and when communication with the spirit is more robust and multifaceted. Spirit mediumship also denotes situations in which the possessed person takes on and identifies with the social role of being a medium for a possessing entity and is an experience of possession that is valued positively. In this usage I follow White, who defines spirit mediumship as a clearly ascribed and recurring role of ritual specialists who act as intermediaries of an identified possessing deity and who identify with the possessing spirit (White 2014, p. 40n11). Spirit mediumship thus usually entails an emically recognized social and cultural role in addition to the phe-nomenological experience of possession. Spirit mediumship is more about the *ability to channel* spirits, while spirit possession refers to the broader *phenomenon* of being entered by spirits, whether in a positive or negative way.

Spirited Enchantment and Ghostly Haunting

Invited Spirits of Prosperity versus Unbidden Ghosts

Some film studies and cultural studies accounts of the persistence of belief in and representations of ghosts and the supernatural in contemporary global cultures have drawn on the notion of modernity as being haunted. These accounts employ psychoanalytic metaphors in which modernity is imagined as entailing a series of exclusions of premodern discourses and practices, which, on the model of Freud's theory of the return of the repressed, return to haunt ostensibly secular modernity in the form of persistent accounts and cinematic representations of ghosts and demons (for example, see Johnson 2014; Fuhrmann 2016). In his account of the revival of the genre of Thai horror films in the early 2000s, Adam Knee describes ghost films as "dealing with the return of the past in supernatural form" (Knee 2005, p. 141). In analysing contemporary Thai horror films, Pattana Kitiarsa argues that "ghosts need to be taken seriously as an analytic category of modernity" (Pattana 2011, p. 202), contending that

[g]hosts and their ghostly presence are the products of modern social marginalisation, made in and through the modernisation process. Ghosts appear and make their presence felt at the various margins of both real and imagined modern social worlds. Thai horror films of late show emotional and intimate sides of modernity, suggesting that modernity has produced a marginalising dark side. (Pattana 2011, p. 202)

These film studies analyses of ghost and horror movies also draw on the notion of the uncanny. The uncanny is mysterious, at once strange and familiar, being a situation of both familiarity and threat manifesting through the same person, object or event. Freud argued that the things we find the most terrifying appear so because they once seemed familiar: "[F]or this uncanny is in reality nothing new or alien, but something that is familiar and old fashioned in the mind and which has become alienated from it through the process of repression" (Freud 1955, p. 364, cited in Israeli 2005, p. 381). Ghostly and uncanny hauntings are indeed one dimension of the field of Thai popular and vernacular religion. But the cults of wealth studied here do not conform to this view of modernity as being haunted by unwanted spirits of its premodern past. The notion of the uncanny—the unsettling return of that which one thought had been overcome—does not fully capture the empirical setting of a modernity in which magic has emerged more strongly than ever in affirmative and adorcistic rather than unsettling ways. In contrast to ghosts, which are typically seen as unwanted and potentially harmful visitations that need to be exorcised, the spirits that are invoked in the magical cults of wealth and associated spirit possession rituals are invited to speak and are actively sought out for their other-worldly wisdom to guide and assist human beings. The spirit mediumship that is a central ritual form associated with the cults of wealth is not an engagement with demons or the monstrous but, on the contrary, aims to bring the supernatural into the human realm so that its special powers can be used to benefit the living. The inhabitants of the spirit world are invoked because it is believed they know more about our world than we do ourselves, and it is their wisdom and supernatural insight that human followers seek to benefit from.

The efflorescence of Thai magical cults of wealth does not reflect the return of a repressed premodernity. As White argues, it is mistaken to "interpret the efflorescence of popular Buddhism as primarily the resurgence of a previously repressed syncretic heritage or polytropic sensibility" (White 2014, p. 194). Rather, we are seeing completely novel formulations of enchanted religiosity. The cults of wealth have emerged from a further working out of the cultural logic of modernity, of the productive capacity of market-based techno-capitalist rationality that, when taken to its logical conclusion, produces seemingly non-rational results. This is not an irruption of repressed unreason. To understand Thai magical cults of wealth we do not need a negative notion of modernity as being haunted. Rather, we need a positive theory of enchantment that imagines magic in a productive relationship with modernity. I develop an account of the production of enchantment in modernity in Chapter Seven.

In the Thai context, Pattana describes ghosts as "angry, vengeful or malevolent spirits of a dead person" (Pattana 2011, p. 203) and he notes that Thailand has a diverse range of ghosts and terms for them, including "demon (*pisat*), ever-hungry ghoul (*pret*), malevolent, internal-organ-consuming spirit (*phi pop*), and monster/zombie (*phi dip*)" (p. 203). In the past, the generic term *phi* was used, often in combination with a variety of qualifying expressions, to denote both spirits whose presence is sought out in adorcistic rituals as well as ghosts whose haunting presence was regarded as needing to be exorcized. In recent decades, however, spirits whose presence is actively sought out in the cults of wealth have largely come to be known by the Sanskrit/Pali-derived term *thep* (from the Sanskrit *deva*) and the royal term *jao* ("lord"), with *phi* now largely implying "vernacular perceptions of ghostly presence and uncanny haunting" (p. 203). White (2014) regards this discursive shift and relabelling of spirits as *thep* and *jao* in adorcistic rituals as part of a process of "upgrading" spirit beliefs and rituals in contemporary urban Thailand.

There is one sense, however, in which accounts of the haunting of modernity do capture the epistemological and theoretical imperative to develop positive accounts of the enchantment of the modern world. As Saler argues, enchantment is part of our normal condition, "and far from having fled with the rise of science, it continues to exist (though often unrecognised) wherever our capacity to explain the world's behaviour is slim, that is, where neither science nor practical knowledge seem of much utility" (Saler 2006, p. 716). He concludes that the discourse of modernity as being disenchanted is "a haunting presence that will not cease to disturb our thoughts until it is reunited with its antinomial partner, 'modern enchantment'" (p. 716).

Fundamentalism

Some accounts of fundamentalism describe it as an anti-modern form of religious expression. For example, Lee and Ackerman describe fundamentalisms as exhibiting "a deep-seated antagonism against the symbols of modernity" (2018, p. 54). In contrast, however, I view the fundamentalist emphasis upon doctrinal purity and rebuilding society from scriptural first principles as betraying distinctly modern preoccupations with purifying belief and a rationalizing reconstruction of knowledge and social life. In this I follow Martin Marty and Scott Appleby, who regard fundamentalism as reflecting the strategies

> by which beleaguered believers attempt to preserve their distinctive identity as a people or group. Feeling this identity to be at risk in the contemporary era, they fortify it by a selective retrieval of doctrines, beliefs, and practices from a sacred past... [R]eligious identity thus renewed becomes the exclusive and absolute basis for a recreated political and social order that is oriented to the future rather than the past. By selecting elements of tradition and modernity, fundamentalists seek to remake the world... (Marty and Appleby 1991, p. 835)

As Charles Keyes et al. point out, fundamentalism is radically opposed to the complexity and hybridity of the enchanted imaginaries that underpin magical ritual: "Fundamentalists point to an authority found in scriptures in order to undermine religious pluralism" (Keyes et al. 1994, p. 12). This trenchant opposition to the pluralism of magical ritual reflects the emphasis on purity that Latour (1993) identifies as a key tenet of purifying ideologies of modernity.

Neoliberalism

Capitalism has developed through several historical phases. This study focuses on capitalism in its neoliberal form, which came to dominate transnational economic and political life in the decades after the end of the Cold War. David Harvey defines neoliberalism as

> a theory of political economic practices that proposes that human wellbeing can be best advanced by liberating entrepreneurial freedoms and skills within an institutional framework characterised by strong private property rights, free markets and free trade. The role of the state is to create and preserve an institutional framework appropriate to such practices. (Harvey 2005, p. 2)

Sherry Ortner observes that while much work has represented neoliberalism as a new and more brutal form of capitalism that has expanded rapidly across the world, anthropologists have also documented "creative adaptations to neoliberalism, as well as resistance movements against it" (Ortner 2016, p. 48). The cults of wealth studied in this book are indeed notable creative adaptations to the neoliberal order in post–Cold War Thailand.

Notes

1. Despite its centrality in Thai discourses of religion, ritual and magic, the term *saiyasat* has a somewhat obscure history. Peter Skilling describes an inscription from Kamphaeng Phet in north central Thailand dated to 1510 CE (BE 2053) that records the meritorious deeds of the ruler of that state, *Chao Phraya* Dharmās'okarāja, and includes one of the earliest references to the term *saiyasat*, which in the inscription has a Sanskritized spelling as *saiyasāṣaṇā* (Skilling 2009, p. 187, citing Prasert and Griswold 1992, pp. 625–40). Skilling notes that George Coedès regarded the term *saiyasāṣaṇā* to derive from the Pali *seyyasāsana*, literally "the excellent religion" (Coedès 1924, p. 159n1, cited in Skilling 2009, p. 187), which in turn derived from the Sanskrit *s'reyas*, "excellent", "superior". Skilling observes that the term *s'reya-s'āsanā* does not exist in Indian Sanskrit literature and its Pali form *seyya-sāsanā* is not known in the Theravada Buddhist literature that derives from Sri Lanka. He adds that while *sāsanā* is the final element of the compound term in this inscription, it would have been pronounced in Thai as *sāt*—that is, *saiya-sat*—and thus would have been a homophone of a compound formed from the Sanskrit term *s'āstra* meaning "text" or "teaching". Later, and indeed modern, Thai spellings of *saiyasat* are based on the Sanskrit term *s'āstra*, with *saiy* subsequently coming to mean magic and sorcery in the later Ayutthaya and Bangkok periods. Skilling observes that significantly more work needs to be undertaken on the origins and development of indigenous Sanskrit- and Pali-derived terms for Buddhism and Brahmanism in Thailand and elsewhere in Southeast Asia.

2. Mérieau notes that this section of the 1932 Siamese constitution closely follows the form of religious freedom enshrined in the 1889 Japanese constitution (Mérieau 2018, p. 12n78).

Part One

Why Religious Modernity Trends in Two Opposing Directions

Chapter One

Fundamentalism against Magic:
The Contradictions of Religious Modernity

Certain developments in Asia, such as those occurring in Thailand, where the dynamism of capitalist production is rivalled only by the drive of diverse forms of ritual activity, both within and outside of Buddhism ... are an affront to occidental myths of modernity.... Religion and ritual are crucial to the life of 'modern' nations, in Asia as elsewhere. They urge us to ... distrust disenchantment, to rethink the telos of development that still informs the models of much mainstream social science. (Jean Comaroff 1994, p. 301)

Practices that continue to treat the world as enchanted ... testify to the existence of realms of practice and, sometimes, institutions that are not premodern and yet are not always fully part of the world modernity brought into being. Sometimes, they can be incorporated into the circuits of capital accumulation. (Sanjay Seth 2013, p. 148)

Introduction: The Making and Remaking
of Magic in Global Modernity

The diverse new forms of supernatural observance and magical ritual apparent in Thailand, and across Buddhist and Confucian East and Southeast Asia (see Yang 2000; Bautista 2012; Brac de la Perrière et al. 2014), demonstrate the intense religious dynamism that emerges in the context of market-centred, mediatized global modernity (Dirlik 2005). The novel forms of magical ritual in Thailand may escape classical definitions of modernity, but they are not premodern traditions.

On the contrary, they are highly contemporary phenomena. As David Lyon contends, "[m]any modernities exist, and they may be shown to have different ways of relating to the religious sphere" (Lyon 2000, p. 21). The Thai cults of wealth provide a lens through which we can see broader processes operating at the global level. This emergence of magical cults of wealth out of the economic and social conditions of late twentieth-century capitalism challenges us to rethink the meaning, character and direction of modernity. Indeed, the efflorescence of spirit cults in the midst of rapid market-based economic growth contradicts classical theories of the relationship of religion and capitalist expansion. As Sanjay Seth observes,

> There are realms of knowing and living in the Western world, as in the non-Western world, that are part of the modern—they are not 'survivals' of premodernity destined eventually to be swept away—but which are neither lived through, nor wholly accessible to us through the categories of the social sciences. (Seth 2013, p. 149)

And as Michael Saler contends,

> The seeming 'universal' distinctions championed by the Western metropole between modernity and tradition, or secularism and superstition, often do not hold up when viewed from the 'periphery' of non-Western cultures negotiating processes of modernisation in complex ways. (Saler 2006, p. 700)

To understand the conditions under which global modernity produces new forms of religious enchantment it is necessary to appreciate the place of magical imaginaries and ritual in the broader conditions of modernity, which have also seen the emergence of diverse forms of often stridently anti-magical religious doctrinalism and fundamentalism. Indeed, how is it that religious modernity has produced new forms of magic alongside anti-magical doctrinalism, sometimes within the same society and religious field? In this chapter I trace the development of understandings of modernity as a multiple set of contradictory processes in which disenchantment and enchantment are each equally prominent moments within a total complex phenomenon. I review the role that studies of religion have had in critiquing accounts that represent modernity as a singular movement of ever-intensifying rationalization. These critical perspectives permit magic and enchantment to be integrated within understandings of modernity. Tracing the history of challenges to ideas of modernity as secular and disenchanting, and the reimagined ideas of modernity that have emerged out of these critiques, provides a way to begin to make sense of the apparent contradictions that empirical research present to us.

As Jean Comaroff observes, in accounting for the multiple directions of religious change we need "to be cognizant of the complexity of the world, to be accountable to its paradoxes" (Comaroff and Kim 2011, p. 176). Justin McDaniel argues that "[t]hese competing forces in modern Thailand—centralization and standardization versus expansion and creativity—are not necessarily something that needs to be resolved by the scholar. Indeed, I do not believe they can be" (McDaniel 2011, p. 159). I agree that these divergent religious processes cannot be resolved in terms of established theories of religion and society. But the social reality of the apparent paradox of ritual-based magic and doctrine-centred religion both assuming growing prominence in rapidly developing Asian societies is a phenomenon that poses pressing questions for studies of religion, and for social science more broadly. I believe that these apparently opposing but historically parallel trends can be resolved if we abandon older notions of modernity as secular and disenchanted and draw on the critical perspectives of analysts such as Bruno Latour. The modern period has been marked by an ideology that pitted rationality against magic, and in which rationalization was represented not merely as one of the processes of modernization but rather as the singularly defining feature of modernity.

Latour lays out processes that constitute modernity as an internally conflicted set of epistemological and extra-epistemological operations that are marked by a divide between purifying, rationalizing ideology and practical hybridity. This bifurcation between purifying ideology and hybridizing practice has led to two distinct forms of religious modernity in Thailand: a doctrinal purification of Buddhism, on the one hand, and a hybridizing proliferation of ritual expression, on the other. Each represents the outcome of the operation across the country's religious field of one of the divided processes of modernity identified by Latour. While the modernity of reformist Buddhism is reflected in the dynamics of purifying rationalization, the modernity of the Thai cults of wealth and other new forms of enchantment is manifested through processes of hybridizing ritual practice.

Modernity is multiple across world regions and between societies. It is also internally divided in each of its locally specific forms. To understand how fundamentalism and magic are both equally modern we need to view modernity as a dual and conflicted set of simultaneous, but often contextually distinct, processes of both rationalization and enchantment. In this book I emphasize the moment and contexts of modern enchantment because they have so often been dismissed as not being modern at all, and it is for this reason that the totality of the modern condition has been misunderstood. It is by studying phenomena that purifying and rationalizing ideologies exclude from their limited understanding of the modern condition that we find processes of modern enchantment. These processes have been widely misunderstood as residues of premodernity waiting to die out rather than inherent aspects of the modern condition itself. Magic has not died out because it is continually being made, and remade, by modernity itself. Indeed, it is only by highlighting the practical, ritual-centred conditions of enchantment that the full scope and operation of modernity can be appreciated. This further reveals that modern magic is not an exotic phenomenon found only in "foreign" non-Western societies. It is an inherent dimension within the global modernity shared by all contemporary societies and cultures, and which merely takes different expressions in different times and places. Thailand's modern magic thus tells us something about the general form of the modern condition, and is not irrelevant to understanding the modern West itself.

Weberianism in Thai Studies

Views that modernity is a historical process of inevitable social rationalization and that magical rituals represent premodern rather than modern phenomena continue to be reflected in some studies of Thai popular religion. While numerous scholars of Thai religion have challenged Weberian theory, these critical perspectives have not been appreciated in some areas of Thai political studies and historiography, which continue to be influenced by notions of modernity as a world historical process of disenchantment. The continuing strength of Weberian theory in these fields of Thai studies can lead to contradictions between empirical accounts of efflorescing supernatural cults, on the one hand, and analyses of the ostensible rationalization of the Thai social order, on the other.

Serhat Ünaldi (2016) provides a recent example of the continuing influence of Weberian sociology in Thai studies. His study of how the Thai monarchy has achieved considerable power and influence over recent decades includes detailed accounts of the importance of supernatural rituals for business and other elites. However, drawing directly on Weber, Ünaldi nonetheless surprisingly argues that we can observe "a gradual delegitimation of royal charisma and … the desacralization of the monarchy" in Thailand, which "may thus be seen as part of a movement towards a more rational political and social order.... [T]he effects of this transformation could lead to a gradual erosion of the charismatic foundations of the Thai kingship" (Ünaldi 2016, p. 13).

In fact, the empirical evidence that Ünaldi presents gives a radically contrary picture; namely, that the monarchy has been increasingly sacralized and the Thai political order remains strongly founded on notions and rituals of charismatic leadership. The tension between Ünaldi's empirical observations and his analyses is introduced because of his commitment to Weberian sociology, even though his evidence points to the further enchantment rather than rationalization of Thai economic and social life. For example, while representing the Ratchaprasong shopping area of downtown Bangkok as a space of instrumental rationality, he nonetheless also observes that "local business owners have simultaneously become religious patrons themselves by setting up Hindu shrines at Ratchaprasong intersection, whose popularity often outshines that of more established royal places of worship" (Ünaldi 2016, p. 24).

Ünaldi draws on Weber's account of charismatic authority, which underscores the importance of a leader's perceived magical powers, in detailing how the late King Bhumibol's (r. 1946–2016) supporters came to perceive his ascribed divine qualities. Yet, while detailing this king's accumulation of charismatic magicality across his long seven-decade reign, which I contend demonstrates the modernity of this expression of enchantment, Ünaldi's attachment to Weber's account of rationalization means that he does not acknowledge that his observations challenge this sociology of modernity. On the one hand, Ünaldi correctly observes that "the monarchy's sacred charisma serves as the most potent source of symbolic capital in Thailand" (Ünaldi 2016, p. 50). Yet, while taking charisma seriously, he nonetheless keeps looking, or hoping, for signs of instrumental rationality: "An accelerating this-worldly orientation among the electorate and the growing significance of instrumental rationality, which had been promoted by the monarchy itself, *might* eventually render charismatic leadership in Thailand obsolete" (p. 23; emphasis added). Ünaldi's study is marked by expressed hopes for a rationalized Thai social order that does not appear in any of his accounts and is in fact counter-demonstrated by the evidence he presents.

Saowanee Alexander notes tensions in Ünaldi's account of King Bhumibol's magical charisma, which emphasizes that the king "inherited his royal charisma from traditional beliefs" while only mentioning in passing that this charisma in fact "gradually accumulated over time thanks to the military and other state agencies as well as the interventions of the United States during the Cold War" (Saowanee 2018, p. 649). That is, while noting the importance of King Bhumibol's magical charisma to the late twentieth- and early twenty-first-century Thai cultural, social and political orders, Ünaldi locates the sources of that charisma in past traditions, representing it as a continuation of premodern beliefs rather than as a very recent product of modern processes. Because of his attachment to Weberian notions of rationalization and disenchantment, Ünaldi represents the power of King Bhumibol's magical charisma as a residue of a past religio-political order, and not as an emergent consequence of Thailand's alternative modernity. As reflected in the following quote, Ünaldi's account of the hypothesized emergence of a Thai social order founded on "instrumentally rational social action" is based on prediction and conjecture rather than on any evidence presented in his book:

> If, due to a reorientation of the general public away from value-oriented to instrumentally rational social action, charismatic legitimacy is no longer seen as the *source* of popular support but as the *consequence* of that support, a shift from charismatic authority towards legal-rational forms may be the consequence. (Ünaldi 2016, pp. 24–25; emphasis in original)

The continuing strength of Weberian sociology can lead to a misrecognition of the recentness of the contours of the contemporary Thai religious field. While not drawing on Weber as explicitly as Ünaldi, the recent study by Craig Reynolds (2019) on the life of the famous Thai policeman *Khun* Phantharakratchadet (1899–2006), renowned for his expertise in *saiyasat* magical lore and ritual, is nonetheless also marked by tensions between the empirical evidence of modern enchantment and an analysis that locates the magic of *Khun* Phan, as he is popularly known, in the past. *Khun* Phan was a driving force behind the renovation of the city pillar shrine in his hometown of Nakhon Srithammarat in Southern Thailand and the cult of magical amulets of the new hybrid deity Jatukham-Ramathep, which is discussed later in this study. In concluding his biography of *Khun* Phan and the history of the magical rituals and amulets the former policeman is famous for in Thailand today, Reynolds places his narrative of *Khun* Phan's magic as part of Thailand's past, stating that his "lifelong quest for *saiyasat* knowledge ... hark[s] back to an earlier age in Thailand.... The *saiyasat* magic that he cultivated belongs to an underdeveloped rural sector that no longer exists in an age when villagers have mobile phones and access to the internet" (Reynolds 2019, p. 157).

In contrast to Reynolds, in this book I locate *Khun* Phan's *saiyasat* firmly within the field of Thai religious modernity, and in Chapter Seven I identify the digital communication technologies noted by Reynolds as one of the productive sources of modern forms of enchantment. Also, despite the evidence he adduces, Reynolds further concludes that *Khun* Phan does not have a place in Thai national history: "National history has little place, perhaps no place, in its narrative for such a figure.... He can be a hero to local people but not a hero in the national story" (Reynolds 2019, p. 157). This is an odd concluding statement given that in 2007 *Khun* Phan received a royal-sponsored funeral attended by then Crown prince and current monarch, King Maha Vajiralongkorn (r. 2016–), two fictionalized action movies have been made about him in recent years, and amulets of the Jatukham-Ramathep deity that he helped produce became a national phenomenon in 2007 and following years. In the context of the conservative monarchist politics of recent decades, Reynolds also overlooks the fact that in his final years *Khun* Phan was regarded by many as the last surviving person to hold the now-obsolete noble title of *khun*, which was conferred by King Prajadhipok (r. 1925–35) in the final years of the absolute monarchy. For this reason, *Khun* Phan constituted a potent symbol of royal authority and influence to monarchists and helps explain why his funeral was attended by the future king of Thailand.

I wish to emphasize that in presenting these critiques of Ünaldi's explicit and Reynolds' implicit Weberian analyses, I am not challenging their otherwise excellent empirical accounts of new forms of magical ritual. Indeed, I draw on details from these two authors' studies in later chapters in this book. I simply point out tensions that are introduced into their respective analyses by a reliance upon Weberian notions, which have been challenged by a number of other studies over the past several decades but which Ünaldi and Reynolds do not engage. This indicates the importance of re-emphasizing the findings of these critical studies, which I now turn to in the following section, as a prelude to developing an account of modernity as a dual, internally conflicted condition. Readers who are familiar with these critiques can skip over this section and rejoin my analysis in the later section, "The Contradictions of Religious Modernity".

Critiquing and Rereading Weber on Modernity and Disenchantment

Enlightenment thinkers endeavoured to trace the progressive and rational goal of human history, and as David Jones observes the sociologies of Durkheim and Weber sought methodologies that "could detect the emergence of increasingly more rational social systems appropriate to the modernity which the physical sciences and their technological knowledge had rendered possible" (Jones 1995, p. 9). In this context, Charles Keyes et al. point out that

> Western theories of modernisation ... presupposed the liberation of people from superstition and time-consuming and expensive rituals so that they could participate in a new rationalised order oriented toward the attainment of self-sustaining economic growth. (Keyes et al. 1994, p. 4)

Douglas Pressman notes that the sociologist Robert Bellah (1970) forecast that "in the ongoing cultural collision between traditionalism and modernity being brought about by capitalist development throughout the Third World, tradition was destined to wither" (Pressman 1993, p. 2). In analysing the history of American studies of Thai culture in the decades immediately following World War II, Pressman summarizes the main tenets of modernization theory as follows:

> Modernisation Theory held that for modernisation to take hold outside the West the overall Western experience with modernity would have to be duplicated.... [I]t substantially implied—just as Max Weber (and numerous others) had asserted regarding the rise of capitalism and science in the West—that religious conceptions of reality which Third World peoples clung to would have to be ... superseded by more rational systems of belief and motivation.... [F]or Third World societies to become modern required that they voluntarily or forcibly leave their old cultural luggage on the threshold. (Pressman 1993, pp. 4–6)

The rise of Thai capitalism since the 1980s, however, has not seen a triumph of rationalizing trends. Rather, this period's more iconic form of religious expression has been a flowering of spirit cults. The experience of recent decades shows that, far from being a brake on economic development, magical religiosity has been an integral part of Thailand's economic transformation. Furthermore, instead of being undermined by capitalism, Thai ritual magic has expanded in parallel with the growth of the economy. In contrast to the predictions of modernization theory, the variety of Thai religion that has suffered the most in the period since the economic boom years of the 1990s is precisely the form that that theory assumed would be the cultural prerequisite for the country's economic development; namely, demythologized interpretations of Buddhist doctrine represented as being compatible with rationality and science. The Thai prosperity cults indicate that, rather than heralding a further triumph of the progress of reason, the country's post–Cold War economic expansion has been associated with a spiritualization and enchantment of the market and capitalist enterprise.

There is general agreement, as Weber argued, that capitalism and religion are intertwined. The further development of global capitalism, however, has revealed it to be as much a force for the enchantment of the world as for rationalization and disenchantment. Over three decades ago, Christine Gray (1986, p. 38) observed that the work of Max Weber, more than that of any other scholar, had been instrumental in determining what issues had been raised in the study of economic change in Southeast Asian polities in the decades after World War II. Gray argued that Weberian approaches to Thai religion, however, had been "unproductive at best and misleading at worst" (Gray 1986, p. 39). Erick White similarly notes that it was because of the influence of Weber that the first generations of anthropologists of Thailand followed existing scholarly presumptions that Buddhism "was primarily a soteriological tradition of other-worldly salvation and only secondarily concerned with satisfying worldly needs" (White 2017, p. 191). Gray critiques Weber for misrepresenting capitalism in a secular frame and failing "to question the irrational and mystic aspects of Western capitalist ideology: beliefs about the magical efficacy of 'work'…; the magical 'efficacy' of the free market; or the magical efficacy of savings (as if savings automatically guaranteed future prosperity)" (Gray 1986, p. 65). These critiques are equally valid in challenging the mystical faith in the market that underpinned post–Cold War neoliberalism. In contrast to Weberian theories of modernization, Gray argues that a major requirement of modern capitalist development in Thailand has been

> the *retention of* traditions of religion and hierarchy. Buddhist rituals are at once a primary mechanism for mediating antinomies, i.e. for satisfying the negative requirements of modern capitalist development under an alien, non-Buddhist power, and the means through which knowledge and power shape and articulate new and alien ideologies. (Gray 1986, p. 80; emphasis in original)

Given the empirical antinomies presented by the development of modernity, some scholars have attempted to reread Weber in order to seek a foundation for a theory of modernity and enchantment. Weber is being rethought in the context of understandings of multiple modernities as well as accounts of the internal duality of modernity within each society.

The Multiplicity of Modernities

Shmuel Eisenstadt's account of multiple modernities provides a critical perspective on why we need to continue using a notion of modernity even as we appreciate the limitations imposed by its origins within European conceptions. Eisenstadt argues that the notion of multiple modernities is a comparative perspective that "goes against the view of the 'classical' theories of modernisation and the convergence of industrial societies prevalent in the 1950s, and indeed against the classical sociological analyses of Marx, Durkheim, and (to a large extent) even of Weber" (Eisenstadt 2000, p. 1). He contends that all these scholars "assumed, even if only implicitly, that the cultural program of modernity as it developed in modern Europe and the basic institutional constellations that emerged there would ultimately take over in all modernising and modern societies" (p. 1). However, Eisenstadt points out that in contrast to this assumption "[t]he actual developments in modernising societies have refuted the homogenising and hegemonic assumptions of this Western program of modernity" (p. 1).

While different modernizing societies have not converged towards a single model of modernity, Eisenstadt also emphasizes that the patterns within each society do not constitute simple continuations into the modern era of the traditions of their respective premodern periods. All modernizing societies share the common experience of a break from premodern patterns of family life, economic and political structures, forms of urbanization, education, communication, and individual lifestyles. However, the forms taken by these respective institutional, cultural and individual dimensions have developed in distinctive ways, "influenced by specific cultural premises, traditions, and historical experiences" (Eisenstadt 2000, p. 2). According to Eisenstadt,

> The idea of multiple modernities presumes that the best way to understand the contemporary world—indeed to explain the history of modernity—is to see it as a story of continual constitution and reconstitution of a multiplicity of cultural programs. (Eisenstadt 2000, p. 2)

One of the most important implications of the term 'multiple modernities' is that modernity and Westernization are not identical; Western patterns of modernity are not the only 'authentic' modernities. (Eisenstadt 2000, pp. 2–3)

Introducing a volume of studies on new religious movements in Southeast Asia, Volker Gottowik develops Eisenstadt's account by arguing that,

[a]s a consequence of the multiplication of modernity, designations for these modernities have multiplied too, with not only 'multiple modernities', but also 'entangled' and 'uneven modernities', 'indigenous' and 'alternative modernities', 'local' and 'vernacular modernities', etc. They all challenge in varying degrees the universality of the concept of modernity and stress that, as an analytic concept, 'modernity' can only be used in the plural or in a localized form. (Gottowik 2014, p. 12)

In considering how, contra Weber, modernity may produce new forms of enchantment, it is important to observe, as Robert Hefner argues, that the past several decades have also shown that capitalism, the driving economic dynamic of modernity, "is neither singular in its organisation nor uniform in its ethics; no less important, its efflorescence is not limited to Western civilisation" (Hefner 2017, p. 267). More to the point, the assumption of modernization theory that a Western-style form of cultural and socio-economic organization would be needed for capitalism to take root in Asia "has been proved ethnocentric and empirically wrong. This is a deeply important lesson, and it is more forcefully illustrated in Southeast Asia than in other areas of the world" (p. 268).

Raymond Lee revisits Weber to consider aspects of his thought that were previously overlooked or underemphasized—in particular, Weber's studies on charisma and magic—for insights on ways to imagine modernity as being productive of enchantment: "By perusing some of Weber's writings on charisma and magic, it may be plausible to argue for an interpretation of his work that envisages the restoration of meaning in a re-enchanted world" (Lee 2010, p. 182). Lee contends that, contrary to many earlier readings of Weber's work, the German sociologist presented a theory of modernity as being constituted by "opposing forces" (p. 189) and that

Weber's view of futurity was dialectical as he focused on a rationalized future as well as on a future that could slip through the iron grip of rationality.... Weber not only addressed the future as the relentless pursuit of progress but also intimated the future as shadowed by currents antithetical to rationality. (Lee 2010, p. 181)

I return to this view of modernity as a dialectical set of contradictory processes below. Nicholas Gane similarly argues that "rationality or rationalization can only be taken as central themes of Weber's work if one ignores the significance of his early writings" (Gane 2002, p. 6). Lee's exploration of charisma and magic in Weber's work leads him to view the sociologist's account of modernity not as a singular unilinear movement towards rationalization and disenchantment but rather as inherently dialectical and complex:

> [C]harisma and magic are not simply anachronisms in the context of social futures being shaped by the forces of disenchantment. If we look a little beyond Weber's work on rationality and ask why he bothered with charisma and magic, then it may be possible to detect an underlying sense of the dialectical in his attempt to describe the complexities of the modern world. (Lee 2010, p. 191)

For Lee, Weber presents us with a view in which "the disenchanted horizon of the modern world was always open to irrational forces that could reconfigure the past as new meanings for the future" (Lee 2010, p. 182).

The Contradictions of Religious Modernity

> The interaction between modernity and religion has resulted in multiple and contradictory reactions, including the apparent paradox that dogma and magic exist side by side in many parts of Southeast Asia. (Volker Gottowik 2014, p. 21)

Hefner observes that, while the decline of religion predicted by Weber, Durkheim "and even the young Geertz and Bellah" has not become the global norm, the new forms of public religious culture that have emerged within consumerist Asian capitalisms "have become more pluralised and agonistic" (Hefner 2017, p. 271). This is clearly evidenced in the conflict between magical and demythologized varieties of Thai religion noted in the introduction. The contemporary field of religious expression is indeed characterized by dialectical opposing tendencies. If we survey the religious landscapes of the world over the past few decades, we find both rationalizing trends, in the form of doctrinal reformism, and also enchanting trends, exemplified in the rise of magical ritual and spirit possession cults. A full theory of religious modernity needs to imagine the contemporary situation as being marked by a dual set of processes that are simultaneously inciting both rationalizing and enchanting tendencies. In various writings, Jean and John Comaroff (Comaroff and Comaroff 1999, 2000) have traced the rise of "occult economies" and the magic of prosperity gospels, on the one hand, and anti-magical religious fundamentalism, on the other hand, to the "radically ambiguous" (Comaroff and Kim 2011, p. 167) impact of neoliberal globalization. The Comaroffs argue that the radical destabilizations resulting from the global triumph of capitalism after the end of the Cold War have seen the rise of social conditions that appear paradoxical in terms of early twentieth-century social theory. They contend that neoliberal capitalism is an economic form marked by "the conjuncture of the strange and the familiar, of stasis and metamorphosis, [which] plays tricks on our perceptions, our positions, our praxis. These conjunctures appear at once to endorse and to erode our understanding of the lineaments of modernity" (Comaroff and Comaroff 2000, p. 293).

Drawing upon Marxian views of capitalism as being structured by inherent contradictions, Arif Dirlik similarly argues that post–Cold War globalization produced "new kinds of contradictions" that differentiate it from the preceding period of twentieth-century "Eurocentric modernity" (Dirlik 2005, p. 7). Dirlik argues that neoliberal global modernity is leading "to the universalization of the contradictions of capitalist modernity, not just between societies, but, more importantly, within them" (p. 7). And, in arguing for more complex analyses that deal with the co-presence of contradictory trends, he states: "Global modernity unifies and divides the globe in new ways. It does not do to emphasise one or the other" (p. 6). Dirlik views neoliberal globalization as having "complicated further contradictions between and within societies, including a fundamental contradiction between a seemingly irresistible modernity and past legacies that ... draw renewed vitality from the very globalizing process" (p. 4).

Michael Saler notes that simplistic accounts are increasingly being replaced by the recognition that modernity is characterized by tensions between seemingly irreconcilable forces and ideas:

> Modernity is defined less by binaries arranged in an implicit hierarchy, or by the dialectical transformation of one term into its opposite, than by unresolved contradictions and oppositions, or antinomies: modernity is Janus-faced. (Saler 2006, p. 700)

Saler's view of modernity as "Janus-faced" and marked by unresolved contradictions and antinomies, based on his analysis of Western history, was prefigured some decades earlier by Christine Gray (1986) in her account of Thai religious modernity as similarly being characterized by contradictions and antimonies. As detailed in Chapter Two, Gray argued that Thai modernity is marked by antinomies that have resulted from its historical engagement with the West in the period when it was globally dominant.

The contemporary religious landscapes of the world require us to view modernity as a fundamentally contradictory set of processes, which in some settings lead to tendencies to purify but which in other contexts proliferate new forms of complex syncretism. Processes, epistemologies and ideologies of rationalization and strenuous purification coexist and contest with equally powerful processes of enchantment, multiplicity and promiscuous mixing. The sociological forces of cultural and social modernization—capitalism, media, techno-scientific technologies—are productive of both rationalization and enchantment at the same time. Richard Jenkins argues that the forces producing both homogeneity and heterogeneity in the modern world cannot be divorced from each other:

> The one entails the other, logically and in everyday social life. Acknowledging this paradox—if that is, indeed, what it is, forces us to recognise the complexity of a world that is neither definitively enchanted nor disenchanted (and which was probably ever thus). (Jenkins 2000, p. 17)

To argue that the world has never been disenchanted is not to deny the strength of modernist forces of disenchantment. Rather, it is to come to a more complex understanding of modernity as incorporating both processes at one and the same time. Jenkins notes that, "in respect of disenchantment and (re)enchantment, modern societies are an array of opposing tendencies, themes, and forces" (Jenkins 2000, p. 13). Van den Akker et al. (2017) have coined the term "metamodernism" to describe the contemporary moment as one characterized by the co-presence of opposites.

As elsewhere in the world, Thai religious modernity is also characterized by the simultaneous development of opposed movements towards both enchantment and disenchantment. Thai Buddhism is being subjected to rationalizing disenchantment in some settings at the same time that new expressions of ritual-based magical enchantment, such as the Thai cults of wealth, are also developing. This contradiction at the centre of the modern Thai religious field is not unique or even unusual. But if neoliberal modernity is an inherently multiple and contradictory set of processes, why has the view that the modern condition is a unilinear historical process of rationalization been so influential? Why, as noted above, is this view still influential in many fields despite the accumulating empirical evidence to the contrary? Drawing on separate studies in the sociology of science and critical historiography, Bruno Latour and Michael Saler respectively argue that views of modernity as a world historical process of rationalization and disenchantment are ideological projects of power. While Latour's and Saler's respective studies are limited to the West, the global impact of discourses of civilization and modernity and the social processes of marketization wrought by colonialism and a globally dominant West mean that their arguments have purchase wherever Western ideologies and technologies have been powerful influences, including in Thailand.

Latour: The Modern Constitution of Rationalizing Ideologies and Hybridizing Practices

As Volker Gottowik notes, the question of what modernity is, is located "between the conflicting priorities of the dis-enchantment and re-enchantment of the world" (Gottowik 2014, p. 9). While rereadings of Weber have sketched the outlines of a more complex theory of modernity, they have not provided an account of how alternative rationalizing and enchanting trends both emerge within the contemporary condition. Nor have they given us a positive account of how modern social forces may actively produce new forms of enchantment, such as is now so apparent in Thailand and other Asian societies. Bruno Latour provides an account of the contradictions of modernity that offers a productive way of understanding the parallel development of opposed disenchanting and enchanting religious moments out of the same modern condition. In *We Have Never Been Modern*, Latour (1993) distinguishes between the intellectual and ideological dimensions of modernity—rationalism, scientism, disenchantment—on the one hand, and its sociological dimensions— capitalism, industrialism, urbanism—on the other. He contends that the intellectual dimension of modernity has never provided an accurate account of the sociological conditions of ostensibly modern life.

Latour argues that as a project of both discursive and social power, modernity is based on a mirage and a misunderstanding of itself. While discursively represented in terms of a great purification and separation of domains of social life, actual lived modernity has proliferated what Latour calls "hybridity"; namely, "impure" intersections of religion and politics, and religion and the economy. Latour presents modernity as a contradictory congeries of an ideology of rationality and discourses of rationalization that overlay actual persistent complexity, or "hybridity". In summarizing Latour's account, Peter Leithart states,

Modernity both purifies *and* hybridizes. That's not what makes modernity unique.... What makes modernity unique is its reluctance to admit that it's doing both.... Why the pretense? Modernity cannot acknowledge hybrids without ceasing to be modern and collapsing back into 'pre-modern' indifferentiation. That we cannot do, because if there is a purification lying at the foundation of all purifications, it is the 'Great Divide,' the temporal division between 'Modern Us' and 'Primitive Them'.... Without the myth of the Great Divide, modernity floats on quicksand, without foundation. We have to keep up appearances, because being modern simply *is* the pretense that We are not Them.... *We Have Never Been Modern* has a Delphic purpose: Latour wants us to 'know ourselves.' It's a lesson in modesty, that We are not so special after all. (Leithart 2014; emphases in original)

Latour argues that the word "modern" designates "two sets of entirely different practices which must remain distinct if they are to remain effective" (Latour 1993, p. 10) in sustaining the illusion that the West is qualitatively different from all previous societies, whether historically in the West itself or geographically in the rest of the world. The actual hybridity at the core of modern Western social life has taken place even as dominant discourses, both in the academy and more widely, have denied this phenomenon and claimed that a great separation of scientific reason from religious unreason has taken place. This is why Latour claims, as announced in the title of his book, that sociologically we have never been modern. That is, the always hybrid conditions of life—even in capitalist, urbanized and mediatized societies—have never conformed to the rationalized and disenchanted image presented in modernist theory.

Latour presents a double critique both of understandings of modernity as a sociological condition and the academic disciplines that claim to have defined and described this condition. In reflecting on Latour's account, Hugh Crawford states: "[T]he repertoire of modern critical analysis has always been internally inconsistent if not outright contradictory, and, more importantly, we have always been at home in the non-modern world, living comfortably with hybrid combinations" (Crawford 1994, p. 578). In detailing Latour's critique of the academic disciplines of modernity, Leithart observes,

For many modernisation theories, the differentiation of spheres is the genius of modernity. Childish primitives that they were (and are), pre-moderns muck everything up. They don't see that economics isn't religion, nor power faith, nor science magic until we moderns come along to tidy them up. (Leithart 2014)

The sociological differentiation of spheres of life that has been de-fined as a structuring characteristic of modernity has in turn been the foundation of the differentiation of specialized modern academic dis-ciplines. In contrast to this presumed differentiation of social spheres and specialist forms of knowledge, however, Latour contends that our social world in fact remains mixed and hybrid, and is not clearly dif-ferentiated. David Lyon similarly argues that sociological theories of modernity have gone astray by focusing on the intellectual dimension at the expense of the practical lived conditions of modernity and, given this, "we may *expect* what from a modernist viewpoint would be called contradictions of belief and practice. Sociology should focus, then, on how people *make a life* rather than just on how they make sense" (Lyon 2000, pp. 51–52; emphasis in original).

Latour describes "purification" as referring to "the world of opin-ions and argument", while hybridity refers to "the world of practices and networks" (Latour 1993, p. 20). Latour's formulation—that the condition we inhabit is split between an ideological level of rationalist modernity and a lived level of non-rationalized practice—provides a model for understanding the parallel development of both new forms of religious reformism and fundamentalism as well as new varieties of magic. While Latour's field of research in science studies might appear to be far removed from the magical cults of wealth considered here, the issues he raises parallel those that confront scholars of efflorescing spirit cults. His insights on the contradictions inherent in the foundations of the modern condition, what he calls the "modern constitution", provide a way to theorize a contemporary situation in which global religious modernity is trending in the opposing directions of both "purificatory" doctrine and fundamentalism as well as "hybridising" magic and ritual. In broad terms, we can say that reformist and fundamentalist movements emphasize doctrine and are ideological, while magic is predominantly focused on practices and the effectivity of ritual. This split between reformist ideology and magical practice is played out through the apparently contradictory trends of religious modernity operating in parallel. Doctrinalism and fundamentalism arise from the ideology of modernity, while modern magic arises within the practical "hybridity" of everyday life.

The Modern Constitution and Interdisciplinary Research

Latour's account of the modern constitution as formed out of a con-tradiction between ideologies of rationalism and hybrid practices not only provides a model for understanding the contradictory purifying and enchanting trends of religious modernity. His elaboration of this theory also provides a comparative frame for a number of the central themes of this study, including the application of an interdisciplinary method, an emphasis on the central place of ritual practice, and the role of contemporary technologies in producing new modalities of enchantment.

As is the case with this study of the proliferation of new cults of wealth in association with spirit mediumship and magical amulets, the empirical complexity Latour encounters in his anthropology of science requires him to continually engage with "hybridity", by which he means the practical intersection in everyday life of "imbroglios of science, politics, economy, law, religion, technology, fiction" (Latour 1993, p. 2)—fields that the "modern constitution" claimed to be distinct and separate. And, as is also the case for scholars of modern magic, Latour's research leads him to study "strange situations that the intellectual culture in which we live does not know how to categorise" (p. 3). He adds,

> Our intellectual life is out of kilter. Epistemology, the social sciences, the sciences of texts—all have their privileged vantage point, provided they remain separate. If the creatures we are pursuing cross all three spaces, we are no longer understood. (Latour 1993, p. 5)

Latour regards anthropology to be the academic field whose methods enable it to conceptualize the "seamless fabric" (Latour 1993, p. 7) of the multiple hybridizations of actually lived existence in both the West and the non-West. Latour argues for a genuine interdisciplinary method that brings the sciences, humanities and social sciences not only into dialogue but also into a common, unified approach that draws upon the ethnographic method of anthropology. Crawford contends that the "current disciplines are both the cause and the symptom of the modern mind, and Latour has written the manifesto for the inter-disciplinarians" (Crawford 1994, p. 579). While beginning its history in the orientalist investigation of "exotic" and ostensibly premodern cultures, Latour argues that ethnographic methods can "come home from the tropics" (Latour 1993, p. 100) and be retooled to reflexively provide insights on the West itself. Such a retooled anthropology that provides the foundation of the interdisciplinary method Latour proposes will "refrain from making any *a priori* declarations as to what might distinguish Westerners from Others" (p. 103).

And like scholars of modern magic, Latour critiques modernism for the misguided belief "that the modern world is truly disenchanted"

(Latour 1993, p. 114). He also gestures towards the productive capacity of modern technologies of capitalism to produce new enchantments: "How could we [moderns] be capable of disenchanting the world, when every day out of laboratories and factories we populate the world with hundreds of hybrids stranger than those of the day before?" (p. 115).

Latour uses the terms "nonmodern" and "amodern" to refer to attitudes and methods that engage all the hybrids that the modern constitution rejects yet nonetheless allows to proliferate in its complex practical intersections. Latour describes this type of hybridity as "polytemporal" (Latour 1993, p. 75) because "[s]uch a temporality does not oblige us to use the labels 'archaic' or 'advanced', since every cohort of contemporary elements may bring together elements from all times" (p. 75). As discussed in Chapter Three, contemporary Thai popular religion reflects this pattern, preserving the past without erasure. In Thai popular religion there is no great divide between past cults and new cults; they are incorporated without exclusions.

Latour argues that the modern constitution—the modern West's attempt to keep processes of ideological and intellectual purification separate from practical hybridity—has become unsustainable. Modernity has now multiplied new forms of hybridity to such an extent "that the constitutional framework that both denies and permits their existence could no longer keep them in place" (Latour 1993, p. 49). There are now so many hybrids "that no one knows any longer how to lodge them in the old promised land of modernity" (p. 131). I return to this theme in Chapter Seven: modernity has expanded to such an extent that it no longer looks the same. Or to put it another way, taking modernity to its logical conclusion reveals the illusions upon which earlier theories of this condition were based.

Modern Disenchantment as Ideology

> The claim that magic has been superseded by modernity is ideological rather than real. (Birgit Meyer 2003, p. 221)

Latour contends that the supposed divide between rational modernity and nonrational superstitious premodernity is a myth, and that the academic disciplines that take this reputed divide as their founding epistemological position are ideological, constituting discourses of power that seek to bring into being the condition that they claim merely to describe. Saler similarly contends that ideas of modern disenchantment are ideological. He asks, "How did Western elites become so enchanted with that incantatory phrase, 'the disenchant-ment of the world'?" And responds, "Elites have enchanted themselves with the spell of disenchantment, but that spell appears to be breaking, leaving a specifically modern, 'disenchanted' enchantment in its wake" (Saler 2006, p. 693). While not explicitly referring to Latour, Saler presents a similar perspective, contending that disenchantment is an ideological project of elites, not an inevitable sociological process, and that enchantment has always been present but has been denied in accounts that misrepresent the social condition that we inhabit.

Drawing on the work of Lorraine Daston and Katherine Park (1998), Saler argues that magical phenomena and marvels have not been expunged from the modern world but rather have been obscured by modernist ideology. Daston and Park argue that the Western social order became disenchanted in the late seventeenth and eighteenth centuries because of social influences, rather than intellectual fac-tors—whether the rise of science, the spread of instrumental reason or the growth of secularism. They contend that in the Middle Ages phenomena regarded as wonders or miracles were viewed as reservoirs of power and as forms of symbolic power over nature, and for this reason they were used to articulate claims to wealth and noble status. Commenting on Daston and Park, Pamela Smith observes that in this period a person who understood wonders "was seen to be capable of controlling a vast system of sympathies and antipathies to gain almost unbounded power" (Smith 2000, p. 420). This is very similar to the forms of analogy and sympathetic magic that characterize Thai pop-ular religion, as detailed in later chapters. After the Enlightenment, however, nature came to be seen as regular and law-abiding rather than following a system of sympathies and antipathies, and in this new epistemological universe "marvels came to connote moral, as well as natural, disorder" and "wonder became a vice, rather than a virtue of the natural philosopher, and found a home in ... popular gazettes" (pp. 421–22). Saler draws on this analysis to argue that, until the Enlightenment,

> elites had maintained a monopoly on wonders, utilizing them for their own political, intellectual, and aesthetic purposes. But with the sixteenth century Reformation and its attendant religious conflicts through the seventeenth century, the masses were using marvels and wonders for their own purposes. (Saler 2006, p. 704)

Elites responded to the threat of anarchy by regularizing nature, "thereby marginalizing wonders as a religious and political rallying cry" (Saler 2006, p. 704), and the discourse of modernity as disenchanted was then "the contingent creation of elites for purposes of prestige" (p. 716). In the seventeenth and eighteenth centuries, a new cultural opposition between the enlightened and the vulgar emerged. Central to the secular understanding of enlightenment as a state of mind and a way of life was the rejection of phenomena regarded as marvels and wonders, which henceforth were defined by elites as disreputable passions to be consigned "to the realm of the vulgar, where [they continue] to flourish within mass culture" (p. 704).

In her account of the genesis of modernism in Germany, Corinna Treitel presents a similar argument detailing how occult practices flourished in this period because "emphasis on achieving satisfaction in this world rather than the next was well suited to the offerings of the modern marketplace and its ability to cater to the ethic of 'personal satisfaction'" (Treitel 2004, p. 710). Treitel observes that occultism in Germany was "admirably suited to the marketing imperatives of the new mass culture, and that occultism flourished rather than diminished in the modern period partly because mass culture was able to bring it to the attention of a wide audience" (cited in Saler 2006, p. 710). This perspective on the close relationship between miracles, magic and popular mass culture in the era of consumer capitalism is especially relevant to the study of Thai cults of wealth. In Chapter Seven I discuss how the commercial mass media have been central to the production of auras of enchantment that envelop new magical cults in Thailand. As Saler notes, Treitel connects fascination with the occult to facets of modernity such as mass consumerism and aesthetic modernism, highlighting "the Janus-faced, 'ambivalent' nature of modernity" (Saler 2006, pp. 708–9).

These various accounts of the relegation of the magical, the wondrous and the marvellous to the realm of the vulgar, where they continue to flourish in European mass culture, are highly relevant to understanding Thai cults of wealth. These new cults of wealth have also emerged in the domain of popular mass cultures of the marketplace; that is, within Thai capitalism. And, significantly for this study, Saler extends his analysis beyond the West to argue that the divide between elite disenchantment and popular magical culture was imposed by Western imperialism on the rest of the world. Drawing on Dipesh Chakrabarty's (2000, p. 89) arguments in *Provincializing Europe*, Saler contends that the binary opposition of Western disenchanted modernity versus ostensibly enchanted non-Western premodernity was more ideological than real, constituting a "conceptual tool for Western colonial purposes that obscured the tensions and contradictions within the modern world" (Saler 2006, p. 699). I draw on this perspective in the following chapter, where I trace how the contradictions of modernity outlined here have dramatically transformed the Thai religious field over the past two centuries.

In summary, even in the modern West only intellectual culture has been secularized and only elite culture is disenchanted. David Lyon argues that the dominance of the double ideology of secularization and disenchantment in many sections of the academy has meant that scholars often overlook the actual continuing presence of religiosity in both modern and modernizing societies:

> [F]aith's fate in the modern world may turn out not so much to be lost in the everyday life-paths of ordinary people, but to be *lost from view* in academic accounts of the modern world. The secularisation of scholarship thus precedes the scholarship of secularisation. (Lyon 2000, p. 24; emphasis in original)

While secularization may refer to the declining strength of established institutionalized religious groups in specific cultural milieu, studies of this phenomenon often say little of alternative spiritualities that may be growing in popularity and influence.

Lyon points out that for much of the twentieth century sociology focussed on the assumed ultimate triumph of "the iron cage of bureaucratic rationality" (Lyon 2000, p. 9), and this assumption has left many academic disciplines ill-prepared analytically to consider the efflorescence of religiosity in late capitalism. Most importantly, many forms of this religious efflorescence have not reflected an anti-modernism that retreats from technology or capitalism. What most challenges theories that view modernity as entailing secularization and disenchantment is that new forms of religiosity have emerged within and through distortions of the supposed "iron cage" of modernist bureaucratic rationality that have been wrought by new technologies and expanding capitalism. Pushed on by new communities formed in cultures of consumerism, the expansion of contemporary conditions into forms that no longer resemble classical images of the modern society have, ironically, provided opportunities for a renewed religiosity. As Lyon puts it, "paradoxically, the cage offers the escape!" (p. 9).

Wouter Hanegraaff (2011) details how magical belief and ritual have survived within modern Western social formations even if until recently they may have been overlooked or largely ignored by scholars whose gaze was blinkered by modernization theory. Lee similarly argues that magic has survived within "the interstices of modernity" (Lee 2010, p. 186), and he describes recent analyses of enchantment as a "de-closeting" of magic: "When the powers of disenchantment recede, magic emerges if only because it no longer faces the disparagement of the rationalized public" (p. 186). Jenkins notes that major epistemological shifts in the sciences as well as the humanities are leading to a reappraisal of the place of enchantment in modernity:

> Even within the scientific community, the frameworks of Newtonian physics are now widely understood to apply only up to a point, beyond which other interpretive models are required. There seems no longer to be a wholly unified epistemological and explanatory framework for understanding the natural world.... This should not necessarily be understood as an erosion of the authority of science, but rather as a potential shift in its centre of gravity towards greater epistemological pluralism. (Jenkins 2000, p. 17)

The Enlightenment view, which framed the broader context of Weber's account of disenchantment and was hegemonic in the West during the nineteenth century, began to fragment in the twentieth century, and Jenkins opines that it may "prove to be the historical exception rather than the rule" (Jenkins 2000, p. 17). Jenkins places the "re-" of "re-enchantment" in parentheses—that is, (re)enchantment—to signal the double phenomenon that modernity never fully expunged magic and has always retained enchanted features, as well as the fact that modernity is actively productive of new modes of magic. He notes that it is now clear that "formal-rational logics and processes can themselves be (re)enchanted from within, or become the vehicles of (re)enchantment. (Re)enchantment can be a thoroughly rationally organised business, particularly with respect to politics, consumption and—arguably the ground of their intersection—the organisation of large-scale events" (p. 13).

The Failure of Modern Social Science

Much theoretical and empirical work remains to be done in integrating these insights into a revised account of modernity. Jenkins contends that, as a beginning, enchantment must "be recognised as an integral element of modernity. Not just as a consequence, or a reaction, but right at the heart of the matter. Acknowledging this encourages an appropriate skepticism with respect to the bureaucratic 'iron cage' and its supposed efficiencies" (Jenkins 2000, p. 22). Simplistic definitions of modernity have failed to capture the intrinsic complexity and multi-directionality of the contemporary world. They have failed because, as partial accounts, they have detailed only one of the contesting directions in which modernity pulls those who live under the spells that are cast by science, technology and capitalism. Modernization theory mistakenly took the moment of rationalization as defining modernity in its entirety and denied the equally modern moment of the production of new forms of enchantment.

Teleological views of modernity as having a singular direction of moving progressively towards reason and rationalization are ideological value judgements or, as in the work of Ünaldi discussed above, beliefs or hopes and do not emerge from empirical analysis of what has actually taken place in modern history. It is noteworthy that in his analysis of the rise of the place of the monarchy in the spatial transformations of modern Bangkok Ünaldi consistently frames his Weberian predictions in the conditional mood, as "might" or "possibly" taking place in the future: "An accelerating this-worldly orientation among the electorate and the growing significance of instrumental rationality ... *might* eventually render charismatic leadership in Thailand obsolete" (Ünaldi 2016, p. 23; emphasis added).

The duality of modernity is only a paradox within rationalist epistemologies that presume to present a totalizing view of all of contemporary existence. Alternative epistemologies and accounts of multiple modernities can accommodate multiplicity and multidirectionality. As a congeries of contingent factors and processes, modernity has had, and continues to have, diametrically opposed tendencies. Supposedly premodern irrational magic and animism are not waiting to die out, and they do not remain in the modern as mere residues of the premodern. Magicality continues to exist because it is being produced and reproduced out of the very conditions of modernity. As discussed in the following section, fundamentalism is also produced out of other combinations and recombinations of modern processes.

Not only has the West misunderstood its own modern self, but the imperial power of the West in its political and economic expansion across the planet has also burdened those who it colonized with mistaken views of themselves. Orientalist knowledge formations of non-Western cultures and societies are doubly in error. Not only do they impose Western views upon the Rest, but these Western views are themselves also fundamentally in error. The West has imposed its misunderstanding of itself upon the rest of the world, sometimes with disastrous consequences. In some places and times, the duality of modernity becomes apparent when political, social and religious movements of purification have critiqued, challenged or even sought to exterminate local forms of enchantment in the name of modern true belief or pure forms of being and existence. As the ideologies of modernity, and the sociological forms of modern life, spread and diverge, they reproduce in distinctive local forms the tensions and contradictions that are fundamentally present in modernity. Hence, we find modern religion—that is, religion that has been transformed and which continues to change in response to ideologies, discourses and technologies of modernity—moving in two directions, both towards rationalized fundamentalism and also towards hybridizing magic.

Escaping the double net of orientalism requires a twofold deconstruction, both of the misperceptions of Western stereotyping of the non-West and also of the West's misperceptions of its own modern self. It is untenable to build fields of disciplinary analysis upon only one of the multiple contradictory processes that make up modernity. A global religious studies and sociology of religion, if they were come into being, would need to address all of these simultaneous trends, not denying the modernity of any of them. They would seek to understand the distinctive conditions under which particular elements of the modern variously incite either fundamentalist or magical views of the world.

The Modern Production of Religious Doctrinalism and Fundamentalism

While the focus of this book is on the modern production of new hybrid forms of magical ritual, it is important to consider for a moment how modernity produces new forms of religious purification. In his account of multiple modernities, Eisenstadt provides insight into how modernity produces reformist and fundamentalist religious movements. As noted above, he emphasizes that, wherever it takes hold, modernity is an inherently conflicted mélange of processes and projects: "As … modernity developed first in the West, it was from its beginnings beset by internal antinomies and contradictions, giving rise to continual critical discourse and political contestations" (Eisenstadt 2000, p. 7). Eisenstadt then argues that while fundamentalist movements outside the West are often articulated in terms of an anti-Western and anti-Enlightenment ideology,

> the distinct visions of fundamentalist movements have been formulated in terms common to the discourse of modernity; they have attempted to appropriate modernity on their own terms…. They share with communist movements the promulgation of totalistic visions entailing the transformation of both man and society. Some claim to be concerned with the 'cleansing' of both…. Like communist movements, they seek to establish a new social

order, rooted in revolutionary, universalistic ideological tenets, in principle transcending all primordial, national, or ethnic units. (Eisenstadt 2000, p. 19)

Jean Comaroff views the rise of fundamentalisms as one response to the uncertainties of neoliberalism, which in some settings incite a "reaching for clearer, seemingly certain, sovereigns, theologies, divinities" (Comaroff and Kim 2011, p. 170). For her, neoliberal precaritization sets "in motion efforts to recover a sense of lost tradition, certain sorts of sovereign force (whether by way of fascism or theology), certain fundamental truths that all assert that 'this is the original text, this is the unambiguous source of power'" (p. 170).

In some non-Western societies, ascendant fundamentalism can also be seen as emerging from the ashes of the global collapse of the Left. The victory of capitalism over centrally planned socialisms and the now global hegemony of the market as the central organizing principle of social and cultural life has been marked by an intellectual crisis in the West and the rise of critical views of modernity such as detailed above. While to a significant extent this has been an intellectual and cultural crisis in the West, the victory of global capitalism has produced material political and economic crises in many former socialist societies, notably in Eastern Europe and the countries of the former Soviet Union. As Comaroff notes in a dialogue with David Kim, the collapse of grand narratives has been a global phenomenon undermining the previously dominant forms of social analysis in both the capitalist West and the formerly socialist East:

Modernist social theory had a confident telos, and a vision of the future—mechanical or otherwise. But this has been severely compromised in our late-modern world. Whether it be Marxist scholarship or modernisation theory, a secular sense of futurity has been dramatically undermined. (Comaroff and Kim 2011, p. 172)

Dirlik provides a more concrete perspective of the intersection of political-economic and intellectual changes over the past three decades:

The decline and fall of socialism in the course of the 1980s opened the way to the globalisation of capital. It also eliminated socialism as a crucial obstacle to cultural appropriations—and, therefore, to the proliferation of modernities, which now find expression in the fragmentation of a single modernity into multiple and alternative modernities. Questioning of Eurocentric teleology in either the capitalist or socialist guise has revealed modernity in its full historicity, and 'geohistorical' diversity... (Dirlik 2005, p. 5)

In the mid-decades of the twentieth century, Marxist-inspired theory was the foundation of anti-colonialist independence movements and trenchant critiques of capitalism and neo-imperialism. But with the collapse of the Soviet Union, the capitalist-turn of now nominally socialist China, Vietnam and Laos, and the end of revolutionary Communist insurgencies in countries such as Thailand, varieties of religious doctrinalism have at times become the new ideological bases for critiques of American neo-imperialism, Western cultural imperialism and more broadly of neoliberal globalization.

In his account of the multiple modernities that have come to inhabit the world, Eisenstadt focuses exclusively on fundamentalist forms of modern religiosity, overlooking the role of magic. There is a need to move beyond Eisenstadt's disenchanted multiple modernities to an account of the contemporary world as also being characterized by enchanted multiple magical modernities. A retreat into fundamentalist doctrinal certainties is not the only possible religious response to the uncertain complexities of neoliberal capitalism. Fundamentalism attempts to resist or manage complexity by reference to principles of simplification. As Keyes et al. observe, "Fundamentalists point to an authority found in scriptures in order to undermine religious pluralism" (Keyes et al. 1994, p. 12). In contrast, modern magic accepts complexity as given and is neither universalizing nor revolutionary. Modern magic in Thailand takes the social, cultural, economic and political orders of modernity as given and draws upon supernatural support to seek to establish advantageous positions within that order. In contrast to fundamentalist religious movements, which in some religions have assumed political forms to define a post-secular non-Western modernity, modern Thai magic is rarely concerned with the West and does not have an anti-Western political or ideological agenda. Given that Thai magic largely ignores the West, it has effectively moved beyond postcolonial anxieties to draw upon the efficacy of ritual in order to gain advantageous positioning within the local form of capitalist modernity that has emerged in Thailand.

The Magic of Modernity: Questions of Interpretation

The perspectives detailed above raise questions of interpretation for studies of "resurgent supernaturalism" and "re-enchantment" in Southeast Asia. One question is whether the widely reported efflorescence of supernatural ritual in Southeast Asia is actual or apparent. Are we seeing an actual intensification of supernaturalism and a sociological expansion of magic in Southeast Asia? Or is it rather that the modernist gaze is retreating, and this alternative perspective now allows us to see more clearly rituals that have always been present but which a rationalist outlook led us to ignore or overlook? The analyses of scholars such as Lee (2010) are ambiguous. On the one hand, Lee claims that magic has survived in the interstices of modernity and becomes visible once again when ideologies of rationalization decline and no longer cloud our vision. On the other hand, he also sees magic as developing from a disenchanted horizon of modernity itself that has the power to reconfigure and produce new meanings for the future. In Thailand it is clear that we now find many new magical cults that are not premodern traditions that somehow managed to survive in the interstices of modernity but which, rather, are novel forms of religious belief and practice. This shows that we need to think of magic not merely as surviving within the interstices of modernity, but rather as emerging and being produced from within the conditions of modernity itself.

Twenty-first-Century Thailand: Modern or Postmodern?

> As soon as we direct our attention simultaneously to the work of purification and the work of hybridization, we immediately stop being wholly modern, and our future begins to change. At the same time, we stop having been modern, because we become retrospectively aware that the two sets of practices have always already been at work in the historical period that is ending. (Latour 1993, p. 11)

A further analytical consideration is whether the magical cults of post–Cold War Thailand should be viewed as modern or postmodern. In previous work I argued that we have entered a postmodern era that represents an intellectual and sociological break from the patterns of modernity, and I wrote of the "postmodernisation of Thai Buddhism" (Jackson 1999a). I am no longer sure, however, that we have passed a transition point from modernity into postmodernity. If the simultaneous emergence of both magical ritual and religious fundamentalism out of the conditions of techno-scientific capitalism confounds predictions of modern social evolution, then this most likely means that we previously had a mistaken view of modernity. The diverse and often opposing religious trends now visible in Southeast Asia and elsewhere may not be postmodern. Rather, they may reflect the coming into focus of the multiple faces of a modernity whose complexity we previously failed to recognize, or refused to acknowledge, because of the dominance of Enlightenment faith in the power and possibilities of reason.

But if we regard postmodernity to denote a condition that has emerged out of processes that take modernity to its logical conclusion, and which produce effects that no longer look "modern" in terms of previous understandings, then perhaps this term may still have some value. Lyon views postmodernity as resulting from the expansion of aspects of modernity "that serve to render modernity less recognisable as such" (Lyon 2000, p. 37). He regards postmodernity as

> a kind of interim situation where some characteristics of modernity have been inflated to such an extent that modernity becomes scarcely recognisable as such.... The inflated characteristics of modernity that give rise to postmodern premonitions, relate above all to communication and information technologies (CIT) and to the tilt towards consumerism.... The growth of CITs and new media augments the power of the image,... encouraging such developments as positional pluralism. But the dynamic of the whole system may be traced increasingly to the demand that consumption levels be constantly raised. (Lyon 2000, p. 7)

Perhaps then postmodernity is not an epistemological or cultural break with modernity but rather a more accurate view of the potentials that have always resided within modernity. With the collapse of grand narratives of reason, perhaps we are now able to see more accurately the multiple contours of the modernity that we have in fact been inhabiting for the past couple of centuries. In the remainder of this study, I use the terms "modern" and "late modern" rather than postmodern, although some of the authors I cite prefer to describe contemporary Thai society and culture as postmodern.

Conclusion

The structure of modernity outlined in this chapter—as a bifurcated and internally contested compound of processes of both purificatory rationalization and hybridizing practice—provides a frame for understanding the apparent contradiction of religious fundamentalism and doctrinal reform emerging alongside magical rituals. Latour's exposition of modernity as a dual system of rationalization *with* hybridization enables us to appreciate that in the contemporary world fundamentalism and magic are *equally modern*. His account also reveals that this is only an apparent contradiction, emerging in rationalizing accounts because of the mistaken view that magic and ritual are residues of premodernity that lie outside religious modernity. It is only within the exclusionary rationalizing discourses of doctrinal reformists, which posit universalizing accounts of religious teachings, that magic and ritual practice are constituted as atavistic others of modernity.

In the next chapter I will discuss how, despite its inaccurate representation of modernity as well as what is understood as "religion", the rationalizing dimension of modernity has nonetheless had a powerful impact on religious life across the globe. This is because the economic and political project of European imperialism empowered rationalizing views of religious modernity as being central to the attainment of Western-style civilization and development. Even though Siam was never directly colonized by a Western power, the imbricated discourses of reason, civilization and development had a transformative impact on all dimensions of social and cultural life, including religious discourse and ritual observance. In the following chapter I detail how the one-sided view of modernity that lay at the heart of Western imperialism and neo-imperialism in the nineteenth and twentieth centuries created tensions and fissures within the Thai religious field. These powerful influences led to a bifurcation within Thai religion between Buddhism represented as "religion" (*sasana*) and *saiyasat* magic represented as "ritual" (*phithi*) or "cult" (*latthi-phithi*). Western discourses of modernity, which assumed hegemonic status on the back of the West's geopolitical dominance, also deformed the academic study of the Thai religious field, often leading to an emphasis on institutional Buddhism and engendering ongoing difficulties in integrating magical ritual into a coherent account of the total field of Thai religion and the full scope of the religious lives of Thais from all backgrounds.

Chapter Two

Buddhist in Public, Animist in Private: Semicolonial Modernity and Transformations of the Thai Religious Field

Introduction

The Thai cults of wealth and associated cult of amulets, divination practices and spirit possession rituals have become increasingly important components of religious expression among many strata of Thai society. However, while a growing number of anthropological studies have explored these phenomena, few histories of modern Thailand have made magical ritual central to their narratives of the country's transformations. This contrasts with the emphasis that has been given to the reform of Buddhism and the institutional role of the Buddhist sangha in modern Thailand (see for example Reynolds 1979, 1988; Somboon 1982; Ishii 1986; Jackson 1989). While the organizational changes of Buddhism instituted by a succession of governments from the beginning of the twentieth century are central elements of many histories of Thailand, the significant evolution of the field of ritual magic that has taken place across the same period is largely absent from narratives of the transformations of Thai society and culture wrought by modernity. Why has modern Thai historiography overlooked magical ritual while emphasizing Buddhism? Furthermore, if the cults of wealth, amulets, divination and spirit possession rituals are indeed central elements of contemporary Thai religiosity, why does the diversity of Thai religion continue to surprise many foreign

---

Sections of this chapter draw on material presented in Jackson (2004a) and Jackson (2004b).

observers and contrast with images of Thailand as an ostensibly Buddhist society? Why does the sociological importance of the cults of wealth appear to be so at odds with many academic accounts and popular representations of Thailand as a "Buddhist kingdom"?

These were issues in my own earlier work. As a post-doctoral researcher in the late 1980s, I studied the history of the political dimensions of Thai religion in the twentieth century. I looked at both the history of state administrative intervention in the organization of Buddhism and the role of military and other elite figures in the Hupphasawan millenarian movement of the spirit medium Suchat Kosonkittiwong. But I lacked a theoretical frame that would enable me to consider state interventions in Buddhism together with elite participation in magical rituals. While senior politicians and military figures participated in both state-administered Buddhism and spirit cults, I published my research separately, as a book on the incorporation of Thai Buddhism within the secular bureaucracy (Jackson 1989) and a stand-alone journal article on the Hupphasawan movement (Jackson 1988). This current book in part emerges out of attempts to resolve tensions between my earlier separate studies of the different rationalizing and enchanting processes that have operated in transforming Thai religion over the past two centuries.

One reason for these omissions and disparities is the rationalist emphasis of the academic disciplines of historiography and political science, which were the frames I worked within in my own earlier research and which I engaged critically in the previous chapter. An additional reason for the neglect of ritual in many studies of modern Thailand is that the significant extent of these practices has at times been obscured by a regime of representation that privileges Buddhism as the public face of religion in a country whose leaders have wanted to represent it to international audiences as civilized, modern and developed. Western political and intellectual power and influence in Siam during the era of high imperialism in the later nineteenth and early twentieth centuries had a major and lasting impact on how the diverse elements of the Thai religious amalgam have been represented on the international stage. As Christine Gray notes, from the middle of the nineteenth century, Siam was a "Western-dominated kingdom-state" (Gray 1986, p. 218). More particularly, the contested character of modernity as parallel processes of purificatory rationalization and practical hybridization that arrived in Siam with Western domination had dramatic transformative impacts on the Thai religious field. The consequent relegation of magical practices, especially among political and economic elites, to more private and less publicly visible spaces meant that some fields of scholarship overlooked the empirical extent, sociological relevance and political importance of ritual, such as the cults of wealth, throughout the period of Siam/Thailand's modernization from the mid-nineteenth century to the present day.

An important Thai response to religious and cultural multiplicity has been to create time and space contexts in which beliefs and rituals associated with doctrinally distinct and at times incommensurable, cosmological and philosophical systems have been separated into different domains, each with its own rules, norms and epistemologies. This pattern of contextualization is called *kala-thesa* ("time-space") in Thai and I describe its expression in Thai religious life in detail in Chapter Three. In the colonial era, this pre-existing system of hierarchically ordered time and place contexts was subjected to an additional, externally imposed, order. Under this Western-imposed regime, some contexts and dimensions of the Thai religious amalgam were relegated to "private/domestic" time and place settings, while others were located in "public/international" *kala-thesa* contexts. This representational regime of images and the formation of a fissure between a public religious domain of Buddhism, now represented as "religion" (*sasana*), and more private spaces of magic, described as "ritual" (*phithi*), "faith" (*sattha*) or "belief" (*khwam-cheua*), emerges from the dissonances and antinomies created by the internally conflicted character of modernity as rationalization alongside hybridization that came as an adjunct to Western geopolitical hegemony in Asia.

In this chapter I trace the impact of Western power in the creation of what I call the Thai regime of images and I consider how this regime has impacted the country's religious field. I describe how the influence of Western colonial-era notions of civilization led Siam's elites to emphasize the Buddhist dimensions of the country's religious amalgam while obscuring the extent of their participation in other forms of ritual. In earlier work (Jackson 2004a) I detailed the operation of the regime of images in Thai gender and sexual cultures. Here I extend that analysis to the field of religious culture and I also engage Michael Herzfeld's (2016) very similar account of cultural intimacy. The public international image of Thailand as a Buddhist kingdom was created in the aftermath of the imposition of Western power over the Thai religious amalgam. For much of the period of Siam/Thailand's self-modernizing engagement with the West since the mid-nineteenth century, a key principle underpinning patterns of spatial and temporal compartmentalization has been the creation of an opposition between, on the one hand, a public domain oriented towards the West and patterned by a largely scriptural image of Theravada Buddhism and, on the other hand, a private/domestic world of belief and ritual in which Buddhism is but one system alongside spirit cults, divination and other forms of magic.

The regime of images has also influenced the study of the Thai religious amalgam, at times leading to an academic focus on Buddhism over spirit cults in accounts of Thai religion in historical and political studies. The regime of images imposed a new form of power over a pre-existing complex amalgam of differentiated time and space religious contexts. This structural divide created in response to the West is now found at all levels of Thai society, in popular religion, in the culture of Western-educated elites and in discourses and accounts of the monarchy. I also contend that we need to revise our histories of modern Thailand to include the transformations of the magical dimensions of religion in the country under the Western-influenced regime of images.

Semicoloniality and the Thai Regime of Images

Several scholars of Thailand have described how modern Thai forms of power are characterized by a concern to monitor and police surface effects, images, public behaviours and representations while being comparatively disinterested in controlling private domains of life. Niels Mulder emphasizes the cultural fetishization of surface effects produced by this regime of power: "Thai society is a presentational society, emphasising formality, conformity, belief in ceremony, while easily taking presentation to be the heart of things" (Mulder 1985, pp. 143–44). Penny Van Esterik describes Thailand as a society that "encourages an essentialism of appearances or surfaces.... The real is hidden and unchallenged. The surface is taken for real" (Van Esterik 2000, p. 4). Rosalind Morris makes a similar argument when she describes this many-sided phenomenon as the Thai "order of appearances" (Morris 2000, p. 173) and a "love of the disciplined surface" (p. 180) that is based on "an overinvestment in appearances" (p. 5). Morris argues that in Thailand's almost two centuries of modernization, political power has not required the creation of a national subjectivity or an essential Thai personhood but, rather, "the appearance or the performance of ideally nationalist behaviour. It requires that one conform oneself to the ideals of the national, and it makes performance the criterion of proper citizenship" (p. 147). Under this modernizing regime, interior phenomena of thought and desire are not monitored, but external shows, performances and public discourses are intensely policed. Morris observes that while the cultural logic of Western societies demands "a relationship of transparency between inner truth and outward appearance", by contrast "the cultural logics that were historically dominant in Thailand permitted appearances and truths to be radically disjunct.... No 'order of things' can be assumed from the signs that meet the eye in Thailand" (Morris 2002, p. 53).

The different "inner" private and "outer" public domains that Morris refers to are not required to conform to a single cultural logic and often operate as largely epistemologically independent domains. This modern Thai regime of images is an internally differentiated form of power that exerts systematically different types of policing and control over actions and discourses that take place or are enunciated in spaces that are culturally demarcated as either "public" or "private". Under this regime, actions performed and statements uttered in contexts of time and place marked as "public" (*satharana*) are more stringently monitored than similar actions and utterances that are restricted to contexts that may be no less empirically visible but that are culturally labelled as "private" (*suan tua*). Here I use "public" to denote visible to the West and "private" to signify not visible to or obscured from the Western gaze. In fact, domestic or private phenomena under the regime of images may be in clear view but presented in such a way as to be considered to be beyond the gaze of Westerners, who it is assumed cannot read Thai or interpret the nuances of Thai forms of comportment or cultural presentation. Indeed, many of the phenomena of the Thai regime of images are "hiding in plain sight".

Under the regime of images, organs of the state—including the civilian bureaucracy, the police force and the military—at times enforce the public/private split and work to ensure that certain "truths" are barred from being stated in public. When a statement or representation is regarded as being excessively disruptive of the "smooth calm" (*khwam-sa-ngop-riap-roi*) of social life then it can be silenced or rendered invisible by the deployment of the legal (and at times extrajudicial) power of the state. The regime of images is thus characterized by official concern with policing the time and place *kala-thesa* contexts, whether public or private, in which an action takes place or a statement is made rather than with enforcing universal norms of acceptable behaviour and speech. Under the regime of images, phenomena are mapped by multiple forms of power whose respective fields of influence are contained within localized and bordered time and place contexts. Emerging in response to the tensions imposed by the internally fractured modernity of the imperialist West, the regime of images developed from the operation of official, bureaucratic and discursive power that enforces a cultural order of *kala-thesa* contextualization.

Some Western observers describe the contrasts between the dual public and private fields of the regime of images as evidence of structural contradictions in Thai culture and society. However, this "contradiction" is only apparent and can better be understood as emerging from patterns of epistemological multiplicity and contextualization. Perceptions of "contradiction" in Thai religious and cultural life arise from observations of the epistemologically distinct contexts of time and place that operate by different logics. But for Thais socialized in the cultural order of *kala-thesa*, the split between the disparate regimes of power over public images, representations and performances, on the one hand, and private practices, on the other, is rarely perceived in terms of "contradiction". Rather, it is understood locally as varying one's behaviour appropriately to suit the normative demands of each context of time and place.

The origins of the modern Thai regime of images lie in the expanding nets of Western political and economic power that defined Siam's semicolonial status as a politically independent but nonetheless subordinate state within the nineteenth-century imperial order in Southeast Asia. Emerging from historically contingent power relations, this regime is neither traditional nor static, but rather is a dynamic and contested system of power/knowledge. For accounts of Siam/Thailand as a semicolonial state during the colonial era, see Rachel Harrison and Peter Jackson (2010). Thailand's semicolonial position in the Western-dominated colonial and Cold War–era world orders has been a major influence in determining the culturally distinctive features of political power and institutional authority in the country. The structural dualities and what, from a Western perspective, are sometimes erroneously labelled as the contradictions of Thai power and knowledge do not reflect a conflict between a residual "tradition" and an emergent "modernity". Rather, the dualities at the heart of the Thai regime of images constitute the very form of Thailand's alternative modernity. As Morris observes,

> The definitive characteristic of the contemporary Thai polity seems to be its duality, its maintenance of two rhetorics of the body and structures of looking. This duality cannot be evaded with reference to a transitional stage. Thailand exists in the nexus of transnationalist capitalist relations and information technologies that define the contemporary world. If its sociopolitical response

to this placement differs from the responses of Western European or other Asian societies, we cannot simply dismiss it as premodern. (Morris 1994, p. 35)

The Thai regime of images is one instance of a more general phenomenon that Michael Herzfeld calls "cultural intimacy", which is a condition he describes as existing in "sore zones of cultural sensitivity" (Herzfeld 2016, p. 2), and which he defines as

> the recognition of those aspects of an officially shared identity that are considered a source of external embarrassment but nevertheless provide insiders with their assurance of common sociality. Cultural intimacy, though associated with secrecy and embarrassment, may erupt into public life and collective self-representation. (Herzfeld 2016, p. 7)

Herzfeld labels this phenomenon cultural intimacy because, he argues, "[n]ational embarrassment can become the ironic basis of intimacy and affection, a fellowship of the flawed, within the private spaces of the national culture" (Herzfeld 2016, p. 34). As an instance of cultural intimacy, the Thai regime of images reflects what Herzfeld describes as

> the desire for control over external images that ... familiar denials and prohibitions express. Such evasive action often flies in the face of all the evidence, but it is sustained by what, to the outsider, can be an infuriatingly imperturbable air of total conviction: if we tell you that these things do not exist, then, as far as you are concerned, they do not exist. But the visitor is still left wondering why so much vehemence should be invested in denying what all the senses affirm. (Herzfeld 2016, p. 1)

Thailand is by no means the only Asian society in which the challenges of the West have led to a bifurcation between a highly policed domain of rationalized purified performances and representations of modernity designated as "public"/"international" alongside a parallel domain of continuously hybridizing practices labelled "private"/"domestic". John Clammer describes Japan, another never-colonized Asian Buddhist monarchy, as

> a society of anxiety, and [it] has been at least since its opening to the West: a society convinced of the workability of its own social arrangements, but deeply concerned that the rest of the world will not recognise it as a real 'civilisation'. Much of its history, at least for the last century, can be read as the attempt to create a front for the world behind which the true sense of uncontaminated being can flourish. (Clammer 2000, p. 165)

Bénédicte Brac de la Perrière notes a similar public/private divide in the religious lives of Burmese elites, who, while engaging in highly visible public displays of Buddhist devotion, continue to worship the spirits at the centre of the national cult of *nat* protective deities:

> Even if the government on the whole neither sponsors nor intervenes in the [*nat*] cult, on a private and individual basis, Burmese officials do participate in it. This is why the most influential spirit mediums are those who have high-ranking military officers or their wives among their clients. (Brac de la Perrière 2007, p. 219)

Herzfeld contends that countries that were historically on the edges of colonial power, such as Siam, often provide the most striking illustrations of the duality of the dynamics at play in cultural intimacy:

> Forced to face both ways—toward the colonial threat from one side and the despised ethnic otherness lurking on the other—they tend to develop especially strong defenses against sharing potentially embarrassing cultural traits with outside observers. Many of these countries belong to the broad category I have broadly dubbed 'crypto-colonial' (Herzfeld 2002)—that is, countries that can lay claim never to have formally fallen under the colonial yoke, but that have experienced its repressive capacities in the form of cultural and social pressures exerted through local elites. (Herzfeld 2016, p. 25)

Herzfeld contends that there is a "geopolitics of cultural intimacy" (2016, p. 45), and the phenomenon emerges in the context of a Western dominated "global hierarchy of value" (p. 3). Non-colonized Siam did not need to wage a war of independence to expel foreign colonizers. Nevertheless, as a part of the effort to preserve national autonomy in the face of the encroachments of an increasingly dominant West, a new form of local power was called into being. The regime of images emerged from this strategic mobilization of local power in the service of preserving Siamese independence. As a strategic response to the challenges that nineteenth-century colonialism presented to national autonomy, the country's absolute monarchy mobilized a new form of power to construct a public field of images of Siam as "civilised" (Thai: *siwilai*; see Thongchai 2000a; Jackson and Harrison 2010). The origins of the modern Thai regime of images as an instrument of power over the population can thus be traced to the intense efforts of Siam's leaders to bring the country to a standard of "civilization" that would satisfy the Enlightenment-informed demands of the Western colonial powers.

While this regime of images was called into being to respond to Western demands for "civilized" behaviour, it simultaneously realized the potential of the indigenous absolutist state, especially in the sphere of public appearances. In contrast, in the private sphere of everyday life, significant disjunctures from public performances of Western-styled civilization were often tolerated and were rarely rationalized to foreign norms. This situation could develop because there was no compulsion from nineteenth-century Western imperialists for non-colonized Siam to reform all levels of its social order. This is why, following Herzfeld, cultural intimacy is especially pronounced in cryptocolonial societies in which foreign powers did not fully overturn local cultural forms or political structures.

The forms taken by cultural intimacy change from one nation-state to another, but within the global hierarchy of value, "State formation often gives rise to this Janus-like adoption of a dual identity, balancing foreign-directed display against sometimes rueful introspection" (Herzfeld 2016, p. 21). Indeed, a defining feature of the Thai regime of images is a rigid demarcation between what is publicly unspeakable, especially in the presence of a non-Thai audience, and what is "common knowledge" in private, local discourses. It is important to emphasize that the split between the domains of public image and private practice that anthropologists have described as a defining feature of modern Thai culture only became linked with institutional and legal power, and hence only assumed its modern form, as an effect of the disjunctures at the heart of Siam's semicolonial response to the challenges of Western imperial power.

Semicoloniality and the Janus-Faced Dualities of Modern Thailand

Christine Gray notes the importance of the regime of images in the actions of Thai political actors when she observes that "Thai leaders' ability to maintain public positions of power is, in large part, a function of their ability to separate hostile (Thai and Western) audiences, contradictory messages, and communication styles" (Gray 1986, p. 27). Gray argues that the arrival of Western geopolitical power in Siam in the nineteenth century produced a series of antinomies within the Thai body politic and elite culture because "the cosmology and symbolic systems of Western and Theravada Buddhist societies are so disharmonic as to be mutually negating" (p. 9). For Gray, the antinomies caused by the arrival of the West account for many of the transformations and continuities from premodern Siam to modern Thailand, which emerged from the need to respond to culturally different and dominant foreign powers at the same time as preserving and buttressing local patterns of rule. This led to the structural duality at the core of the modern Thai cultural, religious and political orders: "[T]he efforts of Thai leaders to mediate the contradictory value systems of East and West comprise Thailand's 'distinct mode of becoming' (*devenir*)" (p. 21).

In his study of the King Chulalongkorn period (r. 1868–1910), Maurizio Peleggi points to this duality and the Janus-faced nature of Siamese power when he argues that the "primary goals of the Chakri reformation were the establishment of the monarchy's authority over a newly bounded 'national' territory and the uplifting of its prestige in the international arena" (Peleggi 2002, p. 9). Thongchai Winichakul also draws on a notion of duality when he argues that *siwilai*, the Thai rendering of colonial-era notions of "civilisation", was as much a performance for local audiences as an attempt to respond to and contain the material power of the countries of the West (Thongchai 2000a). Thongchai further describes the modern Siamese geo-body as emerging amidst two geopolitical forces, one being the local political field of hierarchical "lord/subjects" that was "founded upon the premodern state", the other being the international order that "brought Siam into the global community [and] in which Siam found its humble place" (Thongchai 2000b, p. 54). He points out that this also produced a bifurcation in local forms of knowledge, with one internally oriented and the other externally directed:

> There were two intellectual strategies to negotiate a desirable position in the scale of civilisation. The first was to situate oneself at a desirable position in the comparative, cultural space of civilisation. The second was to measure the great distance one had covered so far, from an uncivilised past, thus ensuring one's place towards the more civilised end of the temporal scale. Neither strategy operated to the exclusion of the other. The major discourses of civilisation in Siam embodied both strategies. (Thongchai 2000b, p. 53)

Epistemic Multiplicity and Buddhist Prestige (*Barami*) in the Regime of Images

As a political construct, the regime of images is not only an effect of Siam/Thailand's subordinate position within a Western-dominated world order. It is also deeply moulded by religious and ethical notions that have long been at the heart of Thai political culture. The principles of hierarchy that structure the regime of images emerge from Buddhist notions of charismatic prestige or *barami* (from the Pali *pāramī*), which originally denoted the perfection of Buddhist ethical qualities. Indeed, *barami* can be regarded as the structuring principle of the Thai multiple episteme of hierarchical time and place *kala-thesa* contexts that provided a foundation for the bifurcated regime of images created in the colonial era. The multiple episteme of the regime of images upholds Buddhist-derived religio-cultural valuations of the charismatic prestige and authority of political actors and institutions such as the military, the monarchy and the nation in the international arena. Like an "image", charismatic authority or *barami* can be enhanced or damaged. The regime of images thus constitutes a religiously informed order of charismatic prestige. Under this regime, legal power operates to maintain prestige, not to support truth, and when an inconvenient truth threatens to damage prestige, then legal power may operate to silence it.

The dominance of the image or representation over reality or truth results from the setting in place of a regime of epistemological multiplicity. When truth is abandoned as a structuring principle in the symbolic domain, then the charm, charisma or prestige (i.e., *barami*) of the image may assume primacy. Public discursive activity conducted under this regime works to construct and uphold the charismatic prestige or *barami* of representations and statements. The performative nature of discourse under the regime of images means that it should be thought of as a system of power/prestige (Thai: *amnat/barami*) rather than a Foucauldian regime of power/knowledge. For in this regime, power is not mobilized in the name of truth (knowledge) but rather to enhance the charismatic prestige of images.

From the perspective of Western rationalist epistemologies, this is not so much a form of knowledge as an instance of cultural ritualism. As Morris notes, "Ritualism is the epithet given to an overidentification with appearances, to the mistaking of form for reality, and even more, to the attribution of reality to form" (Morris 2000, p. 146). As emphasized throughout this study, in Thai vernacular religion, ritual adherence is emphasized over expressions of faith and belief in doctrine. The Thai religious complex can even accommodate disbelief, provided that such a lack of faith is kept separate from ritual observance. Pattana Kitiarsa notes that this situation is stated explicitly in a common Thai idiom: "You may not believe, but never offend [the spirits]" (*at mai cheua tae ya lop-lu*) (Pattana 2002).

In commenting on Baudrillard's account of the society of the simulacrum, Mike Gane notes that there are only two very basic and contrasting cultures ... one based on the accumulation of meaning and effects (and power), the other which is based on symbolic exchanges, a form which ... cancels and annuls the accumulation of power. (Gane 1991, p. 120)

In *The Order of Things*, Foucault (1994) makes a similar distinction between the medieval episteme based on resemblances and association, on the one hand, and the Enlightenment emphasis on rationality, on the other. According to this pattern, the modern Thai regime of images reflects a cultural logic based on resemblances and the accumulation of meanings and ritual forms, which indeed is one of the defining characteristics of Thai vernacular religiosity. That is, the more positive meanings that can be assembled around an image, the greater the *barami* or charismatic authority and legitimacy that results and the greater the prestige value of that image. In their quest for maximal accumulation of positive charismatic images, Thai politicians mirror ritual practitioners' accumulation of deities on their shrines and in their rituals. This accumulative pattern of prestige also structures the religious culture of the Thai monarchy, which combines Brahmanical and Buddhist rituals and teachings in a non-rationalized complex. In Thai royal cults, just as in popular spirit cults and in the quest by politicians for *barami*, the emphasis is on the accumulation of positive images in order to enhance the acquisition of ritually effective power and authority. The existence of doctrinal inconsistencies among the assembled images or accumulated deities in spirit shrines or in royal rituals is no barrier to this process because in the Thai amalgam of multiple, contextualized ritual and religious forms there is no requirement to impose rational or logical consistency among the diverse influences that are brought together.

In the multiple epistemological fields of the context-based Thai regime of images, the prestige of an image may be independent of and separate from its truth-value. A public image may be invalid with respect to a criterion of truth, yet still retain significant prestige or *barami*. This is because the function of discourse within the episteme of images is to establish and enhance the charismatic prestige value of representations through processes of symbolic addition and association, just as is the case in Thai popular religion and the cults associated with the monarchy. Consequently, within the regime of images it is not only the disproving of a representation—the questioning of its truth value—that is feared or which arouses consternation. Equally intense reactions can be incited by challenges to the prestige of a representation.

In some situations, legal sanctions may be invoked when a revered image is damaged by a statement that undermines its prestige, even if that statement is demonstrably true. This is demonstrated in the long prison sentences that have at times been imposed under Thailand's *lèse-majesté* law for the dissemination of factually accurate but unflattering images and accounts of the Thai monarchy that are perceived as damaging its symbolic prestige (*barami*).

Thai notions of a charisma-bearing "image" (*phap-phot*, *phap-lak*) differ from the concept of "image" in media and marketing studies. While there are similarities between a company's emphasis on its corporate image, on the one hand, and the Thai state's emphasis on constructing and protecting valorized images, on the other, the histories of these two phenomena are distinct. The ascendancy of the marketing of images over the selling of products emerged in late-capitalist societies as one aspect of what Jean Baudrillard (1975, 1994) calls the society of the simulacrum. Baudrillard describes the West's post-industrial economy as being increasingly built upon the reproduction and exchange of images, with "real objects" losing their cultural significance amidst mass-reproduced simulations. In contrast, the Thai regime of images emerged in the political culture of the colonial era rather than as a consequence of late twentieth-century post-industrial capitalism. Baudrillard's image is a product of capitalist mass production and the commodification of cultural artefacts—a simulacrum or a copy of a copy that has cultural significance even though it has come adrift from any original instance or true form. In contrast, Thai images are cultural-political artefacts that attain their significance from their relationship to other politically and culturally prestigious images.

Nonetheless, Baudrillard's notion of the image as simulation and Thai notions of *phap-phot* and *phap-lak* (image) share somewhat similar structures, with both denoting representations whose significance does not depend on an anchoring relationship with truth or reality. This similarity means that in the era of globalizing capitalism, the modern business culture of marketing has reinforced the political forces that underpinned the emergence of the regime of images. In Thailand the image-oriented marketing discourses of globalization have contributed to a further incitement of the colonial-era discourses and patterns of politically significant images. I return to this theme in the final chapter to explore how the effects of late-modern processes of mediatization have at times intensified and accentuated pre-existing cultural and religious patterns in Thailand.

The Regime of Images and the Thai Press

One result of the regime of images has been the creation of contextualized spaces that compartmentalize Thai cultural life into private/domestic domains that are typically mediated through Thai language discourses and public/international domains that are often mediated through English and other European languages. In this bifurcated Western-influenced regime, English and Thai language discourses at times operate under different cultural logics—the former in accord with a rational, scientific view and the latter following a more supernatural and magical logic. Christine Gray reports that this transition from "rational" English to "magical" Thai language accounts may occur even in the discourse of a single person. In her fieldwork interviews she noted that

> [a]fter long discussions in English about bank policies, bank officials would invariably switch to Thai, whip out their amulets of Isan meditation monks, and expound on the qualities of these 'true' monks, commonly believed able to fly through the air, to understand the speech of demons and chattering monkeys, and even to converse with angels. (Gray 1991, p. 60)

The English language press in Thailand typically upholds images and attitudes of rational, civilized Siam/Thailand while the Thai language press, for a domestic audience, at times presents events interpreted in magical terms as news. Thai and English language discourses in the country do not always map the same terrain, and the regime of images operates today to structure an effective division of intellectual labour between the English and Thai language press. As a vehicle for public discourses for international circulation, the country's English language press represents the international face of Thailand, while the Thai language press for a domestic readership represents the private/domestic face. The Thai press often operates as if it is published for Thai eyes only, as non-Thais are assumed not to be able, or uninterested, to read Thai. In broad terms, Thailand's English language press, the *Bangkok Post* and *The Nation*, while having somewhat different political slants, nonetheless have historically represented more rationalist perspectives. In contrast, the country's populist Thai language dailies (e.g., *Thai Rath*, *Daily News*, *Khom Chat Leuk*, *Post Today*, *Naew Na*) reflect domestic perspectives. Jeremy Stolow, citing Rajagopal (2001), notes a similar dichotomy in the Indian press regarding accounts of popular religiosity, which he says is marked by the existence of "structured misunderstandings between the 'liberal' oriented English-language newspapers and the more complexly situated Hindi-language papers"

(Stolow 2005, p. 140n19). Stolow states that the English press in India refuses to comprehend the claims of popular religion, which are dismissed as "closed, implacable and impervious to reason" (p. 140n19). Thai Buddhist reformists and the English language press in the country subscribe to what Stolow calls a "hermeneutics of suspicion" (p. 132) of folk and popular religion in that they seek to unmask magic and expose it as a form of deception.

The duality at the heart of modern Thai culture, discourses and politics is reflected in the coexistence of non-rationalized magical and scientific discourses even in some publications oriented to educated Thais. Kasian Tejapira notes that in the 1940s, the weekly newspaper *Mahachon* ("The Masses"), a mouthpiece of the Thai communist movement, included advertisements for astrology services alongside critiques of superstition. These advertisements

> went against every scientistic grain of Marxism-communism, dialectical materialism, historical materialism, or what have you. Be that as it may, this astrological superstition appeared alongside scientific socialism on the pages of the leading propaganda organ of the Thai Communist Party. Even more astounding is the fact *Mahachon* itself made no bones about its opposition to the 'utter nonsense' of astrology. Yet the paper published one advertisement for astrological nonsense after another! One begins to wonder whether it was simply (mis)calculated political camouflage or perhaps something larger, deeper, and impersonal at work—the 'invisible hand' of the market. (Kasian 2001, p. 176)

Kasian suggests that the *Mahachon* newspaper may have accepted advertisements for astrological services, despite their promotion of "superstition", for commercial reasons; that is, to pay for production costs. Historically in Thailand, the message of the market has at times been stronger than the claims of ideology or theory. This same situation can be found in some Thai language daily newspapers and news weeklies today, where one finds anti-superstition articles in the same publication as advertisements for magical amulets. The more intellectual *Matichon* daily newspaper and its sister weekly newsmagazine *Matichon Sutsapda*, as well as some mass-circulation dailies like *Thai Rath*, respond to both the supporters and critics of magical commodified religiosity or *phuttha phanit*. These publications often carry critiques of magical beliefs in some columns while also publishing other columns that take the commercialized cult of amulets as given. These newspapers also often accept large and no doubt well-paying advertisements for new batches of magical amulets. The Thai press, like the Thai populace, reflects a diverse and deeply riven religious landscape of unresolved tensions. The fact that a mid-twentieth-century Marxist newspaper included advertisements for astrology services, however, may also have reflected a situation in which at least some of the Thai Marxists who read the newspaper privately continued to believe in astrology despite presenting a public image of secular atheism that was critical of the supernatural and "superstition".

The contrast between rationalist and magical discourses and accounts of phenomena may even be found within a single piece of published discourse. For example, in some Thai media the elevated spiritual status of the late King Bhumibol, whether as a Buddha-to-be bodhisattva or a virtual god-king *sammatidevaraja* (see Jackson 2007), was regarded to have been demonstrated when his death was marked by supernatural events. Soon after King Bhumibol died in October 2016, *Matichon* daily published a page-one story headed, "Shrouding the city the day the king died—*Thumaketu*—It occurred in the times of the Buddha and Rama 5, Social networks abuzz sharing photos of the miracle".[1] This item reported that on the morning after the king died, a light fog, called *mork thumaketu* by the newspaper, shrouded Bangkok in a morbid dark mist, describing it as a phenomenon that royal chronicles record as having occurred after the deaths of kings in both the Ayutthaya and Bangkok periods, including on the morning after King Chulalongkorn passed away in October 1910. *Thumaketu* is the Thai form of *dhūmaketu*, a Pali term that in the Buddhist scriptures denotes a smoke-like phenomenon (*dhūma*) that is regarded as an omen or sign (*ketu*). Citing Chair Professor Lorm Phengkaeo, a specialist in Thai language, literature and history, *Matichon* reported that the *mork thumaketu* fog had also occurred in ancient north India after the Lord Buddha died and passed into *nibbana*, and is a phenomenon that indicates "a person of great merit has passed away" (*seu khwam theung phu mi bun thi luang lap dap sun*). The article thus linked the Buddha, King Chulalongkorn and King Bhumibol as all being persons of great merit, whose passing was marked by a miraculous phenomenon.

While the *Matichon* article began by focusing on the supernatural character of the *thumaketu* fog, it ended with official statements from the meteorological bureau describing the atmospheric conditions that had produced the fog. The two accounts, one supernatural and the other scientific, were not rationalized or integrated into a single causal narrative. Each interpretation of the origin of the fog was simply reported in succession, one after the other, with the reader being left to make their own assessment of the alternative explanations. Was one account of the fog meant to be more feasible or were both simultaneously valid? Was the phenomenon perhaps over-determined; that is, brought into being by a combination of supernatural forces and natural factors, or perhaps by supernatural forces that can also be interpreted through the lens of science and reason? No resolution of these questions was provided.

Alluding to the pattern of incorporation and contextualization of incommensurable discursive and representational regimes discussed above, Christine Gray observes that "Western values that undercut the indigenous cultural system were publicly adopted in Thailand. Both systems were maintained, sometimes in alternation, and neither fully jettisoned" (Gray 1986, p. 349). Gray also notes that "[w]hat is confusing about the cultural analysis of modern Thai society is that both sets of ideals are simultaneously upheld and rejected by Thai leaders" (p. 74). However, it also needs to be noted that this response to the West was built upon an existing, premodern model that negotiated the tensions between ultimately irreconcilable Hindu- and Buddhist-derived ideologies of royal rule. While taking its current form as a response to Western imperial power and the antinomies of an internally conflicted condition of modernity, the regime of images nevertheless also develops from a premodern setting of *kala-thesa* contextualization as a strategy to negotiate religious multiplicity and which supports deeply founded notions of charismatic authority that continue to lie at the centre of contemporary Thai religious and political cultures. The Thai had already developed a way to negotiate the contradictory cosmological and epistemological systems of Brahmanism, Buddhism and spirit belief through contextualization and compartmentalization before the era of Western imperialism. This existing multiple-epistemological and polyontological regime was then adapted and expanded into the regime of images as a strategy to negotiate the impact of the West and its bifurcated, fractured modernity.

Even though the colonial era has long since ended, the orchestration of the performance of civilization that lay at the foundation of the modern state remains one of the Thai bureaucracy's central preoccupations, and the structure of power that brought the modern regime of images into being remains a key feature of expressions of national culture and identity. Thongchai Winichakul (2000a, 2000b) argues that the construction of images of Siamese civilization was not only a strategic response to the West but was also central to the domestic political project of legitimating the rule of the absolute monarchy in the second half of the nineteenth century and the first decades of the twentieth century. The instituting of the regime of images has always had a dual role, with its domestic legitimatory function providing a basis upon which the absolute monarchy reordered the state bureaucracy and mobilized the population in the name of civilization. The perpetuation of the regime of images long after the end of European imperialism in large measure derives from its continuing value in the domestic political sphere.

While, as noted in Chapter One, Christine Gray presents a critique of the influence of Weberian sociology of religion in Thai studies, she nonetheless retains a somewhat rationalist view of capitalism and modern Thailand. In words that echo Serhat Ünaldi's (2016) hope that the Thai social and political order may in future come to be characterized by more instrumental rationalities, Gray suggests that multiple or Janus ideologies are "transitional, a sign of things to come" (Gray 1986, p. 853). I suggest, however, that the perpetuation of multiple, unrationalized "Janus" faces has been a long-standing Thai political and cultural form. It continues today because it retains value in the contemporary era, with the Thai modernization process based on contextualization being able to conform to multiple cultural logics at the same time.[2] This system of multiple epistemological domains of representation has persisted to the present day because it has proved to be just as suitable to bolstering contemporary political regimes as it was in contributing to the nineteenth-century project of securing national independence in an increasingly Western-dominated world.

Thai Religion in the Imperial World Order: The Regime of Images and the Creation of Janus Rituals

Gray argues that in the domain of religion a key Siamese response to the antinomies presented by the dominating presence of Western modernizing power was the creation of what she calls Janus rituals and practices that can simultaneously be interpreted in two radically different ways by Thai and foreign audiences, respectively. Janus rituals are practices that "appear to embody the ideals of both Western and Thai audiences while having totally different meanings for both" (Gray 1986, p. 234). Janus rituals and Janus discourses are forms of practice and discourse that can be read by non-Thais as reflecting a rational and scientific worldview while at the same time being interpreted by Thai audiences as reflecting a magical and enchanted view. Gray contends that the creation of Janus rituals was a response to the antinomies of civilization and modernity that Siam experienced as it was incorporated into the Western-dominated colonial world order in a subordinate position:

[A] major imperative of Thai capitalist development concerns the elite's ability to mediate antinomies (stave off Western domination and maintain Western support). They satisfied this imperative in part by creating and/or emphasizing 'Janus rituals' that appeared to embody the ideals of both Western and Thai society. (Gray 1986, p. 75)

For example, the purification of Buddhist ritual can at times be read by Western observers as rationalization, a felicitous coincidence when a single action performs a double function within two radically different cultural logics. Gray presents King Mongkut's (r. 1851–68) reform of Thai Buddhism and his establishment of the Thammayut Order of monks before he ascended the throne as a signal example of a Janus ritual, being both "a mode of 'purifying' the Sangha in indigenous eyes" and "of 'modernising' it or making it more 'rational' in Western eyes" (Gray 1986, p. 215). As Gray notes, "Western symbols of 'rationality' … were incorporated into Buddhist paradigms of [ritual] purification" (p. 253). Indeed, Mongkut responded to nineteenth-century Christian critiques of the "superstitious" nature of Thai Buddhism by claiming that his new Thammayut Order eschewed the supernaturalism of the older established Mahanikai Order of monks. He developed

a version of Buddhism that looked pure to the Siamese and 'rational' to Western critics. In conversations with missionaries, he was able to reject the 'superstitious' aspects of existing traditions, which he conveniently identified with Khmer influence, with the Mahanikai and even went so far as to reject the *Traiphum*[3] (Lingat 1933). (Gray 1986, p. 233)

Stanley Tambiah similarly argues that Mongkut's reforms, while interpreted as modernizing and rationalizing by Western audiences, in fact reflected "traditional purification patterns and … enhanced his soteriological claims" (Tambiah 1976, p. 227, cited by Gray 1986, p. 255). Gray observes that Siam's new Janus rituals were like mirrors that "reflected Western ideals back to a Western audience" (Gray 1986, p. 255). To take Gray's metaphor further, Western audiences also often failed to see, or take seriously, what was continuing to take place behind the façade of the Janus mirror. The mistaken assumption of Western observers that a single order of representation unites them with their modern-looking Thai interlocutors can prevent recognition of the fact that the "same" signifier changes its meaning as it circulates between coexisting but not fully commensurable Thai and Western cultural logics. Morris provides an instance of this in a summary of Thongchai Winichakul's (1994) study of the birth of Siamese discourses of geography, observing that in the nineteenth century there was often a confusion and "false correspondence" between Siamese astrology and Western astronomy:

> The seeming translatability of these discourses, [Thongchai] says, permitted a slippage and a movement of one discourse across the horizon of the other, thus inciting a transformation in Siamese thought even as (elite) Siamese thought seemed to be maintaining its autonomy and epistemological authority. (Morris 2002, p. 68)

As Nerida Cook (1992) observes, this duality is highlighted by the fact that in nationalist discourses King Mongkut is lauded as the "Father of Thai Science" because of his skills in astronomy, while astrologers eulogize him as the father of modern Thai astrology because of his expertise in predicting the motions of the planets. Two processes are at work in these cases. First, a Janus ritual is a single ritual or representational form that has the capacity to be interpreted in two radically different and ultimately incompatible ways—one Western and one Thai. Second, under the multiplication of epistemic systems in the regime of images, magical accounts of activities or ritual practices were rendered private or domestic, while rational scientific interpretations were made public for international audiences.

Creation of Categories of "Religion" (*sas–na*) and "Belief" (*khwam-cheua*) in Thailand

Colonial-era Western critiques of elements of the complex amalgam of Thai religious rituals and beliefs have had lasting influences on the forms of power over religious expression. While spirit rituals were decried as superstitious and irrational, and royal Hindu-Brahmanical rituals were at times denounced as signs of oriental despotism, Buddhism by contrast was seen by many Western observers as an enlightened religion that was compatible with Western notions of civilization. This had a significant influence on the religious beliefs that had underpinned the premodern royal political order. In the context of the geopolitical shifts marked by the arrival of the militarily superior Western colonial powers, Patrick Jory observes that the Thai court began to realize that indigenous concepts of power and the premodern political organization of the kingdom were becoming obsolete. From the 1830s,

> the epistemological basis of the Thai intellectual tradition was being questioned by sections of the Thai court. Belief in miracles,

supernatural powers, mythical beasts, premodern cosmologies and religious-historical traditions, even fundamental concepts such as rebirth, were all being reassessed in the light of Western rationalism and science. (Jory 2016, p. 19)

In particular, Jory details the decline of the political-cum-cultural relevance of the *Jatakas*, legends of the Buddha's past lives, from the middle of the nineteenth century. In 1904 King Chulalongkorn wrote an essay denying the canonical authority of the *Jatakas* and reclassifying the stories as folk-tales: "Even more significantly, in denying the veracity of the *Jatakas* and the concept of the bodhisatta king, the king severed the lineage of the Chakri kings from the lineage of the Buddha" (Jory 2016, p. 22).

The critiques of aspects of the Thai religious amalgam as being superstitious or signs of oriental despotism led to the relegation of spirit cults and some Brahmanical rituals to the private/domestic domain and the comparative valorization of Buddhism in the public domain as the public/international face of Thai elite religious expression. This division of the Thai religious amalgam into public and private components was subsequently marked by a discursive divide between "religion" and "belief" based on categories drawn from Western academic studies of religion.

Imperialist Religious Studies, Modernizing State Power and Religious Diversification

Tatsuki Kataoka's study of Chinese temples in Thailand provides insights into how local responses to Western imperialism and the complexities of modernization have influenced the subsequent direction of religious change, both towards doctrinal orthodoxy in some situations and also in the direction of magical rituals in other contexts. Kataoka argues that Southeast Asian religions had to be reinvented in the course of modernization and state-building:

> [E]xisting religious traditions, in accordance with state regulation based on Western standards of religion, have faced growing pressure to fashion themselves so as to fulfill the definition as 'one of many religions' in the sense demanded by the field of comparative religion. (Kataoka 2012a, p. 361)

Western academic definitions of what should be regarded as a "religion", and colonial-era analyses of typologies of "civilisations" in terms of this definition, led Siam to extend state monitoring, supervision and control over the religious amalgam. As part of the effort to create a state recognized as being "civilised" within European discourses of imperialism, Siam's modernizing elites defined some domains of the religious field as falling within the scope of a new category labelled *sasana* or "religion". As Keyes et al. observe, "the Buddhist term *sāsanā*, which today is used as the equivalent of 'religion', only came into general usage in the late nineteenth/early twentieth century" (Keyes et al. 1994, p. 16n4). This created a division in Thai religious life, with many forms of ritual and belief now falling outside of the new official category of *sasana*/religion, and in contrast being labelled as "belief" (*khwam-cheua*) or "faith" (*sattha*). Since the late nineteenth century, official Thai discourses have distinguished between *sasana*—effectively monastery-based Theravada Buddhism, as brought under the jurisdiction of the Department of Religious Affairs (*krom kan-sasana*) within the secular bureaucracy—and non-Buddhist belief and faith, which is rarely administered by the state or occasionally comes under the separate jurisdiction of the Ministry of the Interior.

In some academic and official discourses, rituals and beliefs that fall outside the new category of *sasana*/religion are called *latthi*. Thongchai observes that in modern Thai,

> *latthi* signifies a belief viewed as lower or inferior to an established religion (*sasana*), a view that is not credible, wrong or even dangerous, such as *latthi communit* (Communism) or *latthi boriphokniyom* (consumerism). It is a common word in Thai usage ... that is often used to translate the English '-ism' suffix. It is also usually used for a parochial ideology, a cult, a mystical or folk belief, and for those who are considered superstitious, idiosyncratic or otherwise marginal. (Thongchai 2015, p. 92)

The term *latthi* is usually reserved to describe the beliefs of others with either implied or explicit derogatory connotations. In contrast, terms like *khwam-cheua* ("belief") and *sattha* ("faith") may be used to describe the non-Buddhist beliefs of one's own group and do not have derogatory senses. *Sattha* and *khwam-cheua* refer to one's own non-doctrinal belief, while *latthi* refers to someone else's non-doctrinal, and hence implicitly inferior or misguided, belief. As noted in the Introduction, the modern Thai academic term for forms of cultic ritual, including the cults of wealth, is *latthi-phithi*, which literally translates as "belief-ritual".

Kataoka shows that those domains of Thai religious life that, following the influence of Western ideas, have come to be labelled as "Buddhism" and *sasana*, and which since the reign of

King Chulalongkorn have come under the administration of the Department of Religious Affairs, have been subject to procedural and doctrinal standardization. In contrast, aspects of religious life that are now termed "belief" and "faith", and which have often fallen outside the Western-influenced definition of Buddhism as *sasana*, have had no parallel state supervision or intervention in their rituals, teachings or organization and by comparison have been comparatively free to engage in diverse forms of mixing and blending. This divide between doctrinal and monastic Buddhism defined as religion, on the one hand, and rituals and beliefs, on the other, reflects Latour's (1993) account of Western modernity as a façade of public, purified rationality that masks a hybrid complexity of mixing that evades the boundaries and binary logics of modernist rationalism.

Ironically, the modern, imperialist-driven divisions engendered within Thai religiosity have contributed to the proliferation of new forms of non-Buddhist ritual. Lying outside the scope, and interest, of modern state power, cultic ritual has been largely free to develop and evolve into fascinating new forms in response to changing sociological, economic and technological forces. As will be discussed in Chapter Seven, sources of modern enchantment in Thailand lie outside the domain of state power in new forms of economic organization and communication technologies.

In Thailand, Brahmanical shrines and Chinese Taoist temples are both called *san jao* ("pavilions of the lords"), in contrast to Buddhist monasteries, which are called *wat*. Kataoka observes that neither Taoist temples nor shrines for Brahmanical deities are recognized as "religious places" (*sasana-sathan*) in terms of the official discourse of the Department of Religious Affairs. He argues that the imposition of the Western-influenced categorical distinction between religious expressions labelled as *sasana* (religion) and other forms called *khwam-cheua* (belief) or *sattha* (faith), and the different extent and intensity of modernizing state power exercised over these two domains, has produced a paradoxical situation in the case of followers of Chinese religious rituals in Thailand:

> [While] the followers of Chinese temples claim to be Buddhists in official statistics,… the official status of their temples, with their very syncretic pantheons, is 'non-religious'. Chinese temples, which have been ignored by the state's administrators of religion, demonstrate the gap between the official definition of Buddhism and the religion itself. (Kataoka 2012a, p. 362)

Kataoka further contends that the contemporary "vitality and energy of the religious landscape of Thailand" (Kataoka 2012b, p. 483) emerges from the fact that over the past century the modernizing state has had little interest in supervising or controlling religious activities that came to fall outside the colonial-era definition of Buddhism as religion-*sasana*. While there is now considerable secular bureaucratic oversight of Buddhist monasteries—including the formal registration of Buddhist monks, the setting of the curriculum of Buddhist universities and the awarding of honorific titles to monks—there is no parallel state intervention in or control of the ritual practices or teachings propagated at Brahmanical shrines or Chinese temples. Kataoka notes that since Chinese temples, and I would also add Brahmanical shrines,

> are not recognised as representing religion, they are not forced [by state policy] to select any one institutionalised religion through which to 'purify' their pantheons. This contributes to the persistence of indiscriminative syncretism in the grassroots practices of Thai Buddhism. (Kataoka 2012b, p. 482)

Kataoka sees this situation being to the benefit of Chinese temples in Thailand, as they do not have to compete with state Buddhism and are able to engage in "indiscriminate syncretic worship [which] is also latently sanctioned [by state authorities]" (Kataoka 2012b, p. 461). Jovan Maud (2007) similarly argues that the state-imposed religious order has contributed to the proliferation of new forms of heterodox cultic ritual in Thailand.

In summary, in Thailand the standardization of Theravada Buddhist doctrine and ritual practice, and an intensified syncretization of Chinese and Brahmanical religious expression, have *both* emerged in parallel as effects of modernizing state power. This represents a fascinating instantiation of the divide between discursive rationalization and practical ritual hybridity that Latour identifies as the actual character of modernity. In the religious domain, the imposition of the modern regime of images—itself a response to Western imperialism and the creation of categorical and bureaucratic divisions between official *sasana*/religion and popular belief and faith—has been a productive source of new forms of magic and ritual innovation.

Implicit Relations of Spirit Cults to the Modern State

Jory argues that in response to critiques from the West in the nineteenth century, "[a]ny indigenous practices or doctrines that might be interpreted as signs of 'despotism' or 'superstition' or 'divine kingship' had to be eliminated" (Jory 2016, p. 176). Jory is mistaken in his claim that practices that fell outside the new category of *sasana* were eliminated. The elements of royal cults and elite religious culture that were criticized as superstitious and uncivilized by Western imperialist observers were not destroyed. Rather, they were relocated to new private-cum-domestic zones somewhat separate from the gaze of the critical Westerners. In response to the critiques, Thailand was re-imaged as a "Buddhist monarchy", with the Buddhist dimensions of royal cults and elite religious culture being emphasized in public ritual for international viewing. In contrast, animist and Brahmanical "superstitions" were relocated to private, domestic spaces where they have continued to have genuine religio-political relevance and influence in behind-the-scenes roles. As Kataoka notes, the proliferating forms of "indiscriminate syncretic worship" (Kataoka 2012b, p. 482) have been latently or implicitly supported by state authorities.

The creation of the regime of images in Thai royal and elite religious culture has had differential impacts on the subsequent historical development of both Buddhism and spirit cults. Buddhism was brought under state control in an explicit legal and administrative framework. However, provided they were not regarded as threats to authority in the form of rebellious millenarian cults, spirit cults were largely left out of the state project of harnessing religion to the projects of *siwilai/* civilization, modernization and development.

Yet spirit cults continued to be practised and their rituals and beliefs evolved into ever more elaborate forms beyond the public influence of state power. Spirit cults now have implicit rather than explicit relations to the modern Thai state. The practical relation of spirit cults to the state and to elite religious life is significant, but is not stated in laws or codified in bureaucratic administrative frameworks. As Gray notes, "the most important heterodox aspects of Thai Buddhism are often implicit" (Gray 1986, p. 140). Because spirit cults have an unofficial, but nonetheless genuine, role in Thai political affairs and royal cults, the extent of their influence can only be appreciated through a study of actual ritual practice, not via legal or policy documents. While the modern history of Thai Buddhism can be studied from textual sources and official documents, the history of elite spirit cults needs to draw upon very different ethnographic and cultural studies semiotic methodologies. Indeed, the full actual role and practical significance of spirit cults in elite religious life only becomes visible when one observes the practices of state actors and organizations. This is why it is anthropologists—whose methods provide them with access to the more implicit, private and domestic aspects of religious life—who have written most about Thailand's new magical cults. Anthropology has captured the genuinely influential religious culture of domestic power that came into being with the creation of the regime of images. In contrast, the methods of historians and political scientists often restrict their academic gaze to statutes, policies and the contents of documentary sources, at times limiting their studies to analyses of the formal religious domain of Buddhism/*sasana* that was constituted in modern Thailand as a response to the West.

An Alternative Enchanted History of Thai Modernity

> The lack of attention paid to astrology in Western scholarship has to do with its historical transformation in Western thought, and the consequent antipathy of its scientific successors, to the point where even for the study of those historical periods in our own past where the 'occult' was still acceptable to the majority, it still seems necessary to fight for basic historiographical rights for the subject, and for its human subjects. (Nerida Cook 1989, p. 1)

Impact of the Regime of Images on Thai Studies

The modern regime of images does not merely structure Thai language discourses in Thailand. It has also impacted Western knowledge about the country, both popular stereotypes and academic studies. The dichotomy between public images that can be spoken about and private realities that cannot be named, or are overlooked and remain largely implicit, has been reproduced in some fields of Western Thai studies. As noted, one of the consequences of the imposition of the regime of images across the field of the Thai religious amalgam has been the creation of an international image of Thailand as a "Buddhist kingdom". Many histories of modern Thailand mistake this image for the reality, when in fact non-Buddhist religious rituals have also played important roles in the modern era. Following the emphasis of classical religious studies on Buddhism and its relative denigration of magic as mere ritual, some scholars have mistaken the public/international surface for the totality of Thai culture and social organization.

Pattana argues that the ideological influence of state policies of Buddhist nationalism has led studies of Thai religion to overemphasize the importance of Buddhism in the country's religious complex, with a dominant Buddhist-centred paradigm working "to submerge popular religious beliefs and rituals under the shadow of state-sponsored Buddhism" (Pattana 2005a, p. 462). This academic overemphasis on reformed Buddhism as a defining feature of the modern Thai polity is paralleled by an underemphasis of the extent to which Thailand's lead-ers—appointed, elected and royal—have deployed magical beliefs and rituals across the modern period. While Buddhism may have come to be defined as modern Thailand's pre-eminent religious form, this does not mean that non-Buddhist dimensions of the religious amalgam have been irrelevant to the country's political processes. As Thongchai notes, "[c]ontemporary identity in Thailand is prominently configured through an allegiance of reformed Buddhism with the modern Thai state" (Thongchai 2015, p. 75). While this is true for the public image of Thai national identity, in private and domestic practices even state actors often configure their relations through enchanted and magical rituals. Drawing on some less commonly reported sources that reflect the private/domestic domain of Thai religious life, it is possible to begin to construct the outlines of an alternative history of Thai modernity as being based as much upon magic and supernatural ritual as Buddhism.

King Mongkut

Pattana notes that in many histories of modernizing Thailand no ruler better exemplifies the nineteenth-century political establishment's efforts to construct a rationalist order than King Mongkut: "As King Mongkut steered Siam toward modernisation, one of his chief goals was to eliminate magic, superstition and 'uncivilised' traditions in favour of rationalised Buddhism and Western science, technology and culture" (Pattana 2002, p. 164). Paul Johnson, however, challenges this dominant image of King Mongkut as a "hero of reason" (Johnson 1997, p. 234) and a "pioneer of rationality" (p. 244), arguing that the "stereotyping of Mongkut as 'rational' like the West perpetuates a posi-tivist view of Thai religious development from superstition to science, for which Mongkut plays the mascot" (p. 245). Indeed, the Buddhist dimensions of Mongkut's life have been the focus of much more study by Western scholars than his engagement with Brahmanical and other rituals. In many histories, Mongkut's establishment of the Thammayut reform movement while a monk before ascending the throne in 1851 is interpreted as an effort, as Rosalind Morris puts it, to eschew "the ritualism associated with spirits" (Morris 2000, p. 1). In contrast, Johnson argues that "it is difficult to maintain that Mongkut exercised a consistent Western 'rationality' when his life is examined more closely" (Johnson 1997, p. 236).

Johnson notes that in practice Mongkut relied significantly upon astrology in his rule, and that he presented multiple and distinct faces to different domestic and international audiences: "This points to one explanation for Mongkut's complex and apparently inconsistent 'rationality', namely, that it can be accounted for by the mixed political demands of Thai kingship" (Johnson 1997, p. 239). As detailed in this book, the complex heritage of multiple foreign and domestic influences that intersect in Thai religious, social and cultural life are often managed by a system of *kala-thesa* time and place contextualization whereby different discursive and epistemological fields from diverse cultural, ethnic and religious sources are held apart in largely distinct spaces. This time and place contextualization is found at all levels of the social order, including elite political culture. The multiple contextualized dimensions of King Mongkut's political persona are reflected in the fact that he often signed royal documents, such as the 1855 Bowring Treaty with Britain, with seals in four languages—Thai, Khmer, Chinese and English—each in its own distinctive script. As noted above, Christine Gray alludes to the importance of the regime of images and the contextualization of Thai political life in the modern era when she observes that Thai leaders need to negotiate "separate hostile (Thai and Western) audiences, contradictory messages, and communication styles" (Gray 1986, p. 27).

King Mongkut exemplified the multiple positionalities of Thailand's modernizing elites, presenting different faces to different audiences. Johnson cites Mongkut's institution of Brahmanical rituals as a counter instance to the narrative of his being a "rational Buddhist" king:

> That Mongkut reinstituted and celebrated with great pomp, rituals that he at other times disdained as 'empty' and 'superstitious' seems confusing.... In fact, all of these examples are paradoxical only when logic, consistency, and coherence are seen [through the lens] of the Western, scientific worldview. Mongkut's 'rationality' was negotiated between various interests, of which Western science was only one. (Johnson 1997, p. 251)

In what can be seen as a reference to the Thai system of *kala-thesa* contextualization, Johnson emphasizes that Mongkut's "rationality" was "negotiated among the varying and sometimes competing interests of his time and place" (Johnson 1997, p. 251).

Mongkut's Institution of Phra *Siam Thewathirat as Thailand's "Guardian Angel"*

Few Western histories of nineteenth-century Thailand obseve that Mongkut "invented" a new royal deity, *Phra* Siam Thewathirat (Pali: *Sayamadevādhirāja*), which has continued to be important in the private, domestic rituals of all subsequent monarchs of the Chakri dynasty. In a 2004 article in the Thai language *Nation Weekly*, columnist Rung-arun Kulthamrong quotes Prince Damrong, one of Mongkut's sons, as saying, "His Majesty King Mongkut instituted/ invented (*pradit*)[4] *Phra* Siam Thewathirat in order to worship the spirit of Thailand (*bucha spirit khorng meuang Thai*) in the royal palace" (cited by Rung-arun 2004, p. 78).[5] In a 2007 Thai language newspaper article titled "Guardian Angel of Rattanakosin [Bangkok]", journalist Ram Watcharapradit states that this deity was invoked and named by Mongkut after the 1855 signing of the Bowring Treaty with Britain. At the time, Mongkut is reported to have observed that Siam "had been defeated and lost its independence many times in the past but the country had always survived these dangers. There must then be some protective deity saving the country" (*khong ja mi thepphayada ong dai ong neung thi khoi phithak pok-porng raksa prathet*) (Ram 2007, p. 31). Mongkut had an image of this guardian deity of Siam cast in gold, composed a Pali *khatha* incantation in its honour and had the image installed in the Royal Chapel of Wat Phra Kaeo, where members of the royal family still perform ceremonies in its honour.

Writing in *The Nation*, Thanong Khanthong notes the importance of the cult of *Phra* Siam Thewathirat to the private ritual practices of all Chakri kings since Mongkut:

> In the nineteenth century, King Mongkut, or Rama IV, believed strongly in the gods, or superior beings, which he felt were protecting him, the royal family and Siam from all evils besetting their world. During his time, Burma, Malaya and Vietnam fell to Western imperialism. The king more often than not thanked Phra Siamdevadhiraj for guarding Siam.
>
> The Chakri Dynasty regards Phra Siamdevadhiraj with the utmost reverence. A statue depicting the angel, all in gold and currently situated in the Dusit Palace inside the Grand Palace, is in a standing position and eight inches high. It is meticulously dressed in the form of a mythical god descending from heaven....
>
> Phra Siamdevadhiraj also appears in different forms in literature. Banthoon Lamsam, the president of Thai Farmers Bank, interpreted Mani Mekhala, a goddess in 'The Story of Mahajanak' written by His Majesty the King [Bhumibol], as a sort of Phra Siamdevadhiraj.[6]

Justin McDaniel points to King Mongkut's close connections with the famed magic monk *Somdet* To, who is one of the most important historical figures in the cult of amulets detailed in Chapter Five. McDaniel states that *Somdet* To was the king's favourite monk, adding that "supposedly rationalistic, Western-influenced monarchs, who wanted to purify Thai Buddhism of superstition and non-canonical practices and beliefs" (McDaniel 2011, p. 127) nonetheless had close connections with supernatural traditions. In a footnote to his study of *Somdet* To, McDaniel notes that "[a]n extensive description of King Mongkut's belief in the magical power of ghosts in these important images is described in the chronicle of his reign".[7] Rarely, however, has this "extensive description" been noted in histories of Mongkut's reign written by Western scholars.

Citing Tambiah, Gray observes that in the second year of his reign, Mongkut installed a new *lak meuang* city pillar in the Royal Chapel because his personal horoscope was at variance with that of the existing *lak meuang* (Tambiah 1976, p. 226). Significantly for the analyses presented in this chapter, Gray notes that "[t]his was a private ceremony, presided over by court Brahmins and little remarked upon by Westerners. It has its roots in the Hindu and Cambodian *devaraja* traditions" (Gray 1986, p. 264). Gray also states that the new city pillar represented "'the guardians of the kingdom of Siam', angels who were reincarnations of past Buddhist kings" (p. 264).

While Mongkut has often been represented as a modernizing, rational Buddhist monarch, it is more accurate to say that his actions accorded with the Thai system of time and place contextualization and reflected the application of this established social-cum-cultural order in the creation of the modern regime of images. Under this regime, which came into being as a response to Western critiques of Thai religious and political cultures, the Brahmanical and supernatural elements of his rule were located in a private and domestic realm. Gray notes that Mongkut's sons, "Prince Damrong and King Chulalongkorn [went] to great lengths to modernize Buddhism and convince westerners that it was rational and non-superstitious" (Gray 1995, p. 230). Nonetheless, Gray also notes that "neither Mongkut nor Chulalongkorn ceased active participation in Brahmanical ceremonies, they merely withheld them from the Western gaze" (Gray 1986, p. 278).

King Chulalongkorn

While also often eulogized as a Buddhist king in histories of the modernization of Siam, Mongkut's son and successor, Chulalongkorn, was nonetheless equally eclectic and multiple in his religious interests. Reflecting the dominant historical narrative of modern Buddhist kingship, Thomas Kirsch writes,

Chulalongkorn ... initiated the rationalisation and centralisation of the Sangha, paralleling the organisation of the government. National standards were set for monks.... The overall thrust of these modern developments has been to emphasise the central position of Buddhism in Thai religion and society. (Kirsch 1977, p. 265)

In contrast to this view, however, McDaniel notes that in 1888 King Chulalongkorn also penned the "Royal Rituals of the Twelve Months" (*reuang phraratchaphithi sipsorng deuan*), which in his view showed that the king did not try to create a standard national religion but instead

reveals [Chulalongkorn's] acceptance, if not outright promotion, of diversity in Thai ritual. Moreover, it shows that what was considered proper Thai ritual was not and should not be equated with Theravada Buddhism. In fact, in each month, the rituals described are a mixture of Chinese, Brahmanic, Thervadin, and local.... The divisions and hierarchies between Buddhism, Brahmanism, local and Chinese religions are virtually erased in this presentation. (McDaniel 2011, p. 129)

Thai royal elites have also been active players in the popularization of the cult of amulets. Chalong Soontravanich observes that in 1902 *Chao Phraya* Surasakmontri, commander of an expeditionary force sent to suppress a Shan rebellion in Northern Siam, distributed amulets from an old stupa in Phitsanulok in the mid-north of the country to his troops. When those who wore

IMAGE 3. *Phra* Siam Thewathirat
An image of *Phra* Siam Thewathirat, protective deity of the Chakri dynasty, that was created in the mid-1850s by King Mongkut (r. 1851–68). Mongkut believed the reason Siam remained independent while neighbouring Southeast Asian countries fell under colonial domination was because the country, and the Chakri dynasty, was blessed by a protective divine spirit. (Source: 1997 New Year greeting card.)

the amulets returned to Bangkok unharmed, their magical protection became widely known (Chalong 2013, p. 199). King Chulalongkorn also distributed amulets to his retinue and confidants (p. 205). The king was given a protective *khatha* incantation by the magic monk *Luang Pu* Iam of Wat Nang in Thonburi before he left on his first trip to Europe in 1897.[8] Chalong reports legends that relate how King Chulalongkorn used the protective sacred power of incanting the *khatha* to bring under control a horse that ran wild while he was out riding during a royal tour of Europe.

King Vajiravudh

The reign of Chulalongkorn's son, King Vajiravudh (r. 1910–25), was also marked by a divide between public Western rationality and private supernatural ritualism. While the British-educated Vajiravudh translated Shakespeare and performed modern-style plays, as detailed in the following section he also reinstituted Brahmanical *wai khru* rituals and, in contrast to earlier reigns when Chakri monarchs were associated with the Buddha, he instituted the system of referring to the kings of Bangkok in official discourse as Rama, who in Hindu legend is the human avatar of the god Vishnu. And like his grandfather King Mongkut, Vajiravudh also instituted the worship of a new deity.

Preedee Hongsaton (2018, p. 222) reports that in 1905 and 1906, when he was still Crown prince, Vajiravudh led a party on an official visit to the north of Siam after the suppression of the rebellion by Shan rebels in the region noted above. While in the jungle in the country's north, one of the prince's entourage dreamt of a tall, powerful guardian deity (*asura*). In the dream this deity announced that although there were many threats to the life of the Crown prince, the deity would follow the royal party to protect the future king throughout his time in the deep jungle. Preedee says that Vajiravudh named the deity that appeared in the dream *Thao* Hiranyaphanasun (Pali: *hiranyavanasura*), the "Silver Guardian Deity of the Forest" (Preedee 2018, p. 222). Walter Vella reports that "Vajiravudh heard of the dream and ordered that propitiatory gifts be laid out for Hiranhu. Several people subsequently reported seeing the spirit, the custom of propitiatory gifts became set, and the idea of Hiranhu was established" (Vella 1978, p. 229). Preedee adds that the incident remained vivid in the king's mind:

> [W]hen he ascended the throne [in 1910], he ordered a Brahmanistic ritual to condone the making of four statues of the Guardian. The first he kept personally as an amulet; the second was placed at the Royal Page Department; the third in front of the

royal vehicle and the last one as a statue at the Phayathai Palace. (Preedee 2018, p. 247)

A shrine for the fourth image of this deity was established at the Phayathai Palace in Bangkok, where the king resided while Crown prince. Phayathai Palace is now a museum, and a Thai language flyer describing the *Thao* Hiranyaphanasun shrine is distributed from the museum gift shop.[9] The deity is still worshipped at the shrine today, often by patients from the adjacent Phra Mongkutklao Hospital, which now stands in the grounds of the old Phayathai Palace. As Preedee (2018, p. 223) observes, it is noteworthy that this future king of Siam, who had only recently returned from ten years of studies in England (1893–1903) and grand tours of Europe, the United States, Canada and Japan, "invented" a deity that had no Buddhist origin.

Vella notes that *Thao* Hiran-yaphanasun came to be regarded as the personal tutelary deity of the king, and his divine function was to keep King Vajiravudh and his retinue free from harm. As long as "Hiranhu was propitiated with incense, candles, and food the King would remain safe and well. A portion of the King's food was allotted daily to this royal genie" (Vella 1978, p. 229). Vella doubted that Vajiravudh himself believed in this deity, stating that the monarch supported the belief for the sake of encouraging the common people: "The establishment of Hiranhu as Vajiravudh's personal deity ... enhanced the power and prestige of the King

ท้าวหิรัญพนาสูร
เทพารักษ์ประจำพระราชวังพญาไท

IMAGE 4. *Thao* **Hiranyaphanasun**
Image of *Thao* (Lord) Hiranyaphanasun, the protective deity of Phayathai Palace in Bangkok, that was created in the early 1900s by King Vajiravudh (r. 1910–26) following a dream by a royal retainer. The sun surrounded by a solar halo (*phra athit song klot*) pictured behind the deity is regarded to be a sign of divine magical power. (Source: 2018 brochure distributed by Phayathai Palace souvenir shop.).

[and] lent some strength to all of his programs" (p. 230). Vella appears here, however, to be imposing a rationalist reading on Vajiravudh's honouring of the deity and there seems no reason to doubt that the king did in fact have faith in the protective power of *Thao* Hiranyaphanasun.

Wai Khru: *Royalist Brahmanical Spirit Possession*

Deborah Wong's study of the *wai khru* "honouring the teacher" ritual reveals how the state and monarchy have also contributed to the resurgence of supernaturalism in Thailand in the modern period. The *wai khru* is a ritual honouring of teachers of music and dance that "transfers the spiritual power of the first, primordial teacher to present-day performers" (Wong 2001, p. xvii). All classically trained Thai musicians and dancers "must be initiated by a master teacher before they can actualize the sacred with their bodies and produce the sound and movement that manifest the divine in the human realm" (p. xvii). Wong analyses the figure of the primordial teacher or *khru*—a term derived from the Sanskrit *guru*—also called "the Old Father" (*phor kae*) in *wai khru* ritual, who is invoked in initiation ceremonies into Thai classical performance traditions. In esoteric teachings the Old Father or first teacher of royal-sponsored orchestral music (*piphat*) and dance-drama (*khon*) is identified with the Brahmanical deity *Phra* Isuan—in Sanskrit Ishvara, another name for Shiva. In the *wai khru* ritual the Old Father or Shiva is believed to descend into the body of the initiating teacher or *khru*, who is then a medium for the ritual transfer of the specialist knowledge and charismatic authority of the primordial divine *guru* to the present generation of musicians and performers.

While Thai music and dance-drama teachers distinguish between the invocation of the Old Father in *wai khru* rituals and other forms of spirit possession, Wong observes that from a phenomenological perspective there is little to distinguish the two. Despite a long history of critiques of spirit mediumship by both absolute monarchs and modernizing, post-revolutionary governments in Thailand, Wong details the intimate relationship between modern kings such as Vajiravudh and Bhumibol and the invocation of Hindu deities, protective gods and ancestral spirits in contemporary rituals of initiation into Thai classical music and dance-drama training. Through this she also reveals how official sponsorship of *wai khru* rituals is one factor that has contributed to the growth of spirit medium cults in recent decades. Wong details the pivotal roles of King Vajiravudh and subsequently King Bhumibol in the revival of state-sponsored Brahmanical *wai khru* possession.

Indeed, she notes that royal involvement in *wai khru* initiations was an early twentieth-century innovation of King Vajiravudh as part of his revival of the Brahmanical symbolism of the god-king (*devaraja*): "For the royal performers, [King Vajiravudh] was (as officiant) the source of the spiritual power necessary to them; he was also the King and thus effected a power transfer in the style of the ancient *devaraja*" (Wong 2001, p. 240). Vajiravudh's interest in theatre is well known and is detailed in most histories of modern Thailand. What is less commonly reported in these histories is his support for reviving and expanding the classical Brahmanical rituals of the *wai khru* in his encouragement of the Thai performing arts.

Wong also relates that in the 1970s and 1980s, King Bhumibol, as medium for the auratic power of the Old Father, was chief officiant in *wai khru* ceremonies to re-empower lineages of initiation in state-sponsored training in classical music and dance-drama. These lineages had declined in the mid-decades of the twentieth century when the monarchy and royal traditions were challenged in the aftermath of the 1932 revolution that overthrew the absolute monarchy. King Bhumibol's second daughter, Princess Sirindhorn, was subsequently initiated into the Thai classical music tradition by master teachers who had received their charismatic authority to act as initiating officiants—that is, as mediums—for the Old Father from her father, King Bhumibol.

A book published to accompany the release of the 2011 movie *Khon khon* ("The *khon* people", dir. Saranyu Wongkrajang), about competing *khon* dance-drama troupes in the mid-twentieth century, includes a photo of King Bhumibol officiating at a *wai khru* ceremony in the School of Performing Arts on 5 October 1971 (Saranyu 2011). While Wong does not mention it, here we nonetheless see points of connection between the symbolic sacralization of the monarchy across King Bhumibol's reign (Jackson 2007) and de facto official support for forms of revivified mediumship. The divine associations of Thai kings, both living and dead, are made explicit in spirit medium discourses. Pattana quotes one informant who identifies the spirit of King Chulalongkorn (r. 1868–1910) with the Hindu god Vishnu, and both King Vajiravudh and King Bhumibol are included in the list of deities invoked in official *wai khru* ceremonies performed at the College of Dramatic Arts, with King Vajiravudh's spirit invoked as *Phor Jao*, or "Lord Father" (Wong 2001, p. 143), and King Bhumibol being called "*Luang Phor* [Reverend Father] Bhumibol Adulyadej" (p. 142).

The Buddhist rationalism of modern Thai monarchs such as King Mongkut and King Vajiravudh was contextualized and non-exclusive. Conducting rational Buddhist discourse in international spaces and public forums did not preclude these monarchs from following magical Brahmanical discourse and ritual in domestic spaces and private venues. As will be discussed further in the next chapter, in Thailand's multiple epistemological universe, contradiction only occurs within the logic of a given context, not *between* different hierarchically ordered *kala-thesa* time and place settings.

The Surfacing of Magical Ritual in Thai Public Life

The most important factor behind the continuing power of the regime of images has been the perpetuation of the historical dualities of Siam's, and now Thailand's, semicolonial relationship with the West. In the era of globalization, political power in Thailand continued to present a double picture of a state that looked outwards to more powerful geopolitical influences at the same time that it looked inwards to subject the local populace to the twin demands of international capital and the Thai governing elite. Since the end of the Cold War, however, the formerly private domain of non-Buddhist belief and ritual has increasingly surfaced in public media and spaces from which it had largely been excluded by a modernizing state that was anxious to be seen by Western powers as civilized, rational and scientific. Erick White observes that in recent years, professional spirit mediumship has benefited "from a relative decrease in the stigmatisation of possession by elite religious and political authorities" (White 2014, p. 287). Benjamin Baumann also notes a recent change in the regime of power over the public representation of magical rituals. He observes that while we lack empirically based studies of Thai elites' private religious practices, he nonetheless detects a "magico-animist turn in their public images", stating that,

> The (re)surfacing of 'magico-animism' as an aspect of the elites' public religious configuration is ... a significant change in their public 'self-image' and thus indicative of wider transformations in the cultural logic informing the Thai 'regime of images' and the policing of religious practices in the public sphere. (Baumann 2017, p. 289)

Indeed, over the past couple of decades, there appears to have been a shift in the regime of power that obscured Thai elite participation in magical ritual during most of the twentieth century. No longer always kept hidden or private, elite participation in supernatural ritual has become an increasingly visible and politically significant dimension of the symbolic exercise of power in early twenty-first-century Thailand. In recent years, Thai politicians, military and civilian bureaucrats and members of the royal family, as well as senior business figures and stars in Thai film, music and television, have become increasingly visible participants in various forms of supernatural practice. These ritual practices include astrology, divination, the use of protective magical amulets, and seeking the advice of spirit mediums channelling Chinese, Indian and Thai deities.

This shift was signified in a photograph of 2014 military coup leader and subsequent prime minister, General Prayut Chan-ocha, that was published on the front page of several Thai language newspapers in May 2016. The photograph contrasts with Tambiah's observation that, when he undertook his fieldwork in Thailand in the 1970s, Thai businessmen and soldiers kept their magical amulets hidden behind buttoned-up shirts and uniforms (Tambiah 1984, p. 197). At a press conference held at Government House on 16 May 2016 to discuss

▲ โชว์ของดี...พล.อ.ประยุทธ์ จันทร์โอชา นายกรัฐมนตรีและหัวหน้า คสช. เปิดเสื้อโชว์พระเครื่อง-ของดี (ภาพเล็ก) ภายหลังพระพรหมมังคลาจารย์ (เจ้าคุณธงชัย) ผู้ช่วยเจ้าอาวาสวัดไตรมิตรฯ ได้มอบวัตถุมงคลเพื่อเป็นกำลังใจ ยืนยันเป็นชาวพุทธ ก็ต้องมีพระไว้คุ้มครอง ที่ทำเนียบรัฐบาล

IMAGE 5. Prime Minister Prayut Chan-ocha's Amulets
Page-one newspaper photograph from 2016 of Thai Prime Minister General Prayut Chan-ocha opening his shirt to reveal his personal collection of many magical amulets at a press conference at Government House in Bangkok before an official visit to Russia for discussions with President Vladimir Putin. (Source: *Daily News*, 17 May 2016, p. 1.)

his then forthcoming diplomatic visit to Russia to conduct talks with President Putin, General Prayut unbuttoned his royalist yellow jacket to reveal that he was wearing a plethora of Buddhist amulets on a series of necklaces. General Prayut was prompted to show his impressive collection of amulets to the assembled Thai media in response to a journalist's question of whether he was concerned about meeting with President Putin, who had a reputation for being a tough negotiator. He replied that his many amulets would give him mental stamina in discussions with Putin. The daily newspaper *Khom Chat Leuk* provided the following caption for the colour photograph of General Prayut showing off his amulets at the top of page one of its 17 May 2016 edition:

> Going [to Russia] with amulets (*pai kap phra*): Prime Minister General Prayut Chan-ocha opened his jacket to show his amulets (*phra khreuang*) while issuing a press statement on his [forthcoming] visit to Russia. [He said that he] goes [to Russia] with the amulets and the supporting mental strength (*raeng jai sanapsanun*) that they provide. In his heart he has [the strength] of these amulets, which means that he never shirks or recoils from his duties. (*Khom Chat Leuk*, 17 May 2016).

Daily News also published a similar photograph, including a close-up shot of the prime minister's impressive collection of amulets, at the top of its 17 May 2016 edition and provided the following caption:

> Showing auspicious amulets (*cho khorng di*):[10] Prime minister and head of the National Council for Peace and Order, General Prayut Chan-ocha, opened his jacket to show his amulets (*phra khreuang—khorng di*) after *Phra* Phrommamangkhalajan (*Jao Khun* Thongchai), deputy abbot of Wat Traimit, presented auspicious objects (*watthu mongkhon*) to provide the prime minister with moral support (*kamlang-jai*). [The monk] emphasized that as a Buddhist, the prime minister must have protective amulets (*torng mi phra wai khumkhrorng*). (*Daily News*, 17 May 2016)

Baumann notes that the *Bangkok Post* also covered the same event:

> "I already have many amulets", General Prayut answered as he revealed at least 10 amulets in gold-plated cases on his chest. "I have had these amulets a long time. When I became a soldier, I continued to receive them, like this *Luang Pu* Thuat amulet. But I never count how many amulets I have. They are not heavy because they are in my heart, he said as reporters and officials in the room expressed their awe." ("Prayut's Heart of Gold-plated Amulets", *Bangkok Post*, 17 May 2016, cited by Baumann 2017, p. 288)

Baumann also cites an earlier account in *The Nation* newspaper of former prime minister Thaksin Shinawatra's attempts to enhance his store of beneficial magical power for political ends:

> Prime Minister Thaksin Shinawatra has expanded the battle of his political survival into the realm of black magic, Khmer voodoo, ancient astrology, supernatural and religious beliefs. His dark secret has become well known. Witchcraft and wizardry are now the name of the game. (Thanong 2006,[11] cited in Baumann 2017, p. 288)

In reflecting further on this issue, Baumann observes,

> [T]he surfacing of religious practices in the public sphere that aim at acquiring mystic potency and their association with members of the Thai elite indicates that non-modern epistemological principles always remained meaningful aspects of urban Thai habitus although they were rendered invisible by the purification of Thailand's pubic image of civilized urbanity. (Baumann 2017, p. 290)

The reasons for the public surfacing of magical ritual in the religious lives of Thailand's ruling elites need further exploration. However, the rising influence of theoretical critiques of modernity and its rationalist logics in the Western academy, alongside the declining geopolitical influence of the West and its intellectual, cultural and political heritages, may both be factors. The power of modernist discourses of reason, both in the West and in the rest of the world, is being challenged discursively by poststructuralist critiques and also materially as an epistemological effect of the relative, if not absolute, decline of Western geopolitical power in the context of the economic and political rise of Asia. It is also likely, however, that domestic political factors are influencing the greater public exposure of elite magical rituals. I return to this issue in the Conclusion, where I note how, over the past two decades, the Thai state has increasingly appropriated the cults of wealth to support nationalist and royalist agendas. The growing public visibility of magical ritual parallels the official, but nonetheless still largely implicit, adoption of the cults of wealth within the apparatus of state-sponsored rituals.

Summary

While new forms of magical ritual practice are significant features of the religious lives of Thais from all social strata, the internally divided character of modernity means that this phenomenon has received less attention than it deserves. The ritual lives of many Thais have at times been obscured by a regime of representation that privileges public displays of Buddhist piety and rationalized accounts of Buddhist doctrine. Emerging in response to colonial-period Western critiques of "superstitious" aspects of Thai religious life, this regime of images supported the construction of an international image of Thailand as a "Buddhist kingdom" and contributed to an academic emphasis on the Buddhist dimensions of the Thai religious amalgam, with a comparative devaluing of magical and divinatory ritual. An analytical emphasis on phenomena categorized as "religion" and a relative de-emphasis if not denigration of those described as "ritual" by the discipline of religious studies, together with an empirical obscuring of the full extent of ritual observance among both elites and the general populace, have contributed to a failure to include the transformations of magic within many historical narratives of Thai modernity. Bringing new cults of wealth into focus and ascribing them the full significance that they are due requires more than a merely descriptive method. It also requires a critical perspective that appreciates the extent to which the internal fissures within modernity—as a founding condition of both Western imperialism and the disciplines that now make up the international academy—have contributed to constructing incomplete perspectives of the full scope of the amalgam of Buddhist religiosity and magical ritual that make up the total field of Thai belief and practice.

Even when we engage in the critical revision of perspectives outlined in this chapter, the residual rationalist footprint on religious studies means that current descriptive and analytical categories do not do full justice to the Thai religious-cum-ritual amalgam. We lack a sufficiently nuanced conceptual vocabulary. Before we can appreciate the Thai cults of wealth, we need to do more than critique the forms of modernist discourse and imperial power that have contributed to obscuring key ritual dimensions of the Thai religious field. It is also necessary to engage in the positive task of constructing a conceptual vocabulary and an analytical corpus that enables us to describe and theorize the complexity of the Thai religious field. In the next chapter, I turn to this task of concept building before detailing the main cults of wealth and their symbolic and practical relations to each other and to the closely associated phenomena of the cult of amulets and spirit possession.

Notes

1. *Matichon*, 16 October 2016, p. 1.

2. I should add that elsewhere in her analysis Gray also argues that the impact of capitalism "does not imply an evolutionary progression from sacred to profane modes of social action", but rather "has created a new impetus for the sacralisation of the polity" (Gray 1986, p. 853).

3. The *Traiphum Phra Ruang* is a Thai cosmological text composed in the early Middle Ages and which played an important role in Siamese statecraft until the early nineteenth century.

4. According to the *Thai Royal Institute Dictionary* (2003, p. 497), the term *pradit*, from the Sanskrit *pratiṣṭha*, and the Pali *patiṭṭha*, variously translates as "to establish" (*tang kheun*), "to institute" (*jat tham kheun*), "to build" (*sang kheun*) or "to create" (*taeng kheun*).

5. The quotation is from a publication that Rung-arun (2004, p. 78) describes as "*Somdet Phra Jao Boromwongthoe Kromphraya* Damrong Rachanuphap Speaking To *Mormratchawong* Sumanachat Sawatdikul Na Wangworadit", *Bantheuk Rap Sang*, p. 65.

6. Thanong Khanthong, "Thailand's Future is in the Lap of the Gods", *The Nation*, 26 January 2001.

7. McDaniel gives the source as "Kham Bunnag, *Phra Ratchaphongsawadan Krung Ratanakosin Ratchakan Thi 4* (2550 [CE 2007]: 384–91)" (McDaniel 2011, p. 262n27).

8. In Chapter Five I detail how a postage stamp representing an image of one of *Luang Pu* Iam's famous magical amulets was issued by Thailand Post in 2011.

9. The flyer is titled "*Thao* Hiranyaphanasun, The Protective Deity of Phayathai Royal Palace" (*Thao Hiranyaphansun, Theppharak Prajam Phra Ratchawang Phayathai*).

10. *Khorng di* literally means "a good thing" or "good things", but in the discourse of Thai popular religion the term refers to auspicious amulets.

11. Thanong Khantong, "OVERDRIVE: Thaksin the Wizard Attempts a Supernatural Twist", *The Nation*, 24 March 2006.

Part Two

Thailand's Cults of Wealth

Chapter Three

Context, Hierarchy and Ritual: Theorizing the Total Thai Religious Field

A revision of the western notion of religion is required to understand the complexity of 'multiple modernities' in a globalized world. (Volker Gottowik 2014, p. 7)

Introduction: Strategies for Negotiating Cultural and Religious Multiplicity

The fractured structure of modernity that arrived in Thailand in association with Western imperial power engendered fissures within the total field of religious practice; structurally, administratively as well as in terms of academic analysis. While monastic Buddhism and the canonical Theravada Buddhist scriptures, the *Tipitaka*, came under state administrative control, support and sponsorship, multiform varieties of ritual conducted predominantly by lay specialists outside of monasteries largely fell outside the scope of state interest and bureaucratic oversight. And while scholars affiliated with departments of religious studies, history and politics studied Buddhist monastic structures and doctrine, research on non-monastic cults has predominantly been undertaken by anthropologists. These formal and academic divisions within the Thai religious field belie the fact that the religious lives of large numbers, perhaps the majority, of Thai practitioners from all walks of life cross over and between Buddhist and non-Buddhist ritual observance. To some extent this fact has been obscured by a regime of representation, instituted in response to Western power, that has foregrounded Buddhism while placing ritual practice in a subsidiary position in the background of religious life.

The fracturing of academic research on Thai religiosity between different disciplines, which have focused on Buddhism and non-Buddhist ritual separately, means that to a significant extent we have lacked conceptual categories and theoretical models of the total field that constitutes the religious lives of so many people in the country. This gap also means that we lack generally agreed frames by which to understand new forms of magical practice both in relation to establishment Buddhism as well as the deep history of divination, astrology, spirit possession and other ritual practices. Religious studies has struggled to provide concepts for the structuring patterns of the Thai religious field because its origins in analyses of monotheistic doctrine-based religions has left it largely bereft of ways of imagining a cultural order that is founded upon irreducible, and expanding, difference rather than notions of a uniting set of teachings. Drawing on Erick White's (2014) and Benjamin Baumann's (2017) calls to develop categories that emphasize plurality, assemblages and contestation as defining characteristics of the Thai religious amalgam, in this chapter I engage studies of folk (rural), popular (urban) and official (royal) religious forms in Thailand to present a set of conceptual frames that I suggest help us appreciate the place of the new cults of wealth in the country's sociological landscape and domains of power and authority. In characterizing the fields of Thai vernacular and popular religion in which the cults of wealth are located I propose four concepts and analytical models:

- Polyontologism as an amalgamated non-blended mixing of religious forms;
- The *kala-thesa* "time and space" contextualized separation of culturally diverse ritual forms and a general tolerance of ambiguity, incommensurability and contradiction;
- The hierarchical dominance of Buddhism in structural and symbolic terms; and
- An emphasis on ritual practice over doctrinal harmonization.

I contend that these patterns emerge from Thailand's deep history of cultural and religious multiplicity as elements of a set of strategies to weld the manifold strands of the amalgam of cultic forms into an overarching religious field without imposing any notion of orthodoxy or a singular unitary doctrine. I begin by reviewing debates on how we should characterize the total religious field in Thailand.

The Problem of "Religion" and Debates on the Thai Religious Field

The Thai cults of wealth detailed in the following chapters form a complex of distinct but nonetheless symbolically intersecting movements that share similar ritual features. This complex field of symbolically intersecting cults does not conform to simplistic models of "religion", and the concepts and theories of the field of religious studies do not provide a sufficiently nuanced analytical vocabulary or theoretical repertoire to capture the specificities of this phenomenon. What is more, the distinctive forms of mixing and blending in the symbolic complex of cults of wealth is not captured in current accounts of either syncretism or cultural hybridity. We need a range of new concepts to detail the distinctiveness of the overall phenomenon of the cults of wealth.

The very category of "religion" at the centre of disciplines such as the sociology of religion and religious studies is problematic and has often constituted a hindrance to understanding fields of belief and ritual in Thailand that are multiple, polytheistic and practice-oriented rather than based on expressions of faith in holy texts. The academic study of comparative religion that began in Western universities in the nineteenth and early twentieth centuries drew on the monotheistic, text-based Mosaic traditions of Judaism, Christianity and Islam as its models. As Volker Gottowik observes, "[a]ccording to modern understanding, religion is a clearly distinctive entity with a specific dogma and a specific liturgy: orthodoxy is a main requirement, and ritual is performed merely to symbolize dogma" (Gottowik 2014, p. 15). In this schema it is difficult to conceptualize religions such as Buddhism that lack a creator deity or which, like Hinduism and Chinese religions, place more emphasis on ritual practice than on expressions of faith as the primary means of contact with the divine. And given the collective historical opposition of institutional Christianity, Judaism and Islam to rituals labelled as "magic", the diverse phenomena that fall within this admittedly equally protean category have often been disparaged as superstitions that lie outside of, and in opposition to, the field of religion proper and hence the analytical remit of religious studies. The Eurocentrism and monotheism at the heart of the foundational categories of religious studies means that this academic field has often been unable to describe, let alone analyse, the full diversity of religious phenomena at the global level. Ironically, this foundational analytical and theoretical inadequacy has existed despite an avowed interest in comparative research.

The conceptual and theoretical limitations of religious studies are reflected in the divergences of opinion among scholars about how to characterize Thailand's diverse, complex and multiply intersecting religious landscapes of Theravada Buddhism, Brahmanical and Chinese ritual, royal cults, spirit possession and cults of ritually empowered amulets and other sacred objects. The limitations of the field of religious studies have bedevilled studies of religion in Thailand and in Southeast Asia more broadly, as scholars have struggled to define the complex forms of ritual and mixing found in the region in terms of the categories inherited from European social science. In studies of religion in Thailand, scholars have variously employed notions of "complexity" (Kirsch 1977), "syncretism" (Mulder 1990), "pluralism", and "hybridity" (Pattana 2012). There is still no agreement, however, about how to characterize Thailand's diverse and multiply intersecting religious landscapes. In 1976, Barend Terwiel wrote:

> Many authors state unequivocally that Theravada Buddhists adhere to more than one religious tradition. Apart from 'otherworldly' Buddhism, these Southeast Asian peoples adhere to other strands of religion, generally classed under rubrics such as 'non-Buddhist beliefs', 'folk religion,' 'animism', or 'supernaturalism'. Yet, though virtually all authors recognize this situation, there is no consensus in their views on how the different subsystems are related. (Terwiel 1976, p. 391)

Over four decades later, scholars continue to disagree on whether Thai religiosity is fundamentally "Buddhist" with influences from other traditions or rather is essentially a hybrid or syncretic phenomenon in which Buddhism is one, albeit valorized and privileged, component among others. Justin McDaniel observes that "[t]he lack of consensus of where Buddhism begins and ends remains today" (2011, p. 228), and Patrice Ladwig and Paul Williams state that "[d]espite the widespread skepticism about concepts that try to understand the relationship of Buddhism and indigenous culture, the problem does not disappear" (Ladwig and Williams 2012, p. 11). Of particular relevance to this study is Erick White's view that the novel phenomenon of professional spirit mediumship that lies at the heart of many of the rituals associated with the cults of wealth is "categorically and analytically confounding" (White 2014, p. 11) in terms of the models that earlier generations of scholars used to interpret Thai religious life. As White observes, salient characteristics of professional spirit mediums are that they are possessed by virtuous divinities from the elevated heights of the religious pantheon, they practice mediumship as a full-time vocation, they perceive their vocation as an unabashedly and meritorious Buddhist calling, and they inhabit a robust collective identity as part of a generalised, supra-local and expansive subculture. None of these ... features is easily accommodated within conventional models of possession. (White 2014, p. 13n3)

For White, the key outstanding question is how scholars of Theravada Buddhism in Southeast Asia are to understand the character of the amalgamated religious complexity of this religious field and whether we should

envision the resulting amalgam as either a single integrated syncretic religious system or a conjoined constellation of several distinct and/or alternative religious systems.... In general, the view that this complex amalgamation constitutes a single, integrated syncretic religious system has dominated the interpretation of Theravada Buddhism in Thailand. (White 2014, p. 160)

Given the inadequacies of current analytical categories, White argues that we need new models "to adequately describe and interpret the empirical complexity and diversity of cultural discourses, social practices, and structural relations" (White 2017, p. 198) found in Thai Buddhism. Benjamin Baumann similarly contends that the multiplicity of Thai religious forms makes ethnographies of Thai popular religion difficult, and states that "we need to work on an analytic language that moves our anthropological understanding beyond the paradoxes of qualified modern concepts" (Baumann 2017, p. 66). He maintains that the hypercomplexity of the Thai sociocultural formation requires "a theoretical eclecticism capable of addressing the simultaneity of modern and non-modern cultural configurations that shape the meaningfulness of social practices in contemporary Thailand" (Baumann 2017, p. 162).

White responds to the question of how to understand the diversity of the Thai religious field, not by defining culturally distinct Buddhist and non-Buddhist components, but by expanding ideas of what constitutes Theravada Buddhism. This parallels David Gellner's view that we need to undermine facile assumptions that Buddhism always stands for ascetic values, is opposed to the creation of wealth, is always rational and that monks are uninvolved in magic (Gellner 2017, p. 205). He argues that Buddhist studies needs to be based on a notion of Buddhism that emerges from the beliefs of those who call themselves Buddhist rather than on abstract categories that emerged largely from rationalist Enlightenment ideas:

> If people think they are Buddhist, if they call themselves Buddhist and carry on a ritual, symbolic and religiously experiential life that involves interacting with Buddhist figures in Buddhist idiom, there is something comic about scholars endlessly worrying whether they are really Buddhist. (Gellner 2017, p. 206)

White argues that we need to see "Buddhism as containing plurality, contradiction, and even incommensurability within itself" (White 2017, p. 191), with new models needing to emphasize "plurality, contingency, contestation and agency" as well as foregrounding a "conceptual language of 'formations', 'fields', and 'assemblages'" (White 2017, pp. 198–99). This provides an empirically based understanding of what counts as Buddhism, and White contends that in rethinking Theravada Buddhism we need to explore in detail the "articulation, integration, hierarchy, and boundaries within this composite unity" (White 2017, p. 194) by conceptualizing Thai Buddhism "as a hierarchical composite of multiple religious styles, modalities, or systems working in tandem, either in harmony or in conflict, either loosely or tightly integrated" (White 2016, p. 12). Stanley Tambiah foreshadowed such a reconceptualization of Thai Buddhism as a complex field when he used the expression "formations and amalgams" (Tambiah 1990, p. 137) in referring to religious forms and urged scholars to develop a "phenomenological account of multiple realities and finite provinces of meaning" (Tambiah 1990, p. 101).

Polyontologism: Beyond Syncretism and Hybridity in Thai Religious Studies

The starting point of my reflections in this chapter is the recognition that pluralism, diversity and complexity are defining features of the Thai religious field and have been negotiated and indeed embraced in many areas of Thai cultural life for at least the past few centuries. As Gerrit Gong observes:

> From the dawn of their existence, the Thai states were part of at least three different orders: they were on the periphery of the Chinese commercial and cultural order; in the path of the Indian religious, philosophical, and commercial influence; and part of the multi-centred, multicultural collage of Southeast Asia. (Gong 1984, p. 202)

This polycultural multiplicity is also the defining issue for Thai religious studies, as scholars have struggled to appreciate Thai religion as a complex of multiple, partly discrete yet also intersecting and hierarchically organized ritual-belief systems. Earlier generations of scholars often drew on notions of syncretism to characterize the Thai religious field. However, Pattana Kitiarsa (2005a) has critiqued this "syncretist paradigm" of popular Thai religion for placing institutional Theravada Buddhism in a rigidly paramount position and viewing Buddhism, Brahmanism and animism as isolated and static rather than being in constantly dynamic relations. In contrast, he describes Thai religion as hybrid, in Bakhtin's sense of the mixing of "various languages ... within the boundaries of a single dialect" and which "gives birth to new forms of amalgamation" (Pattana 2005a, p. 467). While he sees hybridization as having been present in Southeast Asian religions throughout history, Pattana argues that the dynamism of Thai popular religion today is different in scale and complexity, with the religious syncretism model having been "outdated by a fast track, cut-and-paste, postmodernizing reality within contemporary Thai society" (p. 487). Rataporn Patamajorn has also drawn on the theoretical frame of hybridity in studying spirit mediumship in central Thailand, observing that in postcolonial studies hybridity refers to "the creation of new transcultural forms within the contact zone produced by colonization" (Rataporn 2007, p. 29).

Even notions of hybridity, however, do not capture the full complexity of Thai social and cultural forms. Ideas of cultural hybridity are based on a binary notion, while historically Thailand has been characterized by polyvalent cultural expressions in which more than two forms are present in contiguous and often intersecting ways. In Homi Bhabha's (1994) account, hybridity refers to situations where two cultural forms merge in a context of differential colonial power relations to engender a distinct, new third space or third category. In Thailand, however, multiplicity and diversity do not function as a critique of imperialist hegemonic unity as in Homi Bhabha's account of cultural hybridity. Rather, differences are foundational and often are not resolved. As Edoardo Siani notes, in Bangkok, "exchange and encounter with alterity [are] part of the everyday.... Foreignness is not new here. It is part of the familiar" (Siani 2018, p. 421). Siani contends that Bangkok is a city that has been "inhabited by deities and spirits originating from other cosmological realms or worlds since its very foundation" (p. 421). White also sees Thai Buddhism as being characterized by foundational diversity: "There is an irreducible plurality, ambiguity and even contradictory character to Theravada religiosity as an ideological, social and institutional phenomenon within late twentieth century Thailand" (White 2014, p. 214). Indeed, foundational diversity characterizes Thai culture more broadly, and strategies for negotiating this diversity are deeply embedded in cultural norms, ritual modes and forms of habitus. Thailand's many religious fields—such as institutional Buddhism, popular religiosity and spirit possession—represent "a wide spectrum of more or less distinct and differing religious beliefs, practices, collectivities and agents" (p. 9).

As Baumann notes, theories of syncretism, hybridity and creolization are not sufficient to explicate the full diversity of Thailand's epistemological and religious complexity because these accounts "overemphasise fusion and the formation of new internally coherent wholes" (Baumann 2017, p. 174). He argues that "the epistemological multiplicity of Thailand's kaleidoscopic socio-cultural configuration … is lost in approaches that emphasise the homogenising effects of global capitalism under syncretic readings of hybridity" (p. 223) and further observes that "[t]he rarely addressed irony of poststructuralist approaches in area studies research is … that while poststructuralism tries to transcend rationalist dualisms, its critical potential remains premised on the presence of dualist thinking" (p. 46). Justin McDaniel similarly contends that theories of religious hybridity, whether based upon Mikhail Bakhtin (1981)[1] or Homi Bhabha (1991), are lacking because both reduce religious phenomena "to unified products of diverse influences or parts" (McDaniel 2016, p. 930).

Based on her research on divination and healing rituals among the Giriama people of coastal Kenya, who draw on both folk and Islamic beliefs, Janet McIntosh (2019) argues that notions of syncretism and hybridity fail to account for all pluralist religious practices. Like Baumann and McDaniel, McIntosh contends that the theoretical tool kit for considering religious encounters and comingling has been impoverished by an overemphasis on a presumed coherence in religious belief and practice:

> The concept of syncretism also risks conflating the myriad forms that religious pluralism can take. Although some scholars define syncretism in terms of the combination of disparate religious elements into inconsistent and conflicting new configurations, more commonly the term refers to the mingling of religious material that might once have been incompatible but is now rendered whole and compatible—or at least is pushed in that direction. *The Oxford English Dictionary*, for instance, defines syncretism as 'an attempted

union or reconciliation of diverse or opposite tenets or practices'. (McIntosh 2019, p. 114)

McIntosh reports that in Giriama religiosity, "religious plurality is not about reconciling Islam and Giriama Traditionalism into a new, 'systemic' whole, but rather about drawing on both while continuing to mark them as distinct. More than one religion may be used, but the religions are juxtaposed rather than blended" (McIntosh 2019, p. 116). Giriama ritual practice is based on a patterned alternation between two systems of supernatural power, each of which has its own spiritual forces and its own terms of address. This pattern of distinct, contiguous but non-blended sources of religious potency has close parallels to Thai popular religion and the symbolic complex of cults of wealth detailed in Chapter Six. McIntosh argues that notions of syncretism and hybridity fail to capture this pattern of religiosity because they imply that the trajectory of religious change is "from conflict and discrepancy to consilience, harmony, synthesis, integration, 'cross fertilization,' and other terms that imply the fusion of difference into a new whole" (p. 115). The syncretistic or hybrid image of distinct religions merging into a new, coherent system is influenced by "Western and Abrahamic premises about the very category of religion" and "by the presumption that religions are by definition systems of 'belief' that are integrated, internally consistent, and preoccupied with universal 'Truth'" (pp. 115–16).

In words that closely echo White's call to develop an account of Theravada Buddhism as a "composite unity", McIntosh contends that a new model is required to account for religious pluralism that preserves "discontinuity between loci of religious power" (McIntosh 2019, p. 112). She calls this model "polyontologism", which she defines as an emic stance that is recognized by cultural insiders and which acknowledges the mystical potency, and the ontological reality, of more than one set of religious or cosmological forces:

> In polyontologist practice, the plural ontologies are not modeled as 'ultimately one,' nor are their associated deities or forces semiotically aligned or equated.... Differences between the systems in question are (emically) recognized and upheld by practitioners.... [T]he differences are not erased or minimized because practitioners are not ideologically expected to be consistent in their beliefs or committed to a single tradition of practice.... No attempt is made to assimilate the potentially contradictory premises of each system because there is no ideological prioritization of consistency to begin with. (McIntosh 2019, p. 117)

McIntosh observes that even today it remains a challenge for many scholars of religion "to wrap their minds around an approach to religion that embraces a multiplicity of potentially contradictory cosmological options, which indicates that "we have some distance to travel to come to grips with religion's many futures" (McIntosh 2019, p. 118).

The type of polyontological practices described by McIntosh in Kenya are also found in Thai popular religion, such as the division of responsibilities between Buddhist monks and Brahmin priests in many rituals. In August 2018, I observed a five-day *ngan somphot* ritual to request blessings and wealth from the deity Jatukham-Ramathep at the City Pillar Shrine in Nakhon Srithammarat in southern Thailand, which is now a central locale for the empowerment of the Jatukham-Ramathep type of amulets that will be discussed in Chapter Five. Within the setting of this multi-day ritual complex, Buddhist and Brahmanical ritual specialists performed highly contextualized and separate roles. There was no ambiguity, and no hybridity. Buddhist monks performed chants of blessing from the Buddhist canon, the *Tipitaka*, before the Brahmanical rituals began, and then left the scene and returned to their monasteries. Once the monks had departed, the Brahmins began to perform their rituals, using hybrid *khatha* incantations that invoked Hindu deities in the context of a Buddhist cosmology. McDaniel notes that amulets of Hindu deities are often "forged in rituals performed by both Buddhist monks and Brahman priests working together" (McDaniel 2011, p. 276n83). White describes two rituals at a monastery in Chumphon province in Southern Thailand in 1996, one being a ceremony to consecrate a new shrine to the spirit of King Chulalongkorn and the other a robe donation ceremony to the monks residing at the monastery. Both spirit mediums and Buddhist monks participated in the two events, but in neither ceremony

> was there any significant or sustained communication between professional spirit mediums and monks, nor was there any coordinated or joint ritual action. While both monks and mediums occupied the same ritual space for a select period of time and had a prominent role to play in the total composite sequence of ritual action, they slid past each other interactively in an almost frictionless way. In many ways at an interactive level they each respectively almost seemingly failed to or refused to acknowledge each other's presence as significant participating ritual actors. (White 2014, p. 178)

White calls this type of contextualization of distinct ritual orders "inclusive syncretism". He observes that the conjoint presence of both ordained Buddhist monks and lay spirit mediums in the rituals detailed above, which were performed in the same space,

> conformed in many ways to a principal of segregation that is also implied by the religious regime of inclusive syncretism. In both temporal and spatial terms, monks and mediums under the terms of inclusive syncretism carry out relatively segregated lives and activities.... [R]elations of hierarchical dominance between [monks and mediums] are encoded within the framework of inclusive syncretism. (White 2014, p. 179)

In his study of traditions of ritual healing in Thailand, Louis Golomb reports what can be described as a polyontological setting, observing that most of his Buddhist informants "recognised the possibility of numerous magical traditions with independent sources of knowledge and power" (Golomb 1985, p. 105).

Edoardo Siani also reports a situation that mirrors McIntosh's account of polyontologism. When asking Thai diviners (*mor du*), astrologers and spirit mediums (*rang song*) their understandings of their practices, he found no single belief system but, rather, "competing cosmological narratives" that represent what he describes as the "cosmological multiplicity" (Siani 2018, p. 417) of Thai popular Buddhism: "As the Thai Buddhist cosmos multiplies, it eludes cosmological treatises, revealing itself to be negotiable, dynamic and always in the making" (p. 420). Nonetheless, he did find that Buddhism provided a foundation for all the forms of "cosmology making" engaged in by ritual specialists: "The only cosmological notion that is unquestioned, and that indeed plays a crucial role in different narratives, is the law of *karma* ... as a natural, moral and ultimately political principle that determines individuals' positions in the sociocosmic hierarchy" (p. 420).

Not only Thailand is characterized by this form of non-rationalized multiplicity. Benedict Anderson argued that "contemporary Javanese political culture is ... a heterogeneous, disjunctive, and internally contradictory complex of traditional and Western elements, with a lower degree of internal logic and coherence than in the past" (Anderson 1972, p. 5, cited in Baumann 2017, p. 166). Religious and other forms of negotiating multiplicity also emerge from Thai political history. Visisya Pinthongvijayakul notes that in the Northeastern province of Chaiyaphum, spirit shrines and Buddhist monasteries are twin realms of power, and this non-exclusive religious schema is reminiscent of the workings of the premodern polity in the region, whereby a chiefdom on the periphery of two powers might seek protection from both: "Premodern chiefdoms in northeast Thailand ... simultaneously paid tribute to both the Bangkok and Vientiane [Lao] courts. The present religious practice reprises a premodern form of power relations in the multi-concentric mandala system" (Visisya 2018, p. 71). Visisya contends that political dynamics, as well as the religious system in northeast Thailand, are informed by the fact that this region's "peoples have encountered a multitude of imposed authorities throughout history" (p. 73). In discussing religiosity across the Mekong river in Laos, John Holt similarly observes that the religious system of the Lao can be described not so much in terms of syncretism between a cult of spirits and Buddhism but rather as separate and complementary ontologies (Holt 2011, p. 255).

The Thai Religious Field as an Amalgam

We have often relied on metaphors drawn from other fields in imagining the diverse forms and varieties of cultural mixing. For example, biology and botany supplied the term "hybridity", which as noted above is now used to denote the mixing of two cultural patterns to merge into a distinct third form. This notion, however, does not capture the polyontological multiplicity detailed here. We need a more extended analytical vocabulary to enable us to distinguish different forms of cultural and religious mixing, and also the forms of power that underpin the various responses to negotiating cultural difference. In seeking to better characterize the Thai religious field, metallurgy offers us the term "amalgam", which denotes an inhomogeneous mixture of dissimilar metals. In this I follow a number of scholars, including White (2014), who uses "amalgam" in his critical study of Thai religious complexity, Tambiah, who also uses the term "amalgam" in his account of the "interlacing" of rituals in Southeast Asian religions (Tambiah 1985, p. 320), and Irene Stengs (2019), who similarly draws on this term in characterizing the cult of the spirit of King Chulalongkorn (see Chapter Four). I suggest this notion provides a more accurate image for the overall form and character of the complex of cults of wealth within the Thai religious field, which together constitute an unalloyed amalgam of Buddhist, Hindu, Chinese and other rituals and beliefs.

An example of the type of religious amalgam found in Thailand is the existence of parallel "Buddhist" and "Hindu" *khatha* or incantations to worship the deity Brahma at the Erawan Shrine located at the Ratchaprasong intersection in downtown Bangkok. In 2011, a large billboard adjacent to this shrine advertised a royal-sponsored ritual to sacralize statuettes and amulets of the Erawan Brahma. The

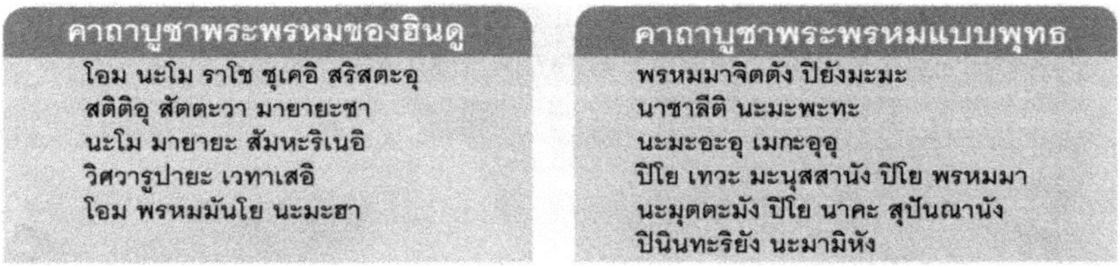

คาถาบูชาพระพรหมของฮินดู	คาถาบูชาพระพรหมแบบพุทธ
โอม นะโม ราโช ชุเคอิ สริสตะอุ	พรหมมาจิตตัง ปิยังมะมะ
สติติอุ สัตตะวา มายายะชา	นาซาลีติ นะมะพะทะ
นะโม มายายะ สัมหะริเนอิ	นะมะอะอุ เมกะอุอุ
วิศวารูปายะ เวทาเสอิ	ปิโย เทวะ มะนุสสานัง ปิโย พรหมมา
โอม พรหมมันโย นะมะฮา	นะมุตตะมัง ปิโย นาคะ สุปันณานัง
	ปินินทะริยัง นะมามิหัง

IMAGE 6. Hindu and Buddhist Incantations for the Erawan Brahma
Dual "Hindu" (left) and "Buddhist-type" (right) *khatha* incantations to request the blessings of the Erawan Brahma, reflecting the amalgam-like form of combining without blending that characterizes the religious multiplicity of Thai vernacular religion. (Source: Poster at Erawan Shrine, Ratchaprasong Intersection, Bangkok.)

advertisement noted that devotees of the Brahma image at the Erawan Shrine have the option of honouring the deity with either a "Hindu worship incantation" (*khatha bucha khorng Hindu*) or a "Buddhist type incantation to worship *Phra* Phrom (Brahma)" (*khatha bucha phra phrom baep phut*), with the Hindu incantation being written in Sanskrit and the Buddhist one written in Pali. Here, Brahmanical and Buddhist rituals were not merged into a single hybrid but rather were kept apart in separate ritual forms that could be practised in honour of the same deity in the same location.

The amalgam-like ritual complex of Thai vernacular religion tames pluralism and incorporates diversity within a frame that both preserves difference and ensures that it remains subservient to a greater order. As detailed below, the multiple constituents of the Thai religious field are hierarchically ordered under Buddhism. Nonetheless, within this overall hierarchy, Thai vernacular religious culture can incorporate difference while normalizing it in a system where even rapidly proliferating diversity supports and enhances the status quo rather than threatening or challenging it. This is a highly malleable and expandable cultural formation, eminently suited to interacting with and incorporating foreign elements while not erasing or overwhelming pre-existing local and indigenous forms.[2] This situation is not only found in Thai religious culture but is also a more general characteristic in many cultural domains in the country. In discussing trends in Thai architecture in the twentieth century, Lawrence Chua observes,

> Modernity did not erase these older cosmological associations and ways of thinking about space but was itself transformed in the encounter. Rather than displacing one another, two competing ideologies were sustained.... One approach did not simply yield to another. Rather, the modern [architecture] could sustain

heterogeneous and discordant temporalities—the past, present, and future—within a single structure while also supporting conflicting philosophical, political, literary, and artistic views. (Chua 2018, p. 334)

The Thai religious field is a non-rationalized amalgam or multiplicity. In terms of belief, there is no single, overarching logically consistent Thai religious doctrine. Rather, there are multiple, sometimes discrete, often overlapping, co-extensive sets of religious beliefs that, as detailed below, are united in a hierarchical order at the level of ritual practice. As McDaniel observes,

> the ability to retain and maintain several seemingly mutually exclusive belief systems is common in Thailand. If we study an individual's evolving religious repertoire, then we do not need to fit their actions and beliefs into a cultural system, rationale, or single religious tradition. (McDaniel 2011, p. 226)

McDaniel critiques analysts who devalue multiplicity of belief and attempt to impose a single rational order on the Thai religious field: "Why can't we expect that a person will hold and act upon simultaneous, multiple ideals? Why don't we see this as an advantage? Why is consistency or orthodoxy seen as the ideal?" (McDaniel 2011, p. 227). In this amalgamated religious field constituted of multiple, and often incommensurable, teachings, synthesis takes place at the level of ritual and practice without discursive rationalization. Structure is not established or instituted by processes of rationalization or doctrinal uniformity. Rather, as detailed below, the order of the field of the Thai religious amalgam is instituted by a ritual-centred and practice-based hierarchy in which Buddhism is in a paramount position.

The Additive Logic of Thai Vernacular Buddhism

Buddhism in real life is accretive. (Gombrich 1971, p. 49)

In his account of the prosperity cult of *Jao Mae* Kuan Im, Nidhi Eeoseewong observes that "[t]he Thai system of belief is able to increase the number of spirits and gods indefinitely" (Nidhi 1994, p. 90). Tambiah notes that Thai religious multiplicity is based on an accumulative approach to ritual, with "the addition of meaning through the cumulation of similar or related connotations" (Tambiah 1985, p. 164). Deborah Wong similarly notes that the intersection of Buddhism, Hinduism and spirit cults in Thai religious practice "reflects an additive approach to ritual belief in Thailand that stretches over several millennia" (Wong 2001, p. xviii), while McDaniel emphasizes the valuing of "abundance" (*udom sombun*) in Thai religious ritual: "Generally, in Thai Buddhism 'more is more'" (McDaniel 2011, p. 67). Shrines, McDaniel writes, are "sites of accretion" (p. 67) made up of a vast array of images, murals, texts and teachers that are constantly added to, repaired and rearranged. This cultural logic of ritual "abundance" or "plenitude" (*udom sombun*) in Thai Buddhist monasteries and spirit shrines prevails in contrast to the seemingly austere Buddhist doctrinal ideals of non-attachment and asceticism:

> Altars … are crowded with gifts, bowls, clocks, incense, and small images. Colorful and intricate murals often fill nearly every open space on the walls. The doors are carved from top to bottom with inlaid mother-of-pearl or gold filigree. One gets the sense of overflowing wealth. (McDaniel 2011, p. 67)

Nerida Cook observes that astrology is an important component of the Thai interest in "abundance" and maximizing ritual efficacy, commenting that in Thailand,

> Astrology provides schedules for the timing of significant events, enabling participants to attempt to maximise the efficacy of activities by ensuring that they are performed when auspiciousness is at a peak; and similarly it enables dangerous undertakings to be performed when malefic forces are minimal. (Cook 1989, p. 12)

In Thailand, astrology, formally called *horasat* or colloquially *du dao* (observing the stars/planets), is not always a clearly defined field and, in addition to temporal calculations of the movements of the planets across the heavens, can also include diverse forms of prophecy and divination, including dream interpretation, the study of omens, palmistry and numerology.

McDaniel further observes that, "[i]n Thailand, the evolution of a personal repertoire usually takes the form of accretion. Thai religieux seem to add to their individual repertoires but rarely subtract.… Abundance is valued" (McDaniel 2011, p. 226). Adam Chau argues that Chinese religious ritual is also characterized by a logic of "efficacy maximisation through ritualist-multiplication" (Chau 2011, p. 560), and Volker Gottowik observes that this emphasis on addition and accretion is a broader feature of cultic ritual:

> Cult religions do not define their knowledge about their gods through notions of what is 'true and false', but accept, according to Assman (2003, p. 28), contradictory statements: the main concern is not the risk of worshipping false gods, but rather of neglecting an important deity (Assman 2003, p. 38). (Gottowik 2014, p. 38)

IMAGE 7. Spirit Medium Shrine 1
Images installed on a temporary shrine of a spirit medium set up outside the Shri Maha Mariamman Hindu Temple on Silom Road in Downtown Bangkok in October 2010. The mix of images of Hindu, royal and Buddhist spirits and deities reflects the multiple religious cultures making up the often-idiosyncratic amalgams in individuals' repertoire religiosities. From left to right: Krishna, King Chulalongkorn, Ganesh, Buddhist naga serpent deity, and Durga. Spirit mediums from around Thailand who channel Hindu deities attend the annual Navaratri Festival at the Shri Maha Mariamman Temple, one of the oldest Tamil Hindu temples in Thailand. (Photo by the author.)

We find a similar ritualistic multiplication to maximize charismatic magico-symbolic efficacy in both popular and royal ritual in Thailand. Indeed, the royal Buddhist-Brahmanical complex can be seen as an attempt to maximize the magical-charismatic authority of the monarchy by a logic of ritual addition of both Brahmanical and Buddhist forms. As Wong argues, "[t]he Buddhist power of merit [*barami*] and the 'Brahman' power of *saksit* are joined in certain men, and they are not mutually exclusive. If anything, the felicitous intersection of these trajectories seems to amplify power" (Wong 2001, p. 83). And, as Thai society has become more culturally and ethnically complex over the centuries, so too has Thai religiosity become more diverse as new elements have been incorporated into the expanding vernacular pantheon to become parts of the religious repertoires of individuals. Thus, the deities of the cults of wealth are not worshipped to the exclusion of

IMAGE 8. Spirit Medium Shrine 2
Images on another temporary spirit medium shrine set up near the Shri Maha Mariamman Hindu Temple in Bangkok on the occasion of the Navaratri festival in October 2010. While this is a Hindu festival celebrated at a Tamil temple whose officiants are Indian Brahmin priests, the images include Chinese deities, reflecting the mixing of Indian and Chinese religiosity in Thai professional spirit mediumship and the repertoire religiosities of devotees of the cults of wealth. Top row of larger images left to right: Ganesh, Kuan Im with many arms, Kuan Im, Durga, and Durga. Bottom row of smaller images: Shiva, Krishna, Ardhanarishvara (hermaphroditic deity of Shiva with Parvati), Durga, and two Chinese deities. (Photo by the author.)

older gods but in addition to those religious figures, and the rituals of these cults are not practised exclusively but in addition to existing practices of Buddhist merit making.

Thai popular religion and the cults of wealth are domains of hyper-presence, of overdetermined and intersecting cultural, political and ethnic histories, where magical power (*saksit*) and charismatic authority (*barami*) are intensified by a quantitative accumulation of the many sources of the culture from both the present and the past at one time and place, producing a surfeit of symbolizations. It is often as if Thai popular Buddhism references all its historical sources, reflecting a desire to bring all of the past into the present. This produces a concertina effect in many Thai ritual settings, as if all past moments are required to condense into one place in an intense visual experience of power that Rosalind Morris (2000, p. 115) describes as "baroque" but which is always lavishly ornate and transcends any single cultural logic. Morris describes Thai Buddhist temples and spirit shrines as sites of "representational excess" (Morris 2000, p. 122), with the excessive cultural richness of Thai popular religious culture producing the effect of a "delirium" (p. 107). Given the additive principle that more is always better, "truth" or "doctrine" cannot be the guiding principle in structuring this religious order. As detailed below, it is for this reason that non-epistemic principles of hierarchically structured ritual practice are the foundation of the order established among the multiple, incommensurable doctrines of the diverse cults in Thai popular Buddhism.

Tensions within the Thai Religious Amalgam: Contradiction and Tolerance of Ambiguity

Scholars of Thai religion often specialize in studying one aspect of the religious field, whether monastic Buddhism, spirit possession or new reformist movements. These focused studies often present contrasting accounts of the religious field because the phenomenon under observation does indeed operate by principles that are distinct from those of other dimensions of the complex multiple amalgam of Thai vernacular religiosity. Ambiguity and contradiction are central features of this amalgam, which in popular Buddhism places primary emphasis on embodied ritual practice and much less emphasis on intellectualizing and rationalizing religious behaviour. In contrast to the purification or extermination of ambiguity that Volker Gottowik says is a characteristic of the modernization of religion in Islamic societies such as Indonesia, in Thailand we continue to find tolerance of ambiguity in modern magical religion. Gottowik cites Thomas Bauer as defining the concepts of "cultural ambiguity" and "ambiguity tolerance" as "the coexistence of different ethnic and religious groups … and the practice of living concurrently in more than only one of them (Bauer 2011, p. 39)" (Gottowik 2014, p. 20).

The inability of scholars to agree on the fundamental structuring characteristics of the Thai religious field noted at the beginning of this chapter not only emerges from the limitations of the analytical categories of religious studies. It also derives from there being historical, and ongoing, tensions among the various dimensions of the religious amalgam, which have not merged or hybridized into a single internally coherent structure. There is lack of agreement among scholarly specialists about the character of Thai religion because it is not harmoniously integrated but rather is constituted as a field of multiple contestations. While Thai ritual practice is accumulative and emphasizes abundance, the religious complex of Buddhism, Brahmanism and spirit cults nonetheless retains internal tensions.

One of the major tensions within the Thai religious amalgam is between doctrinal reformist Buddhism and the diversity of ritual-based forms of magical practice. Unlike most other constituents of the religious amalgam, doctrinal Buddhism does place rationally consistent views of the cosmos and notions of "pure", "true" and "genuine" belief and practice at the centre of its understanding of religion. Morris observes that "the belief in spirit possession today offends scripturally oriented Buddhists, who see in the claims to spiritual presencing precisely the same ontologizing gesture that is prohibited in the Buddha's teachings of impermanence" (Morris 2000, p. 146). She notes that scripturally oriented Buddhists "eschew the ritualism associated with spirits and view it as a profane and excessively visible residue of primitive and animist belief" (Morris 2000, p. 1). Morris also describes the tensions between Buddhist monks and spirit mediums, many of whom are women, gay men and trans women:

> Monks, who are believed capable of achieving magical powers through the study of texts and meditation practice, often deride [spirit] mediums for a lack of learning, and mediums and their clients point to the relative merit of their possessing spirits (most of whom are supposedly highly learned Buddhists) as the sources of their own relative potency. (Morris 2000, p. 85)

Indeed, as noted in the previous chapter, in official discourses doctrinal Buddhism is defined as a "religion", *sasana*, in contrast to other forms of ritual devotional practice, including the cults of wealth, which are described as forms of "ritual" (*latthi-phithi*) or "belief" (*khwam-cheua*). In Chapter Two I discussed the historical origin of the binary opposition of "religion" (*sasana*) and "ritual" (*latthi*) in the impact of Western colonial-era notions of civilization. Even though doctrinal Buddhism places a rationalized view of pure and true religion at its core, the overall system of the practice-based Thai amalgam can incorporate this because consistent belief or doctrine is not a key criterion for inclusion in the more ritually oriented dimensions of the religious field. Followers of ritual-based cultic forms are not necessarily made anxious or concerned by doctrinal Buddhism, even though reformist Buddhists often criticize cultic ritual, because they view it as one more, albeit hierarchically and politically valorized, component of the religious amalgam alongside their own rituals and beliefs. The tensions between doctrinal and ritual-based religion are experienced more acutely by the followers of reformist Buddhism than by the followers of cultic ritual. It is the followers of reformist Buddhism, therefore, who most often articulate the tensions and contradictions within the Thai religious amalgam, not the followers of "belief" or "ritual". Drawing on the forms of Western religious studies summarized at the start of this chapter, doctrinal Buddhists often critique ritual-based forms of magic, which they see as superstitious accretions that sully the pure Buddhism that they seek to institute and protect.

Because they are typically more articulate about their religious beliefs and views on matters of doctrine, reformist Buddhists often receive greater attention in international media and academic circles. This greater representational presence of doctrinal Buddhism can skew the perceptions of some observers, who may fail to recognize the full extent of the popularity of ritual-oriented movements. As detailed in the previous chapter, Western discursive and political power has significantly influenced representations of Thai religiosity as well as Thai religious studies. As an effect of the regime of images, doctrinal Buddhism is at times mistakenly represented in international settings as the totality of Thai religion. This is because this form of religiosity, based more on doctrine and discourse, conforms to Western stereotypes of what constitutes "religion", and because of the privileged hierarchical position of Buddhism in the Thai religious amalgam detailed below.

Tensions between Brahmanical Devaraja and Buddhist Dhammaraja Conceptions of Thai Kingship

It is not only Thai popular religion that is marked by multiplicity and tensions. Thai royal cults that combine Buddhist and Brahmanical beliefs and rituals are also constituted by fundamental tensions. F.K. Lehman observes that a "troublesome conceptual dissonance" (Lehman 2003, p. 24) exists between Brahmanical ideas of royal divinity and Buddhist notions of the meritorious power (*barami*) of Thai kings, while Robert Heine-Geldern argues even more strongly that "[t]he theory of divine incarnation as found in Hinduism ... is incompatible with the doctrine of the Buddhism of the Hinayana [i.e., Theravada]" (Heine-Geldern 1942, p. 23). Christine Gray similarly observes that "[t]he idea of an ambiguous duality (or multiplicity) of natures was already central to the [Thai] royal tradition, as Reynolds (1972) and Tambiah's (1976) works have demonstrated" (Gray 1986, p. 309). She adds that the combination of Brahmanical and Buddhist ideologies, religious cosmologies and rituals of kingship produces an "inherently multidimensional nature of the [Thai] king", with structural "ambiguities" and "dualities" (p. 109) in a Thai royal tradition that is based on two coexisting and "potentially contradictory cultural codes and ideologies of power" (p. 120). Gray notes that while the *devaraja* cult was downplayed in the nineteenth century in response to Western critiques of "oriental despotism", it was never expunged and "has persisted as the basis of concepts of the king's sovereignty", becoming a "source of tensions and ambiguities that periodically surface" (p. 117).

Multiple Royal and Popular Religious Epistemologies

The dissonances between Brahmanical and Buddhist notions of royal rule, which are both equally foundational to Thai royal cults, have had defining influences on Thai religious and cultural epistemologies. When the politically dominant religious forms of a society are structured by a foundational tension, if not contradiction, then popular demotic forms of religiosity that develop in that context will of necessity be deeply impacted by those foundational incompatibilities. Thai cultural epistemologies have been forged out of the negotiation of the foundational tensions and contradictions within both royal and popular religiosities in a context of multiple, coexisting cultural and religious traditions. As Gray observes, the history of Buddhism and Buddhist kingship in Thailand is a "'layering of traditions' which gives rise to multiple paradigms for action" (Gray 1986, p. 144). Thai religious and political cultures are built upon this foundational unrationalized multiplicity and, in turn, the society's complex, multiple and hierarchized religious formation is the foundation upon which a complex, multiple and hierarchical social order has developed. As will be outlined in Chapter Seven, this pattern has been further accentuated, not undermined, by the conditions of late modernity and consumer capitalism.

Thailand preserves and alternates between Buddhist and Hindu symbolisms and rituals as well as between different versions of kingship. This doctrinal ambiguity is preserved and subsumed within a state ritual complex that emphasizes correct ritual practice (orthopraxy) over doctrine or belief (orthodoxy). In a sense, there is no public orthodoxy of royal cults. There is no text or official public discourse that resolves the tensions between the Brahmanical and Buddhist dimensions of Thai royal cults. There is, however, a tightly structured practical royal ritual orthopraxy. As was the case in the rituals described above, doctrinal tensions are kept to one side in royal rituals where Brahmin priests and Buddhists both officiate, albeit in spatially and temporally distinct settings within ritual events.

Time and Place (*Kala-Thesa*) Contextualization in the Thai Religious Amalgam

One of the most important processes by which diversity and tensions within the amalgam of the Thai religious complex are managed is contextualization. This contextualization needs to be clearly distinguished from processes of cultural or religious hybridization in which two distinct modalities or cultural forms merge into a new "third space" (Bhabha 1994). In Thai "time and place" (*kala-thesa*) contextualization, religio-cultural differences are preserved in contiguous bordered spaces rather than merging into a blended hybrid. Indeed, contextualization and compartmentalization are also key principles of the broader Thai social structure and they emerge in part from the multiplicity of the Thai religious system, whose components remain ambiguously differentiated.

Nidhi Eeoseewong has presented a detailed account of the contextualization of multiple forms of difference in his analysis of Thai ideas of spatiality (*pheun-thi*) and space and time (*kala-thesa*). As Nidhi emphasizes, "[h]uman beings live amidst spatialities and times (*pheun-thi lae wela*)" (Nidhi 1991, p. 180) and "worldviews are founded on notions of space and time" (p. 181). In his account, Nidhi variously uses the formal term "spatiality" (*pheun-thi*) and the local cultural category "time and space" (*kala-thesa*) to denote ritually bounded cultural domains and social spaces. He argues that Thai social and cultural spatialities are bounded and multiple, with each zone having a distinct set of rules of conduct and behaviour:

> In Thai thought spatiality has many characteristics that are the opposite of contemporary ideas of space. Spatiality in Thai thought is not a single, unbounded plane but rather is divided into sections by clearly marked dividing lines. Each section of spatiality has specific, distinctive features.... Hence, in each sectional space there are different laws (*kot*) that must be followed. When humans cross from one spatiality to another they need to behave according to another, different set of laws (*kot*) or *dhamma*. (Nidhi 1991, p. 183)

Nidhi maintains that "Thai people look upon spatiality and time as discontinuous sections (*pen suan-suan mai seup-neuang-kan*). Whatever one does has to be undertaken 'correctly according to time and place' (*thuk kala-thesa*), an idiom that cannot be directly translated into English because Westerners (*farang*) do not think about time and space in a Thai way" (Nidhi 1991, p. 191). Nidhi contends that English terms such as "proper", "appropriate", "impeccable" and "correct" do not fully capture the meaning of the expression *thuk kala-thesa*—"to be correct according to time and place"—because each society's ideas are based on a radically different worldview with incommensurable notions of time and space. Penny Van Esterik (1999, p. 277) describes the notion of *kala-thesa* (from the Sanskrit *kāla-des'a*, "time-place") as denoting contextual sensitivity to the setting for actions and statements in a society that is characterized by multiple forms of power over social life and cultural expression (Van Esterik 1999, p. 278). According to Baumann, *kala-thesa* "describes the embodiment of the relational logic that structures Thailand's hierarchical social organisation" (Baumann 2017, p. 229).

Nidhi argues that Thai *kala-thesa* spatialities have clear borders or boundaries (*khorp-khet*) in both the horizontal and vertical dimensions (Nidhi 1991, pp. 184–85). The vertical divisions of Thai spatialities are forms of hierarchy, and Nidhi provides the example of the gendered hierarchicalization of Thai contexts that gives men privileged access to more spaces than women. He contends that Thais "construct the boundaries that separate different spatialities by means of ritual (*phithikam*)" (p. 183) and that all Thai people are socialized and conditioned to instinctively respect the divisions between and amongst different spatialities.

Moving between different spatialities also changes the subject who inhabits each *kala-thesa* setting, and Nidhi maintains that "[w]hen humans cross from one spatiality to another they need to change themselves (too)" (Nidhi 1991, p. 183). Van Esterik similarly observes that *kala-thesa* contextual sensitivity leads to the formation of multiple identities that "slip easily over each other like tectonic plates" (Van Esterik 1999, p. 278). On the multiplication of Thai contextual subjectivities, Nidhi observes,

> An important principle of entering another spatiality is that of changing oneself, because each spatiality has its own specific characteristics. A person in one spatiality cannot enter another spatiality without changing their status (*sathana*) or condition (*saphap*). Not to do so may lead to dangerous or inauspicious (*mai-pen-mongkhon*) consequences. (Nidhi 1991, p. 187)

He gives as an example government offices that display signs that say, "Government Office: Please Dress Politely" (*sathan-thi ratchakan prot taeng-kai suphap*), where Thais need to adapt their dress and bodily comportment before they can enter these locations in order to conform to the specific performative norms of that time and place:

> Government offices (because they are official locales [*khorng luang*]), hence are placed at a different level from ordinary spatialities.

Government offices exist at a higher level than ordinary spatialities and citizens do not dare enter these locales without changing their selves, at the very least by changing their clothing. (Nidhi 1991, p. 189)

The signs ordering one to dress politely in government offices have meanings that extend beyond clothing. They are signs that mark the divide between lower ranked spatialities outside government offices and the higher ranked spaces of government service. A person who sees these signs does not only have to check their clothing before entering the government office, they also have to compose their demeanour and manners (*samruam kiriya-marayat*) much more than normally, because he/she well realises that they are entering a spatiality at a another [higher] level. (Nidhi 1991, p. 189)

Nidhi says that the personal transformation involved in moving from one bounded, rule-defined spatiality to another has several aspects: (1) changing one's physical presentation, such as one's dress; (2) changing one's behaviour, "which has the result of producing a different personality (*bukkhalikkaphap thi taek-tang*)" (Nidhi 1991, p. 191); and (3) changing oneself by ritual means, such as conducting protective rituals before starting a journey or undertaking the ritual practices of ordination before becoming a Buddhist monk. A person who can enter more numerous and diverse spatialities than others, or who enters spatialities barred to ordinary people, is said to possess "special powers" (*itthirit*) (p. 187). Nidhi uses the term *itthirit* to denote the ability to enter special social and cultural domains, an expression that in Thai ritual discourses refers to "magical power".

In local discourses, those who transgress the norms of time and place contexts are criticized for not knowing how to "locate them-selves appropriately" (*wang tua mai mor-som*), acting "wrongly for the time and place" (*phit kala-thesa, mai thuk kala-thesa*) or "not knowing the [right] time and place" (*mai ru-jak kala-thesa*). Van Esterik notes that despite the centrality of *kala-thesa* to Thai life, most Westerners have difficulty in noticing the divides between time and place contexts:

Even after many years in Thailand, one seldom knows when boundaries are crossed, when one has *phit kala-thesa* [acted wrongly for the time and place context], only that the coming together of time and place and relationships is not quite right, that either the knowledge of contexts or persons was incomplete or inaccurate. (Van Esterik 2000, p. 39)

Baumann calls the implicitly marked liminal frontiers between *kala-thesa* contexts "phantom walls" (Baumann 2017, p. 230). Nonetheless, Van Esterik notes that

> [c]hildren are taught from birth to recognize *kala-thesa*, lest they *phit kala-thesa* (make an error in *kala-thesa*). But in my experience the concept is rarely talked about or written about, except to correct children. It is so deeply taken for granted among Thais that I knew the concept years before I learned the word. (Van Esterik 2000, p. 228)

While not referring to the term *kala-thesa*, which as Van Esterik notes is rarely verbalized explicitly, several scholars have nonetheless remarked upon the phenomenon in a variety of ways. Andrew Johnson observes that the Thai "religious system is not seamless, rather it rests upon internal contradiction and division" (Johnson 2015, p. 293). Tambiah notes that Thai cultural logics are not based on binary or exclusionary notions of "either/or", with participation in Western and traditional systems not regarded as being "fraught with conflict", even for Western-educated Thais, because this state of affairs "is aided by the different contexts of their relevance and therefore their insulation from direct confrontation" (Tambiah 1977, p. 129). Tambiah states that his Thai informants found "no reason … why all systems of knowledge [Thai and Western] could not co-exist, without one finding it necessary to supplant another according to some exclusive criteria of falsifiability and experimental proof" (Tambiah 1977, p. 129). Golomb observes that even those he describes as "devout Buddhists" may participate in "non-sectarian, syncretic curing ceremonies of magical-animism. They have effectively partitioned their ritual participation into two distinct spheres of activity: parochial formal religious observance, and supernaturalistic rites wherein both ingroup and outgroup religious symbols may be used for practical, therapeutic purposes" (Golomb 1985, p. 278). Golomb further states that "alternate participation in poorly integrated animistic and nonanimistic belief systems is achieved without cognitive dissonance by isolating inconsistent beliefs in separate conversational or ritual contexts" (p. 105).

White emphasizes that "contextually situated and bounded practices" (White 2017, p. 196) form the analytical ground of Thai religious life, also noting the "context-dependent" character of Thai "cultural identity and social positionality" (p. 197) more broadly. As Nidhi emphasizes, "[n]ot only uneducated rural people, even members of the urban middle class who adopt *farang* (Western) ways, may unconsciously behave or have attitudes based on old Thai notions of spatiality" (Nidhi 1991, p. 182). Baumann describes contemporary magical epistemologies in Northeast Thailand as "non-modern" and contends that

> [m]ost persons born and raised into contemporary Thai language games have thus incorporated this simultaneity of modern and non-modern epistemologies as essential aspects of a shared Thai habitus…. The contextualized validity and practical meaningfulness of these seemingly opposed epistemologies for individual actors varies, however, along socio-cultural features. (Baumann 2017, p. 29)

Jovan Maud also notes the complex negotiation of the boundaries that separate the multiple spatialities of the diverse amalgam of cults that pattern Thai religious life:

> Such interactions require the complex interplay of boundary crossing and boundary maintenance, of recognition and incommensurability, and of sameness and difference. In the context of the [Buddhist] robe offering ceremony, as with other cross border religious interactions in southern Thailand, it is the complex negotiation that takes place, where boundaries and differences are simultaneously elided and evoked, problematised and realised. (Maud 2007, p. 379)

The contextual specificity of meaning between different religious systems in the Thai amalgam may even result in the same phenomenological event being mapped by different religious logics. As noted above, the Brahma image at the Erawan Shrine in Bangkok may be worshipped by either a "Hindu" or a "Buddhist" *khatha* incantation. Marjorie Muecke describes a ritual in Chiang Mai in northern Thailand in which a female medium was possessed by the spirit of one of the Lord Buddha's closest followers, Moggalana, and at which Buddhist monks were present. She notes that spirit mediums described the ritual in Brahmanical terms as *phithi kan yok khru*, "the ritual to ceremonially honour one's initiating master", while the monks used Buddhist terminology to describe it, calling it *phithi kan khao phansa*, "the ritual of entering the Buddhist Lent rainy season retreat" (Muecke 1992, p. 101). Baumann emphasizes that time and place contextualization not only separates different ritual spaces, it also differentiates multiple epistemological systems:

> *Kala-thesa* determines not only which practices are performed, but also the validity of Thailand's multiple epistemologies and thus how to interpret a practice in a given context. It is thus not only the performed practice that changes with 'time and place', but

also its meaning. This contextuality of meaning is even harder to grasp for modern minds than the contextuality of social practices. The difficulties Western observers have to notice the boundaries monitored by *kala-thesa* are [compounded] by the fact that they are invisible and manifest only as embodied aspects of Thai habitus. (Baumann 2017, p. 229)

The contextualized multiplicity of Thai cultural and religious life also impacts the academy beyond anthropology and the study of religious culture. Soraj Hongladarom presents a view of the enterprise of philosophy in Thailand in "situations where visions of what constitute the good life and so on collide, a conception that changes the aim of philosophy from establishing truth to seeing what good could come out of … unfinalisable arguments" (Soraj 1996, n6). In effect, Soraj describes the enterprise of philosophy in Thailand as an intellectual negotiation of the incommensurable discourses that make up the amalgamated multiplicity of Thai culture:

Philosophy in this conception is not a state where one is at one with Reality, nor a movement toward that Reality, but a contested, conflicting condition where parties agree on some very basic condition needed for arguments to get going, such as the use and rules of logic, but disagree on almost everything else. (Soraj 1996)

Soraj positions his view of Thai philosophy as being radically different from Western philosophies' aim of finding universals. In contrast, Thai philosophizing is an anti-universalist form of thought that emerges from the context of multiple incommensurable discourses.

To re-emphasize, the lack of agreement on how to describe and theorize Thai religion detailed above results not only from the complex, multi-cultural mix of traditions and rituals but also because distinct processes of mixing of these diverse traditions take place, and current theories of cultural blending do not always clearly differentiate among these various processes. In some situations the boundaries between different traditions are dissolved and there is indeed hybridization into a distinct new "third space" form.

For example, the *khatha* or formulaic incantation used by the magic monk *Luang Phor* Khoon—whose cult of wealth is described in Chapters Four and Six—to sacralize amulets was a hybrid of Brahmanical and Buddhist terms. As reported by *The Nation*:

[*Luang Phor* Khoon] said that although the *ma-a-u* chant he uses during the [amulet sacralization] rite was reminiscent of the Vedic *a-u-m* chant to invoke the Hindu gods, it was comprised of the initials of the Maha Moggalana, a Buddhist saint, and two of Buddha's noted disciples: Ananda and Upali.[3]

Khoon's blessing chant shows the hybrid form of his ritualism and can be seen as a Buddhacization of an originally Brahmanical ritual, reversing the Hindu mystical sound of creation, *aum*. Peter Skilling notes that while the language of Buddhist ritual chants is Pali, the formulas recited by Brahmins in Thailand are often in "a thoroughly hybrid Pali-Sanskrit-Thai. Even when a text may appear to be in Pali, it may be written in Thai syntax and verse" (Skilling 2009, p. 186). Skilling also notes that Saveros Pou describes the hybrid language used in Khmer religion as "Khmero-Pali" (Pou 1991, pp. 13–28). Justin McDaniel makes a similar observation: "When Thais compose Pali, they often incorporate a number of Sanskrit spellings. There is certainly a Sanskrit-Thai-Pali-Khmer hybrid language in magical texts in Thailand. This is so distinctive that one could argue that it is a new Pali dialect specific to this genre" (McDaniel 2011 p. 276n86). There are numerous other examples of hybridity in modern Thai history, such as the "European-Sino-Siamese" hybrid architectural style of King Mongkut's hilltop palace, Phra Nakhon Khiri, built in Petchaburi Province west of Bangkok in 1859, which Somphong Amnuay-Ngerntra states, "reflects a transitional period in Siamese aesthetics between traditional eclecticism and aspiring modernism" (Somphong 2007, p. 76). The clothes of the royal court in the King Chulalongkorn period, such as the male *chut phra ratcha patan*, were a hybrid of Thai and Western Victorian-period styles.

In some situations in the Thai religious amalgam, one tradition is incorporated within another in a subordinate form by being re-interpreted, such as when Hindu deities are incorporated into Thai Buddhism not as creators or masters of the cosmos but rather as protectors of Buddhism. In other settings, however, such as ones Nidhi describes in time and place contextualization, the boundaries between traditions are preserved and there is tension about boundary preservation and maintenance. In the case of the cults of wealth, the different cultural and religious sources of this amalgam are not merged into a single undifferentiated hybrid form. Their original forms are preserved and placed side by side. Thai, Hindu and Chinese gods are not merged, but rather their respective images are placed side by side on spirit medium ritual altars, and different Thai, Chinese and Hindu spirits possess mediums in sequence, one at a time. The contextualized, additive logic of Thai popular religion—including spirit mediumship, the cult of amulets and the cults of wealth—preserves and does not obscure the visual and other forms of distinctiveness of its diverse cultural sources.

Furthermore, different hybridizing and contextualizing processes of mixing are not necessarily mutually exclusive. They may both take place within the same ritual event, and individual religious practitioners negotiate these multiple traditions by drawing on multiple processes by which they relate, or differentiate. In the complexity of modern Thailand, as well as in the multiplicity of premodern Siam, there have been and still are multiple strategies and diverse processes of engaging and living across cultural, ethnic and religious plurality. While there are spaces of contextualized *kala-thesa* differentiation, in other locales we may find hybridized third spaces.

Bénédicte Brac de la Perrière (2016) describes the religious field of contemporary Burmese religiosity as also being marked by a form of contextualization, which she describes as the "autonomisation" of different religious "lines". Regarding spirit possession in modern Burma, she observes,

> The increased autonomy of spirit possession does not mean that it stands apart from the overall religious system. On the contrary, one of the aspects of autonomisation is that the cult is both in constant interaction with, and is normatively separated from, Buddhism. More precisely, this constant interaction is built on the physical separation of ritual institutions. (Brac de la Perrière 2011, p. 167)

Brac de la Perrière defines autonomization as a "dialogical process in the delimitation of the domains of practices in the religious sphere" and argues that this is central to "processes of sustaining hierarchy" (Brac de la Perrière 2011, p. 180). Indeed, patterns of hierarchical organization are another central feature of Thai vernacular religiosity.

Under the Hierarchical Dominance of Buddhism

Some scholars have attempted to decentre Buddhism as the defining nucleus of Thai religiosity. These accounts have challenged the view that Thai vernacular religion should be viewed solely through the lens of Buddhism and propose a model in which the various dimensions of belief and ritual reflect and grow from an underlying substrate of belief and ritual. Following Nicola Tannenbaum, Deborah Wong proposes that the Buddhist, Hindu, Chinese and spirit dimensions of Thai religiosity may all share a common underlying belief structure, and that

> Buddhism may be part of deeper [historical] patterns of belief, and that models positing multiple religious systems at work in

Southeast Asia may miss the ways that they are part of broader, more encompassing belief. (Wong 2001, p. xviii)

McDaniel also presents an account of Thai religion in which the Buddha is not the prime actor and Buddhism is not the most important tradition, arguing that "[d]espite having central cultural axioms, there is no core of Thai Buddhism" (McDaniel 2011, p. 15). Given this, he maintains that in academic studies

> it would be wise to stop describing different shrines, images, amulets, rituals, texts, and liturgies as Brahmanic, Mahayanist, tantric, esoteric, royalist, animistic, or even syncretistic. Thai religious practices reflect a great deal of what William Connolly has described as 'tolerance of ambiguity'.... [O]bjects and practices are valued because of their relation to certain events, people, and places, not because of their ability to articulate Buddhistness, Brahmanicness, Thainess, or localness. (McDaniel 2011, p. 17)

Rather than focusing on analysing Thai popular religion in terms of the extent to which it conforms to categories such as Buddhism, Hinduism or Brahmanism, McDaniel says we should instead study what he calls "the epistemic characteristics of macrolevel Thai culture or religion" (McDaniel 2011, p. 9). Peter Vandergeest makes a similar point in his study of Buddhism in southern Thailand in the nineteenth and early twentieth centuries, arguing that

> [r]eligious practices in Songkhla were *an assembly of rituals, practices, and meanings which cannot be identified primarily with any single tradition in a totalising manner.* Rather, they were structured by the social context of the nineteenth century in Songkhla.... Cultural practices are best understood as the historical outcome of a multiplicity of practices with diverse origins in specific historical contexts which, for heuristic purposes, can be seen in terms of different interpretive domains (Buddhism, folk-Brahmanism, and so on). (Vandergeest 1993, p. 862; emphasis added)

Buddhacization and Buddhocentrism

Nonetheless, while it is vital for analytical models of Thai religiosity to address the multiplicity and internal pluralism of the religious field, it is equally important to recognize that this system is deeply patterned by hierarchies that locate the various elements in stratified relations of superiority and inferiority. In her account of the autonomization of different dimensions of the religious field in Burma, Brac de la Perrière emphasizes that this type of contextualization supports a definite religious hierarchy. Brac de la Perrière observes that, in Burma, ceremonies to honour the Thirty-Seven Lords or *nats* that involve spirit possession "cannot be performed in a [Buddhist] monastery compound or in a pagoda" (Brac de la Perrière 2009, p. 199). She maintains, "It is important to emphasise that the physical separation between the spirit cult and Buddhist practices serves to differentiate the two domains within the Burmese religious sphere. This construction has a very specific function: to maintain hierarchy by keeping Buddhism separate, pure, and superior. It is mainly a normative separation" (Brac de la Perrière 2011, p. 168). Even though there is a spatialized contextual separation of the spirit possession cults, these ritual forms are legitimized by "encompassment within the Buddhist system of values" (Brac de la Perrière 2009, p. 201). Spirit cults in Burma, as in Thailand, are "entangled in the overarching Buddhist idiom" (Brac de la Perrière 2009, p. 197).[4]

Similarly, in Thailand, there is no doubt that Buddhism is the most prestigious religious form and creates the frame within which all other elements of the complex amalgam assume their place. The amalgam of Brahmanism, Chinese rituals and spirit cults is hierarchically ordered under the overall dominance of Buddhism. Through most of Thai history, political edicts have defined Buddhism as the supremely authoritative religion, followed in order of prestige (*barami*), but not in order of truth-value, by Brahmanism, and then by spirit cults. Pattana Kitiarsa's account of the Buddhist-centred form of religio-symbolic power that structures the placement of images of deities on altars in Thai spirit medium shrines makes this relationship clear:

> The statue of Buddha is always positioned at the top [of altars], since he is regarded as the supreme deity in Thai religious cosmology and since Buddhism is the country's state sponsored religion and has traditionally formed its sociocultural foundation. (Pattana 2005a)

Gray emphasizes the dominance of Buddhism in the Thai religious order and its incorporation of Brahmanism and other elements: "In the Theravada polities of Southeast Asia, Hindu deities became encompassed within the Buddhist cosmology as guardians of the Buddha, and Brahmanic rituals, within Buddhist rituals" (Gray 1986, p. 114). Gray uses "Buddhacisation" to denote "the historical and cultural processes that position new beliefs and practices within an overarching Buddhist soteriological framework" (p. 127). She contends that there has been a progressive historical Buddhacization of the Thai religious field, with state power leading to monastic Buddhism being located at the acme of the hierarchy of the religious amalgam:

By the end of the Fifth Reign [of King Chulalongkorn, r. 1863–1910], Brahmanic rituals were well enclosed within Buddhism in the process of encompassment or 'Buddhacisation'. The gods of the Hindu pantheon had been designated as mere guardians in the Buddhist cosmos. (Gray 1986, p. 306)

The recent building of shrines to Chinese Mahayana bodhisattvas and Hindu deities within Thai monastery compounds not only shows the symbolic expansion of Theravada Buddhism into new domains but also the incorporation of originally non-Theravada rituals and cults within the overarching frame of Thai Buddhism. McDaniel describes the proliferation of shrines to Hindu deities in recent years as "expanding the Thai Buddhist repertoire" (McDaniel 2011, p. 154), while Gray (1986, p. 765) notes that this appropriation of new religious elements is an act of domination in which originally non-Theravada forms are subject to the ritual and symbolic dominance of Buddhism.

Wong's account of the *wai khru* "honouring the teacher" ritual provides an example of the superiority of Buddhism in relation to Brahmanical rituals and beliefs. *Wai khru* is a form of ritual possession when an empowered initiating teacher channels a deity regarded as being the original guru and founder of a lineage of spirit mediums or artistic specialists. Depending on the setting, the foundational deity-cum-teacher may be addressed as "The Old Father" (*phor kae*) or regarded to be an ascetic *reusi*. During this ceremony, which is usually held annually, the initiating teacher empowers his or her disciples by being possessed by the spirit of the original teacher as well as the collective spirits of all other past teachers within the lineage. As Erick White observes, it is through this experience of possession "that unbroken continuity and perfect transmission is ensured by recreating and reproducing on a regular annual basis that original transcendent moment emblematic of the original revelation, transmission, and acquisition of esoteric knowledge" (White 2014, p. 47). In Northern Thailand this ritual is called *yok khru* ("raising up the teacher [in a ritual of honouring]") and it is conducted by spirit mediums as well as by artists and performers of different genres of classical dance and drama to honour and reconfirm their relationship with their initiating *khru*.

While Buddhist monks do not perform the actual *wai khru* ritual and are not present at the invocation of the Old Father or ascetic *reusi*, they nonetheless bless the space in which the ritual will subsequently take place as well as the assembled participants before the Brahmanical invocations begin. Buddhism thus authorizes and blesses this Brahmanical-cum-animist ritual, and the sequence of rituals for the *wai khru* ceremony shows that Buddhist ritual, in this case monks' chanting of blessing recitations from the *Tipitaka*, acts as a foundation upon which Brahmanical magic is enacted. In the Thai religious amalgam, the *saksit* magical power of Brahmanical and other forms of ritual is thus enabled by the authorizing *barami* or charismatic authority of Buddhist rituals, which typically take place before and, at times, spatially separate from, but nonetheless contiguous with, Brahmanical ritual.

While Buddhism is ritually superior, it is nonetheless important to emphasize that within vernacular Thai Buddhism, as opposed to reformist doctrinal Buddhism, the hierarchical superiority of Buddhism is not brought about by expelling non-Buddhist religious forms. Rather, non-Buddhist expressions of religiosity are incorporated in ritually inferior positions within a potentially expandable sphere of Buddhacized sanctity and influence. Gray describes the renovation of temple buildings in Buddhist monasteries, which now often include shrines to non-Buddhist deities, as a type of bricolage in which the modern sponsors of renovation

> appropriate objects and practices with distinct historical and/or regional values [and] recontextualise them, thereby imbuing them with new meanings…. By thus combining them with a new set of elements, the bricoleurs have thus created a new tradition or mythology that retains the old meanings of its elements as part of the new. In the Theravada tradition such acts of appropriation are acts of dominance, the stuff of domination, the primary mechanism through which history and myth is created, represented and appropriated. (Gray 1986, p. 765)

Jovan Maud notes that the success of the political-cultural project of forging a national Thai identity in the twentieth century has freed "individual laypeople from the burden of locality, allowing them to see the entire nation as a domain of choice" (Maud 2007, p. 101). This has permitted originally local cults to achieve national status. He nonetheless emphasizes that the "profusion of heterodox forms and practices in modern Thailand" does not replace Buddhism "as the symbolic core of Thai society" (p. 104). Irene Stengs also affirms that Thailand's "new religious movements need to be positioned in relation to the kingdom's official religious institution: the Buddhist sangha (order of monks)" (Stengs 2009, p. 25).

Maud highlights the role of the state and state-sponsored Buddhism in the proliferation of new religiosities. He contends that the Thai state continues to act as "guarantor of the symbolic order" (Maud 2007, p. 98), with its hegemonic domination of the country's cultural landscape underpinning recent religious diversification. Maud argues that all the new religious forms "retain an unacknowledged dependence on nationally prescribed hierarchies of value" (p. 4) in which institutional Buddhism and the religious figure of the Buddha are paramount. Despite their apparent diversity, the many new prosperity cults "continue to depend on an underlying unity which is largely provided by 'the state'" (p. 98). Maud further notes that, while the diversity of new prosperity cults might seem to challenge "a unitary vision of [Thai] religion, they also participate in, and reproduce, uniform hierarchies of value" (pp. 98–99).

White similarly maintains that the culture of professional spirit mediums "is thoroughly immersed within the dominant and encompassing Theravada Buddhist milieu that … defines the normative religious imagination in contemporary Thailand" (White 2014, p. 431). He notes that "professional spirit mediums have consistently sought to refashion and reconceptualize their religious identity so that it more closely resembles the roles of both folk Brahmanical practitioners and Buddhist monks" (p. 131). White contends that the process of Buddhacization observed by Gray in the 1970s is continuing today as professional spirit mediums pursue "a legitimating strategy of religious upgrading in the wake of the rise of modernist reform and establishment state Buddhism" (p. 290). This strategic upgrading of the spirit mediumship that is central to many of the rituals of the cults of wealth is reflected in a range of domains. While the spirits of older forms of spirit mediumship were usually identified as *phi*, a generic term that denotes "numinals" (Baumann 2017, p. 17) of many varieties, the spirits of the new cults are almost always referred to either by the honorific title *jao*, "lord", the Pali/Sanskrit-derived term *thep* (*deva*, "deity") or the royal-cum-Buddhist title and classifier of *ong*. The shrines of professional spirit mediums are now also referred to with royal vocabularies, often being described as *tamnak*, "an abode of a lord". Consultations with a spirit medium, especially one who channels an elevated deity, are also described in royal terms as "to have an audience with" (*khao fao*).

As a result of the religious upgrading or Buddhacization of spirit possession rituals, White notes that the distance between Buddhism and Buddhist monks, on the one hand, and spirit mediums and spirit possession, on the other, has narrowed considerably in recent decades. Nonetheless, most of this narrowing has been asymmetrical and has primarily consisted of spirit mediums reconceptualising their identities, practices and goals so that they are now more thoroughly defined, both in their minds and in the minds of their followers and clients, in terms of normative Buddhist beliefs and practices, goals and desires, roles and institutions. (White 2014, p. 105)

While professional spirit mediums have sought to establish pragmatic linkages with receptive Buddhist monks, neither the Buddhist sangha nor most Buddhist monks "have significantly refashioned their ideological, social or ritual relations with regards to spirit possession or spirit mediums" (White 2014, p. 96). Indeed, while the rise of professional spirit mediumship has been paralleled by a "selective relaxation" (p. 104) of the opposition between spirit mediumship and Buddhism, this has not occurred without opposition from some reformist monks and laypeople. As Rosalind Morris notes, "[Buddhist] doctrine frowns on mediumship as fiercely as mediums claim to be good Buddhists" (Morris 2000, p. 108) and there is ongoing contestation over the prestigious labels of "Buddhism" and "Buddhist" in the Thai religious amalgam.

Tambiah's (2013) model of the galactic polity can be drawn upon here, where a high degree of local political and religio-symbolic autonomy is granted on condition that Buddhism is ritually acknowledged as being superior. The Thai religious amalgam is a galactic polity of greater and lesser deities, in which the Buddha is located at the apical centre. I here revise my earlier position (Jackson 1999b, p. 316), where I argued that Buddhism had become less important relative to Brahmanism. In the light of Maud's and White's studies and Gray's arguments about Buddhacization, I now agree that new cults of wealth have emerged within an overarching Buddhist imaginary that preserves, and indeed further elaborates, the Buddhist-centred hierarchy of Thai religion.[5]

The alternative, and apparently competing, academic views that, on the one hand, Thai religion is Buddhist, and on the other, that Buddhism is just one component of a broader religious complex, are not necessarily mutually exclusive. Rather, these contrasting perspectives may reflect observations made from different standpoints within the hierarchy of the Thai religious amalgam. If one looks down from the top of the hierarchy, the Thai religious amalgam looks Buddhist and decidedly male-centred. If one looks from the bottom up, however, the religious complex may appear more female-centred and oriented towards spirit rituals. If one views Thai religion from the bottom up, Buddhism appears as one part of a broader religious complex, which nonetheless provides the structuring patterning for the hierarchical relations amongst the diverse cultic elements. Furthermore, if one views Thai religion through the gender lens of male roles and political leadership, then it is more Buddhist. But if one views the hierarchy of the Thai religious amalgam through the alternative polarizing gendered lens of the place of women, and of gay men and trans women, then it is less Buddhist and more focused on spirit cults. As an academic enterprise, religious studies has tended to look at Thai religion from the top down and as Buddhist, while anthropology, and especially feminist anthropology, has often looked from the bottom up and viewed the amalgam as a complex in which Buddhism is but one cult among many others.

The Primacy of Ritual: Polytropy and Hierarchy in Vernacular Thai Buddhism

Southeast Asia is a crossroads of many religious influences, which have always been treated syncretically. One precondition for this basically peaceful syncretism is the fact that the different religious communities largely eschew orthodoxy and content themselves with their followers' commitment to a particular ritual practice (orthopractice). (Gottowik 2014, p. 7)

Inconsistencies between the doctrines of different strands of the Thai religious amalgam, both in popular religion and in royal cults, are also managed by placing greater emphasis on correct ritual practice (orthopraxy) than on correct belief (orthodoxy) (see Jackson 2003, p. 19). This accommodation permits a high degree of symbolic interpenetration amongst Theravada and Mahayana Buddhism, Brahmanism and spirit cults. As McDaniel notes, in Thailand it is often hard to define someone's beliefs: "Statements of belief are a rarity in Thai culture.... Thai Buddhists often define themselves by what they do rather than what they believe" (McDaniel 2011, p. 13). However, "[w]hile beliefs are rarely articulated, [ritual] technologies are commonly defined, compared, and implemented" (p. 13).

The question of how to characterize societies marked by expanding religious complexity based more on ritual than on doctrine is not unique to Thailand. The complexity and diversity of religious ritual and belief in South Asia and China present similar analytical challenges, and scholars in these fields have explored responses that offer productive contributions to studies of religion in Thailand. Given that mainland Southeast Asia has long been a site of intersections between and among India and China, bringing studies of religion in these latter regions into dialogue with accounts of ritual practice in Thailand and neighbouring Southeast Asian societies can help establish a frame for comparative analysis, especially given that scholars researching all these regions struggle with similar issues of categorization and theorization. In this regard, the account by Michael Carrithers of ritual polytropy in India is especially valuable in understanding how the contextualized hierarchical order of Thailand's Buddhist-centred religious amalgam is held in place.

In words that ring true for scholars of religion in Thailand, Carrithers observes that studies of Indian religiosity need to come to terms with "a degree of slipperiness, an ability to be enthused by now one religious figure and now another, and perhaps throughout to maintain worship of a third ... that is ... difficult to bring decisively within the grasp of scholarship" (Carrithers 2000, p. 832). And like scholars of Thailand, Carrithers seeks to understand the religious forms of a "variegated civilisation, where one is brought daily into necessary and necessarily peaceable contact with persons of many practices and beliefs" (p. 835).

Carrithers notes that in attempting to characterize the pervasive religious pluralism across South Asia, scholars have drawn on expressions such as "Indic eclecticism", the "fluidity of attitude towards religious identity", and the "complex and often shifting nature of religious identity" (Carrithers 2000, p. 833). He finds all these attempts to grasp Indian religiosity inadequate, however, and proposes an alternative model that he terms "ritual polytropy". For Carrithers, polytropy refers to the

> eclecticism and fluidity of South Asian religious life. I coin the word from the Greek *poly*, 'many', and *tropos*, 'turning', to capture the sense in which people turn toward many sources for their spiritual sustenance, hope, relief, or defence.... This points to a cosmopolitanism in social and spiritual relations which I take to be the norm, rather than the exception, in South Asia. (Carrithers 2000, p. 834)

Carrithers argues that polytropy "captures more faithfully the nature of the Indian material" than the term "syncretism", which he contends suggests a putatively pure original against which syncretism is contrasted as a decay or corruption (Carrithers 2000, p. 836). For Carrithers, polytropy is an always already existing religious condition of foundational multiplicity rather than a secondary, derived condition from any original form of religious purity.

White references Carrithers' account when he describes Thai popular religiosity as "polytropic" (White 2014, p. 36n9), and Adam Chau has drawn on Carrithers to study religion in China, which he describes as "religiously plural" (Chau 2011, p. 556) and where, as in India, "each person is necessarily surrounded by and encounters on a daily basis, holy persons and deities of different religious traditions" (p. 566). In this setting, as is also the case in Thailand, people develop "a general reverential attitude towards all these holy persons and deities, all the while being more or less conscious of the differences between these sources of power and authority" (p. 556). In Thailand, as in China and India, vernacular religiosity is marked by a general attitude of reverence while remaining aware of the differences between multiple sources of power and authority of diverse religious figures. Indeed, Carrithers' account of polytropy in India echoes themes that Nidhi explores in his account of the multiple *kala-thesa* contexts of Thai cultural and religious life: "[P]olytropy points to a fact of life in a cosmopolitan society, namely, that one may routinely be different persons at different times ... and may enter into different relationships as different persons" (Carrithers 2000, p. 840). Like Nidhi and Van Esterik, who observe that Thais assume different identities as they move between diverse ritually distinguished *kala-thesa* contexts, Carrithers states that the plurality of worship in India,

> corresponds to the plurality of identity and interest that anyone in such a complex civilisation as India's might have.... To be able to move smoothly from one role to another in the multiplicity of relationships that comprise daily life in a complex civilisation constitutes the very condition of civil peace. (Carrithers 2000, p. 860)

Carrithers' analysis suggests that Nidhi and Van Esterik's accounts of a contextualized multiplicity of subjectivities is not unique to Thailand but rather is a more general cross-cultural condition in complex multicultural and multireligious societies. He argues,

> [T]he very existence of a complex civilisation must rely—*naturally*, so to speak—on a plurality of identities for its members alongside a corresponding breadth of differing social relations. And this breadth goes—again *naturally*, at least in India—with a breadth of holy persons and a multiplicity of clients. (Carrithers 2000, p. 860; emphases in original)

The many parallels between Thai vernacular religion and polytropic Indian and Chinese religiosity help us understand why Indian and Chinese deities have been increasingly appropriated within modern Thai religious observance and form central elements of the cults of wealth that are described in the next chapter.

The Centrality of Rituals of Respect

Of particular relevance to studies of religiosity in Thailand is Carrithers' argument that the forms of ritual expression and social relationship that emerge from South Asian cosmopolitanism "are hierarchical and manifested through deeply ingrained and highly stylized corporeal and sensual acts of worship, *puja*" (Carrithers 2000, p. 835). Carrithers contends that the key religious attitude in Indian religious systems is not faith in doctrine but rather "respect", which is expressed through embodied ritual practice rather than through statements of belief or doctrinal faith. Carrithers views Indian polytropic religious life as being united across traditions through shared ritual forms of reverence, which are embodied in the practice of raising the joined palms in the gesture called *anjali*. Similarly, in Thailand, the fundamental religious attitude in both popular religion and royal cults is not based on any statement of belief or profession of faith, but rather is an embodied demonstration of respect, *bucha* (from the Sanskrit/Pali *puja*), which is also manifested by bringing the palms of one's hands together at the level of the chest or the head in the gesture of *wai*, which is the Thai term for *anjali*. As Carrithers observes of South Asia,

> *Puja* expresses a relationship, not a concept, just as a handshake may express a relationship. This social character is demonstrated by the absolutely minimal act necessary to *puja*, the *anjali*, the obeisance with joined prayerful hands and the inclination or prostration of the body toward the divine person. (Carrithers 2000, p. 835)

And like the gesture of the *wai* in Thailand, in India the *anjali* is "central to the everyday social recognition of other persons.… Just as one already knows how to greet a stranger with decorum and esteem, so one knows how to greet a strange god" (Carrithers 2000, p. 835). Carrithers emphasizes that the central religious attitude of respect embodied in the ritual gesture of the *anjali* is not a rationalized expression of doctrine: "The thought which goes with the *puja* is not scholastic or finely discriminating, but practical and interactive, arising from deeply felt corporeal attitudes" (p. 836). He adds,

> The gesture of *puja* makes no discrimination, has no theology, and makes no commitment other than respect.… [T]he habitus of *puja* is to a degree inherently indiscriminate, making worship of many holy persons not just possible, but likely. (Carrithers 2000, p. 852)

It cannot be emphasized too strongly that the embodiment of religious respect is also the foundation of the hierarchies of ritual in Thailand, where "stylized corporeal and sensual acts of worship" are also called *puja*, pronounced locally as *bucha*, and are enacted with the gesture of the *anjali*, described by the term *wai*, which in Thai is not a noun but a verb; that is, "to show ritual respect to". Significantly, in Thailand inquiries about one's religious affiliation are not expressed in terms of "What religion do you believe in?" but rather "What religion do you *respect?*" (*nap-theu sasana arai?*). Thailand's diverse religious elements are not united by a single intellectual doctrine. Rather, they cohere through a common attitude of respect—of *nap-theu*, "to show respect to"—which is physically embodied in the *wai*. It is not what one believes, in any epistemological sense, but rather what one respects, honours (*nap-theu*) and worships (*bucha*) in terms of an embodied hierarchical relation expressed through the *wai* that determines religious affiliation and association in Thailand.

In India, Carrithers maintains that "actions speak louder" (Carrithers 2000, p. 850), and he gestures towards the performative dimension of *puja* and *anjali* as bringing into being the religious orientation that they visually and viscerally reflect—"*Puja* does not run on theories: it possesses its own autonomously compelling obviousness as spiritual action, written into the body of worshippers in childhood" (p. 851). I discuss the role of the performative effects of ritual in generating new modalities of enchantment in Chapter Seven. And, as in Thailand, Indian polytropic religiosity is an open system: "[R]elationships to holy persons in India are analogous to friendship … in that one can have many friends … and one can always add new friends" (Carrithers 2000, p. 856).

Thai Repertoire Religiosities

Carrithers' account of Indian polytropy is very similar to Justin McDaniel's (2011, p. 105) account of Thai religious repertoires and David Lyon's account of postmodern religiosities as a "bricolage of beliefs": "The idea of making up your personal bricolage of beliefs, choosing what fits and what does not, appears to be a popular mode of religiosity or spirituality today, especially in North America" (Lyon 2000, p. 18). In the mix of religious and ritual traditions in India, China and Thailand, as well as the late-modern West—all of which are marked by cultural processes of blending and individual strategies of negotiating multiplicity and difference—there are considerable opportunities for personal variation in religious practice.

While there may be practical conformity in terms of rituals of respect across the Thai religious field, in the common embodied attitude of the *wai*, individuals construct their own repertoires and arrive at their own often idiosyncratic understandings and interpretations of their religious lives. As Edoardo Siani (2017) found, even among ritual practitioners there is significant diversity in terms of how rituals are understood and explained. Giuseppe Bolotta (2017) cites Pattana on the importance of altars in Thai religious life and argues that altars in homes and offices, as well as in the ritual spaces of diviners, spirit mediums and other ritual specialists, are sites that express an individual's religious repertoire: "[A]ltars in their symbolic and physical sense bring together deities from diverse backgrounds and origins; the altar is the sacred site where the religious hybridisation of popular beliefs actually takes concrete form" (Pattana 2005a, p. 484, cited in Bolotta 2017). For Bolotta, the altar

> marks sacred boundaries and requires specific patterns of ritualized conduct. Religious icons, statues of deities and other objects are hierarchically arranged on the altars of urban spirit shrines as well as in ... Buddhist temple halls.... The position of worship elements on the altar, therefore, reflects both cosmological and political dimensions. (Bolotta 2017)

Bolotta reports that even some Thai Catholics participate in the rituals associated with new prosperity cults, observing that Bangkok Catholics, "[l]ike most Thais,... revered Rama IX [King Bhumibol] with near religious devotion" (Bolotta 2017). Some of Bolotta's Catholic informants created "household altars at home, where they worshipped icons of Jesus and the saints alongside the other numerous entities that inhabit the Indo-Buddhist pantheon in Thai popular religion ... Chinese and Indian deities, Buddhist monks, and Thai kings, especially Bhumibol (Rama IX) and Chulalongkorn (Rama V)" (Bolotta 2017). And it is not only the general populace that constructs idiosyncratic personal religious repertoires. Members of the Thai economic and political elites, including monarchs, also create their own personal repertoire religiosities. In Chapter Two I detailed how King Mongkut (r. 1851–68) and King Vajiravudh (r. 1910–26) each instituted novel forms of personal ritual around newly invented deities.

Conclusion: Living across Religious Diversity

Modern Thai religious observance is characterized by an expanding number of ritual forms that derive from diverse Buddhist and non-Buddhist sources. These diverse ritual forms are not merged into a single, integrated hybrid but rather remain distinct in a religious totality that is best described as a polyontological amalgam of non-homogeneous expressions. While not merging under a single rationalized cosmology, the amalgam of the Thai religious field nonetheless exhibits structuring patterns and regularities that hold its many units together in a coherent, if often contested, whole. Key structuring processes are the contextual separation of ritual forms and their combination into a pyramidal hierarchy in which Buddhist ritual and teaching and the personage of the Buddha are acknowledged as possessing supreme authority and prestige. At the level of individual religious observance, this multiple, contextualized hierarchy of cosmologies and spiritual figures is negotiated by an embodied ritual practice of respect that does not require or necessarily expect explicit affirmations of belief or faith.

The emphasis on ritual in the Thai amalgam is a pragmatic response to cultural and religious multiplicity: the need to bring diverse, contextually differentiated forms within an overarching frame. It is not possible to synthesize incommensurable doctrines from different religions without a forced, perhaps violent, imposition of some notion of orthodoxy. It is possible, however, to bring incommensurable religions into something approaching a harmonious, if complex and contested, whole if each is accorded a contextually delimited space within the social body where its belief system can operate autonomously. These multiple contexts of incommensurable religious ontologies can be joined if the glue that bonds them abjures doctrine and questions of orthodoxy and is instead based on the imposition of expected common forms of ritual expression.

Ritualism in Thai vernacular religion does not emerge from an anti-intellectual rejection of doctrine or philosophy but rather from the practical need to build religious lives across multiple belief systems that are often epistemologically irreconcilable. *Kala-thesa* contextualization and the emphasis on ritual emerge from Thailand's deep history of ethnic, cultural and religious multiplicity as central elements of a set of strategies to weave together doctrinally discordant systems. The fact that Buddhism is placed in a superior, hierarchically dominant position in this system of ritually bonded contexts demonstrates that forms of power are invoked in forming the Thai religious amalgam. However, this is a form of power that incorporates doctrinal differences without requiring adherence to any single teaching or cosmological schema, instead insisting on conformity to performative norms and common ritual forms of respect across all religious contexts.

In the following three chapters I detail the new cults of wealth that have come to form increasingly prominent elements of the expanding amalgam of the Thai religious field. In Chapter Four I describe some of the most important royal, Chinese, Brahmanical and Buddhist cults of wealth. In Chapter Five I detail how the cults of wealth intersect with two other emergent dimensions of enchantment in the modern Thai religious amalgam, the cult of amulets and professional urban spirit possession cults, while in Chapter Six I describe how the processes outlined in this chapter have contributed to the separate cults of wealth forming into an amalgamated symbolic complex. The formation of this symbolic amalgam in the late 1990s and early 2000s also marked the sociological transition of the cults of wealth from marginal to mainstream expressions of religious life. Together, the following three chapters reveal how the Thai cults of wealth constitute a ritual amalgam that is structured by a dynamically evolving and hierarchically patterned spatial and temporal compartmentalization of its diverse Theravada and Mahayana Buddhist, Brahmanical, Chinese and other elements.

Notes

1. The analytical focus on binary structures that lies at the heart of theories of hybridity is made clear in the following account by Mikhail Bakhtin of hybrid linguistic constructions: "What we are calling a hybrid construction is an utterance that belongs, by its grammatical (syntactic) and compositional markers, to a single speaker, but that actually contains mixed within it two utterances, two speech manners, two 'languages', two semantic and axiological belief systems. We repeat here there is no formal—compositional and syntactic—boundary between these utterances, styles, languages, belief systems; the division of voices and languages takes place within the limits of a single syntactic whole, often within the limits of a single sentence" (Bakhtin 1981, pp. 304–5, cited in Baumann 2017, p. 160).

2. However, this system is only able to fully incorporate foreign elements that are prepared to bow to the Thai framework and accept a subordinate position within it. Christianity, Islam and Judaism cannot be expected to become part of the Thai pantheon so long as they retain their claims to unique and universal revelation. Nonetheless, in their incorporative form of vernacular Buddhism, some Thai Buddhists have included Christian images. Frank Reynolds notes that the iconography and structures at the popular Wat Phai Rong Wua monastery in Suphanburi Province west of Bangkok include a Christian church, a mosque, a Hindu temple and a Chinese Buddhist temple that were constructed by an abbot who saw himself as being truly Thai, truly Chinese as well as truly European (Reynolds 1978, p. 198). The controversial spirit medium Suchat Kosonkittiwong also included Christian imagery at his Hupphasawan temple complex in Ratchaburi Province (see Jackson 1988).

3. "Those Not-so-Magic Charms of *Luang Phor* Koon", *The Nation*, 21 September 1995, p. A5.

4. George Condominas (1976) argued that hierarchicalization has a deep history in Southeast Asian spirit possession cults and predates the arrival of Buddhism.

5. I note here Thongchai Winichakul's observation, expressed in a conversation, that "othering" in Thai culture is rarely a process of negating or destroying ethnic or cultural differences but rather is centrally concerned with establishing hierarchy.

Chapter Four

Thailand's Cults of Wealth: Royal Spirits, Magic Monks, Chinese and Indian Deities

Introduction

Thailand's modern cults of wealth emerge from diverse cultural, historical and religious origins, reflecting the deep history and the more recent intensification of the society's polycultural complexity as detailed in the previous chapter. Each cult has a distinct history, has developed around a particular divine or magical figure, has its own forms of ritual expression and often also possesses its own shrines and sites of worship and pilgrimage. While having precedents in the religious valuing of prosperity in Thai Buddhism, all of the cults of wealth considered in this study are recent religious phenomena that only took their current forms in the later decades of the twentieth century. Four main categories of cults of wealth can be distinguished based on the type of deity or spiritual figure that is the focus of ritual devotion: cults of Thai kings and other royal personalities; cults of Chinese deities; cults of Hindu gods; and cults of magic monks, both living and dead, from Thailand's Theravada tradition. In this chapter I describe the most prominent Thai cults of wealth in each of these four categories, pointing out their recentness, their differences from earlier Thai magical cults, their intimate associations with the market and their popularity among middle class and elite Thais. I begin by detailing older cults of prosperity that formed the religious setting from which new movements have emerged and diverged.

Sections of this chapter draw upon material detailed in Jackson (1999a) and Jackson (1999b).

174

"Buddha Never Said Profit is a Dirty Word":[1]
Precedents for the Modern Cults of Wealth

An emphasis on improving luck and acquiring wealth is not a wholly novel feature of vernacular Thai religiosity. The diverse cults of wealth represent a contemporary, commodified expression of long-standing patterns of Theravada devotionalism. Christine Gray emphasizes that there is "an elective affinity between Buddhism and capitalist expansion" (Gray 1986, p. 100) and that "Theravada Buddhism does not preclude a positive valuation of the pursuit of wealth, nor does it rule out a positive connection between the pursuit of wealth and the pursuit of salvation" (p. 43). Rather, Gray observes,

> [T]his-worldly and supra-worldly activities are inherently complementary, because monastic and economic activity are seen as having a mutually beneficial effect on each other. Success in one domain guarantees success in the other, and vigorous market activity is potentially an expression, albeit indirect, of religious duty. (Gray 1986, p. 41)

Barend Jan Terwiel (2012, p. 13) argues that Theravada Buddhism did not gain acceptance as a focus of the ceremonial life of the Siamese court in the early middle ages merely by virtue of its philosophical doctrine. Rather, he contends, Buddhism was viewed as being efficacious in providing ceremonies to ensure the kingdom's prosperity as well as playing a pivotal political role in providing a legitimating rationale for the monarch's right to govern. Terwiel relates the adoption of Theravada Buddhism by Siam's ruling elites to its perceived ability to draw on supernatural support to promote economic prosperity and to provide a political ideology of rule. In brief, Buddhism has been linked to wealth and power from its adoption in Thai kingdoms, and Justin McDaniel argues that historically in Thailand neither Buddhist monks nor religious laity placed value on *nibbana* or ultimate salvation but rather practised Buddhist rituals for "protection from sickness, poverty, and disaster, as well as order and predictability" (McDaniel 2008, p. 13). McDaniel contends that in the Thai Buddhist tradition, "[o]rder was valued over tradition, safety and wealth over emptiness and asceticism, and ritual technology over meditational achievement" (p. 14).

Furthermore, Thai ritual magic has long been relied upon to promote commercial activities. Small traders in markets display phallic-shaped amulets, *palat khik*, positioned with the head of the phallus facing the customer, alongside their items for sale to promote economic "fertility". Historically, Theravada Buddhist rituals in Thailand have included blessings for prospering and prosperity as part of promoting the well-being of the faithful, with it being customary for Thai monks to end sermons with blessings for "happiness (*khwam-suk*) and prospering/prosperity (*khwam-jaroen*)". It is also customary for Buddhist monks to bless the opening of a new shop or the inauguration of a new commercial undertaking, and there is a long association in Buddhist legend between the power of Buddhist saints to bless material activities and the attainment of wealth. Precedents for the modern prosperity cults can be found in the honouring of the *arahant* or saint Siwali (Pali: Sivali), a contemporary of the Buddha, and in the worship of the goddess Nang Kwak, long regarded as a patron deity of Thai shop owners.

According to a devotional booklet dedicated to Siwali and titled *If You Want Good Luck and Fortune Worship Phra Siwali, The Arahant Who Possessed Great Fortune* (P. Suwan 1996), Buddhist legend relates that this early member of the sangha remained in his mother's womb for seven years, seven months and seven days before being born, a numerologically auspicious miracle that conferred him with "great fortune", *mahalap*. The term "fortune", *lap* (from Pali: *labh*), has multiple connotations in Thai, denoting the good fortune to achieve spiritual enlightenment as well as material prosperity. While a relatively minor figure in Thai Buddhism, images of Siwali, who is represented as a wandering ascetic monk (*phra thudong*) carrying a furled parasol over his shoulder, are not uncommon in monasteries, and statuettes of this Theravada saint of fortune are sold in all Thai amulet markets.

Perhaps the most popular Thai prosperity cult before the 1990s was focussed on the figure of Nang Kwak, "the beckoning lady", the popular name given to Suphawadi (Pali: Subhavadi), a female figure from Buddhist legend. According to a devotional booklet (Wiphuthayokha 1997?) dedicated to Nang Kwak, at the time of the Buddha, a Brahmin family that made its living from trade had a beautiful daughter named Suphawadi. As the family travelled the North Indian countryside, selling goods from their wagon, they chanced to meet the *arahant* Kassapa, and after listening to his sermon they became followers of the Lord Buddha. As the family took leave of the saint, he blessed their young daughter, saying, "May your wishes be fulfilled and may you progress and prosper with wealth, silver and gold from your trading enterprise." Sometime later the family met another *arahant*, Siwali, the saint of fortune detailed above. Siwali gave Suphawadi the same blessing that had been conferred by Kassapa. From that time, the family's business flourished and they became extremely wealthy, attributing their good fortune to the blessings of the two *arahants*. Images of Suphawadi or Nang Kwak represent her as a smiling, dark-eyed, Indian-looking young woman sitting in a kneeling position with her right hand raised in a beckoning gesture. The action of beckoning with the hand is called *kwak* in Thai and Nang Kwak literally means "the beckoning lady". Shop owners believe that her image beckons customers and improves business. Before the rise of the late twentieth-century prosperity movements, an image of Nang Kwak could be found installed on an altar attached to the wall of almost every small to medium-sized store and restaurant in Thailand. In the 1990s, Nang Kwak came to share her space on shop altars with images of King Chulalongkorn, the Chinese bodhisattva Kuan Im, Hindu deities and diverse prosperity monks detailed in the rest of this chapter.

It also needs to be noted that the religion of the Southern Chinese who migrated to Thailand in large numbers in the nineteenth and early twentieth centuries, and whose descendants now make up a considerable proportion of Thailand's middle classes and commercial and business elites, also included a significant emphasis on "gods of

IMAGE 9. Nang Kwak *Pha Yan*
A magically inscribed *pha yan* (*yantra* cloth) with an image of Nang Kwak, "The Beckoning Lady", a spirit who is at the centre of one of the oldest Thai cults of wealth. With her right hand raised in a beckoning gesture, her image is found in stores across Thailand, where she is believed to promote business and beckon customers into the store. (Source: Wat Phra Mongkhon Bophit, Ayutthaya, 2003. From the author's collection.)

wealth" (Alexeiev 1928). These various premodern Theravada and Chinese religions of wealth were antecedents of the 1990s prosperity cults. The distinctiveness of the newer cults lies not so much in their orientation towards wealth and prosperity per se but in their social prominence and political relevance. A key question considered in later chapters is what transformed devotion to commercially gained wealth from a minor strand to a dominant mode of religious expression in Thailand in the later decades of the twentieth century.

From Protection to Prosperity: Changing Emphases in Thai Magical Ritual

Another distinguishing feature of the new cults of wealth is that they reflect a shift in the emphasis of Thai magical ritual from securing protection to promoting prosperity. Amulets and other ritual objects associated with the cults of wealth, and the *keji ajan* or magic monks who are believed to have the spiritual authority to sacralize and magically empower (*pluk sek*) them, were originally regarded as having apotropaic or protective powers to ward off evil and prevent harm. However, as the Thai economy expanded rapidly in the latter decades of the twentieth century, these objects and ritual specialists also came to be regarded as having the capacity to enhance luck and increase opportunities for success in careers and business. The double impact of processes of mediatization and commodification emphasized in this study and addressed further in Chapter Seven is especially evident in the contemporary form of the cult of amulets in Thailand, first de-scribed in detail by Stanley Tambiah (1984). Reflecting on Tambiah's much-cited study, Pattana Kitiarsa notes,

> Amulets have evolved in meaning from symbols of traditional protective power to conduits of supernatural influence on economic success. This significant shift reveals the power of print and broadcast media that has accelerated the 'spatial and social mobility' of religious messages to wider audiences. (Pattana 2012, p. 101)

The relation of the cult of amulets to the cults of wealth is detailed in Chapter Five. Justin McDaniel identifies the acquisition of potency in Thai magical ritual as a contextual manifestation of the cultural value of "abundance" (*udom sombun*) (McDaniel 2011, p. 18). Drawing on McDaniel's account, Benjamin Baumann notes,

> The cultural value of abundance, which implies that mystic potency can be accumulated through the acquisition of animated objects

and their adding to already existing configurations, manifests most visibly on public and private spirit shrines and house altars throughout the country. (Baumann 2017, p. 310)

Erick White is of the view that the fact that the ritual arts of efficacy in Thailand utilize "idioms of prosperity, longevity, security, harmony, plenitude, and recovery" (White 2016, p. 8) predisposes them to having a greater role in a market economy centred on wealth creation. Baumann also observes that the enhancement of security and prosperity and the acquisition of what he terms "mystic capital" (Baumann 2017, p. 309) and mystic potency are central to Thai vernacular religion, with an emphasis on multiplication, fecundity and increase being the objective of ritual: "The acquisition of mystic potency ... implies an increase in prosperity, security and well-being in 'Thai religion'", with security and prosperity being "tangible manifestations of one's mystic potency" (p. 311).

These related ideas—of protection from harm leading to success, prosperity and wealth—are embodied in the dual royal figures of King Chulalongkorn and King Bhumibol, who are at the centre of cults of wealth related to the monarchy. The images of these two kings are often paired in ritual and religious settings as dual icons of the cult of the monarchy. In these settings King Chulalongkorn is ascribed the apotropaic role of having saved Siam from colonialism and ensured national independence and sovereignty in the nineteenth century, while King Bhumibol is linked with progress, prosperity and wealth in the latter twentieth and early twenty-first centuries. King Chulalongkorn is represented as having secured the foundation of modern national sovereignty in the nineteenth century, which in turn enabled King Bhumibol to rule over an era in which capitalist Thailand could prosper in the modern world economy.

In the intersecting symbolic complex of the cults of wealth detailed in Chapter Six there is often an oscillation and interplay between images and discourses of protection and prosperity, victory and wealth, and success and progress. These dual sets of symbolisms reflect the fact that this cultic complex is an integral cultural constituent of Thailand's contemporary political economy, which needs to be seen as a single domain. Army and police followers of *keji ajan* magic monks may emphasize the protective apotropaic dimensions of the sacral power of amulets, while middle-class professionals and businesspeople may emphasize the power of amulets to engender success, prosperity and wealth. However, just as the army, police and business interests continually interrelate in Thai political economy, so too these two dimensions are part and parcel of the same religio-symbolic field, like the two faces of the coin-shaped amulets described further in the next chapter.

The transition from protection to prosperity as the focus of much Thai magical ritual is exemplified in the history of the cult of ritually empowered amulets. Chalong Soontravanich (2013) argues that the desire for protection from crime and violence in the turbulent years after the end of World War II and during the insurgencies and re-gional conflicts of the Cold War era were significant influences on the rise in the popularity of Buddhist amulets. Senior policemen and law enforcement officers, such as the legendary policeman *Khun* Phantharakratchadet (1899–2006), whose biography has been detailed by Craig Reynolds (2019) and who initiated the Jatukham-Ramathep variety of amulets described in Chapter Five, popularized the minted form of amulets as protective talismans.[2] Thai soldiers fighting com-munist insurgencies within the country and as allies of America in the Indochina wars were also key players in the rise of the modern cult of amulets. Gray reports that Praphat Charusathien, commander-in-chief of the Thai Army from 1964 to 1973, thought amulets were important because they protected soldiers in battle:

'Soldiers have a popular custom of having amulets to boost morale. Amulets protect them ("strengthen the heart")', he said. 'Soldiers respect different monks and amulets because they are good luck and auspicious.' (Gray 1986, p. 616)

As the Thai economy grew rapidly from the early 1980s, amulets evolved from being protective talismans for policemen fighting bandits and soldiers fighting communists to being seen as magically productive agents that increase wealth and prosperity.

Prosperity Cults of Thai Royal Figures

The Cult of Sadet Phor Ror. 5: *Worshipping the Spirit of King Chulalongkorn and the Thai Monarchy*

The cult of the spirit of King Chulalongkorn (r. 1868–1910) or King Rama V is among the most ubiquitous of Thailand's prosperity cults. The worship of King Chulalongkorn appears to have begun in the 1960s,[3] and at the height of the economic boom decade in the 1990s its most important ritual site was the equestrian statue of the king that stands in the middle of the Royal Plaza in front of the Anantasamakhom Throne Hall in Bangkok. Among followers of this cult, the spirit of King Chulalongkorn is variously called *Sadet Phor R. 5* ("Royal Father of the Fifth Reign") or more simply *Sadet Phor* ("Royal Father") or *R. 5* (*ror. ha*), "The Fifth R." This latter expression is an abbreviation of the official title "The Fifth Reign (*ratchakan*) [of the Chakri Dynasty]" by which this king is often known in Thai. In devotional literature and in official discourses King Chulalongkorn is also often called *Phra Piyamaharat*, "The Dearly Beloved Great King", and the annual public holiday in remembrance of his death on 23 October 1910 is called "The Day of the Dearly Beloved Great King" (*wan piyamaharat*). This prosperity movement draws on Brahmanical ideas of the *deva-raja* or "god-king", and Nidhi Eeoseewong summarizes the beliefs of followers of this movement as follows:

> After King Chulalongkorn passed away, he was reborn (*sathit*) in a spiritual realm (*phop*) as a divine being (*thep*), and because of his great mercy (*metta*) for all human beings he disseminates his charismatic power (*phra barami*) to aid and look after those who have faith in him. He has manifested miracles (*patihan*) on many occasions, which are confirmations of this faith. (Nidhi 1993, p. 11)

Irene Stengs also notes that for followers of the cult of King Chulalongkorn this king "is believed to have been reborn in one of the heavenly abodes as a divine being, a guardian angel (*thep, thewada* or *deva*)" (Stengs 2009, p. 84).

During the economic boom years in the mid-1990s, tens of thousands of the faithful flocked to the equestrian statue of the king in the Royal Plaza in Bangkok each Tuesday and Thursday evening, the days of the week associated with King Chulalongkorn's birthday and "teacher's day", respectively, in Thai astrology. This caused traffic jams and forced the Bangkok Metropolitan Administration to impose no-parking and no-hawking restrictions in the immediate vicinity of the statue. Followers sat on mats laid out on the asphalt around the statue and set up foldaway tables as temporary altars on which they displayed devotional offerings believed to have been loved by the king in life: French cognac, Cuban cigars, fruit and pink roses. Incense and candles were also lit, and garlands of marigold flowers were offered to the statue, being ritually placed on the pedestal and then returned to the devotees to be taken home as spiritually empowered mementoes. A specially composed Pali incantation or *khatha* seeking King Chulalongkorn's blessing was chanted by followers praying for a boon while kneeling before the statue. A Thai classical dance troupe and orchestra were often on hand, ready to be hired to perform by those who wished to entertain the spirit of the monarch in ritual fulfilment of a boon that had been granted.

While the equestrian statue of King Chulalongkorn in Bangkok provided a geographical focus of the movement in the 1990s and early 2000s, the image of the king is now found throughout Thailand. Large numbers of jewellery shops in the country as well as many gift stores sell amulets with Rama V's image, which are worn as lockets or hung from motor vehicle rear-view mirrors. Altars or *hing bucha* ("shelf for worship") with one or more images of King Chulalongkorn are found in many small and medium-sized shops across the country as well as in department stores. It is also common to find images of King Chulalongkorn, often together with images of the late King Bhumibol, near the most important Buddha image in Thai monasteries; that is, within the heart of the country's most sacred Buddhist spaces.

Erick White notes that King Chulalongkorn is now regarded "as a *bodhisattva* and a guardian deity of the Thai nation and its citizens" (White 2014, p. 6). Jean and John Comaroff observe that "appeals to the occult in pursuit of the secrets of capital generally rely on local cultural technologies: on vernacular modes of divination or oracular consultation" (Comaroff and Comaroff 2000, p. 317). Thailand's royalist prosperity cult can be seen as one such local cultural technology deployed in pursuit of the secrets of capital. In Thailand the monarchy plays a similar symbolic role to that of anti-colonialist resistance heroes in formerly colonized Southeast Asian countries. The saintly aura that surrounds the memory of martyred independence heroes like José Rizal in the Philippines accrues to the monarchy in Thailand; in particular, the divinized image of King Chulalongkorn. In nationalist historiography, Chulalongkorn is credited with having preserved Siam's independence in the face of French and British imperialism and having set the country on a self-determined course to modernity and economic development. Chulalongkorn's two grand tours of Europe in 1897 and 1907, when he met kings, queens, prime ministers and presidents, symbolized independent Siam's claim to be seen as an equal of colonial-era European states.

Devotees believe this king's spirit can intercede to improve sales, draw in customers and promote wealth. In 1997, *The Nation* columnists writing under the pseudonym Chang Noi observed,

[T]he image of Chulalongkorn lives on in the present day. It has become the focus of a form of national cult.... The image [of the king] turns up on racks of posters between Bon Jovi and Madonna; on shrines at shops, restaurants, go-go bars and brothels; among the ranks of Hindu and Chinese deities called upon to provide good fortune; and partnered with images of monks like *Luang Phor* Khoon who also offer comforting promises of good fortune. For the mass of people ... [King Chulalongkorn is] part of superstitious belief in the power of fate and fortune.... The idea that development would reduce the role of superstition now belongs to the past. We know instead that development simply turns superstitious practice into a commercial opportunity.[4]

In his study of the cult of *Sadet Phor Ror. 5*, Nidhi observes that amulets and images of King Chulalongkorn are associated with "improving commerce" and "making you loved and trusted by people who meet you, so you can conduct your business undertakings successfully" (Nidhi 1993, p. 31). He believes the rapid rise in the popularity of the movement in the early 1990s reflected the needs of an expanding commercial middle class whose business interests and lifestyles were not addressed by existing religious forms. Nidhi also emphasizes the novelty of the cult of *Sadet Phor Ror. 5* and describes the King Chulalongkorn prosperity movement as being different from previous personality-based cults in Thailand in that it was not originally associated with rituals that sought supernatural assistance in assuring invulnerability (*khong kraphan*), seeking love potions (*ya sane*) or acquiring sudden wealth by winning the lottery. Rather, he observes that the aim of followers of this cult is to "seek an increase in wealth from one's own business" (p. 32). But while amulets and images of King Chulalongkorn may not originally have been associated with the more traditional Thai supernatural interests that Nidhi lists, my observations on visits to shrines in the mid to late 1990s suggest that these ritual objects had become incorporated within established patterns of Thai supernaturalism.

Stengs locates the King Chulalongkorn cult as lying at the intersection of modern forms of Buddhist kingship in Thailand, with "divine kingship, Buddhist ritual, spirit cults and potent objects" (Stengs 2009, p. 4) emerging from mass media and consumerism. Like Nidhi, Stengs emphasizes that, "[a]lthough drawing on tradition, the King Chulalongkorn cult is first of all a specific, contemporary phenomenon of the late twentieth century" (p. 4). She also contends that the King Chulalongkorn cult needs to be understood "in the context of the general promotion of the Thai monarchy, and of King Bhumibol in particular. In fact, the ever more exalted expectations of kingship in the person of King Bhumibol formed the core of the King Chulalongkorn cult" (p. ix). Stengs also contends that the rise of cults around the figures of King Chulalongkorn and King Bhumibol "for a large part reflects increasing individual preoccupations with acquiring and consolidating wealth" (p. 24).

IMAGE 10. King Chulalongkorn and King Bhumibol New Year Card
A 1997 New Year greeting card combining images of King Chulalongkorn (top), King Bhumibol (bottom) and *Krommaluang* (Prince) Chumphon, a son of King Chulalongkorn revered as the founder of the Thai navy and also the focus of a spirit cult. This image of King Bhumibol with two other royal figures whose spirits are regarded as being at the centre of distinct cults of wealth reflects the way in which the contemporary monarchy is symbolically associated with new forms of religious enchantment.

While the worship of the spirit of King Chulalongkorn is arguably the most widespread and elaborated royal prosperity cult, other kings and royal figures are also the focus of cults of the monarchy. Significant cults also exist for the Ayutthaya-period King Naresuan (r. 1590–1602), revered for his campaigns to free Ayutthaya from Burmese control; King Taksin (r. 1767–82), who re-established the Siamese state after the Burmese destruction of the old capital of Ayutthaya; and Abhakara Kiartivongse (1880–1923), known among devotees by his royal title of *Krommaluang* Chumphon, a son of King Chulalongkorn regarded as the founder of the modern Thai navy as well as an adept in *saiyasat* magical lore and healing traditions.

Prosperity Cults of Chinese Deities

The Prosperity Cult of Jao Mae *Kuan Im (Guan Yin)*

Kuan Im is the Thai rendering of Guan Yin, the name given by the Chinese to a female form of the Mahayana Buddhist bodhisattva Avalokites'vara (Thai: Awalokitesuan), whose Sanskrit name Nidhi Eeoseewong (1994) glosses as "the lord who looks down (upon us with mercy)". In Mahayana Buddhism, Avalokites'vara is considered to be the bodhisattva of compassion, and in China this saint-god is believed to be a blessed being who takes a female form and assuages the suffering of the faithful. In China, Kuan Im is also the focus of a fertility cult and her assistance is sought by women seeking to fall pregnant. In Thailand, Kuan Im is commonly given the honorific title *Jao Mae* ("Lord Mother") and is also called the "Goddess Dressed in White" (*thephi nai chut khao*) and "The Blessed Mother of Mercy" (*phrae mae metta*). Nidhi (1994, p. 79) regards the worship of Kuan Im to have similar commercial objectives to the cult of King Chulalongkorn, with followers of both devotional movements seeking good luck, fortune and wealth (*chok, lap, khwam-mang-khang*). He states that "[i]n Thailand Kuan Im is somewhat akin to a goddess of commerce" (Nidhi 1994, p. 86), which reflects her long-standing associations with fertility, wealth and prosperity in Chinese religious practice. In Thailand this female avatar of the bodhisattva Avalokites'vara is also closely linked to the Toaist Nine Emperor Gods Festival. This festival is celebrated during the first nine days of the ninth month of the Chinese lunar calendar and is popularly called the Chinese Vegetarian Festival (*thetsakan kin je*; see Cohen 2001, 2008).

The popularity of Kuan Im in Thailand is reflected in the widespread availability of amulets and other products bearing her image as well as a large volume of often anonymous devotional literature

IMAGE 11. Kuan Im *Pha Yan*
A magically inscribed *pha yan* (*yantra* cloth) with an image of *Jao Mae* (Lord Mother) Kuan Im. This image reflects the incorporation of the Chinese Mahayana Buddhist bodhisattva within the symbolisms of Thai magical ritual. Thai text to the lower left of the image of Kuan Im reads "Worship and your business will be good", while the Chinese characters on the lower right of the image read "Travel safely". The latter is an inscription commonly found in Chinese temples, which suggests this ritual item may have been marketed to Chinese tourists in Thailand. (Source: Wat Phra Mongkhon Bophit, Ayutthaya, 2003. From the author's collection.)

(e.g., *Bot-suat bucha jao mae Kuan Im* [1997?]; *Chiwa-prawat lae phra khatha jao mae Kuan Im phothisat* [1997?]; Klum Bua Hima [pseud.] 1993). Nidhi (1994, p. 80) notes that images of Kuan Im are now often found on shop altars beneath those of King Chulalongkorn or members of the royal family such as the late King Bhumibol. Unlike the King Chulalongkorn prosperity movement, the worship of Kuan Im in Thailand has no single shrine or geographical focus, with numerous sacred sites devoted to her. These sites are called *samnak* or *tamnak*, "temples" or "palaces", if they have resident spiritual specialists such as spirit mediums of the deity and *san jao* or *sala*, "abodes of the lord" or "shrines", if they house an image of the goddess. Kuan Im temples are located separately from Theravada Buddhist monasteries. But since the 1990s it has become increasingly common for shrines with her image to be found within the grounds of Thai monasteries. Nidhi notes that in the first half of the 1990s the worship of both King Chulalongkorn and Kuan Im began to be incorporated within Theravada Buddhism:

> [The King Chulalongkorn and Kuan Im movements] ... have arisen and developed outside the monastery [i.e., outside of Buddhism] and also tend to be followed outside the monastery. Nevertheless, even though the cults of King Chulalongkorn and *Jao Mae* Kuan Im arose outside the monastery, they have very quickly spread extensively within the monastery, which makes these two ... cults so exceptionally interesting. (Nidhi 1994, p. 106)

The integration of the worship of Kuan Im into state and royal-sponsored Theravada Buddhism is also shown by the installation of a statue of this bodhisattva at Wat Bowornniwet, the country's most important royal monastery, where male members of the royal family traditionally spend their period as an ordained monk. A metre-high Chang dynasty bronze image of Kuan Im was donated to this royal monastery in the second half of the 1990s by a wealthy Sino-Thai patron, and in January 1998 Wat Bowornniwet placed half-page colour advertisements in the Thai language press to promote the sale of gold, silver and alloy replica images of the statue to raise money to build a *sala* or shrine to house the new image within the monastery. In this advertisement Kuan Im was referred to by her more formal Mahayana title of *Phra* Awalokitesuan (Sanskrit: Avalokites'vara), with the name Kuan Im placed in parentheses afterward.[5]

The Cult of Kuan Im and the Integration of the Sino-Thai

The rise of the worship of Kuan Im as a goddess of wealth and commerce among ethnic Thais and her integration into Theravada

Buddhism reflect an increasing openness to appropriating Chinese religious elements in Thai popular religion. This incorporation of Kuan Im into Thai religion also reflects an invigorated self-confidence on the part of the Sino-Thai communities and their pride in their Chinese cultural heritage. Kevin Hewison (1993), Kasian Tejapira (1997), Gary Hamilton and Tony Waters (1997), and Craig Reynolds (1998), among others, have written of the renewed cultural confidence of Thailand's Chinese and their central role in redefining what it meant to be Thai in the "era of globalisation" (*yuk lokaphiwat*).

Christine Gray uses the term "Sinocisation" to denote "the mechanism, often religious, through which successive generations of Chinese immigrants are integrated into the [Thai] polity" (Gray 1986, p. 128). Gray here refers to a period in the earlier decades of the twentieth century when the Chinese in Thailand were minoritized by restrictive policies and when they were encouraged, and at times legally required, to become more Thai. Gray also traces the processes by which increasing numbers of elite and middle-class Chinese have become enfranchised as Thai citizens by participating in Buddhist ritual:

> Participation in Theravada Buddhist merit-making ceremonies was and remains a passport from 'Chinese' to 'Siamese' identities and occupations: from that of trader to official. This dynamic accounts for much of the vitality of Theravada Buddhism: Buddhist merit-making rituals flourished as a mechanism for the mediation of 'ethnic' occupational categories. (Gray 1986, p. 191)

Gray thus describes the adoption of Theravada beliefs and rituals by Sino-Thais as a ticket to achieving upward social mobility in the Thai social order. Participation in Thai religious and ritual life as a means of claiming and demonstrating loyalty to the Thai nation is especially clear in the career of the controversial Sino-Thai spirit medium Suchat Kosonkittiwong, who founded the millenarian Pusawan and Hupphasawan movements in the 1970s (see Jackson 1988). Suchat's teachings, which drew on Buddhist figures from legends and Thai cultural history, can be seen as having been influenced by his perception of his inferior social and political position in Thailand because of his ethnic Chinese background. Suchat claimed,

> One's nationality is simply something determined by circumstances. Even though I am only a Chinaman's son I still dare to say that I love Thailand. I love Thailand more than many Thais who are now selling out their nation.... Wasn't it the son of a Chinaman, *Phra Jao* Taksin Maharaja, who reclaimed our independence? (Anan 1981, p. 143.)

Taksin, who is widely believed to have had Chinese parentage, was an Ayutthayan general who defeated the invading Burmese after the destruction of the former capital of Ayutthaya in 1767 and subsequently established a new Thai capital at Thonburi, opposite modern Bangkok. Hailing from a poor background, Suchat claimed a position in Thai society by channelling the spirits of famed Buddhist monks and a Hindu-Buddhist deity called Brahma-Chinnapanjorn. He also effected a Sino-Thai religious accommodation by incorporating the worship of Kuan Im among the spirits of the Theravada figures he channelled.

Since the 1980s, however, we have seen the reverse process: not ethnic Chinese adopting Thai ways but rather ethnic Thais participating in and adopting Chinese religious ritual practices. This process can be regarded as a progressive Sinification of the field of Thai popular religion in which ethnic Thais have adopted Chinese rituals to enhance their own status and wealth. Since the 1990s, the once strongly defined Thai-Chinese ethnic divide has become blurred to such an extent that Thais with no Chinese heritage now appropriate Chinese ritual to enhance their status within the hierarchical Thai social order in which wealthy Chinese have become what Gray calls a "new merchant nobility" (Gray 1986, p. 29).

Chinese influences on Thai Buddhism are far from new, with Chinese architectural elements being found in several urban monasteries from the early Bangkok period, such as Wat Suthat. Never before has a Chinese Mahayana deity, however, played such a prominent role in Thai religious life or inhabited the ritual space of Thai monasteries. It is now not uncommon for ethnic Thais from diverse backgrounds to claim a personal relationship with Kuan Im, to wear amulets of her image and to refrain from eating beef as expressions of their piety.

The rise of the cult of Kuan Im as a goddess of commerce and wealth is a cultural indicator of the further social and political integration of Thailand's ethnic Chinese population into narratives of "Thainess". The 1990s saw a more complete enmeshment of the Sino-Thai population into national political, cultural and religious life and the blurring of the Thai/Chinese distinction in the development of the hybrid social form that Nidhi calls *jek* and which Kasian calls *luk-jin* or urban Thai culture.[6] Nidhi notes a devotional publication listing the followers of a large Kuan Im shrine in Bangkok, which includes the names of many senior Thai civil servants and serving military officers as well as Sino-Thai businesspeople, commenting that, in a situation such as this being '*jek*' is becoming a social condition unrelated to ethnicity.... [I]t is becoming somewhat meaningless to talk of '*jek*' or 'Chinese' (*cheua jin*) in contemporary Thai society because it is not possible to say precisely where the identifying characteristics (*ekkalak*) of this group differ from that of Thais. Hence, one may say that the cult of Kuan Im is widespread amongst urban 'Thais'. (Nidhi 1994, p. 80)

As Gray observes,

[I]n studying the relationship between economy and religion in Thailand, one is studying 'ethnic' relations: the reciprocal impact of waves of Chinese immigrants on a [Thai] religious tradition whose roots are South Asian. Most important, one is studying the history of the constantly shifting representation of 'Thai' versus 'Chinese' people ... and ... the history of ritual, of control over the media of symbolic domination (Bourdieu 1977). (Gray 1986, p. 63)

What is significant in the emergence of the worship of Kuan Im as a Sino-Thai or *jek/luk-jin* urban synthesis is that the appropriation of Chinese religious culture by the Thai has been just as important as the appropriation of Thai culture by immigrant Chinese. The contemporary religious prominence of Kuan Im emerges from a parallel Sinicization of the Thai as well as a Siamization of the country's ethnic Chinese communities.

The appropriation of Chinese religious culture extends beyond the incorporation of the worship of Kuan Im into Theravada devotions. Ritual products associated with many of the prosperity movements, including those of King Chulalongkorn and prosperity monks such as *Luang Phor* Khoon, also reflect a strong Chinese aesthetic, with a preponderance of the auspicious colour red and a common preference for Chinese-style Thai lettering (See Chapter Six).

This cultural and religious openness to appropriating Chinese religiosity also suggests that the Sino-Thai population has been sufficiently "Siamised" that their economic success and prosperity during the economic boom years was able to be read as a Thai national success story, and not just the success of one ethnic sector of the population. The Sino-Thai population has long dominated the Thai economy (see Krirkkiat and Yoshihara 1983; Akira 1996) and was a dominant local force in the country's economic boom (see Pasuk and Baker 1995). However, in a context where *jek/luk-jin* was equated with urban Thai, then *jek/luk-jin* economic success was read as Thai success, and *jek/luk-jin* culture became Thai culture, and a prestigious and admired part of Thai middle-class urban culture at that. It was for this reason that large numbers of ethnic Thais have had few qualms about incorporating Chinese elements into their devotional practice since the 1990s.

The integration of Kuan Im into Theravada religiosity has also been facilitated by an indigenization of this Chinese figure. The worship of the Mahayana bodhisattva has been resignified within Thai religious expectations in the process of her appropriation. Nidhi (1994) observes that Kuan Im was first worshipped in Thailand as a goddess

IMAGE 12. *Luang Phor* **Khoon Souvenir Fan**
A souvenir hand-held fan featuring a design that combines a photo of *Luang Phor* Khoon (Reverend Father Multiply) squatting with jewellery and wads of Thai banknotes along with images of Chinese deities and religious figures, sold from his monastery Wat Ban Rai. This souvenir item demonstrates the amalgamation of Chinese Mahayana Buddhist and Taoist religiosity with Theravada Buddhism in the cults of wealth. The Chinese figures are the bodhisattva Kuan Im (top right); a Chinese Buddha image called "Multimillionaire Tycoon" (top left); the eight Taoist immortals (left and right); and the three Chinese deities of fortune, prosperity and longevity (bottom). The Thai text reads: "Fan in gold; multiply wealth a hundred thousand million times; fan away pain, suffering, illness, danger and evil." The Chinese character on the left means "good fortune, happiness, luck", while the character on the right means "safety, peace". These are common inscriptions in Chinese temples. (From the author's collection.)

of commerce, and her cult has been incorporated in a hybrid form within the context of what he describes as pre-existing Thai "spirit religion" (*sasana phi*) and Theravada belief. Nidhi (1994, p. 85) details the varieties of mixing of Thai and Chinese elements in Thai Kuan Im temples in terms of the types of "worldly happiness" (*lokiya suk*) that followers hope to be granted by the goddess. These include the wish to improve business, obtain wealth and fortune (*chok lap*), find a good marriage partner, have peace and happiness in one's life, have a long life, be blessed by having mercy (*metta*) bestowed upon oneself, be free from enemies, and to have sons. In being acculturated within a Thai religious frame, Nidhi contends that Kuan Im has also come to be linked with more typically Thai interests such as finding lucky lottery numbers and solving relationship problems. In her role as a granter of boons, this Siamized Kuan Im is often given a title accorded to other beneficent feminine beings within the Thai pantheon, *jao mae* or "Lord Mother", while in her role as an expounder of ethics to promote commerce she is given the title *phra mae*, "Reverend Mother". In summary, Nidhi contends that Kuan Im has been incorporated within Thai popular religion in a hybridized form, with many of the visibly Chinese elements of contemporary Thai religion being a mere clothing that dress persistent patterns of Thai supernatural beliefs. According to Nidhi, "[e]ven though the external form of the cult is Chinese, many of the Kuan Im temples, that is, at the usual type of spirit medium shrines, some mediums channel Kuan Im and other [non-Chinese] deities gods (*thep*) at the same time" (Nidhi 1994, p. 90). Nidhi adds that "Kuan Im has become just another god or spirit (*phi*) within the Thai system of belief, which is able to increase the number of spirits and gods indefinitely" (p. 90).

Nidhi (1994) says that in the mid-1990s the cults of King Chulalongkorn and Kuan Im reinforced each other, with the King Chulalongkorn cult responding to the political needs of the urban middle class while the Kuan Im cult responded to the cultural needs of this group. As will be discussed in Chapter Six, as the Thai economic boom years continued into the 1990s, there was increasing blending of the different cults of wealth into a symbolic complex or amalgam of prosperity movements. Both the King Chulalongkorn and Kuan Im cults reflected the increasing role and importance of the middle class in Thailand. Significantly, neither cult emerges from the official Buddhist religion, although, as Nidhi (1994, p. 79) predicted, both cults would ultimately be incorporated within official (*thang-kan*) Thai religion, which indeed came to pass by the turn of the new century.

The boom years accelerated the dissolution of the divide between the Thai and Chinese ethnic-cultural groups. Thailand's prosperity in this period was founded upon social stability that, to a significant extent, emerged from the cultural and religious integration of the Thai and the Chinese under the uniting signifier of the market. At a broader level, the symbolic mixing and religious convergence of the complex of prosperity movements detailed in this book reflects the story of the economic, social and political integration of state-aligned power elites, urban professionals, Sino-Thai business groups and the rural and urban working classes into a new social formation under the integrating socio-economic structure of market capitalism.

Prosperity Cults of Hindu Deities

Hindu deities such as Brahma, Ganesh and Rahu have also become the focus of prosperity movements and spirit medium cults in Thailand in recent decades. Indeed, Hindu deities, generally called *thep* (from the Sanskrit *deva*), are replacing Thai spirits (*phi*) in many urban spirit medium cults. Shigeharu Tanabe notes that in spirit mediumship in Northern Thailand,

> [t]he tutelary spirit possessing a spirit medium is almost invariably a powerful male deity, often derived from the past mysterious power-holders featured in Khon Müang [Northern Thai] mythologies and folktales…. Yet this traditional pattern of tutelary spirits has been gradually undermined by Bangkok-based deities since around the 1970s; these include Hindu gods like Siva, Narai [Vishnu], Phra Phrom (*Cao Phò* Erawan). (Tanabe 2002, p. 57)

As noted previously, the expansion of Thai magical religiosity is not simply a re-incitement of "traditional" forms; it is the emergence of new configurations of magical belief and ritual that are often replacing older varieties of religious expression. The intimate associations between the cults of wealth and new forms of urban professional spirit mediumship are discussed in the next chapter.

Hindu deities have been incorporated into the Buddhist pantheon as guardians of the Buddha's *dhamma*. Pattana Kitiarsa notes that in popular belief the spirits of revered Thai kings, such as King Chulalongkorn, are often linked closely with Hindu gods, especially Vishnu. He cites one interviewee, a seventy-one-year-old medium for King Chulalongkorn's spirit from Khorat in Northeast Thailand, as stating that "[a]ll Thai kings are descended from Vishnu. Rama V [King Chulalongkorn] was reborn as a god in heaven after his death. He is a *thep*, not a mere spirit (*phi*). *Thep* also follow Buddha's teachings;

I can tell this from the fact that the reigning king has to pay homage to a Buddhist monk" (Pattana 2012, p. 28).

The growing popularity of the worship of Hindu deities and their association with cults of wealth is reflected in the significant number of shrines for these gods in the upmarket Ratchaprasong shopping district of downtown Bangkok. The first shrine to a Hindu deity established in this area was the famous Erawan Shrine to Brahma built in 1956 to protect the Erawan Hotel, now the Grand Hyatt Erawan Hotel. Serhat Ünaldi reports that complications faced in the construction of the Erawan Hotel caused suspicions about malevolent supernatural influences:

> Advice was sought from Rear Admiral Luang Suwicharnpat, who, apart from being a doctor in the Navy with a pronounced interest in alternative medicine and spiritual healing, practiced meditation and astrology. He diagnosed that the date for the laying of the hotel's foundation stone had been inauspicious and advised the board of directors to build a shrine for Brahma in front of the hotel to protect it from evil spirits. Brahma, the Hindu god of creation, was thought to embody the four virtues of the Buddhist *dhammic* principles. In due course, the Fine Arts Department molded a four-faced statue of Brahma out of plaster covered with gold leaves. The Erawan Shrine was opened, together with the hotel, on 9 November 1956. It was the first of many spiritual sites in the Ratchaprasong area. (Ünaldi 2016, p. 129)

Ünaldi observes that the deity Brahma at the Erawan Shrine has become so popular that is has evolved into an unofficial guardian spirit of the city, becoming, "in effect, the shrine of Bangkok, overshadowing the *lak müang* [city pillar] shrine in the old royal section of the city (Keyes 2006, 4)" (Ünaldi 2016, p. 188). Ünaldi also notes that according to data compiled by the Than Thao Mahaphrom Foundation, which administers the Erawan Shrine, about 1.2 million people visit the shrine each year: "The foundation itself owes its existence to the popularity of the shrine. Because donations from believers rapidly exceeded the amount needed for its maintenance, the foundation was established in 1969 to look after the surplus money and use it for charitable purposes" (Ünaldi 2016, p. 187).

The many shrines to Hindu deities in the Ratchaprasong area are now promoted in tourist literature. Ünaldi notes that the sacred Hindu shrines that have sprung up around the Ratchaprasong intersection have been commissioned by business leaders (Ünaldi 2016, p. 187). The July 2017 issue of the Thai Smile Airline inflight magazine *We Smile* included an article in parallel English and Thai language texts titled in English "Walk of Faith: Ratchaprasong Square Trade Association Invites You to Visit 8 Gods in One Walk" ("Walk of Faith" 2017, pp. 32–35).[7] This article detailed the eight shrines dedicated to different Hindu deities now located in the Ratchaprasong area. As the inflight magazine stated, "[w]hen it seemed that the deity Brahma brought abundance to the area, more shrines were built for the sake of prosperity" (p. 33). The Thai version of this text states that it is "entrepreneurs" (*phu-prakorp-wisahakit*) in the Ratchaprasong area who have installed the additional shrines, observing that all eight shrines can now be visited in only thirty minutes, and all are conveniently accessible from the pedestrian skywalk that links major department stores and the BTS Skytrain network in the Ratchaprasong area, with signage to each shrine. The eight shrines to the Hindu deities in the area and the blessings conferred by each are detailed as follows:

> Ganesh (Thai: *Phra Phikkhanet*): Shrine located in front of the Isetan Department Store at the Central World shopping complex. "Considered the god of success, creativity and new beginnings. It is important to start your journey with Ganesh as he will bring about a successful end and remove all obstacles in your way" ("Walk of Faith" 2017, p. 35).

> Trimurti (Thai: *Phra Trimurati*): Shrine also located in front of the Isetan Department Store at Central World. "The most supreme god in the Brahman-Hindu religion, with the power to help you find and keep your soulmate" (p. 35). This Trimurti statue, which represents the three major Hindu deities Brahma, Shiva and Vishnu in a single form, has also become popular with women and gay men seeking blessings in finding a partner, especially on St Valentine's Day.

> Umathevi (Thai: *Phra Mae Umathewi*): Shrine located in front of Big C Ratchadamri. "Worship the mother of the universe, and you will find victory over enemies" (p. 35).

> Lakshmi (Thai: *Phra Mae Laksami*): Shrine located on the fourth floor of the Gaysorn Village mall. "As the goddess of beauty, prosperity, wealth, fortune and success in business negotiation as well as wealth, Lakshmi will bring bounty to those who worship her and lead a virtuous life" (p. 35).

> Jatulokbal (Thai: *Thao Jatulokban*): Shrine located on the fourth floor of the Gaysorn Village mall. "This deity watches over the four cardinal directions to keep the world peaceful and protect all humans from danger" (p. 35).

> Erawan (Thai: *Thao Mahaphrom*): Shrine is located beside the Grand Hyatt Erawan Hotel. "As the creator of all things and one of

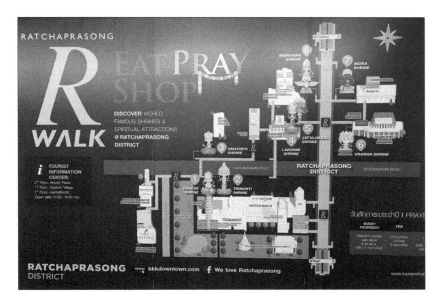

IMAGE 13. "Eat, Pray, Shop" – Ratchaprasong Skywalk, Bangkok
A 2019 tourist information display board map on the Ratchaprasong Sky Walk in downtown Bangkok that links public transport, shopping malls and shrines for eight Hindu deities. The sign, which conveniently labels each shrine on the map from 1 to 8, implores tourists to "Eat, Pray, Shop", indicating the explicit mix of consumerism, relaxation and religiosity in new prosperity cults in Thailand.

the trinity of the supreme divinity, Brahma is also filled with mercy. He can bless and grant any type of wishes for his worshippers" (p. 35).

Indra (Thai: *Thao Amarintharathirat* or *Phra In*): Shrine is in front of the Amarin Plaza mall. "Known as the protector of the virtuous, Indra will expel visible and invisible evils as well as protect businesses" (p. 35).

Narayana (Thai: *Phra Narai* or *Phra Wisanu*): Shrine located in front of the InterContinental Hotel. "As one of the deities that forms the supreme trinity, Narayana will bring about happiness, career success and the ability to overcome obstacles" (p. 35).

The Brahma Cult of Wealth

The image of Brahma at the Erawan Shrine in the Ratchaprasong shopping district of Bangkok has become the centre of a distinctive cult of wealth that is now visited by thousands of Thai and overseas Chinese tourist visitors every day. This deity and his shrine are also patronized by members of the highest echelons of Thai society. On

19 February 2011, Princess Ubolrat, eldest daughter of King Bhumibol, officiated in a ritual to cast and consecrate images and amulets of the Erawan Brahma on site at the shrine. The name given to these images was "The Blessed Ubol Brahma, Bestowing Blessings" (*Phra Phrom Ubon Bandan Prathan Phorn*), which included the first element of the princess's own name, Ubol (from the Pali *upala*, meaning "a lotus"). The "deity image consecration ritual" (*phithi thewaphisek*) was conducted by 199 Buddhist monks, all described as being *keji ajan* or magic monks (see below), as well as the royal Brahmin priest *Phra Ratchakhru* Wamathepmuni and invited Brahmin priests from India.

The ritual was advertised in advance on a large, prominent billboard across the road from the shrine, and several Thai newspapers carried colour four-page inserts of this ritual. These inserts advertised that the images of Brahma could be purchased (*bucha*) from three hundred offices of Thailand Post around the country, with funds to go towards one of the princess's royal charities: "One Heart, Helping those in Need" (*neung jai chuay leua phu prasop phai*). The ritual was initiated and organized by the "Miracle of Life Foundation", whose patron is

IMAGE 14. The Erawan Brahma in Bangkok
Image of the Hindu deity Brahma at the Erawan Shrine in downtown Bangkok on the cover of a 2006 paper-back book titled *The Blessed Brahma: The Deity Who Bestows Wealth and Prosperity* by Thotsaphon Jangphanitkul (Bangkok: Comma Design and Publishing). A large volume of devotional liter-ature for the deities of the cults of wealth is published in Thailand and sold through bookstores as well as at news-stands and convenience stores across the country.

Princess Ubolrat, with Pradit Phatharaprasit, then deputy minister for finance, as head of the event organizing committee. A text promoting purchase of the images and associated amulets made clear the intersection of beliefs in protection from harm and the promotion of business success and prosperity that are at the heart of the Thai cults of wealth:

> Brahma is the great deity (*mahathep*) who created the world, the lord (*thepphajao*) of creation, who has mercy and power (*anuphap*) over human destiny, who comes to the aid of others. Lord Brahma bestows happiness and success in life. When one prays to honour Brahma, the Lord will grant wisdom in the conduct of one's career, protecting and keeping one far from enemies, granting strength and insight in resolving manifold problems. Hence it is appropriate that companies, stores, hotels, resorts, hospitals, factories, enterprises, government offices, educational institutions, monasteries, public welfare centres, villages and individuals of faith should install an image of the deity to ensure an auspicious life.

The Prosperity Cult of Ganesh

The worship of the elephant-headed deity Ganesh, the son of Shiva and Parvati in Hindu belief, has also increased rapidly in recent years. Revered as the deity of new beginnings and the remover of obstacles, Ganesh is considered to be generous and benevolent and to have a special affinity with the creative arts. The annual festival dedicated to Ganesh in the Hindu ritual calendar, Ganesh Chaturthi (also called Vinayaka Chaturthi), is increasingly practised at Ganesh shrines in Thailand, which have expanded in number across the country since the early 2000s. Arratee Ayuttacorn and Jane Ferguson note that persons involved in sales, such as estate agents, car purchase financers and car dealers, are prominent among the followers of the expanding cult of Ganesh (Arratee and Ferguson, 2018, p. 7). McDaniel also notes that the worship of Ganesh is closely linked with wealth: "Ganesh is said to protect those with money and help those without it get it" (McDaniel 2011, p. 158).

Ruchi Agarwal and William Jones date the rise of the Ganesh cult in Thailand to the years immediately following the Asian economic crisis in the late 1990s and observe that in Thailand this deity is acquiring new roles and functions. The growing popularity of this deity is "reflected in a rapidly expanding trade in Ganesa images and icons displayed in shopping mall exhibitions in a variety of forms, colours, shapes and sizes" (Agarwal and Jones 2018, p. 121). They also observe that the rapidly growing popularity of the cult of Ganesh is seen in "the existence of [Ganesh] iconography in Buddhist temples, private and public shrines, market areas and other public places", as well as in the growing popularity of Ganesh ritual celebrations at locations such as the Shri Maha Mariamman Tamil Hindu temple on Silom Road in Bangkok (p. 122). The rapid increase in the popularity of Hindu deities is reflected in the iconography at the Wat Saman Rattanaram Buddhist monastery in Chachoengsao Province east of Bangkok, which has a giant image of a reclining pink Ganesh, as well as Rahu and Erawan. In 2016 and 2017, the giant statue of Ganesh at this monastery was advertised on a billboard along an elevated expressway in Bangkok, which described the image as the biggest Ganesh statue in the world.

In a reflection of the rapid changes in focuses of devotion in Thai popular religion, one shrine on Pinklao Road in the Thonburi area of Bangkok that was originally dedicated to Shiva in the early 1990s was refurbished and rededicated to Ganesh in 2009. This shrine had first been inaugurated in a ritual officiated by Princess Bejaratana Rajasuda (1925–2011), the only daughter of King Vajiravudh (r. 1910–25) (Agarwal and Jones 2018). An especially popular shrine to Ganesh is located in the Huay Kwang district of Bangkok and has become well-known in the capital as a site with many fortune tellers.

Arratee and Ferguson have studied a new Ganesh museum and a shrine to the deity in the northern Thai city of Chiang Mai, established respectively in 2013 and 2014, also noting that Ganesh images are now found in many Buddhist monasteries and Ganesh amulets are common across Thailand, reflecting "a new commoditised sacrality" (Arratee and Ferguson, 2018, p. 5). One Ganesh follower whom they interviewed stated, "[w]hen I need money, I will ask Ganesh for assistance. Because of him, I am able to dream of a lucky number, and when I play it in the lottery, I always win. Also, Ganesh helped me get a good price when I sold a property" (p. 5).

Numerous spirit mediums channel Ganesh, and Arratee and Ferguson note that the rituals of spirit possession associated with the cults of deities such as Ganesh employ new communication technologies that allow devotees to consult these gods, through their human mediums, over the phone or via the internet. One Chiang Mai informant, Anna, who consulted a spirit medium over the phone, stated, "Ganesh possessed the medium and advised me how to deal with colleagues.... I believe in Ganesh and whenever I have problems, I pray for him to release the obstacles and help me to find a solution" (Arratee and Ferguson, 2018, p. 6). Anna continued to consult Ganesh (and the spirit medium) by phone for the next two years, and rather

IMAGE 15. Streetside Shrine to Ganesh
A shrine to Ganesh, Hindu deity of success, on the pavement outside a store in Bangkok in 2019. Decorated with 100-baht Thai banknotes and surrounded by images of three other Hindu deities—Shiva (left), Lakshmi (right), Durga (above)—this shrine indicates the hopes for financial success and the mixing of the worship of multiple deities in the devotions of Thai followers of cults of wealth. (Photo by the author.)

than describing remunerating or paying the medium for her services Anna said that she was making merit by sending money to help the medium in Bangkok (p. 5). As noted in the introduction, the commercial aspects of the Thai cults of wealth are typically represented through discourses of religious merit.

Arratee and Ferguson note that members of the royal family, including Princess Ubolrat and Princess Soamsawali, former wife of the present king, King Maha Vajiralongkorn, have visited the new Ganesh shrines in Chiang Mai: "Photographs of these royal visits are proudly displayed in the respective establishments, giving the sites legitimacy and the sacred aura that surrounds the royal family within Thai culture" (Arratee and Ferguson 2018, pp. 8–9). Agarwal and Jones observe that "[c]elebrity endorsements of Ganesa are common in Thailand, as the elephant god has historically been seen as a patron of the arts" (Agarwal and Jones, 2018, p. 131). Reflecting on the intersection of religious rituals and commercial and financial interests in the Ganesh cult, Arratee and Ferguson conclude:

> The Ganesha cult occupies a religio-cultural space where Buddhism and Hinduism converge with the economy, consumer practices and cultural identity.... [I]t makes use of orthodox Buddhism,

but beyond the sangha-sanctioned space of the temple, while at the same time looking to Hindu traditions to bring meaning and efficacy.... [T]he new Ganesha cult brings people together in a frenzy of merit-making and spending. (Arratee and Ferguson, 2018, p. 9)

The Prosperity Cult of Rahu

Rahu is another Hindu deity who has become popularly linked to cults of wealth in recent years. Since the early 2000s, the semi-privatized national postal authority, Thailand Post, has become especially active in the production and marketing of ritual objects and literature relating to different cults of wealth. I summarize the many recent Thailand Post stamp issues representing the devotional figures at the centre of the cults of wealth in Chapter Six. In March 2019, Thailand Post sent an email to all of its philatelic standing order customers, including this author, marketing a book titled *The Deity Rahu: The Great Bodhisattva Deity* (*thep phra Rahu: borom thewa phothisat*), by one *Ajan* Lak Rekhanithet. The book was described as including historical information on Rahu and his place in astrology and Theravada Buddhism, while *Ajan* Lak is reported as being a member of the "Institute of Predictive Sciences" (*sathaban phayakorn-sat*), which seems to be an organization established and led by Lak Rekhanithet himself. This book on Rahu was advertised together with another publication, *The 2019 Astrologers Diary*, jointly authored by *Ajan* Lak Rekhanithet, *Khru Hon* (astrology teacher) Phattana Phattanasiri and *Ajan* Tuangthip Panjawarakul.

In the email advertisement, Lak Rekhanithet is described as a "leading astrologer of Rattanakosin" (*hon ek haeng krung rattanakosin*), and Rahu is said to be "a great deity, the supreme bodhisattva deity" (*maha thep borom thewa phothisat*) who has the "charismatic authority" (*barami*) and "divine power" (*thewanuphap*) to change one's horoscope from bad to good. *Ajan* Lak's book was advertised as coming together with an amulet of Rahu riding on the divine bird Garuda, which is said to have been empowered in "magically powerful Buddha-deity sacralization rituals in the four regions of the country" (*phithi phuttha-thewaphisek an saksit 4 phak*) so that those who receive the auspicious object together with the book will have "their bad luck turned to good and receive good fortune and money" (*chok-lap ngoen-tra*). The statement that the amulets underwent a double Buddhist and Hindu "deity" sacralization ritual and identification of this Hindu deity as a bodhisattva, a future Buddha, reflects the Buddhacization of Hindu belief and ritual in contemporary Thai popular religion. This

IMAGE 16. Advertisement for an Amulet of Rahu
A 2019 Thailand Post advertisement for an amulet of the deity Rahu, Hindu god of eclipses, riding on the divine bird-deity Garuda, official symbol of the Thai state and monarchy. Produced by Lak Rekhanithet (pictured left), described as "the leading astrologer of Rattanakosin [Bangkok]", this advertisement was sent by email to all subscribers to Thailand Post's philatelic sales service and reflects how state agencies actively produce and market ritual products associated with cults of prosperity.

marketing of a book and an amulet dedicated to Rahu by the national post office not only reflects the popularity of the cult of this deity but also the extent to which cults of wealth have become mainstream religious phenomena in Thailand.

Keji Ajan: Magic Monks of Prosperity

Many Buddhist monks, both living and dead, have also become nationally prominent figures linked to cults of prosperity. The monasteries of these monks are often sites of pilgrimage, their images are placed on house and shop altars as expressions of personal devotion, and amulets blessed by them or which bear their image are worn to promote business as well as to provide protection from harm. The popularity of monks linked to cults of wealth would appear to represent a recent, and rapid, transformation within Thai Buddhism. Just over three decades ago, Gray wrote: "A monk who uses his energy and patience (*khanti*) towards advancing this-worldly goals is brought low on the purity scale. Worse yet, he might be a 'false' or deceptive monk" (Gray 1986, p. 587). This is no longer the case. Since the 1990s, many monks have been publicly involved in the blessing and promotion of material prosperity. Many of these "magic monks" or *keji ajan* are reputed to possess supernatural powers and their names are often perceived as being auspiciously linked to good fortune and wealth. Pattana describes a magic monk or *keji ajan* as follows:

> A magic monk refers to any monk who has acquired knowledge and skill pertaining to magic, superstition, or supernatural power and puts them into practice.... A magic monk is a monk widely regarded for his charisma and magical or supernatural potency. He at least must be widely recognized and revered by his followers through events that define his supernatural potencies such as his amulets saving lives of disciples or followers, giving winning lottery numbers, or providing healing magic, etc. (Pattana 2005b, p. 211)

While magic monks operate within the existing social institution of Thai monastic Buddhism, Pattana emphasizes that they use various forms of magic "as an instrument to obtain wealth, fame, and reputation, which are not necessarily expected by the Sangha" (Pattana 2005b, p. 214). He also emphasizes the intimate relationship of magic monks with capitalism and commerce, observing that while *keji ajan* may behave like spirit mediums or fortune tellers, they "forcefully argue that [their] agency has ... a firm ground in the existing structure of Thai syncretized religious traditions. Monks practising magic and dealing with the temple's mundane businesses have become increasingly common in Thai Buddhism" (p. 215).

The Keji Ajan Somdet *To and* Luang Phor *Thuat*

One group of *keji ajan* in the cults of wealth are linked to the monarchy, the nation and state ideology. *Somdet* To and *Luang Phor* Thuat (also commonly called *Luang Pu* Thuat) are among the most important *keji ajan* who are linked to the monarchy and these two monks are also central figures in the modern cult of amulets. McDaniel observes, "If *Somdet* To is the patron saint of central Thailand, then *Luang Phor* Thuat has become the patron saint of southern Thailand" (McDaniel 2011, p. 242n67).

Somdet To, also known as *Luang Phor* To and more formally by his ecclesiastical title *Somdet Phra* Phutthachan Phrommarangsi, was a high-ranking monk in the nineteenth century when he was abbot of Wat Rakhang Khositaram in Bangkok. McDaniel calls him "the most powerful magician and ghost tamer in Thai history" (2011, p. 5). He is famous in Thai legend as the monk who exorcized the ghost of *Mae* Nak, a spirit who is believed to have haunted her husband and killed residents of the Phrakhanong district in eastern Bangkok in the nineteenth century. In director Nonzee Nimibutr's 1999 film version of the *Mae* Nak legend, *Somdet* To chants the *Chinnapanjorn Khatha* (Pali: *Jinapañjara gāthā*) incantation to heal and release the spirt of Nak.[8] Widely revered as a defender of Siam, *Somdet* To is associated with the cult of the monarchy in several ways. He is regarded to have been a son of King Rama II (r. 1809–24) by a non-royal wife and in his senior years he was the Pali language teacher of the young Prince Chulalongkorn, the future King Rama V. And like Chulalongkorn, he is represented as a nationalist hero who helped preserve Siamese independence against imperialist incursions. In one story, French gunboats involved in the 1893 Pak Nam incident—when France challenged the authority of Siam to expand its empire in Indochina—were said to have been held off by the power of amulets that *Somdet* To had sacralized. McDaniel relates this story as follows:

> When the [French] gunboats started approaching the Grand Palace [in Bangkok] several laypeople and monks rushed to Wat Rakhang and Wat Chayasongkhram on opposite sides of the river. They knew that before he died *Somdet* To had buried several valuable amulets underneath two large stupas. *Somdet* To, many believed, had commanded a certain group of followers to go to these large stone stupas and chant a protective chant, the *Jinapañjara gāthā*, continuously. This chanting empowered by these buried amulets

IMAGE 17. *Somdet* To and King Chulalongkorn Greeting Card A 1997 New Year greeting card combining images of *Somdet* To (top), a nineteenth century magic monk famous for his amulets and the Chinnapanjorn *khatha* protective incantation; King Chulalongkorn (lower right); and *Krommaluang* (Prince) Chumphon, a son of King Chulalongkorn revered as the founder of the modern Thai navy and for his knowledge of *saiyasat* magical practices. This image reflects beliefs that these three figures drew upon royal-cum-Buddhist charismatic authority (*barami*) and magical *saiyasat* skills to preserve Siam's independence during the colonial period.

would create a powerful magical barrier across the river and defend the city. The French gunboats were supposedly magically repelled by the chanting and the amulets. (McDaniel 2011, p. 55)

Amulets reputed to have been sacralized by this monk, as well as more recent talismans that bear his image, are among the most famous and valuable auspicious objects in Thailand today.

Jovan Maud notes that *Luang Phor* Thuat is believed to have been a Buddhist monk who lived during the seventeenth century and wandered the landscape of what is now Southern Thailand. This monk is associated with several miracles, most famously turning saltwater fresh with the touch of his foot, earning him the common appellation *Luang Phor Thuat Yiap Nam Thale Jeut*, "The Venerable Ancestor Who Treads on Saltwater [and turns it into] Freshwater" (Maud 2007, p. 8). In 1954, *Phra Khru* Wisaisophon, the abbot of Wat Chang Hai monastery in Pattani province in Southern Thailand and locally known as *Ajan* Thim, began producing amulets depicting *Luang Phor* Thuat: "In a short time these amulets gained a reputation for providing their wearers with invulnerability and became very popular among the armed forces, especially the Border Patrol Police" (p. 199). Maud also notes that *Somdet* To and *Luang Phor* Thuat are often associated with each other in popular iconography (p. 199).

Magic Monks with Commercially Auspicious Names

Another group of *keji ajan* who are especially closely associated with the cults of wealth have names whose meanings coincidentally relate to notions of abundance, increase, fecundity and prosperity, such as *Luang Phor* Ngoen (Reverend Father Silver/Money) and *Luang Phor* Khoon (Reverend Father Multiply). Many ritual products associated with the cults of magic monks play upon the commercially auspicious meanings of the names of these *keji ajan*. These devotional products and associated literature, produced by laypeople, often display a high degree of creative licence. For example, in 1997 one Wet Worawit published a booklet titled *The Auspiciously Named Spiritual Teachers Ngoen and Sot*, which was a compilation of the biographies and miracles attributed to *Luang Phor* Ngoen, the nineteenth-century abbot of Wat Bang Khlan in Phichit Province in mid-north Thailand, and *Luang Phor* Sot, the twentieth-century abbot of Wat Pak-nam Phasicharoen in Thonburi, across the Chao Phraya River from Bangkok.[9] The Thai term for "cash" is *ngoen-sot*, a fortuitous combination of the names of these two well-known monks who lived in different periods and apparently never met in life. The distinctive personality cults of these two monks had never previously been linked before the book's lay author-publisher combined the names of *Luang Phor* Ngoen and *Luang Phor* Sot to create a symbolic frame for the explicit worship of "cash" (*ngoen-sot*). In the introduction to his book, Wet states that the publication would be of special interest to readers who make their living from trading and business "because 'cash' (*ngoen-sot*) is something that everyone wants". Wet also included the following advertorial subheading on the book cover: "Including a photo to worship cash (*bucha ngoen-sot*) and an incantation to call in cash", written and blessed by another monk named *Phra Ajan* Sri-ngoen ['blessed money'] Aphatharo.

IMAGE 18. Devotional Poster of Ten Auspiciously Named Magic Monks
A devotional poster of ten *keji ajan* magic monks with auspicious names arranged in sequence so their names— Kaeo Waen Ngoen Thorng Man Khong Jaroen Suk Sot Cheun—spell out a message of prosperity and wellbeing in Thai: "Jewels, rings, money and gold are secure; prosper, be happy and refreshed."

Another example of the creative use of the names of magic monks in ritual objects is a framed devotional picture produced by the Phorn Patihan ("Miraculous Blessing") Company sold from the gift section of the Thai Tokyu Department Store in Bangkok's Mahboonkhrorng Centre in 1997. This devotional image combined the images of nine monks in a sequence so that their names read out an auspicious message. The names of the nine monks were Ngoen, Thorng, Man, Khong, Khoon, Jaroen, Suk, Sot and Cheun, and the message formed from their names read, "Wealth (*ngoen-thorng*) Security (*man-khong*) Multiplies (*khoon*), Progress (*jaroen*), Happiness (*suk*), Joyfulness (*sot-cheun*)". The following additional message was added beneath the images and names of the monks: "Enhancing the charisma (*barami*) of the devotee, great fortune, business progresses, wealth flows in, complete health."

Large Thai corporations were also active participants in this creative use of the names of magic monks. On 1 January 1997, as the speculative fever of the Thai economic boom was at its peak and just a few months before the onset of the dramatic crash of the Asian economic crisis, Petroleum Thai or PT Co. Ltd (since reformed as PTG Energy Co. Ltd), a major gas producer in the Gulf of Thailand and owner of service stations across the country, placed full-page advertisements in national newspapers. These advertisements wished PT customers a happy New Year and included the images of six magic monks, Reverend Fathers Ngoen, Thorng, Man, Khong, Jong and Jaroen, arranged in order so that their names formed the Thai sentence meaning "Money and gold are secure; may you prosper". The following New Year message was printed under the images of the magic monks: "May this year be a great year with money and gold flowing in … with best wishes from PT."[10]

The Prosperity Cult of Luang Phor *Khoon:* *"Reverend Father Multiply"*

One of the most prominent of the magical prosperity monks during the years of the Thai economic boom was *Luang Phor* Khoon, whose name and title translate as "Reverend Father Multiply".[11] At the height of the economic boom in the mid-1990s, this aged abbot of a remote monastery two hundred kilometres northeast of Bangkok emerged as the most prominent religious figure in Thailand, achieving superstar status with a mass nationwide following amongst all sections of society. *Luang Phor* (Reverend Father) Khoon Parisuttho, abbot of Wat Ban Rai monastery, was widely believed to possess supernatural powers of prophecy, healing, conferring luck and warding off harm, and he became the focus of a national cult that emphasized the acquisition of wealth and power. Born in 1923, Khoon Chatponlakrang was ordained as a monk in 1944 and lived alone in the forests of Northeast Thailand for several years, developing a reputation for possessing supernatural powers. He began casting amulets in his own image in the 1950s when he became abbot of Wat Ban Rai in Dan Khun Thot District of Nakhon Ratchasima Province. He died in 2015, and his remains were granted a royal-sponsored funeral in early 2019.

In the 1990s, *Luang Phor* Khoon's activities were often front-page stories in national newspapers. His image and cult objects, such as the many types of amulets he sacralized, are found in homes, stores, marketplaces, taxis, buses and a plethora of other locations across the country. At the height of his popularity in the 1990s, sales of these products brought hundreds of millions of baht into the coffers of his monastery Wat Ban Rai each year. Khoon's followers included former prime ministers, the then head of the Royal Thai Army, members of the royal family and senior businesspeople as well as hundreds of thousands of ordinary Thai men and women from all walks of life. The anonymous author of one hagiographical biography of Khoon stated that "it would not be wrong to say that he is the most prominent Buddhist teacher of this period" and that Khoon is "the only monk whom people all over the country respect and have faith in" (*Luang Phor Khoon Parisuttho* [1996?], p. 11). Khoon became a cultural icon, approaching the status of a patron saint of wealth.

What distinguished the cult following of *Luang Phor* Khoon from other personality-based Buddhist movements in Thailand was its dramatic transformation in the 1990s from a local to a national phenomenon, being sponsored by the highest echelons of the Bangkok military and civilian elites, and its unabashed support for wealth creation. The abbot's popularity was founded on faith in his supernatural power to multiply good luck and to enhance good fortune and wealth. The ongoing popularity of *Luang Phor* Khoon after his death and the continuing association of his name with the multiplication of wealth is shown in the title of a 2016 book on amulets titled *The Most Popular Million Baht Amulets, Big Silver, Big Gold, Increase X Multiply [Khoon] X Rich: Amulet Specialists Handbook* (Wisan 2016?).[12] The title of this publication played on the meanings of the names of the four monks whose amulets were reviewed, being a handbook of the amulets sacralized by *Luang Pu* To, whose name means "Reverend Grandfather Big"; *Luang Pu* Phoem, whose name means "Reverend Grandfather Increase"; *Luang Phor* Khoon, "Reverend Father Multiply"; and *Luang Phor* Ruay, whose name means "Reverend Father Rich".

IMAGE 19. *Luang Phor* **Khoon DVD**
DVD of a movie dramatizing the life of the magic monk *Luang Phor* Khoon ("Reverend Father Multiply") titled "I'll make you rich" (*ku hai meung ruay*). The DVD pack included a *Luang Phor* Khoon amulet (centre) of the "I'll make you rich" series sacralized in 2004. This DVD was sold from 7-Eleven convenience stores in February 2015, just three months before the magic monk died in May 2015.

Summary

While originating from diverse royal, Chinese, Hindu and Buddhist sources, the many Thai cults of wealth all share the emphasis on plenitude and abundance (*udom-sombun*) that McDaniel (2011) identifies as a defining feature of Thai Buddhism. In contrast to older cultic forms, which were historically associated with local deities and protective tutelary spirits with limited geographical spread, the deities and spirits worshipped in the cults of wealth have achieved national relevance and are not restricted to any one site or locality. The cultural diversity of the sources of the cults also reflects the polycultural complexity of Thailand and indicates how the ethnic plurality of the society is represented symbolically and ritually in the religious field. Cross-ethnic participation in the cults manifests in the ways formerly Chinese deities have been incorporated into Thai patterns of worship and Hindu deities have been Buddhacized as protectors of the Buddha's dispensation (*sasana*). The accommodation and appropriation of Chinese and Indian deities to Thai religious patterns also reflects the dominant position of Theravada Buddhism in structuring the hierarchy of the expanding pantheon of deities that form the devotional focus of Thai vernacular ritual practice.

The cults of wealth are not the only new forms of magical ritual to have emerged in Thailand in recent decades. Cults of magically empowered amulets and innovative forms of professional spirit mediumship are two other modalities of modern enchantment that have evolved within the expanding field of Thai popular religion since the middle of the twentieth century. While distinct autonomous domains, the cults of amulets and professional spirit mediums intersect with the cults of wealth, and in the next chapter I describe how these additional religious innovations form important aspects of the material and ritual dimensions of the prosperity movements.

Notes

1. Catherine Fox, "Flaky Biz", *Australian Financial Review Boss Magazine*, April 2006, p. 57.
2. Policemen continue to be major players in the cult of amulets as reflected in a 2011 book titled *Auspicious Amulets of Famous Policemen* (Ek Angsanon 2011).
3. The origins of the cult of King Chulalongkorn predate the economic boom. Barend Jan Terwiel notes that amulets with the image of King Chulalongkorn were already popular at the time of his research at a rural monastery in Ratchaburi Province west of Bangkok at the end of the 1960s (Terwiel 2012, p. 70).
4. Chang Noi (pseud.), "Lessons from History: Globalisation Revisited", *The Nation*, 26 December 1997. p. A5.
5. *Khao Sot*, 5 January 1998, p. 23.
6. Nidhi's term for Thailand's ethnic Chinese, *jek*, derived from the Tae Jiw (Teo Chiu) Chinese dialect, was originally a colloquial term with derogatory connotations in Thai. In the 1990s, however, *jek* was resignified and appropriated within some Thai academic discourses to describe those ethnic Chinese who have adopted Thai language, religion and culture, and in this usage it has parallels with the Malay term *peranakan* used

to describe the Straits Chinese. Suchit Wongthes, former editor of the popular *Art and Culture* (*Sinlapa Watthanatham*) monthly magazine to which Nidhi has been a frequent contributor over the years, was one of the key popularizers of the academic use of *jek*. Suchit's 1987 book *Jek Pon Lao* ("Jek mixed with Lao") was a deconstruction of notions of essential Thai culture and ethnicity, claiming that Thai was in effect a blending of Chinese and Lao. But not all Thai intellectuals like this academic use of *jek*. Thammasat University political scientist Kasian Tejapira (1997) prefers the less loaded expression *luk-jin* ("Chinese descendent") to refer to Sino-Thais.

7. The Thai title of the article was *Sen-thang haeng sattha: Samakhom phu-prakorp-wisahakit nai yan ratchaprasong chuan ruam sakkara 8 ong-thep phan Ratchaprasong Walk*, which translates as "Path of Faith: The Association of Ratchaprasong Entrepreneurs Invites You to Worship 8 Deities via the Ratchaprasong Sky Walk".

8. See McDaniel (2011) on the importance of this *khatha* incantation in contemporary Thai popular Buddhism.

9. *Luang Phor* Sot is also regarded as the spiritual source of the Wat Phra Dhammakaya movement.

10. *Matichon Daily Newspaper*, 1 January 1997 (BE 2540), p. 16.

11. Khoon's name is also a homonym of the national flower of Thailand, the Golden Shower Tree (*Cassia Fistula*), whose formal name in Thai is *Ton Ratchaphreuk* (from Sanskrit meaning "the royal tree") and whose popular name is *dork khoon*. While Khoon's name meaning "to multiply" is pronounced the same as the name of this tree, the two words are written differently in Thai script.

12. The Thai title of this book was *Rian Yort Niyom Ngoen Lan To Ngoen To Thorng, Phoem X Khoon X Ruay, Khu-meu Sian*. In this book title the multiplication sign "X" was placed between the names of three monks, Reverend Fathers Phoem ("increase"), Khoon ("multiply") and Ruay ("rich"): "Phoem X Khoon X Ruay". Also, the name of *Luang Phor* To, whose name means "big", was used as an intensifier in association with the names of Reverend Father Ngoen ("money") and Reverend Father Thorng ("gold"); i.e., To Ngoen ("big silver/money"), To Thorng ("big gold").

Chapter Five

Empowered Amulets and Spirit Possession: Material and Ritual Dimensions of the Thai Cults of Wealth

Introduction: Autonomization and Contextualization of Modalities of Modern Enchantment

Followers of the cults of wealth engage with the deities at the centre of these ritual forms in a number of ways. Each deity and spirit in the cults has a dedicated *khatha*, a mantra or incantation usually composed in a mix of Pali and Sanskrit that is chanted by the devotee when worshipping or requesting a boon or blessing. These *khatha* are often written on boards attached to the base of public shrines that house images of the deities in order to facilitate ritual worship by the faithful. If a requested boon is granted, then it is incumbent upon the devotee to recompense and thank the deity in a ritual called *kae bon*. Each deity is believed to have a set of personal preferences, and the type of *kae bon* ritual performed will depend on the particular likes and interests attributed to the boon-granting spirit. Some deities, such as Brahma at the Erawan Shrine in Bangkok, are believed to enjoy being entertained by Thai classical dance and music, and a troupe of professional dancers and musicians is always present at this shrine ready to be hired to perform for the deity by devotees whose boons have been granted. Other deities are believed to enjoy particular forms of food or drink, and offerings of these items may be placed at the deity's shrine in a ritual expression of thanks.

Sections of this chapter draw on material presented in Jackson (1999a).

Thailand's cults of wealth also lie at the intersection of two other major phenomena that are distinctive emergent features of the Thai religious field and which reflect novel modalities of ritual enchantment; namely, the cult of amulets sacralized by magic monks and professional spirit mediumship. One of the most widespread and popular ways of demonstrating attachment to a deity, or to request a spirit's helping presence, is to own or wear an amulet bearing an image of the god. Sacralized amulets are an especially notable category of ritual objects that represent the deities and spirits of the cults of wealth. As Justin McDaniel notes, the cult of amulets in Thailand has expanded well beyond representing figures that relate directly to Theravada Buddhism:

> [T]here are many amulets of Chinese deities and *bodhisattas*. Moreover, there are hundreds of different types of amulets in Thailand that do not depict Buddha images or Buddhist monks. They depict Hindu deities, royal family members, local goddesses and gods. (McDaniel 2011, p. 196)

The faithful can also seek to communicate directly with a deity associated with a cult of wealth in a spirit possession ritual mediated by a professional spirit medium who channels that god.

The cults of wealth, the cult of amulets and professional spirit mediumship are three distinct but intersecting phenomena that have all emerged as novel expressions of Thai popular Buddhism since the middle of the twentieth century and which represent autonomous expressions of ritual and material religious practice. Each has distinctive sets of ritual specialists: Buddhist monks and Brahmins in the case of the cult of amulets and professional lay men and women in spirit possession cults. This parallels the rise of autonomous "lines" of magical ritual in modern Burma, where Bénédicte Brac de la Perrière (2011) identifies cults of spirit possession and of magical sages called *weikza* (Brac de la Perrière and Rozenberg 2014) and *bobogyi* (Brac de la Perrière and Munier Gaillard 2019) as distinctive domains of ritual practice. The proliferation of multiple lines of magical ritual also reflects the *kala-thesa* time and place contextualization of Thai religious life. In Thai the distinctive localities associated with each new ritual form are often given different names: the shrines for images of deities associated with the cults of wealth are usually called *san-jao* ("palaces of lords"); the monasteries of magic monks who sacralize amulets are called *wat*; while the residences, "abodes" or "palaces" of professional spirit mediums may be called *samnak* or *tamnak*. However, while being recognized as distinct in terms of separate sites of ritual practice that have different labels in local discourses, the faithful may move between

IMAGE 20. Chinese Dragon Dance at the Erawan Shrine in Bangkok
A Chinese dragon dance troupe entertains the image of Brahma at the Erawan Shrine in downtown Bangkok in 2016. The dragon dance troupe was hired by a family of overseas Chinese tourists who had returned to Bangkok to thank and honour Brahma for granting a boon requested on a previous visit to the Thai capital. While *kae bon* rituals to thank Brahma for boons granted usually involve hiring a Thai classical dance and music troupe to entertain the Hindu deity, this instance demonstrates the ritual innovation that often emerges when Thai, Hindu and Chinese religious cultures mix in the cults of wealth. (Photo by the author.)

all three lines of the cults of wealth, amulets and professional spirit mediums in seeking to enhance their material and physical wellbeing. The follower of a cult of wealth may worship at the shrine (*san-jao*) of the deity whose blessing they seek, visit the monastery (*wat*) of a magic monk who makes and sacralizes amulets bearing an image of the deity, and also seek to communicate directly with the spirit at the palace (*tamnak*) of a professional spirit medium who channels that deity.

The three religious lines of cults of wealth, amulets and spirit possession are also in constant interaction with each other as well as with mainstream Buddhism, even as they are "built on the physical separation of ritual institutions" (Brac de la Perrière 2011, p. 167). Modern enchantment takes multiple forms in both Thailand and Burma, where Brac de la Perrière observes that the autonomous yet continually interacting character of the several new lines of magical practice in that neighbour of Thailand provides rich opportunities for ritual specialists to adapt to changing conditions by "providing a niche for alternative modernities, a place for bricolage" (p. 180). Erick White refers to the multiple alternative religious modernities in Thailand when he observes that professional spirit mediums "constitute just one thread within the more generalized cacophony of innovative and alternative religious forms that seek to claim an accepted foothold within the legitimizing aura of mainstream Thai Buddhism in what can now be called a Post-Reform, Post-Establishment Buddhist era" (White 2014, p. 289). In this chapter I describe the material dimensions of the cults of wealth in the closely allied cult of amulets and the central place of spirit possession in the rituals associated with the cults.

The Cult of Amulets among Thailand's Power Elites

Thailand's magic monks are at the centre of a nationwide, and increasingly international, cult of sacralized amulets that are not only believed to protect the wearer and help them increase their wealth and prosperity but are also highly valuable and sought-after objects in their own right. Sacralized amulets come in a variety of forms, including tiny metal Buddha images, small tablets made from baked clay (*phra phong*), small rolled metal cylinders inscribed with magical formulae and inserted under the skin of the upper arm (*takrut*), and medallions (*rian*) made from bronze or alloys of precious metals. Round or oval-shaped metal amulets are called *rian klom*, while rectangular stamp-shaped amulets are called *rian sataem*—literally, "stamp coins". An additional form of ritual object are *pha yan* ("*yantra* cloth"), which are small rectangular pieces of cloth printed with images of deities and inscriptions of blessing verses and magical incantations. Amulets and *pha yan*—in formal discourse called "auspicious objects" (*watthu mongkhon*) or colloquially "holy objects" (*phra khreuang*)—are believed to acquire magical powers from the *khatha* incantations that *keji ajan* monks chant over them. To be sacralized or empowered (*pluk sek*), amulets must be chanted over by monks for extended periods, sometimes in rituals repeated each night for several months. Amulets are commonly worn as pendants or hung from a motor vehicle's rear-view mirror like a St Christopher medallion. A thriving market in amulets exists throughout Thailand, with stores and markets dedicated to the trade and a wide range of magazines and books that detail the characteristics and prices of amulets produced by various famous monks. In the amulet trade, the purchase price of these objects is euphemistically called their "worship value" (*kha bucha*) or "rental price" (*kha chao*) rather than the more mundane term of "price" (*rakha*), which is used to denote the purchase of other marketable products, commodities and services. As noted in the Introduction, the spending of money to purchase these spiritual objects is symbolically associated with religious practice and the accumulation of merit rather than mundane investment.

While amulets are sacralized by Buddhist monks, the devotional figures represented on these talismans are not necessarily associated with monastic Buddhism. Amulets with images of Hindu deities, Kuan Im, King Chulalongkorn and other royal figures from Thai history are just as common as those that bear images of famous monks or revered Buddha images. These ritual objects thus represent a site of symbolic intersection among the various cults of wealth and form an important component of the symbolic complex of cults that I detail in Chapter Six.

The cult of amulets, and of the magic monks who ritually empower these auspicious objects, is a cultural form that reflects speculative capitalism and the intimate relationship between sacral authority and economic and political power in modern Thailand. This is especially clearly revealed in the participation of Thailand's power elites in the cult of magical amulets and the high honour accorded to *keji ajan* magic monks. Christine Gray notes that many informants during her research in the late 1970s were ardent amulet collectors. She reports one interview with a royal secretary:

> The royal secretary pulled out an amulet he was wearing. It was imprinted with the image of Royal Grandfather [i.e., *Luang Pu*] Phang,[1] a famous meditation monk from Manchakiri District in Khon Kaen [Northeast Thailand]. He had received this amulet from Major-General Pow Sarasin, the head of the narcotics board, who had sponsored a *kathin* [monks robes offering] ceremony at *Luang Pu* Phang's meditation retreat. An interview with Pow Sarasin revealed that one of his assistants, a native of Sakon Nakorn [in northeast Thailand], had first brought him news of *Luang Pu's* miraculous exploits. (Gray 1986, p. 615)

In 1979, Gray interviewed a young assistant-vice-president of Bangkok Bank who had graduated with an MBA from an American university about the bank's support for *kathin* robes offering rituals. She asked,

> Was he wearing an amulet? He immediately pulled one out from under his shirt and spoke enthusiastically of the monk whose image it contained. The monk was a meditation monk in *Acaan* Man's Thammayut line, famous for his magical powers (including

his ability to read minds and fly through the air). 'This monk knew the true meaning of religion', he said. 'He really did not care about the world.' (Gray 1986, p. 847)

The extent of support for the cult of amulets among Thai politicians is demonstrated in a 2010 book titled *Auspicious Amulets of Famous People* (*Phra di khon dang*, Khao Sot 2010) that detailed the favourite amulets of senior members of the then Democrat Party–led government. The first chapter of the book was dedicated to the personal collection of then prime minister Abhisit Vejjajiva, who described his amulets of *Luang Pu* Thuat and Jatukham-Ramathep.[2]

The marketization of amulets in Thailand is distinctive and the scale of the industry now found in the country is not matched anywhere else. Chalong Soontravanich (2013) argues that the Thai cult of amulets is a recent phenomenon that only assumed its current form and scale in the period after World War II. Gray also notes the recentness of the Thai cult of amulets:

> A Thai anthropologist who had done fieldwork in the North said that the custom of wearing amulets with the images of monks was a new one, restricted mostly to people in Bangkok. (Traditionally amulets took other forms: cloth, stone, tiger fangs.) Military leaders, bureaucrats and technocrats alike coveted these amulets, regardless of whether they claimed Chinese ancestry or saw themselves as modern economists. (Gray 1986, p. 615)

Like Gray, Chalong notes that the rise of the cult of amulets reflects a major transformation in the relations among Buddhist ritual, sacred objects and the economy. He observes that before the nineteenth century,

> Thais strictly separated the sacred domain from the profane.... Sacred religious objects, Buddha images in particular, were to be kept in the monastery, the only place of purity and sanctity. Outside the monastery, especially in a private residence, lay the profane domain suitable for profane objects and worldly activities. (Chalong 2013, p. 188)

This began to change in the mid-nineteenth century, first among the Bangkok elite. Chalong contends that the rise of a bourgeois middle class in Thailand in the nineteenth and early twentieth centuries not only led to a modern, materialistic and scientific way of thinking but also reinforced belief in supernatural power. In the past, Buddha images were regarded as sacred images for public worship, but in the more individualized society of bourgeois capitalism the image of the

Buddha was relocated to an amulet, with this personalized image of the Buddha "becoming a medium or an agent of ... magical power" (Chalong 2013, p. 190).

IMAGE 21. BTS Skytrain Tenth Anniversary Amulet
Newspaper advertisement for a specially commissioned amulet of the nationally famous magic monk *Luang Phor* Ngoen, whose name means "Reverend Father Money". The amulet was distributed to passengers on Bangkok's BTS Skytrain network from King Bhumibol's birthday on 5 December 2009 to celebrate the tenth anniversary of the BTS public transport system. Large corporations in Thailand are prominent sponsors of the cult of amulets, especially ritual objects of auspiciously named magic monks associated with the cults of wealth. (Source: *Khom Chat Leuk*, 2 December 2009, p. 14.)

Similarities between Amulets and Currency

The reproduction of images of kings, Buddha images, Chinese and Indian deities and famous monks on amulets also occurred after another major cultural transformation. In premodern Siam, portraiture had been a taboo as it was believed that if one's image was made or one's portrait was taken it would shorten one's life. This belief was overturned during King Chulalongkorn's reign, when the royal family adopted photography and became avid enthusiasts of the new technology of image production. Chalong notes that "[t]he most revolutionary change affecting the Buddhist amulet cult was caused by the introduction of photography and coin-minting technology during the mid-nineteenth century" (Chalong 2013, p. 191). Originally introduced into Thailand to make currency, these technologies were "soon applied to the making of commemorative medals" (p. 191). The new photographic and coin-minting technologies meant that medals and amulets were stronger and lasted longer and the images they carried were also much clearer and sharper.

Indeed, there are many similarities in terms of physical shape, constituent metals, method of production and terminology between the modern form now taken by Thai amulets and coinage in circulation. In Thai, metal amulets are often called *rian phra khreuang*, an expression that includes the same term, *rian*, used to refer to coinage as well as to many currencies based on the decimal dollar. The Thai term *rian* derives from the Portuguese and Spanish *real*, which denoted the coinage of these two early colonizing powers in Southeast Asia. The first Siamese coins with an image of a monarch were minted in the reign of King Chulalongkorn. There is thus an intimate symbolic intersection between coins and amulets, which, as ritually empowered objects that signify wealth, are regarded as being magically empowered to bring in more wealth to the owner, and that also have monetary value as collectible items. The intersection of the cult of amulets and the cults of wealth is further reflected in the fact that handbooks for collectors and investors in Thailand often include valuable amulets, coins and banknotes in the same publication.

The Cult of Amulets and Fund Raising

Benedict Anderson provides insight into the importance of amulets to Thai monastery finances in the context of what he describes as "the triumph of a consumerist culture" (Anderson 2012, p. 93). Anderson notes that the late abbot of Wat Phai Rong Wua in Suphanburi Province west of Bangkok, *Luang Phor* Khom (1902–90), was explicit about the importance of amulets to the finances of his monastery in the period after World War II. He cites an interview with *Luang Phor* Khom in which the abbot stated:

> We wanted to construct a wat for the Buddhist faith but we didn't know how to find money. When we saw that people liked magical and sacred objects, we decided to enter the trade.... I made millions of Buddhist amulets, big and small. I made so many that I forget the total number. But I made them in good faith. (Anderson 2012, p. 43)

After *Luang Phor* Khom died in 1990, it was found that Wat Phai Rong Wua was in substantial debt. The monastery's lay finance committee "[f]airly quickly mass-produced amulets of the deceased abbot ... to ease the *wat's* economic difficulties" (Anderson 2012, p. 57).

The movement of the cults of wealth from the social margins to religious mainstream in Thailand is indicated by the large number of state agencies that now sponsor the production of sacralized amulets, which have become central features of the material culture of the prosperity cults, for a wide range of fund-raising purposes. Chalong reports that a five-thousand-seat convention centre of the new main campus of the university for the Mahanikai Order of monks, Mahachulalongkorn Rajavidyalaya University in Ayutthaya, was built with a budget of 500 million baht "financed entirely by the proceeds of amulet sales" (Chalong 2013, p. 184). McDaniel notes that the sale of Ganesh amulets and images has grown in such popularity that the International Thai Studies Conference held at Thammasat University in 2008, an academic meeting of over four hundred foreign and Thai scholars and opened by Princess Sirindhorn, was funded largely by the sale of Ganesh images:

> The original idea for this fund-raising was initiated by Dr Anucha Thirakanont, director of the Thai Khadi Research Institute and professor at Thammasat University. He commissioned Phra Raja Khru Wamathepmuni, the head of the Brahman sect of Thailand, for the ritual consecration of the images.
>
> The consecration ceremony was performed at the Brahman temple by the head of the Brahman sect himself. The Brahman ceremony was also 'enhanced', as Anucha stated, by a Buddhist ceremony at Wat Suthat. This is indeed the first time a secular academic conference was funded by the sale of statues of an elephant-headed deity. (McDaniel 2011, pp. 207–8)

Serhat Ünaldi (2016, p. 31) notes that in September 2007, on the occasion of the renovation of the Giant Swing (Phra Sao Ching Cha) in the old city of Bangkok, a historical site of royal Brahmanical rituals, the Bangkok Metropolitan Administration produced miniature replicas of the swing, souvenir books, special edition stamps and two sets of Giant Swing amulets for sale. One set of these amulets bore the picture of *Phra* Trimurti, the Hindu trinity of Brahma, Vishnu and Shiva combined in one image and believed to be a potent source of wealth. The other set of amulets depicted *Phra* Sri Sakyamuni, the main Buddha image in the nearby Wat Suthat monastery. The amulets were made from materials that included wood from the poles of the old Giant Swing mixed with the remains of other sacred objects from previous significant occasions such as the celebrations for the eight-ieth birthday of King Bhumibol's mother, the late Princess Mother Srinagarindra, in 1980. McDaniel comments on the importance of the commercial aspects of the cult of amulets in Thailand as follows:

> Social critics and scholars who lament the crass commercialism of the 'amulet craze' often fail to mention the collateral social services enabled through the funds generated by the craze…. In this way, amulets can be seen as a great benefit to Buddhist communities rather than a local cultural corruption of traditional Buddhist values. (McDaniel 2011, p. 208)

The Cult of Luang Phor *Khoon Amulets*

In the 1990s, the marketing of amulets sacralized by the magic monk *Luang Phor* Khoon, who was described in the previous chapter, be-came a multi-million-baht industry. His monastery of Wat Ban Rai became the focus of this trade in spiritually empowered products, with Khoon himself located at the symbolic centre of an industry that commodified and marketed his charisma (*barami*). The author of one manual describing the plethora of *Luang Phor* Khoon amulets that were produced in the final decades of the monk's life states that he sacralized his first batch in 1969 (Saengphet [1994?]). Thai soldiers fighting communist forces in Laos and Vietnam in the early 1970s who wore these amulets were reported to have been miraculously saved from danger during armed engagements. Khoon's reputation in Khorat province and across Thailand's northeast for miraculously empowered amulets dates from this time. But it was after the disastrous collapse of the shoddily constructed Royal Plaza Hotel in Nakhon Ratchasima in 1993, when the Thai press focussed on survivors who were reported to be wearing *Luang Phor* Khoon amulets, that his cult achieved national scale. Writing in *The Nation* in 1994, Nithinand Yorsaengrat reported,

> In the 1970s, *Luang Phor* Khoon's fame grew. Thai soldiers, officials, politicians and businessmen from everywhere visited him to ask for his amulets.

However, it was after the 1993 [Royal Plaza] hotel collapse that the monk really came to the fore. Today, some of his more famous followers include [former prime minister] Gen. Chatichai Choonhavan, Supreme Commander ACM Voranart Apicharee, and Permanent Secretary for Labour, Sawai Bhramanee.[3]

Nithinand also reported that in the mid-1990s Khoon's monastery received 100,000 baht each weekday and a million baht on weekends from the sale of blessed amulets.[4] A large proportion of these donated funds were used to finance welfare projects. In 1992, Khoon donated 91 million baht to schools in the Northeast, and in 1993 he gave more than 200 million baht to support rural public health services. In 1995, Khoon's projects included a 190-million-baht college in his home district of Dan Khun Thot and a 30-million-baht monks' hospital in Nakhon Ratchasima city.

Speculative investment in Khoon's amulets became a prominent feature of the cult in the mid-1990s. In 1995, *The Nation* reported that because of increasing demand, prices for many types of *Luang Phor* Khoon amulets had "skyrocketed from Bt20 to between Bt1,000 and Bt10,000 each, but the abbot said he condones this increase as a means to finance his planned projects to benefit the public".[5] At the same time, Khoon's most famous amulet reportedly sold for 400,000 baht, with these high prices spawning an active trade in fakes.

Some reformist Buddhists criticized *Luang Phor* Khoon for being part of what they claimed was a well-orchestrated public relations programme involving many lay people associated with Wat Ban Rai who made money from the sale of his amulets. The monk was criticized for selling superstition and promoting the commercialization of Buddhism. Supporters of *Luang Phor* Khoon responded that he did not use the money for himself but donated funds from the sale of amulets to charitable projects. Nonetheless, it is not clear what proportion of donated funds was used for these welfare projects. In response to questions about financial accountability, in 1995 Khoon told *The Nation*: "Donations are carefully documented to ensure that the money goes to the proper causes", but he also added that he "could not be completely sure there was no abuse of donated funds."[6] Considering the role of press and business interests together, it can be said that the *Luang Phor* Khoon phenomenon was significantly influenced by media owners and newspaper editors who were eager to promote sales with stories of miracles and by entrepreneurs interested in profiting from commodifying Khoon's supernatural charisma.

Commodifying Charisma: Sponsoring and Naming Amulets

Batches or *run* of *Luang Phor* Khoon blessed amulets were often given a name, which was either inscribed on the amulet itself or printed on the box in which it was sold. Before the 1990s, *Luang Phor* Khoon's amulets were given more traditional names. Early batches in the 1970s and 1980s were called "school batches" (*run rong-rian*), intended to be sold to raise funds to build a community school, or "*bodhi* leaf batch" (*run bai pho*), the name of an ancient Buddhist symbol referring to the bodhi tree under which the Buddha Gotama is said to have attained enlightenment. From the early 1990s, however, the names of many batches of Khoon's amulets were explicitly linked with money making. The following sample of the names of batches produced in various years in the first half of the decade provides an indication:[7]

1990 – "Fortune, Success, Increase" (*run lap phon phun thawi*).

1990 – "Multiplying Fortune" (*run khoon lap*). Here Khoon's name was used in its literal meaning "to multiply" as an element of the name of the amulet batch. Many subsequent batches also employed this device of including Khoon's name in the title in the sense of "to multiply".

1993 – "Rich for sure" (*run ruay nae*).

1993 – "Doubly Multiplying Wealth" (*run sap thawi-khoon*).

1993 – "Doubly Multiplying Prosperity" (*run mang-mi thawi-khoon*).

1993 – "Tycoon Multiplying Wealth" (*run jao-sua khoon lap*).

1993 – "Requesting an Increase in Wealth" (*run khor phoem sap*).

1993 – "Multiplying wealth, multiplying silver, multiplying gold" (*run khoon lap, khoon ngoen, khoon thorng*).

1994 – "Paying off debts" (*run plot ni*).

Behind-the-Scenes Middle Men: The Cult of Amulets in the Hands of Lay Committees

The production of amulets is often sponsored by laypeople in order to raise funds for charitable activities or to support construction or renovation of Buddhist monasteries or pagodas. It was lay sponsors who paid for the production of the batches of amulets and who chose the names in the list detailed above. As Khoon told *The Nation*:

> 'Sponsors of the amulets always have the design and inscription of their set of amulets ready before asking my permission to produce them. I always give my permission—now, many sets of amulets have been produced.... I forget how many,' *Luang Phor* Khoon said,

adding that he did not really care much about the inscriptions. The sponsors always gave the money they earned from sales of the amulets to charity, according to the monk. He said he normally gets up at 3 am and blesses new amulets until dawn, then goes to greet his followers, hundreds of whom visit his temple every day.[8]

Khoon's relations to wealth thus emerged from the ludic semiotic activities of his followers, and commercial exploiters. It was Khoon's lay followers who first played upon the association of his name with multiplying wealth. The form of Khoon's amulets and other ritual products associated with his cult were thus largely determined by the "market", with the design and naming of such products being in the hands of lay sponsors, who were often business interests who had an eye to maximizing sales amongst believers.

In her study of the connections between the ritual economy mediated by monks and the rise of Thai capitalism in the country's provincial areas in the 1960s and 1970s, Gray describes the important role of "ambitious entrepreneurs" who sought ritual connections from magic monks. She observes that Buddhist monks became "important and unacknowledged business intermediaries … who helped powerful entrepreneurs from Bangkok to form ties with influential rural monks and their followers" (Gray 1986, p. 577). Lay people have thus been key players in the emergence of Thailand's new ritual economy, the size of which remains obscure because it is signified in terms of "religious merit" (*bun*) rather than being described as commercial profit. Gray emphasizes the importance of behind-the-scenes laymen in the development of this ritual economy and the commodification of ritual that has taken place since the 1960s:

> Low-ranking men from the forests and nearby villages report the news of the miracles performed by [magic monks] to district officers or to other low-ranking government officials. These men then pass the news or 'stories' upwards in a chain of command until it reaches their superiors in Bangkok…. These 'big men' (i.e. *phu yai*) may 'go to see for themselves' if the rumors are true, and, if they believe them, arrange *kathin* [robes offering] ceremonies leading to the temple of the monk in question. (Gray 1986, p. 649)

Gray contends that the "missing pieces" in the story of the rise of new forms of commodified popular ritual at the national level have been the roles of

> lay advisors [*makkhanayok*] to Buddhist temples, whose job it is to act as liaison between the Buddhist clergy and the Buddhist laity. It also corresponds to the role of the *sanghakiri* (now the Department

of Religious Affairs), the government department whose job it is to act as a liaison between the Sangha and the government. (Gray 1986, p. 638)

Gray calls these men, who are almost always anonymous, "go-betweens", and she describes how it is often former monks who, upon leaving the sangha and resuming lay life, take on work as decision makers and organizers of the magical economy. While these go-betweens "are socially invisible and their actions undiscussed" (Gray 1986, p. 640) because they are junior in the hierarchical Thai social order, they nonetheless play a central role in linking wealthy sponsors and patrons to magic monks and their ritual authority. Gray adds that "[m]ost government agencies have a particular employee who plays this role in their merit-making ceremonies. He is usually a former monk of common birth who comes from a rural area" (p. 639). She also notes that during the period of her research the then Department of Religious Affairs kept extensive files on Buddhist monks and played the role of intermediary between rural monks, the Sangha Council and the royal palace (p. 669).

Marketing the Magical Aura of Amulets

The efficient nationwide marketing of *Luang Phor* Khoon amulets was shown in an advertisement published in *Thai Rath* on 24 October 1996 (p. 18) for a batch of amulets and talismans collectively named "Doubly Multiplying Prosperity" (*run mang-mi thawi-khoon*), whose production was sponsored by *Phra Khru* Athornsasanakit (Suthep Aphakaro), then abbot of Wat Hua Lamphong in central Bangkok. Prices ranged from 10 baht for a pressed clay *phra phong* amulet to 35,000 baht for a sixty-gramme gold miniature statue of Khoon. The items could be ordered by telephone reservation from a wide range of locations across Thailand, including twelve monasteries in Bangkok, each with its own sales office; twenty-seven amulet sales centres (*sun phra khreuang*) in Bangkok; three large amulet markets in Bangkok (Phanthip Plaza at Pratunam, Jakrawan Phra ["amulet universe"] in Banglamphu, and Queen Plaza at Wang Burapha); twenty-two gold and jewellery shops in Bangkok; and also from twenty-one provincial locations. Credit card orders were welcomed. In this advertisement Khoon is referred to as "His Powerful Holiness Reverend Father Khoon Parisuttho, the Divine Being of the Land of Isan" (*phra det phra khun than Luang Phor Khoon Parisuttho thepphajao haeng daen Isan*), and the accompanying text states that Khoon had given permission to his followers to produce these objects in order to raise funds to build hospitals, schools and other deserving projects. The advertisement claimed that the investment value of these auspicious objects would be ensured by their being produced in limited numbers and by their availability being restricted to orders placed before a specified closing date. In summary, the production and marketing procedures adopted by those associated with the *Luang Phor* Khoon industry in auspicious objects ensured that the items would retain a guaranteed investment value.

The Cult of Jatukham-Ramathep Amulets

The cult of amulets has continued to expand in the early twenty-first century, and new focuses of ritual and speculative attention regularly appear. Since *Luang Phor* Khoon died in 2015, the cult of his amulets has subsided somewhat as he is no longer alive to bless new batches of auspicious objects. However, in 2007, a decade after the Asian economic crisis, another type of amulet that bore the image of the twin deities Jatukham-Ramathep became a national phenomenon. The two deities at the centre of this amulet cult, Jatukham and Ramathep, are legendary founders of the southern Thai city of Nakhon Srithammarat. An ancient shrine with their separate, twinned images is located adjacent to the main pagoda of Wat Mahathat in that city, and these dual gods are believed to be protective deities (*thewarak*; Pali: *deva-raks'a*) of the Buddha's relic located in that monastery's stupa. The twinned deities have long been believed to possess supernatural potency among Buddhists in the south of the country, and the compound name Jatukham-Ramathep means "The Deity Rama of the Four Houses" (Wright 2007).

The intersections of state authority, Sino-Thai business interests, spirit mediums, the cult of amulets and Buddhism in the emergence of new cults of deities of wealth is reflected in the origins of the Jatukham-Ramathep amulets. In the 1980s, a new police chief in Nakhon Srithammarat, Lieutenant-General Sanphen Thammathikun, decided to refresh the city's horoscope and renovate the city pillar shrine. Rachelle Scott (2007) notes that local authorities felt renovation of the old city pillar shrine was required because a number of people believed the area of the shrine was cursed. A group of local Sino-Thai businessmen urged Sanphen to consult a spirit medium at a Chinese shrine near Wat Nang Phayam, a monastery that is dedicated to the mother of the Jatukham-Ramathep deity. The medium drew a strange image and recommended that the lieutenant-general consult *Khun* Phantharakratchadet, a retired policeman and a respected local authority on ritual magic, to interpret the image.

According to some biographies, Butr Phantharak, or *Khun* Phan as he is widely known, was born on 18 February 1898 and died on 6 July 2006, which would have made him 108 upon his death. As Craig Reynolds notes, 108 is a highly auspicious number in Thai Buddhism as it is "the number of marks on the soles of the Buddha's feet" (Reynolds 2019, p. 32).[9] As the *Bangkok Post* reported, *Khun* Phan was "believed to be the last commoner holding the noble title of *Khun*", a title abolished after the overthrow of the absolute monarchy in June 1932.[10] *Khun* Phan appears to have received the name Phantharakratchadet as part of the conferral of the noble title.[11] *Khun* Phan was regarded to be a local hero, who in his earlier years as a policeman had helped restore law and order to the once gangster-ridden province of Nakhon Srithammarat. As the *Bangkok Post* noted, "[t]he late policeman was famous for his expertise in incantations and was a disciple of Jatukarm-Ramathep, believed by worshippers to be the guardians of Nakhon Si Thammarat city."[12]

Reynolds reports that *Khun* Phan was able to identify the image drawn by the spirit medium for Lieutenant-General Sanphen as a composite of the guardian deities protecting the reliquary at Wat Mahathat:

> When the policeman [Sanphen] returned to the shrine to report the news, the spirit of Jatukham-Ramathep spoke through the medium, saying, 'I've been waiting for you for a thousand years! Now I'll tell you how to build the city pillar shrine.' (Reynolds 2019, p. 141).

Scott states that in order to purify the space of the old, supposedly cursed city pillar shrine, the image of the newly instituted compound deity Jatukham-Ramathep was made of wood from a takian tree, "a wood with strong associations to the lottery…. Mae Takien Thong is a female spirit whom Thais believe inhabits Takien trees. Many believe that she reveals lucky lottery numbers on the surface of her body (the trunk of tree)" (Scott 2017, p. 235). Reynolds reports that amulets of the image of the double-headed Jatukham-Ramathep deity were struck and sold to the public to raise funds to build the new city pillar shrine for the city (Reynolds 2019, p. 56). In 1987, *Khun* Phan was a key figure in the production and consecration of the first batch of Jatukham-Ramathep amulets (p. 10) and he presided at the formal consecration of the image of the "new" compound deity at the renovated city pillar shrine on 4 August 1987, which was also attended by then prime minister General Prem Tinsulanonda, a southerner from Songkhla.

Khun Phan's royal-sponsored cremation was held at Wat Mahathat in Nakhon Srithammarat at the end of February 2007, an event that was presided over by then Crown Prince Vajiralongkorn and his then consort HRH Princess Srirasmi. It was reported that a hundred thousand people attended the cremation.[13] In reporting *Khun* Phan's cremation, a *Bangkok Post* journalist wrote:

> Sociologist Narong Boonsuayfan, of Nakhon Si Thammarat-based Walailak University, said he believed most of the people attending the cremation were more interested in the talismans than in the bravery and good deeds of the late policeman. 'The Jatukarm-Ramathep phenomenon is a reflection of Thai people's obsession with money. They went to the cremation to get the talisman and then make money from it,' he said.[14]

After *Khun* Phan's death in 2006 and his royal-sponsored cremation in February the following year, the type of amulets established by the former policeman became a national phenomenon. Pattana Kitiarsa notes,

> At the height of its popularity in 2006 and 2007, the Chatukham-Ramathep amulet was the most sought-after talisman in the country, and the production, circulation, and consumption of this religious commodity had created a multi-billion-dollar industry. (2012, p. 111)

The rapid nationwide rise in popularity, and the huge sums of money spent on amulets, of the previously obscure figure of Jatukham-Ramathep was a major news story in 2007. The sums of money spent on mass-produced amulets of Jatukham-Ramathep were so large that this ostensibly religious phenomenon was reported widely in the business sections of newspapers and made front-page news in business magazines. Wipha Jiraphaisan (2007) cites an unquoted source on the size of the Thai amulet industry in 2007 as stating sales for non-Jatukham amulets sold in that year totalled 15–20 billion baht, while sales of Jatukham-Ramathep amulets alone totalled 10 billion baht, equalling 1.5 per cent of Thailand's GDP for that year. One item published in the Business Section of the *Bangkok Post* reported that "[t]he Jatukarm-Ramathep craze has brought good fortune to the country's newspapers, which recorded 10.47% growth in advertising spending in July [2007] due almost entirely to the amulets."[15] This news item also reported that the funds spent on amulets, such as those of Jatukham-Ramathep, were so great that the Bangkok office of the international Nielsen Media Research company was keeping records of spending on press and media advertising for *wathu-mongkhon* or "sacred objects".

At the height of the popularity of Jatukham-Ramathep amulets in July 2007, Nielsen reported that 111.54 million baht had been spent on this category of advertising in the Thai press in one month, which was fourteen times the amount spent a year previously in July 2006:

> The first seven months of the year [January–July 2007] for the [sacred object] category accounted for 465.78 million baht, against 69.35 million a year earlier.
>
> Mass-market Thai-language newspapers received the lion's share of the amulet ads but the party appears to be over. The law of supply and demand has caught up with the amulets and their prices have fallen like a stone—some can now be bought for five baht each or even bought in bulk.[16]

The *Phra* Jatukham-Ramathep amulet craze represented a religious phenomenon that was subject to the economic laws of supply and demand. Demand for the amulets waned in the second half of 2007: "The oversupply of amulets including the sale of fake ones caused prices to drop sharply."[17]

Nonetheless, on 29 March 2008, just one year after the amulets had become a phenomenon across the country, the national postal authority, Thailand Post, issued a special set of twelve Jatukham-Ramathep postage stamps. Each stamp in the set was valued at nine baht, when the domestic postage rate for a letter at the time was only three baht.

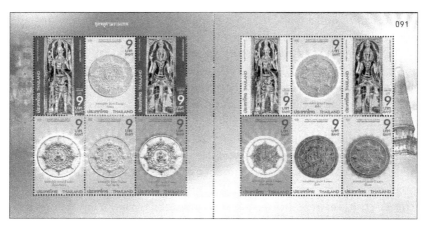

IMAGE 22. Jatukham-Ramathep Stamps
Set of twelve stamps of various images and amulets of the hybrid deity Jatukham-Ramathep issued by Thailand Post in March 2008. Thailand Post issued these stamps less than a year after Jatukham-Ramathep magical amulets became a national phenomenon, reflecting the responsiveness of national organizations to new forms of the cults of wealth. Each stamp's value of 9 baht and the stamp sheet total value of 108 baht reflect the numerological significance of these numbers in Thai magical lore.

Giving the stamps a value of nine baht can be interpreted as a numerological link to King Bhumibol, King Rama IX. Furthermore, nine
times twelve (the number of stamps in the set), equals 108, which, as
noted above, is an auspicious number in Thai Buddhism and was the
reputed age of *Khun* Phan when he died in 2006. The importance of
magical numerology in the Thai cults of wealth is detailed further in
the next chapter. *Thai Stamp Bulletin*, the official philatelic organ of
Thailand Post, advertised the special stamp issue under the heading,
"Power of Faith and Belief" (*phalang haeng sattha lae khwam-cheua*).
The accompanying text in broken English dates the oldest amulets to
1987, the year in which the Nakhon Srithammarat city pillar shrine
was renovated and rededicated to Jatukham-Ramathep, and notes
its hybrid Brahmanical/Buddhist sources and supernatural import:
"Present [i.e., nowadays], Chatukham-Rammathep is high received
respects all over by believing that it's supernatural power in all fields
to be comparable to Sun and Moon for getting rid of the darkness
of the earth."[18] The issuing of the Jatukham-Ramathep stamp set by
the national post office demonstrates the extent to which the cult of
amulets has become a mainstream religious phenomenon. I discuss
other recent stamp issues that represent the cults of wealth in Chapter
Six.

Spirit Possession and Ritual Dimensions of the Cults of Wealth

Spirit cults are prominent in popular Thai religious practice, and spirit
possession rituals are associated with many of the cults of wealth, including the worship of Indian deities, the Mahayana bodhisattva Kuan
Im, royal personalities such as King Chulalongkorn, and deceased
magic monks. Not all spirit medium cults are related to the cults of
wealth, and not all followers of the cults of wealth participate in spirit
possession rituals. Indeed, spirit possession is often criticized and at
times has been denounced by reformist Buddhists. Nonetheless, there
is a significant overlap between the cults of wealth and rituals of spirit
possession, and the two sets of phenomena share a number of similarities. Notably, the cults of wealth and spirit cults have both grown in
number and prominence over the past few decades, they are both highly
commodified religious forms and there is a significant overlap in the
communities of devotees who follow both religious forms. Like the
cults of wealth, contemporary professional spirit possession cults are
just as much for the winners from Thailand's economic development
as for the losers. Spirit possession cults are accessed by all levels of Thai

society, including the rural and urban poor, the professional middle classes in government service and the private sector, the wealthy, and the military and police. In a study that presented a regional synthesis of forms of spirit possession across mainland Southeast Asia, George Condominas (1976) noted that, historically, institutional spirit possession has been present at all levels of social organization—including lineages, villages and polities—and has served diverse functions from the therapeutic to promoting prosperity and maintaining territorial integrity. Condominas also argued that Southeast Asian spirit possession is typically embedded in complex religious configurations, often dominated by Buddhism, and is based on a conception of the person as formed by a plurality of souls and according to which multiple spirits are manifested in succession in possession rituals in a hierarchical order.

At the height of what is often described as Thailand's modernizing developmentalist period during the Cold War, sections of Thailand's military elites participated publicly in supernatural cults linked with spirit mediumship. In the 1970s, the Hupphasawan movement of the spirit medium Suchat Kosonkittiwong attracted followers from among the most senior and powerful sections of the Thai military and political establishment (Jackson 1989). Spirit mediums are sought out by all levels of Thai society in their engagements with global modernity and they provide symbolic means to empower followers to become active beneficiaries of the new economic order. Unlike millenarian movements or forms of religious fundamentalism, modern spirit possession cults in Thailand assume the capitalist order as given and seek to locate their followers advantageously within that order.

Indeed, a key parallel between the cults of wealth and new forms of spirit possession is their common association with the market economy. Spirit mediums not only channel deities at the centre of the cults of wealth but they have now also become professional specialists who make their living from performing spirit possession rituals for clients. Erick White observes that professional spirit mediums are widely reported in the Thai mass media and they "occupy a position of socio-cultural dominance in relation to other forms and traditions" (White 2014, p. 37) of spirit possession in Thailand. And just as the cults of wealth are recent modern phenomena, the forms of professional spirit mediumship that are now efflorescing in Thailand and across mainland Southeast Asia are also contemporary forms of religious expression, and not static survivals from the premodern past (see Bénédicte Brac de la Perrière and Peter A. Jackson 2022). Speaking comparatively of the growth of spirit possession and shamanistic ritual across East and Southeast Asia, Ruth Inge-Heinz observes,

> Wherever we find shamans today, their shamanism cannot be purely a relic from the past.... No religious form survives thousands of years without change. New shamans appear when old values and beliefs break down. Whenever socio-economic or political changes force a society to move into unknown territory, shamanic practices emerge from elementary levels. (Heinze 1988, pp. 30–31)

Rosalind Morris notes that under the influence of Western discourses of reason and science, in the nineteenth and early twentieth centuries spirit mediumship in Thailand came to be imagined as an "interruption of the nation's modernity" (Morris 2000b, p. 459). Indeed, she adds that, "thirty years ago, spirit mediumship itself was imagined as being on the verge of disappearance" (p. 458). However, in contrast to this situation only a few decades ago, she notes a dramatic increase in the numbers of practising spirit mediums in Chiang Mai in the final decades of the twentieth century, of the order of several hundred per cent. Like the cult of amulets and cults of wealth, the phenomenon of professional spirit mediumship dates from the period after World War II. White (2014, pp. 259ff) notes that Walter Irvine's informants reported that there were only about 30 mediums in Chiang Mai in the 1950s, but the number had grown to 250–300 at the time of his research in 1977 (Irvine 1982, p. 317). Marjorie Muecke reports that in Chiang Mai "between the late 1950s and late 1970s there was a six-fold increase in the proportion of spirit mediums per 1000 population" (Muecke 1992, p. 97). Shigeharu Tanabe (2002, p. 65n2) and Morris (2000a, p. 236) both reported between 800 and 1,100 mediums in the city in the 1990s.

The Centrality of Spirit Possession to Popular Thai Buddhism: Monks as Mediums

Increasing numbers of scholars (e.g., Muecke 1992; White 2014; Visisya 2018) now argue that, in contrast to earlier research that viewed spirit possession cults as being distinct from Buddhism, spirit mediumship is a central and increasingly important element of Thai Buddhism. Several decades ago, Stanley Tambiah described Thai religiosity as having a "double relationship to the divine through priesthood and possession" (Tambiah 1970, pp. 369–70), pointing to the intimate relationship between Buddhism and spirit possession in Thai popular Buddhism. And Muecke observes that "[b]oth monks and mediums are socially acknowledged as privileged channels of communication between humans and the supernatural…. Both groups, mediums and monks, aspire to the same end, an end that each group complements the other in achieving" (Muecke 1992, p. 102).

Pattana Kitiarsa (2005b), Visisya Pinthongvijayakul (2015) and Bernard Formoso (2016) have all challenged the stark contrast between Buddhism and spirit possession, and between monks and mediums, that was characteristic of earlier studies of Thai Buddhism. White argues that "[t]he phenomenon of spirit possession is not only more widespread, commonplace, and valued among Theravada Buddhists than classical anthropological models argue, it is also more deeply entangled with normative Buddhist ideology, ethos, and practice" (White 2017, p. 191). Recent studies provide examples of Buddhist monks and mediums collaborating in rituals, monks deferring to the authority of mediums, monks becoming possessed, and laity treating possession as a technique of ritual prowess that parallels or even rivals monasticism (p. 193). Pattana has sought to erase the categorical divide between Buddhism and mediumship. Taking practice rather than scripture as his starting point, Pattana describes magic monks (*keji ajan*) and spirit mediums (*rang song, khon song*) as both representing forms of mediumship (Pattana 2012). He describes magic monks who sacralize and empower amulets as practising a modified form of mediumship in which they invite an *ong tham*, which Pattana describes as a "dhammic calling" or "superagency", to guide their actions: "Every magic monk needs … a superagency … a powerful god, goddess, or other deity, who owns and exercises his or her agency through a human mouthpiece or medium with communicative capability and ritual expertise" (Pattana 2005b, p. 213). Pattana gives the example of one group of followers of a monk of the Thammayut Order in Northeast Thailand who observe a magical practice called *wicha duangtham*, "the knowledge of the *dhamma* orb", and whose superagency is referred to as an *ong tham*, "a *dhammic* being", which denotes the spirits of Buddhist *arahants* who lived at the time of the Buddha (p. 213). When in meditation, the followers of *wicha duangtham* speak in tongues, which is described as *phasa tham* or "dhammic language". In this case we have a set of ritual practices that closely mirror spirit possession but which are framed within a Buddhist symbolic and discursive context. Pattana describes Thai magical Buddhism and mediumship as complementary forms and components of a single religious complex. As White notes, Pattana "identifies the experience of possession as foundational to the charismatic authority of both spirit mediums (possessed by virtuous gods) and magical monks (possessed by a virtuous dharmic essence)" (White 2014, p. 297).

Spirit mediums share some similar functions with magic monks in the spiritual and psychological services offered to their clients. As Pattana notes, both categories of ritual specialists practice magic and claim to have gained supernatural powers in the name of their super-agency, with the assistance of various kinds of magic, and "[t]hey both receive money and some other rewards from their clients" (Pattana 2005b, p. 219). The types of services offered to devotees/clients for fees by both magic monks and spirit mediums include eliminating bad omens or the reduction of misfortune and strengthening good fate (*sadorh khrorh*); astrological fortune telling (*du duang*); spraying sacralized holy water to ward off bad luck and provide protection from evil spirits (*rot nam mon*); enhancing or renewing one's lifespan (*tor ayu/seup chata*); exorcizing bad spirits (*lai phi/khap porp*); setting up a house or altar for a guardian spirit (*yok san phra phum*); blessing a new car, house or office (*joem rot, joem ban, joem samnak-ngan*); and providing tips for winning lottery numbers (*bai huai, hai chok hai lap*).

While doctrinal Buddhists maintain a clear distinction between the spiritual insights of Buddhist monks that derive from meditative practice, on the one hand, and the statements of spirit mediums when possessed by deities, on the other, the line between Buddhist insight and possession is often blurred. Buddhist monks may not invoke the discourse of "possession" (*khao song*), but they do employ the notion of having meditation-inspired "visions" (*nimit*) and they also invoke the prophetic and revelatory power of dreams. Jovan Maud notes that the current national popularity of images and amulets of the legendary Southern Thai monk *Luang Phor* Thuat, who was described in Chapter Four, came from the vision of one monk, *Ajan* Thim:

> As the result of a series of visions and other 'discoveries', *Ajan* Thim proved himself to be the primary and privileged 'medium' through which the essence of *Luang Phò* Thuat came to take material form. It needs to be emphasised, however, that *Ajan* Thim never claimed to be possessed by the ancestral saint. His 'mediumship' derived from his superior ability 'to see the world as it really is', especially his superior sensitivity to the presence of *Luang Phò* Thuat, and the authority that derived from them. (Maud 2007, p. 201)

Kazuo Fukuura describes the way that a Buddhist monk he studied in Northern Thailand negotiated the fine ritual distinction between the rituals of possession and Buddhism:

And it is striking to note that there is a Buddhist monk who is possessed by a village guardian spirit. As a medium, the monk does not perform any services for clients, but he organizes the annual ritual for worshipping the spirit in a local event around his temple, inviting many spirit mediums to participate. This kind of ritual is generally called *yok khu*, or the 'ritual of worshipping deceased masters'. It is held annually by each medium, and on this particular occasion, the host medium invites the other mediums to join in. (Fukuura 2011, pp. 112–13)

Kaj Århem (2016a, 2016b) argues that a "possession complex" lies at the heart of regional forms of animism in Southeast Asia. Historically, deceased ancestors were the beings who are invoked in Southeast Asian animism. While recent research confirms that possession remains at the heart of Thai popular religion, including the cults of wealth, it has undergone a number of significant changes. Pattana argues that urban spirit mediumship in Thailand is a novel phenomenon that constitutes a distinct new field within Thai popular religion and which has emerged only in the last few decades. He traces its genealogy to a convergence of "Buddhist millennialism, the persistence of folk spirit-medium cults, the consequences of rural-to-urban migration and rapid urbanisation, the influence of court Brahmanistic rituals, and the influences of Chinese and Indian communities in urban areas" (Pattana 2012, p. 16). White also argues that professional spirit mediumship is not merely a reworking of pre-existing ancestral and guardian spirit cults but rather is a complexly articulated form of emergent religiosity that draws upon many distinct traditions of popular religion, including folk and court Brahmanism as well as Chinese and Hindu spirit mediumship (White 2014, p. 273). Muecke similarly reports that "the spirit medium cults now on the rise in northern Thailand serve not ancestral spirits [as in the past], but *thewadaa*, the spirits of figures of regional or national, historical and religious significance. *Thewadaa* derive from the Brahmanical system of deities" (Muecke 1992, p. 98).

White contends that professional spirit mediumship is fundamentally different from other indigenous forms of Thai mediumship because of its entrepreneurial or professional—that is, commercial—nature (White 2014, p. 123). Pattana (2005b) uses the expression "urban spirit medium cult" (*latthi-phithi song jao khao phi*) to distinguish this type of spirit cult from the traditional village ancestral cults that Århem describes in his account of the Southeast Asian possession complex. White summarizes the key distinguishing characteristics of professional spirit mediums as being: (1) a reconceptualization of beliefs, practices and experiences as being more explicitly Buddhist;

(2) a transformation of part-time practitioners into full-time professionals with a calling; and (3) the creation of relatively autonomous religious subcultures and social worlds, which is also the case for other dimensions of popular religiosity (White 2014, p. 354).

White argues that in light of recent studies of the expanding spirit possession cults in Thailand and neighbouring Southeast Asian societies we need to fundamentally rethink classical models of possession and Buddhism. He points to "plural, fluid and contested understandings of possession" in complex and multiple relations with diverse forms of Buddhism in Thailand, stating that "[w]e cannot posit a singular Buddhism in dialogue with a singular spirit possession. Rather, we have multiple projects for envisioning Buddhism in dialogue with multiple modalities of spirit possession" (White 2017, p. 195).

The cults of wealth overlap significantly with the pantheon of lords (*jao*) and deities (*thep*) at the centre of Thai professional spirit mediumship. Spirit mediums speak of "lineages" or "lines" (*sai*) of possessing deities from different cultural or ethnic categories, such as *sai Thai* (Thai deities), *sai Jin* (Chinese deities), *sai Khaek* or *sai Hindu* (Indian deities) (White 2014, p. 87). White identifies four lineages or categories of deities among professional spirit mediums: (1) deified royalist figures from Thai history; (2) gods from Hindu and Buddhist mythology; (3) Chinese Buddhist bodhisattvas and figures from Chinese mythology; (4) and spirits of highly accomplished Buddhist virtuosos such as revered monks (p. 85).[19] These are precisely the same categories of deities that are at the centre of the cults of wealth, and White notes that mediums often serve as "the central officiants" in the rituals associated with the prosperity cults (p. 106).

In the subculture of Bangkok's professional spirit mediums, the lineages of *Thai, Jin* and *Khaek/Hindu* are signifiers of three discrete but powerful sources of sacral power. White maintains that these three sets of terms no longer mark ethnic identity or national origin but instead point to civilizational regimes of supramundane cosmological and ritual efficaciousness that can be accessed by Thais from all backgrounds. In a study of a shrine to a Chinese deity in the Southern Thai town of Krabi, Eric Cohen describes the officiating spirit medium as "a southern Thai 'religious entrepreneur', with only tenuous links to a Chinese ancestry, who serves as a professional Chinese spirit medium, though he identifies himself as a Buddhist and has even been ordained as a Theravada monk" (Cohen 2008, p. 85).

Thai, Jin and *Khaek/Hindu* also function as a framework for organizing combinations of these three "lineages" in the ritual lives of mediums, with many being possessed by idiosyncratic amalgams of deities from two or all three of these three lineages (White 2014, p. 88). Bangkok's professional mediums now treat public celebrations of Chinese and Hindu spirit possession as extensions of their own subcultural cycle of festivities and celebrations, "regardless of the fact that Chinese and Hindu religious officiants do not regard these festivals in this light and are even somewhat critical of the presence of professional mediums at those events" (p. 130). This blending of multiple Thai, Chinese and Indian religio-cultural lineages reflects the intersections found in the symbolic complex of the cults of wealth that I detail in the next chapter. The de-ethnicization of these civilizational regimes of ritual is also a further marker of the integration of Thailand's Sino-Thai into the mainstream of Thai social, cultural and political life.

Summary

Twenty-first-century Thailand presents a picture of an extremely dynamic complex of contextually distinct and ritually autonomous, but nonetheless intersecting, religious "lines", each of which is changing rapidly and is also having significant impacts on other dimensions of Thai religious life. This represents additional complexity for what was already a highly diverse and multiple-structured universe of religious rituals, doctrines and specialists.

The complexity of the intersections among the cults of wealth, the cult of magically empowered amulets and professional spirit mediumship in contemporary Thailand challenges established models of Theravada Buddhist religiosity. To add to this complexity is the fact that the different cults of wealth also intersect in symbolic forms, commercial spaces and in ritual objects in contextualized amalgams that do not conform to theories of religious syncretism or cultural hybridity. Beyond the distinctive rituals, devotional and supplicatory incantations, shrines and sacred sites associated with each prosperity cult, from the late 1990s media representations and mass-marketed ritual objects increasingly combined symbolisms of many of the cults in one location, forming a symbolic complex that linked the cults into a loosely integrated religious formation. The amalgam of the symbolic complex of the cults of wealth reflects the polyontological and contextualized form of mixing without combining outlined in Chapter Three. I detail the symbolic complex of the cults of wealth in the next chapter, describing how it reflects widespread patterns found across the Thai religious field. The formation of the symbolic complex of prosperity cults also represents a significant sociological transition as the cults moved from originally marginal positions to the centre of national religious life.

Notes

1. *Luang Pu* Phang (1902–82) was of the lineage of the meditation master *Ajan* Fan, who in turn was of the lineage of the famous meditation master *Ajan* Man. Gray states that *Ajan* Man (1870–1949) became famous in the 1960s, sometime after he died, when his relics came to be regarded as having magical properties.

2. Other politicians and their favourite amulets detailed in this book were Niphon Phrormphan, deputy head of the Democrat Party, who displayed his *Somdet* To amulet; Anuthin Chanwirakul, leader of the Bhumijai Thai Party; Jorngchai Thiangtham, former minister of communications; Suvat Liptapallop, former deputy prime minister, who described his *Luang Phor* Khoon amulets; Prasopsuk Bundej, president of the Senate in 2010; Nikhom Wairatphanit, senator for Chachoengsao Province and deputy president of the Senate; Direk Theungfang, senator for Nonthaburi Province; Chaloemchai Sri-orn, senator for Prachuapkhirikhan Province and deputy head of the Democrat Party; Somsak Prisananananthakul, head of the Chat Thai Phattana Party; and Samphan Thorngsamak, Democrat Party MP for Nakhon Srithammarat Province.

3. Nithinand Yorsaengrat, "The Humble Face of Buddhism", *The Nation*, 3 March 1994, pp. C1–C2.

4. Ibid.

5. "Those Not-so-Magic Charms of *Luang Phor* Koon", *The Nation*, 21 September 1995, p. A5.

6. Ibid.

7. Summarized from *Luang Phor Khoon Parisuttho* [1996?] and Saengphet [1994?].

8. "Those Not-so-Magic Charms".

9. The auspicious number 108 also occurs in other settings in Buddhist teachings. The *Samyutta Nikaya* of the Pali canon includes the *Atthasatta Sutta*, "The Exposition on 108", in which the Buddha lists 36 past feelings, 36 future feelings and 36 present feelings, totalling 108.

10. Woranuj Maneerungsee, "Media Advertising: Jatukarm Amulets Good News for Papers", *Bangkok Post*, 10 August 2007, Business Section, p. B1.

11. Reynolds translates the former policeman's new name as meaning "duty-bound to protect the power of the king" (Reynolds 2019, p. 61).

12. "Talismans Draw Huge Crowd to Cremation", *Bangkok Post*, 23 February 2007, p. 3.

13. Ibid.

14. Ibid.

15. Woranuj , "Media Advertising".
16. Ibid.
17. "Religion: Jatukarm Craze on the Wane, but Faith Intact", *Bangkok Post*, 13 August 2007, p. 1.
18. Verbatim text as published, *Julasan Khao Sataem Thai* (Thai stamp bulletin), 2008, no. 1, pp. 16–17.
19. What links all these lords and deities is that they share a common designatory particle in Thai, *ong*, while, in contrast, the older Thai category of possessing spirits, *phi*, are classed as *ton*. Among spirit mediums, a person who has a propensity towards possession or is in a state of possession is described as *mi ong*, "having *ong*" (White 2014, p. 86n60). Members of the royal family are also described by the same classifier *ong*. In contrast, the classifier *khon* is used to denote all other human beings. This linguistic feature reveals links between the monarchy and high-level deities in the new phenomenon of professional spirit mediumship. Indeed, court Brahmins have played a role in the rise of professional spirit mediumship, with White noting that individuals and families that claim to be descendants of royal court Brahmins have been active in numerous ways within the subculture of professional spirit mediums (p. 275).

Chapter Six

The Symbolic Complex of Thai Cults of Wealth

Introduction: From the Margins to the Centre of the Thai Religious Field

Since the mid-1990s, images and representations of the diverse range of Thai prosperity cults detailed in the previous chapters have increasingly occurred together in the same locations. They have appeared jointly among the images installed on spirit medium shrines, in collections of amulets and other ritual objects, in the symbolism of commercial products such as on New Year greeting cards, and on official postage stamps. While the figures associated with these movements are the objects of distinct devotional cults, an increasing symbolic collocation and interpenetration of the different strands of the Thai cults of wealth has become increasingly evident.

For example, On 5 December 1998, the birthday of the late King Bhumibol and at the height of the Asian economic crisis, *Khao Sot* daily newspaper carried an advertisement for a set of five gold images that included Kuan Im in her form with a thousand arms (*Kuan Im phan meu*); Kuan Im in a meditation pose (*Kuan Im pang samathi*); Ganesh; the Lord Buddha being protected by a serpent naga king (*Phra nak prok*); and the magic monk *Luang Pu* Thuat. All these images had been sacralized in a *pluk sek* magical empowerment ritual on 27 November 1998 under the sponsorship of the then Sangharaja or

---

Sections of this chapter draw on material presented in Jackson (1999a), Jackson (1999b) and Jackson (2016).

Supreme Patriarch of the Thai sangha at Wat Bowornniwet, the most important royal monastery in Thailand. The advertisement stated that funds raised from the sale of these diverse images were to be used to renovate Wat Wachirathammawat monastery in Phitsanulok Province in the country's mid-north. In addition to showing their growing intersection, this example also indicates the extent to which deities and spiritual figures associated with the Chinese, Hindu and Theravada cults of wealth had become mainstream religious forms that had been brought within the scope of state-sponsored official Buddhism by the final years of the 1990s.

In this chapter I show how the coming together of representations of the different cults of wealth in diverse fields reflects the structuring principles of vernacular Thai religiosity outlined in Chapter Three. The symbolic complex is an amalgam of representations of discrete, non-syncretized cults that—while all being found in the same ritual sites, commercial locations and mediatized spaces—remain ontologically distinct. The examples of the symbolic complex detailed in latter sections of this chapter reflect the polyontological character of this emergent phenomenon in the Thai religious field and the continuing significance of contextualization, or joining without merging, in contemporary Thai religious life. While the deities in the cults of wealth are typically new additions to the expanding Thai pantheon, and the commercial purposes for which their assistance is sought represent a shift from the traditional apotropaic focus of Thai *saksit* magical ritual, the structuring patterns of the new cults reflect continuities and historical associations with older forms of ritual observance. Indeed, the primacy of ritual practice over doctrine and teachings is a key dimension of continuity between older forms of magic and the symbolic complex of cults of wealth. The symbolic complex has only been able to emerge as an amalgamated field of representations because the contextualized, polyontological multiplicity of cults is held together by the common embodied attitude of ritual respect that devotees exhibit towards all the deities and spiritual figures. After outlining the notion of a symbolic complex, I detail how the additive logic of Thailand's polyontological and contextualized field of religious ritual is reflected in the representational logic of this amalgam.

While followers of the different cults of wealth may not be required or expected to hold to a single doctrinal view of the focuses of their devotion, they do nonetheless share common understandings of the symbolic references and associations of numbers, colours and incantatory phrases that enable them to ascribe significance to images and representations of different deities and spirits. Numerology and astrologically significant colours are key features of the symbolic complex that build links among the ritual figures. I detail how the structuring patterns of vernacular Thai religiosity are expressed in the symbolic complex in the novel and previously secular domains of commercial enterprises, advertising and mass marketing. I then provide examples of the expansion of the symbolic complex of cults of wealth from spirit medium altars to commercially mass-produced ritual objects, postage stamps and other situations. The continuing expansion of the scope of the domains across which the symbolic complex of cults of wealth is found reflects the progressive incorporation of these ritual forms within mainstream religiosity among Thailand's economic and political elites.

Symbolic Complex

In the anthropology of religion, "ritual complex" describes heterogeneous and intersecting forms of popular belief—linked more through common patterns of ritual observance than by statements of faith or doctrine—that characterize much vernacular religious practice in Southeast Asia and China (see, for example, Cohen 2001, p. 50; Wong 2001, p. 163; Formoso 2010, p. 15). Drawing on the notion of ritual complex, I use "symbolic complex" to describe the mediatized and other symbolic fields of representation within which the various deities and spiritual figures of the Thai cults of wealth are made accessible both visually and materially, and through which they are often marketed as objects of ritual consumption. Symbolic complex expands the idea of ritual complex by denoting the relocation of images of ritual significance from traditional locations on altars and in shrines to the commodified domains of print, visual and electronic media as well as on commercially produced ritual objects. Symbolic complex also denotes the fact that the diverse deities and supernatural personages worshipped in the Thai prosperity cults are not linked by a common doctrine but rather by a collective aura that emerges from their physical and visual collocation in the same ritual spaces or in the same commercial media. As detailed further in the next chapter, this mediatized aura is an important force contributing to the production of new forms of enchantment. Irene Stengs uses "amalgam" to denote something similar to what I describe as the symbolic complex of prosperity cults, noting that "[t]he King Chulalongkorn cult is clearly but one element in the amalgam of cults that constitutes Thai popular religiosity today" (Stengs 2009, p. 177). She also adds that in Thai popular Buddhism the King Chulalongkorn cult is "part of an interrelated and versatile repertoire of practices, beliefs and symbols surrounding a wide variety of charismatic and magical figures" (p. 178).

Erick White draws on my notion of symbolic complex when he observes that the pantheon of possessing deities in the contemporary community of professional spirit mediums reflects "a larger shared symbolic complex of supramundane entities active within the cosmos [of] popular Thai Buddhist religiosity" (White 2014, p. 330). He is of the view that the most unusual aspect of the efflorescence of Thai popular religiosity in the 1980s and 1990s "was the deepening symbolic and social interconnections between these otherwise relatively independent practitioners, movements and associations" (p. 328). White regards this symbolic complex as being unusual because it constitutes an amalgam of "diffuse national 'cultic' movements with no specific leader, no overarching institutional organisation, and no primary centre of collective worship" (p. 255). Nonetheless, he suggests that the symbolic interconnections among the different cults of wealth provide "intriguing indications of deeper historical interrelationships between different strands of popular religiosity which suggest the hidden role that various forms of popular religiosity have played in each other's historical emergence and constitution" (p. 329). Indeed, the longer-term history of Thai vernacular religion over the past couple of centuries remains to be written, and in Chapter Three I sketched outlines for the beginnings of an alternative history of Thai modernity that places magical ritual at the centre of narratives of the country's transformations since the middle of the nineteenth century. In the following section I consider some of the structuring principles of the symbolic complex that I hope bring to light aspects of the "hidden role" of "the deeper historical interrelationships" among the cults of wealth that White refers to.

An Implicit Religio-Symbolic Complex

The overall phenomenon of this complex of new cults—some of which are Buddhist, some Brahmanical, some Chinese and all thoroughly capitalist—has not been given a single descriptive label in Thai. Nonetheless, the increasing penetration of economic and commercial forces and symbols into Thai religious practice is often critically labelled as *phuttha phanit* or "commercialized Buddhism" and has been widely denounced by reformist Buddhists, both monks and laity. Pattana Kitiarsa uses the expression *phuttha phanit* to refer to the cults of prosperity in ways that are similar to my notion of the symbolic complex.

Pattana states that "[t]he occult economy produced by and maintained through the cults of *phuttha phanit* represents the most compelling embodiment of popular religiosity in contemporary Thailand" (Pattana 2008b, p. 140). He adds that the cults of *phuttha phanit* emerge from "fertile syncretic religious traditions [of] Theravada Buddhism, folk Brahmanism, animism, supernaturalism, magic and the worship of Chinese and Indian gods and goddesses" (p. 131).

While the symbolic complex is not formally identified as a unified phenomenon in Thai discourses—whether popular, academic or official—taken as a whole it constitutes a distinctive religious phenomenon that, since the 1990s, has become a de facto national religion of wealth incorporating elements of state-sponsored Buddhism while placing prosperity at the symbolic and devotional centre of ritual practice. The collectivity of prosperity movements came to be linked symbolically with nationalist narratives of Thai development, growth and cultural pride; narratives that in earlier decades had been related to state-sponsored Buddhism. By the time of the onset of the economic crash in July 1997, the prosperity cults had come to link the general populace, Sino-Thai business interests, the state and the monarchy under the comforting symbolic roof of royal spirits, Chinese and Indian gods, and magic monks. The cult of the monarchy is also a central feature of the symbolic complex, especially the figures of King Chulalongkorn and King Bhumibol. King Bhumibol has represented several roles in the mythos and symbolism of the cults of wealth. He is variously represented as a bodhisattva king, a *devaraja* whose semi-divine powers include both protection and prosperity, and he is also seen as an ethical religious model, following his own personal spiritual quest.

Stengs critiques my notion of symbolic complex as "missing the point" that the elements of the complex are "rooted in the same Buddhist cosmology" and that in an earlier study (Jackson 1999b) I presented the symbolic complex "as a separate object in Thai social reality" (Stengs 2009, p. 295n48) from Buddhism. As I hope to have made clear in the previous chapters, I do not see the symbolic complex of prosperity cults as being separate from Thai Buddhism, and this misunderstanding of my account may have arisen because, as detailed in this chapter, the symbolic connections and associations among the cults are often more implicit than explicit.

Precedents for the Symbolic Complex

Precedents for the forms of symbolic intersection among diverse figures of the cults of wealth can be traced to the 1960s and 1970s.

The controversial spirit medium Suchat Kosonkittiwong (see Jackson 1988), who founded the Pusawan and Hupphasawan movements, channelled several key figures of what, a couple of decades later, would become the prosperity cults. Suchat developed a complex religious system that combined elements of Thai and Chinese spirit beliefs, Theravada prophecies of the future Buddha Maitreya, and Brahmanically influenced beliefs in a benevolent world spirit (Pali: *loka viññaṇa*; Thai: *lok winyan*) that guided human history. Suchat used his idiosyncratic religious system to support a stridently nationalistic and anti-communist political position. With financial support from influential followers, Suchat began an extensive construction programme at the Hupphasawan religious complex in Ratchaburi Province west of Bangkok in the 1970s. Large statues of Jesus, Mary mother of Jesus, the Buddha, the future Buddha *Phra Sri* Ariya Maitreya in the form of the bodhisattva Kuan Im, the Hindu gods Shiva and Ganesh, and the Thai Kings Taksin and Rama I were built on the summit of Khao Tham Phra (Monk's Cave Mountain) in the complex. These statues, only some of which were ever completed, reflected an early instance of the symbolic complex.

Suchat saw himself as responding to the threat of communist subversion in Thailand and he claimed that the spirit world had chosen three bodhisattvas to help Thailand through that difficult period; namely, the spirits of the magic monks *Luang Pu* Thuat and *Luang Pu* To, as well as the legendary figure of Mahabrahma Jinnapañjara. The central roles of *Luang Pu* To, also known as *Somdet* To, and *Luang Pu* Thuat in the cults of wealth is described in Chapter Four. In Suchat's system, King Mahabrahma Jinnapañjara (Thai: *Thao Mahaphrom Chinnapanjorn*) was a legendary follower of Moggalana, a disciple of the Buddha. Justin McDaniel (2011) has detailed the importance of the *Chinnapanjorn Khatha* (Pali: *Jinapañjara gāthā*) incantation, which is popularly attributed to *Somdet* To, in popular Thai Buddhism. *Somdet* To's evolving role in popular Thai Buddhism is especially interesting as the forms of protection and guidance his spirit and his magically empowered amulets are regarded as conferring have changed in different historical periods. As detailed in Chapter Four, in the colonial era, *Somdet* To was regarded as having saved Siam from European imperialism. During the Cold War, Suchat saw him as saving Thailand from communism, and in the era of neoliberal globalization he has been seen as a protector of the Thai economy who helps his followers establish financially beneficial relations with new sources of wealth. This reflects the historical transformation of the forms of supernatural protection that the spirits of the cults of wealth have offered at different points of Thailand's modern history.

The Religious Algebra of the Symbolic Complex of Prosperity Cults: Logics of Resemblance and Association

Associations among the cults of wealth in the symbolic complex, described in detail below, are often effected by semiotic links based on what McDaniel calls the "religious algebra" of Thai ritual life (McDaniel 2011, p. 119). Barend Terwiel (2012, pp. 72–73, 166–69) and Stanley Tambiah (1984, pp. 295, 375n2) have detailed the magical significance of signs and numbers in Thailand. While McDaniel maintains that there is no core to the diverse and dynamic components of the complex of rituals and beliefs that make up the Thai religious field, he nonetheless contends that the numerological and other forms of symbolic association constitute "a common logic at the very foundation of Thai Buddhism that links the body of the Buddha and the body of each human being in a universal algebraic net" (McDaniel 2011, p. 119). In this religious algebra the person and teachings of the Buddha play pivotal symbolic roles:

> [T]he phases of the moon, the days of the week, the parts of the body, the names of Buddhist texts, previous Buddhas, famous teachers are seen as existing in their own syllabic, mathematical, temporal, and spatial relationships…. Those adept in this Buddhist algebra … are able to reveal a network of power that is accessible to everyone provided they know the access codes. (McDaniel 2011, pp. 119–20)

McDaniel adds:

> The letters, numbers, and drawings used in the formulas are indices, not symbols. They are believed to directly cause events or protect objects if chanted, drawn, or tattooed correctly and with the right focus. These equations do things. They solve problems. (McDaniel 2011, p. 103)

Ritual objects associated with Thailand's prosperity cults, like many other forms of popular and royal cultic worship, draw upon a logic that regards spiritual power (*saksit*) and charisma (*barami*) as being acquired, transferred and accumulated through symbolic relationships of resemblance, similitude and association. Within Thai vernacular religion, a similarity of appearance, sound or meaning between objects, symbols or words is often taken as indicating a similarity of the spiritual power that they possess. White notes that the magical attitude towards the world in Thai vernacular Buddhism is based on beliefs in a hidden "homology and correspondence across the multiple dimensions and levels of the cosmos, and the presumption that such correspondences can be exploited by those who are knowledgeable about the nature of those interdependencies and linkages" (White 2016, p. 5). Tambiah observes that the cosmological scheme of Thai spirit mediumship and magical cults operates by means of "correspondences, sympathies and antipathies, identities and differences between the microcosm of man and the macrocosm of the universe" (Tambiah 1977, p. 98). In this cosmology "there is no separation between the workings of 'moral laws' and ... 'natural laws'; the [Buddhist] concept of *dhamma* encompasses both" (p. 98), and for this reason "events in nature and cosmological notions are considered to be interrelated and to affect one another" (p. 128). This scheme brings together "various systems of instrumental knowledge, such as meditation, alchemy, astrology and healing" (p. 116). In discussing metaphors and magic in Thai healing traditions, Louis Golomb observes that Thai ritual specialists cross boundaries between different healing traditions in "agile leaps" that are,

> facilitated by the liberal application of metaphorical principles that permit them to identify analogies between vaguely similar physical, mental and behavioural phenomena.... 'Metaphor' here is not restricted to analogies drawn with linguistic symbols; rather it also links such diverse nonverbal media as humidity, temperature, taste, smell, color, shape, gesture, melody, emotion, and personality. (Golomb 1985, p. 139)

By this cultural logic, the fact that a monk reputed to possess supernatural abilities is named Khoon, which means "to multiply", is taken to indicate that his powers include the capacity to "multiply". Indeed, in his devotional cult, *Luang Phor* Khoon was believed to have possessed the power to multiply spiritual qualities such as merit (*bun*) that Thai Buddhists have traditionally sought from religious participation. However, in a period when wealth became the national obsession, and when becoming rich was interpreted as relying upon accumulated merit, *Luang Phor* Khoon was also believed to be capable of multiplying the personal wealth of the faithful. This belief was rendered explicit in photographs of the monk handling large sums of money that appeared on ritual objects associated with his movement.

In *The Order of Things*, Foucault describes a similar logic as having underpinned medieval Western discourses:

> Up to the end of the sixteenth century, resemblance played a constructive role in the knowledge of Western culture. It was

resemblance that largely guided exegesis and the interpretation of texts; it was resemblance that organised the play of symbols, made possible knowledge of things visible and invisible, and controlled the art of representing them. (Foucault 1994, p. 17)

Tambiah notes that Foucault presents

a vivid picture of the doctrine of signatures whose chief concept of 'resemblance' maintained that words and things were one, that the name of a thing was an essential part of it, its signature, and a system of resemblance held everything together. The seventeenth century developed a different view of language in terms of 'representation' in which language related to the world in an arbitrary way. (Tambiah 1990, p. 21)

In writing of the similar logic of resemblance in Vietnamese vernacular religion, Paul Sorrentino observes,

These properties are typical of what Philippe Descola has coined as "analogism" (2005: 280–281, 409–412), a predominant concern for coherence in a universe seen as being of a potentially infinite diversity, textured by relations of correspondence between elements of various natures, such as colours, chemical elements, parts of the human body or of the cosmos, deities, stars or hours of the day. This coherence need not be permanent. On the contrary, societies with a strong analogic tendency are endowed with numerous practices aimed at finding ad-hoc coherence in complexity, such as astrology, physiognomy or numerology. The Chinese (and Sino-Vietnamese) 'penchant for correlative cosmology' (Verellen, 2003: 26; see also Granet, 1934) is archetypical of such concern. (Sorrentino 2022)

A second, related principle operative in Thai vernacular religion and ritual practice is that of association, whereby objects and people that are not necessarily regarded as being similar are nonetheless believed to transfer sacral power by virtue of a relationship of contiguity or contact. For example, when an array of sacred and ritually empowered (*pluk sek*) images is placed in proximity then the space within which they are collocated is believed to possess an intensified power. Christine Gray notes that "interactions between king-deities and lesser beings have soteriological significance" (Gray 1986, p. 107), with the sight or touch of the king having *saksit* power and *barami* authority. This principle of association is closely related to the additive logic of Thai popular religion described in Chapter Three, under which the accumulation of icons, images and symbols of different deities and spiritual figures—even if those figures are from disparate doctrinally unrelated religious traditions—is regarded as intensifying the magical power that can be accessed by the faithful.

It is the operation of the semiotic principles of similarity and association under the overall logic of accumulation and addition that makes shrines and altars in Thailand often appear "cluttered", "busy" and "baroque" to Western observers, combining a seemingly eclectic array of diverse deities and images. The principle of association and the additive logic of Thai religion means that the faithful believe that access to blessings and supernatural power is enhanced by the greater the number of empowered symbols and images that are collocated within the space of a shrine or temple. The design of many of the ritual objects of the cults of wealth, such as the *Luang Phor* Khoon lucky banknotes described below, emerges from the operation of these principles.

Magical Numerology in the Symbolic Complex

Magical numerology is an important element of the religious algebra of Thai popular Buddhism and is a key factor in the design of ritual objects associated with the symbolic complex of prosperity cults. In the Introduction I noted that many expecting Thai mothers decide to give birth by caesarean section so they can choose an astrologically auspicious birth date for their child. Christine Gray notes that in Thai belief the odd numbers three, five and seven are propitious (Gray 1986, p. 221), with odd numbers being seen as auspicious and representing life, while even numbers are "inauspicious, representing death and sickness" (p. 739). Pattana Kitiarsa (2012, p. 40) notes that Thai magical numerology is intimately linked with providing tips for winning lottery numbers, and the numbers five and nine are especially significant in the Thai cults of prosperity, with multiple overlapping associations that overdetermine the magical significance of each of these numbers.

Magical Significance of the Number Five

Five is the number assigned to the reign of King Chulalongkorn (r. 1868–1910) who, as the fifth monarch of the Chakri dynasty, is also called Rama V in English and in Thai is referred to as *Ratchakan Thi 5*, "(The King of) the Fifth Reign". Devotees of the prosperity cult of King Chulalongkorn call him *Sadet Phor Ror. 5*, "Royal Father of the Fifth Reign". In English, the kings of the Chakri dynasty are often called Rama and assigned a number according to their reign. In this system, King Chulalongkorn is called King Rama 5. McDaniel notes that the number five also has historical and symbolic resonances:

"The historical Buddha is often depicted as being surrounded by five disciples on his deathbed.... In Thailand, it is commonly believed that there are five Buddhas in this epoch, including the historical Buddha" (McDaniel 2011, p. 48). Terwiel notes the importance of the number five in rituals to sacralize amulets:

> The [sacralization] ceremony should be held on a day when the 'spirits are strong': an ominous, portentous day on which it is inadvisable to cremate corpses, such as a Saturday or a Tuesday. The fifth day of the fifth lunar month is especially suitable for sacralisation. That is also why there is a great demand for tattoos on this day. (Terwiel 2012, p. 72)

Luang Phor Khoon said that he only implanted *takrut* amulets on Saturdays because Saturday is a "strong day" (*wan khaeng*) of the week, which helped him confer the greatest magical power (*phalanuphap*

IMAGE 23. Magical Numerology of Kings Rama 5 and Rama 9
A 1997 New Year greeting card with an image of King Chulalongkorn, his royal insignia and the number of his reign, "555", on the left and King Bhumibol, his royal insignia and the number of his reign, "999", on the right. The Phra Thinang Chakri Maha Prasat palace built by King Chulalongkorn in the nineteenth century and names of the two kings are in the centre of the design. The design of this card reflects the numerological significance of the numbers five and nine in Thai magical lore and their importance in prosperity cults of the Thai monarchy in which Kings Chulalongkorn and Bhumibol are linked with narratives of Thai national independence, success and wealth.

saksit) to the object during the ceremony. *Takrut* are a type of spirit-ually empowered amulet made of small square rolls of metal foil, often gold, that are inscribed in sacred Khom or Cambodian script, rolled into a small cylinder and implanted beneath the skin of the upper arm as protective charms.

Magical Significance of the Number Nine

The number nine is significant in both Thai and Chinese beliefs. In the Thai Buddhist sangha, the highest and most prestigious level of clerical Pali language studies is called *parian tham 9*, and monks who have achieved this level of Pali studies are honoured by being placed under the personal patronage of the king. Nine-tiered umbrellas are placed over Buddha statues on the altars of royal temples and over the head of the king at his coronation. The ninth heaven is the highest level of Buddhist heaven, symbolic of *nibbana*. There are nine auspicious planets (*nopphakhrorh*) in Thai astrology and nine is the highest value digit. Gray notes that in Thai Buddhism "[t]he number nine stands for the best, the brightest, the highest and most pure and auspicious objects in the kingdom" (Gray 1986, p. 738). She adds that "[n]ine stands for kings, for the Buddha, for enlightenment and for progress, 'stepping forward'" (p. 458). Indeed, in Thai the number nine (*kao*) is a close homophone of the term for "progress" (*kao*). The primary sense of *kao* is "to step" or "a step", and the compound term *kao-na*, literally "to (take a) step forward", also means "to progress" or "advance". This coincidence enables the Thai expression for the late King Bhumibol Adulyadej, *ratchakan thi kao*, "(the King of) the Ninth Reign (of the Chakri Dynasty)", to have a second meaning of "the reign that progressed" or "the reign marked by progress". As the ninth king of the Chakri Dynasty, in English, King Bhumibol is often called King Rama 9.

In Chinese belief, the ninth day of the ninth lunar month is also the apogee of the celebrations of the festival of the Nine Emperor Gods, the Taoist deities at the centre of the Chinese Vegetarian Festival (*thetsakan kin je*) that is now celebrated nationally in Thailand and has become associated with the cult of Kuan Im. In his study of the Nine Emperor Gods Festival in Phuket, Erik Cohen (2001) notes that in Chinese belief the number nine is considered a masculine (*yang*) number. As two masculine numbers occur on the ninth day of the ninth lunar month, the time when the Nine Emperor Gods Festival is celebrated, this date is called a double ninth as well as a double masculine. It is the day on which it is believed that the male principle *yang* reaches its annual apogee, and marks the beginning of the rise of the *yin* female principle (Cohen 2001, p. 48).

The wealth-associated significance of the number nine pervades Thai cultural, commercial and political life. For example, at New Year in 2005, the Tourism Division of the Bangkok Metropolitan Administration placed a full-page colour advertisement in the *Bangkok Post* Business Section titled "Venerating 9 Temples to Welcome the New Year of 2005".[1] This advertisement stated that "to begin a new life by merit-making is to give your life a great fortune" and went on to note that the customary ritual of venerating nine monasteries and shrines in Bangkok "is considered a creation of auspiciousness to the life" (actual English text). The nine Buddhist monasteries and spirit shrines listed and the customary type of merit that is believed to be attained from worshipping at each location were as follows: Wat Suthat, "widening vision and creating charm to all people"; Wat Chanasongkhram, "victory over obstacles" (the name of this monastery means "victorious in war"); Wat Arun, "Prosperous life"; the City Pillar Shrine, "Discard problems, lengthening life, more fortune"; Wat Kalyanamit, "safe trip, more friendship"; Wat Rakhang, "Well-liked by others"; Wat Phra Kaeo, "Coming wealth"; Wat Pho, "Peaceful life"; and Chao Phor Seua Shrine, "More power and value".

IMAGE 24. Thailand Post Stamp of Kuan Im
A postage stamp representing the Chinese Mahayana Buddhist bodhisattva Kuan Im (Guan Yin). In addition to being valued at the auspicious price of 9 baht, Thailand Post issued this stamp special issue on the numerologically significant date of 9 September 2009, with the date 09 09 09 printed on the selvedge edging of the sheet above the stamp. Thailand Post is prominent among state agencies that actively market products related to the cults of wealth by drawing on beliefs in auspicious numbers, colours and designs.

Auspicious Numbers in Thai Business and Politics

Many people in Thailand are willing to pay premiums for vehicle licence plates and mobile phone numbers with strings of nines or other lucky numbers. Thai government agencies participate actively in the commodification of these auspicious numbers, colloquially called "beautiful numbers" (*boe suay*) or "beautiful numerals" (*lek suay*) in Thai. On 27 November 2016, during the hundred-day official mourning period after the death of King Bhumibol, the Office of the National Committee for Broadcasting, Television and Telecommunications held its first online auction for a range of "beautiful" (*suay*) or auspicious mobile phone numbers, with the money from sales going into the department's consolidated revenue. The online auction opened at the auspicious time of 9:09 a.m. The largest number of bids was received for the number 09 8888 8888, regarded as an "auspicious number" (*lek mongkhon*) not only because it begins with the number 9 but also because the numeral 8, here repeated 8 times, is regarded as an upright version of the mathematical symbol for infinity ∞.[2] The number 8 is also regarded to be luckiest digit in Chinese belief. The second- and third-highest bids were received for the mobile phone numbers 06 5555 5555 and 09 5555 5555, which include the number 5, signifying King Chulalongkorn. Even the winning bids were made in terms of amounts of money that were beautiful numbers or *lek suay*. The winning bid for the phone number 09 8888 8888 was 8,100,000 baht. The figure of 6,900,000 baht was successfully bid for the number 06 5555 5555, and 6,898,888 baht was bid for the number 09 5555 5555. This suggests that the bidders had most likely received ritual advice on the amounts to bid to be successful.[3]

The policies and actions of a succession of Thai civilian and military prime ministers have also reflected the political significance of the number nine. In 2002, the *Bangkok Post* reported that then prime minister Thaksin Shinawatra ordered that the national budget be adjusted so that the number nine would be prominent in the figures:

> Folk superstition, political marketing or genuine fiscal prudence? Cabinet ministers yesterday approved a token 100-million baht cut to the fiscal 2003 budget, bringing total spending to an auspicious figure of 999.9 billion. The Budget Bureau had originally proposed a budget of one trillion baht, but Prime Minister Thaksin Shinawatra called for spending under the PM's Office to be cut back to reach the 'lucky nines' figure.[4]

That is, following a cut of 100 million baht from the previously planned annual budget of a trillion (1,000,000,000,000) baht, the final national budget for the 2003 financial year came to 999,9000,000,000 baht—a total that included four lucky nine figures.

Charles Keyes notes that the political destiny of the leader of the September 2006 military coup against former prime minister Thaksin, General Sonthi Boonyaratglin, who is a Muslim, "hinged heavily on the auspicious number nine.... The coup took place on the 19th day of the 9th month [September] in the Buddhist year 2549 [CE 2006]. The day following the coup, General Sonthi appeared on TV at 9:39 a.m., 'It was the number nine all the way.' (*The Nation*)" (Keyes 2006, pp. 25–26). And following the advice of his personal astrologer, General Prayut Chan-ocha, the leader of the May 2014 coup against Thaksin's sister and then prime minister Yingluck Shinawatra, timed the start of his first post-coup cabinet meeting for 9:00 a.m. on Tuesday, 9 September 2014.[5] That is, the first cabinet meeting of the coup-installed government was held at the ninth hour of the ninth day of the ninth month.

Following the death of King Bhumibol in October 2016, the auspicious associations of the number nine were inscribed and embodied in a range of ways. *The Nation* reported a boom in customers wanting tattoos of the number nine inscribed on their bodies or having their hair shaved in the shape of the number nine.[6] Across the country, government agencies and private organizations coordinated their members in mass formations that, when viewed from above, took the shape of the Thai numeral nine. These mass formations, called *prae aksorn* or "transforming [oneself] into a letter/numeral", were a symbolic embodiment in which the Thai populace collectively formed themselves into the shape of the numeral nine.

Auspicious Colours Associated with Kings' Birth Days

In Thai astrology the day of the week on which one is born is significant. Colours are also magically significant in the design of cultic objects as, in Thai tradition, an astrological rule deriving from Hindu mythology assigns an auspicious colour to each day of the week (see Cornwel-Smith 2013, pp. 162–65; Ünaldi 2014, p. 212). The auspicious colour for each day of the week is associated with a Brahmanical deity regarded as the protector of those born on that day. Colour schemes of ritual objects associated with the cults of wealth are especially important indicators of symbolic associations with the monarchy; in particular, the cult of King Chulalongkorn, as well as that monarch's association with the late King Bhumibol (Jackson 2009). King Bhumibol was born on a Monday, a day whose auspicious colour is yellow, while King Chulalongkorn was born on a Tuesday, whose auspicious colour is pink. In ritual objects associated with the cults of wealth, the colours yellow and pink often stand in as visual indicators of these two kings and of the beliefs associated with their respective cults. For example, *The Nation* reported that "[o]n Thursday [13 October], the day of [King Bhumibol's] passing, a couple of thousand people, dressed in pink or yellow, had gathered outside Siriraj Hospital to pray for the ailing King's recovery."[7] The *New York Times* reported that "[t]hrongs of people had gathered at Siriraj Hospital on Thursday afternoon as rumors of the king's death spread. Many wore pink, the color thought to bolster his health."[8]

Symbolic Integration of the Prosperity Cults

The symbolic complex of prosperity cults can be seen as representing what David Lyon describes as the postmodern process of dedifferentiation in the field of religion. The dedifferentiation of consumption, for example, refers to a breakdown of the traditional distinction between shopping and cultural activities, such as when cultural spaces like museums and galleries spawn branded merchandizing shops and when shopping malls include cultural attractions such as performances and leisure zones. Indeed, airports, as well as many train and bus stations, are now increasingly difficult to distinguish from shopping malls. Lyon notes that dedifferentiation "accentuates the consumer culture, in which consumption becomes an order of life" (Lyon 2000, p. 5), and is a phenomenon that also affects religious practice. In the 1990s, the Pantip Plaza shopping mall in the Pratunam area of Bangkok was an early example of the dedifferentiation of religion in Thailand. Pantip Plaza became popular as a shopping complex where one could buy religious icons alongside personal computers, software, mobile phones, DVDs and other digital communication technologies. Lyon emphasizes that the commercial and media-driven processes of dedifferentiation have the capacity to override logical contradictions that may exist among the diverse phenomena that effectively come to be integrated into a unified symbolic domain:

> The proliferation of distinctions, in popular music for instance, can produce situations in which differences become less significant, and in which supposed contradictions between different spheres start to disappear. At this point the cultural reservoir can be drawn on increasingly at will. Dedifferentiated categories such as 'world music' and 'fusion' illustrate this tendency. (Lyon 2000, p. 44)

In Thailand, capitalist processes of dedifferentiation accentuate the contextualized polyontological character of Thai popular religiosity and contribute to the repertoire religiosities and the bricolage approach to religious practice described by McDaniel (2011) and Gray (1986). In this setting, tensions and logical contradictions between the doctrines and traditions of different religious figures can lose their power to inhibit interaction or mutual borrowing. The collocation of elements of the symbolic complex in commercial spaces as detailed below also mirrors their juxtaposition in ritual spaces such as on the altars of spirit mediums. Commercial processes that have underpinned the development of the symbolic complex of prosperity cults mirror many of the ritual processes and characteristics of popular Thai religion described in Chapter Three. In the final chapter of this book I consider the ways in which capitalism and new media have accentuated many of the characteristics of Thai popular Buddhism. Processes of dedifferentiation that parallel the pre-existing characteristics of Thai popular religion are revealed in several notable features of semiotic integration within the symbolic complex of prosperity cults:

- *Interpenetrating Sacred Spaces*: The installation in sacred spaces dedicated to one religious figure of images and cultic objects linked with one or more of the other prosperity cults.
- *Patterns of Accumulative Worship*: Where individuals integrate the worship of figures from all strands of the symbolic complex of prosperity cults into their personal devotions.
- *Symbolic Integration in Commercial Space*: The commercial manufacture of similarly designed lines of ritual products—including statuettes, amulets, wall posters, framed pictures, greeting cards, calendars and ornamental clocks—which represent many elements of the symbolic complex.
- *Symbolic Intersection in a Single Ritual Object*: The production of ritual objects that combine images, texts or other references to the diverse strands of the prosperity cults in a single item.

Interpenetrating Sacred Spaces

In the second half of the 1990s, it became increasingly common to find images of King Chulalongkorn installed within Buddhist temples and for shrines dedicated to the Chinese Mahayana bodhisattva Kuan Im to be located within the walls of Thai monasteries, as the ritual spaces of the different prosperity movements began to converge within the sacralized domain of Theravada monasteries. As Nidhi Eeoseewong

(1994) observes, while the cults of King Chulalongkorn and *Jao Mae* Kuan Im first emerged outside Buddhist monasteries, by the early 1990s their iconography and rituals had moved within the sacralized space of Thai *wat*. Shrines to Hindu deities such as Ganesh and Brahma have also become increasingly common additions to Thai monasteries. There is also a commercial dimension to this interpenetration of sacred spaces. Localities sacred to one of the prosperity cults—such as the monasteries of magic monks, the King Chulalongkorn equestrian statue in Bangkok, and Kuan Im temples—have often come to include sales offices or souvenir shops from which it is possible to buy ritual objects relating to the full panoply of the movements, not merely the devotional products associated with the spiritual figure that is the focus of that locality.

When I visited the King Chulalongkorn equestrian statue in Bangkok in December 1996, August 1997 and August 1998, hawkers sold icons and objects dedicated to all the prosperity cults from the backs of pick-up trucks parked in rows. One could visit the equestrian statue and return home with a *Luang Phor* Khoon amulet or an ornamental wall clock decorated with an image of Kuan Im. Or one could visit shops attached to the monastery of a *keji ajan* prosperity monk such as *Luang Phor* Khoon and return home with a King Chulalongkorn amulet and a statuette of Kuan Im, both of which had been blessed by the resident abbot. Just as Thai department store chains sell the same lines of clothes, toiletries and other consumer items across the country, so too the devotional products of the cults of wealth are standardized and made available nationally by retail sales networks that link the sacred localities of the various movements with commercial outlets. Commercial forces represent devotional objects associated with the different prosperity cults within common lines of products, creating a market-based symbolic convergence.

This phenomenon is far from being unique to Thailand or to Asian religions. Roman Catholic amulets, statuary and other devotional objects sold from religious shops around the Christian world also display a similar market-based standardization. Indeed, the numerous shops selling devotional products located across the Vatican City in Rome—from the colonnades of St Peter's Square to the base of the cupola of the dome, immediately outside the Sistine Chapel and throughout the Vatican Museum—are strikingly similar to Thai religio-commercial spaces. Geremie Barmé (1996) also observed a similar phenomenon in the commercial standardization of memorabilia associated with the posthumous cult of Mao Zedong in 1990s China.

At the height of *Luang Phor* Khoon's popularity in the 1990s, his monastery of Wat Ban Rai, located in the middle of rice fields fifty kilometres northwest of the provincial centre of Nakhon Ratchasima, was the focus for large numbers of stalls and shops selling religious icons, images and pictures for the full range of prosperity movements, and was a prominent example of the interpenetration of sacred spaces. On visits to this monastery in August 1997 and again in August 1998, I observed a hierarchy of religio-commercial spaces within and immediately outside Wat Ban Rai. A shop selling only *Luang Phor* Khoon religious objects and staffed by half a dozen lay men and women occupied one corner of the main sermon hall, a large two-storey building that also housed Khoon's private rooms and the monastery offices. Next to the sermon hall, under aluminium roofing, more than fifty lay men and women had their own small stalls selling a variety of religious objects for all the prosperity movements as well as local handicrafts and herbal remedies. And lining the street immediately outside the monastery, a row of shops also sold objects associated with Khoon as well as King Chulalongkorn and Kuan Im. In the 1990s, Wat Ban Rai was unusual even by Thai standards in that the amount of space inside the monastery walls that was dedicated to selling devotional objects was larger than the space devoted to religious activities.

Patterns of Accumulative Worship

In Chapter Three I observed that Thai vernacular religion is characterized by an accumulative logic. This accumulative logic is especially pronounced, and indeed heightened, in the symbolic complex of prosperity cults and is reflected in an accumulative approach to the worship of figures associated with the movements. These patterns of accumulative worship are reflected in the range of spirits that are channelled in the expanding professional spirit possession cults associated with the cults of wealth. Writing of the shrine of a Northern Thai spirit medium, Rosalind Morris states:

> One cannot help but be dazzled by the baroqueness of its interior, the myriad icons, the array of dishes, the countless joss sticks that burn. Here is the statue of the fasting Buddha, of the Buddha in meditating position, of the Maitreya Buddha of the future. Here is the iconic protector of business, Gwan Yin, the bearer of financial luck. There is the image of King Chulalongkorn, and of King Mongkut, of Taksin. Here is Queen Camadevi.[9] (Morris 2000a, p. 115)

Similarly, Andrew Johnson notes that amongst the spirit mediums with whom he conducted research in Chiang Mai in the early 2000s there existed

> an interlocking hierarchy that combines Indic gods, animist spirits, and the spirits of dead kings. In the city of Chiang Mai … the swiftly changing community of spirit mediums has overlapping sovereignties and hierarchies that elide attempts at categorization. (Johnson 2017)

In 1997 the magazine *Mahalap* ("great fortune"), which reported stories of Thai professional spirit mediums, produced a two-volume guide on what were described as "leading mediums (*rang song*) from all over Thailand" (*Poet Pratu Tamnak Song* [1998?]). Volume one of this guide included accounts of thirty-eight mediums, with the spirits that they channelled representing a cross-section of the famous monks, royal spirits and Chinese and Brahmanical deities of the cults of wealth. The *Mahalap* book described three mediums as being channels for Kuan Im and another three as being possessed by the spirit of King Chulalongkorn. Of the remaining thirty-two nationally prominent mediums profiled, four channelled the spirits of other Thai kings and queens; fourteen channelled Hindu deities (three channelled Brahma and one channelled Ganesh); and the rest were possessed by a diverse range of spirits.[10] Nidhi Eeoseewong (1994, p. 90) has noted that it is not uncommon for mediums to channel more than one spirit—for example, with Kuan Im being channelled in sequence with a Brahmanical deity—adding a further fascinating instance of the interpenetration of prosperity religions within the "spiritual space" of an individual medium's trance state. Erick White describes the religious statuary in the compound of the Garden of Dharma, the spiritual centre of a family of Brahmin priestly experts who claim descent from the court Brahmins of the Chakri dynasty, and that he visited in the mid-1990s, which included images of the Hindu deities Durga and Ganesh, Sukhothai-style Buddha images, various Chinese deities and a large gold statue of King Chulalongkorn (White 2014, p. 4).

In the 1990s it became common for the dashboards of Thai taxis, buses, trucks and private cars to display an array of icons and amulets with images of King Chulalongkorn, Kuan Im and prosperity monks such as *Luang Phor* Khoon and *Somdet* To. In August 1998 I rode in a Bangkok taxi owned and operated by a driver in his forties who had migrated to the capital from Ubon Ratchathani province in Northeast Thailand a decade earlier. The dashboard of his taxi displayed an array of amulets representing King Chulalongkorn, various sacred Buddha

images such as *Luang Phor* Sothorn or *Phra* Phutthasothorn at Wat
Phra Phutthasothorn in Chachoengsao Province east of Bangkok, several famous monks and Kuan Im. When I asked if he honoured (*nap
theu*) *Jao Mae* Kuan Im too, he replied that although he did not have
any Chinese ancestry, he honoured all the deities and sacred spirits
(*nap theu mot*). In this conversation the driver said that the current
period was one in which "*Luang Phor* Khoon was booming" (*pen yuk
Luang Phor Khoon boom*) or becoming extremely popular. Here, the
then recently borrowed English word "boom" conflated meanings of
rapid economic growth and cultic popularity, reflecting the intersection of economics and popular sentiment in the rapid growth of the
Luang Phor Khoon prosperity cult. This also shows how the language
and symbolism of the economy came to intersect with many aspects of
religiosity and cultural production during the economic boom period.

Privately published devotional literature provides another indicator
of the integration of the different prosperity movements in the religious
practices of individuals as well as the polytropy and repertoire religiosity
of Thai popular religiosity. One example of this literature is a pocket-
book titled *The Charisma of Phra Siam Thewathirat: Bestowing Peace
upon the Nation* (*Barami phra Sayamthewathirat* 1997), which was sold
from bookstores in 1997. This booklet was published by the family-run
Liang Chiang publishing house in Bangkok as an expression of the
family's religious devotion and a filial honouring of their great-grandfather, Lippo Sae Tiaw, who migrated from Southern China and
established the business in 1916. This publication gives an idea of the
range of deities and monks honoured by a Sino-Thai business family
in Bangkok in the late 1990s. The book opens with a quote from the
late King Bhumibol on the value of the Buddhist ethical perfection
(Pali: *pāramī*; Thai: *barami*) of "effort" (*khwam-phian*) and hard work in
creating individual and collective wellbeing, and then reproduces a series of Pali-Thai incantations dedicated to becoming a multimillionaire
(*khatha mahasethi*), blessing money (*khatha sek ngoen*) and increasing
one's attractiveness and charm (*khatha sane*). The remainder of the book
reproduces colour images and special *khatha* incantations dedicated to
honouring the following deities and spiritual figures:

- *Phra* Siam Thewathirat, the patron deity of the Chakri monarchy,
  whose image appears on the cover and to whom the booklet is
  dedicated (this deity was described in Chapter Two);
- The *Phra* Phutthachinarat Buddha image in Phitsanulok Province
  in mid-Northern Thailand, widely regarded to be one of the most
  beautiful Buddha images in the country;

- *Phra Mae* Kuan Im, with a devotional *khatha* in the Tae Jiw Chinese dialect transcribed into Thai script;
- King Chulalongkorn, here called *Phra Piyamaharat Ratchakan Thi 5*, "the Beloved Great King of the Fifth Reign"; and
- Ten well-known Buddhist monks, including five linked with the cults of wealth: *Luang Phor* Ngoen Phutthchot of Wat Bang Khlan in Phichit Province; *Luang Phor* Sot Janthasaro, also known as *Phra* Mongkhonthepmuni and *Luang Phor* Wat Pak Nam; *Luang Phor* Khoon Parisuttho; *Somdet* To (here called *Somdet Phra* Phutthajan To Phrommarangsi); and *Luang Pu* Thuat. The other five monks listed are *Phra Ajan* Man Bhuridatto, a respected Northeastern meditation master; *Jao-khun* Nor Ratratchamanit, a former abbot of Wat Thepsirin in Bangkok; *Luang Pu* Khao Analayo; *Luang Pu* Waen Sujinno, the late abbot of Wat Doi Mae Pang in Chiang Mai province; and *Luang Phor* Kasem Khemako, from Lampang Province in Northern Thailand. Four of the monks in this latter group were honoured with visits by the late King Bhumibol during his reign, while before his ordination *Jao Khun* Nor was a close friend and confidant of King Vajiravudh.

The use of an opening quote from King Bhumibol in this book is revealing in several respects. The term *khwam-phian* is a translation of the Pali word *viriya* (Thai: *wiriya*), the moral perfection or *barami* that is at the centre of the *Mahajanaka Jataka* tale of one of the Buddha's past lives that King Bhumibol (1999) revised and that became a best-selling publication in the years after the Asian financial crisis. The relationship of King Bhumibol's ethical pronouncements to the magical blessing of wealth is also explicit here, showing how individual worshippers draw on the image and words of the late king as a figure who blesses wealth and who also provides a symbolic frame for the prosperity cults.

Symbolic Integration in Commercial Space

While the integration of the prosperity cults became increasingly visible in the intersection of their ritual spaces and in patterns of accumulative worship, it was in commercial space that the symbolic interconnections among the movements was often most pronounced. Commercial spaces where the full panoply of religio-commercial symbols was displayed included markets for amulets and religious icons, greeting card and gift displays in department stores and gift

IMAGE 25. Signs for Computer Equipment and Amulets at Pantip Plaza, Bangkok
A sign for computers, video games and CDs (left) side by side with a sign for amulets (right) at Pantip Plaza, a major shopping mall in Bangkok, in 1997, reflecting the close association of modern communication technologies and the cult of amulets in contemporary Thailand. The sign on the right reads, "Amulet Centre: Bought for Good Prices". (Photo by the author.)

shops, and private shrines in shops and offices. Within these spaces, amalgamated symbolisms of the prosperity cults created a semiotic effect of unity.

Bangkok has long had markets, called *talat phra*, dedicated to the sale of icons and amulets, and these commercial spaces predate the economic boom years of the 1980s and 1990s and the efflorescence of the cults of wealth. Some of the older more established *talat phra* in Bangkok are located at Wat Mahathat, at Wat Ratchanada on Ratchadamnoen Road and at the Jattujak Park weekend market. During the boom years, however, new *talat phra* appeared in Bangkok shopping centres such as at Wang Burapha, Banglamphu, Pantip Plaza on Petchaburi Road, Ngam-wong Wan shopping mall and many other locations. In its integration of capitalism and religiosity, Pantip Plaza was one of the most interesting *talat phra* in Bangkok. This mall on Petchaburi Road in the Pratunam commercial district of Bangkok was built in the early 1980s, and in the 1990s it became a shopping centre dedicated to selling computer hardware and software as well as magical amulets and religious iconography, with some stores in the multistorey complex selling both computers and amulets. In the 1990s, Pantip Plaza was a commercial space where the latest electronic technologies were sold side by side with supernatural talismans. Combining in one space the electronic and digital magic of the technological present with charismatic magic, Pantip Plaza demonstrated the "hi-tech" relevance of Thai supernaturalism and the compatibility of this belief system with late capitalism and its information technologies.

The accumulative approach to worshipping figures associated with the prosperity cults described above was also reflected in the semiotics of the production, display and retailing of devotional products. Producers of objects as diverse as New Year greeting cards, wall posters, decorative framed portraits, religious statuary and amulets manufactured their product lines to almost identical specifications, with images of King Chulalongkorn, Kuan Im, Indic deities, *keji ajan* magic monks and members of the royal family often becoming interchangeable design elements. The display of these items within retail spaces such as on department store shelves further reinforced the semiotic effect of unity. In the 1990s one could find rows of greeting cards, shelves of statuary and glass cases of amulets in which all the different versions of a particular product line—such as ornamental King Chulalongkorn, Kuan Im and *Luang Phor* Khoon alarm clocks—were displayed side by side. The production of lines of products to the same design specifications and their juxtaposition on shop shelves reflect the requirements of mass production and marketing. However, the market-driven logics of production and retailing also created semiotic effects that mirrored and re-intensified the accumulative logic that underpins the ways in which the different elements of the symbolic complex are in fact consumed and ritually worshipped. Thai producers of ritual objects were able to manufacture all elements of the symbolic complex of prosperity cults to common design specifications, and retailers were able to sell them from the same shelves and display cases, because devotional consumers already perceived the different religious figures as being related.

At the height of the Thai economic boom in the 1990s, retail displays of New Year greeting cards provided prominent and ubiquitous instances of the collocation of all elements of the prosperity religions within commercial space. In December 1997, I surveyed displays of Christmas and New Year greeting cards in several department stores and malls in Bangkok: Merry Kings at Saphan Khwai, Mahboonkhrorng at Siam Square, Robinson at Silom, and Zen at the World Trade Centre. I also surveyed the Robinson shopping mall in the northeastern city of Udonthani. In all these shopping complexes, more than half of all greeting cards on sale had images relating to one or other prosperity movement, often in association with images of King Bhumibol and other members of the royal family.

In 1997, the Interproduct Company produced a series of similarly designed cards with images of Kuan Im (three designs), *Luang Phor* Khoon, King Bhumibol with his late mother the Princess Mother, King Bhumibol with King Chulalongkorn (two designs), and King Taksin. The same company also produced a second series of similarly designed cards with images of Kuan Im (three designs), Rama V, *Luang Phor* Khoon, King Bhumibol (three designs), King Bhumibol with King Chulalongkorn (two designs), King Bhumibol with *Luang Phor* Khoon, King Taksin, and Princess Sirindhorn.

The T.S. Card Company produced a series of cards with the message "May You become Rich" (*khor hai ruay*) printed on the cover. One card in this series superimposed the message "May the Economy be Good, May your Business Flourish, and May You be Rich the Entire Year" (*khor hai setthakit di kha-khai di ram-ruay talort pi*) engraved on a porcelain plate painted with a traditional Thai design. This company also produced a second series of cards that symbolically linked King Bhumibol and wealth by superimposing images of the monarch on representations of old Thai banknotes from the 1940s and 1950s. The T.S. Card Company continued the banknote theme on yet another series of cards designed to look like banknotes and including messages relating to wealth. One card in this series printed the message "This Year You Will be Rich" (*pi ni ruay*) in Chinese-style red letters on top of an image of the Grand Palace and a portrait of King Bhumibol. Another card printed the single word "Rich" (*ruay*) in bright red letters in the centre of its banknote-styled design together with images of the magic monks *Luang Phor* Ngoen and *Luang Phor* Sot so that their names spelled the word "cash" (*ngoen-sot*).

In all the stores surveyed, cards with images from the symbolic complex of prosperity movements were displayed together on one set of racks, while cards with Western-style Santa Claus and Christmas tree designs were displayed on separate racks. The fact that more than half of all New Year greeting cards on sale in the late 1990s represented an image of one or other element of the complex of cults of wealth suggests that card manufacturers believed these images were likely to be the most popular with Thai consumers, and the prominence and sheer number of these greeting card displays around the country indicated the popularity of these images and the prosperity movements in general.

Symbolic Intersection in a Single Devotional Object

The symbolic integration of the cults of wealth is also shown by products that combine elements from more than one movement within a single image or object. For example, the incorporation of the worship of Kuan Im into Theravada Buddhism was prominently evidenced in the cult of *Luang Phor* Khoon, who blessed icons and images associated with the Mahayana bodhisattva as readily as those from the Theravada tradition. On the occasion of the annual Chinese Vegetarian Festival in October 1995, The Mall department store chain placed full-page advertisements in the Thai language press to promote the sale of 1.2 × 2 metre colour posters of Confucius as a child paying ritual homage to Kuan Im.[11] Customers who purchased at least 500 baht worth of goods from a branch of The Mall during the festival could buy the poster for the special price of only 499 baht, reduced from the usual price of 2,000 baht. The advertisements reproduced the poster and at the bottom-left included a photo of *Luang Phor* Khoon squatting on his haunches and smoking a homemade cigar. It was stated that Khoon had blessed the printing of this poster, and holy water consecrated at a blessing ceremony had been used in the mixing of the inks in the printing process. This example demonstrates the interpenetration of Thai and Chinese religiosity in a commercial context, with a Theravada monk blessing a Chinese Mahayana bodhisattva as well as the founder of Confucianism at the request of a department store chain. Purchasers of the poster produced by The Mall could thus obtain multiple blessings from three religious and ritual traditions in one item, with the blessing of figures from Chinese Mahayana and Confucian traditions by a nationally famous magic monk representing the extent of the integration of Thailand's Chinese community into the nation's social and cultural life.

Reverend Father Multiply Lucky Banknotes

A series of "lucky banknotes" (*thanabat khwan thung*) apparently produced by people associated with *Luang Phor* Khoon provide another instance of the symbolic collocation of elements of the complex of prosperity cults on a single devotional object. First produced in 1994 and based on colour copies of actual banknotes denominated in 100, 500 and 1,000 baht, the lucky banknotes combined symbols of protection against evil and victory over foes, together with images and symbols of wealth. In the second half of the 1990s, these lucky banknotes, selling for as little as 10 baht a piece, were used widely by small traders as good luck talismans to increase business. When they first appeared in October 1994, the lucky banknotes created some controversy because in their design the image of King Bhumibol that appeared on all Thai legal tender during his reign was replaced by an image of a smiling *Luang Phor* Khoon, squatting on his haunches and handling large wads of apparently real Thai banknotes.[12] Khoon's followers initially announced that they planned to take legal action against those who had produced the lucky banknotes. As reported by *The Nation*,

> The followers stressed that neither they nor the monk were involved in producing the notes, adding that the production of such notes is defamatory to His Majesty [King Bhumibol]. Members of the Wat Ban Rai Committee said they had banned the sale of the lucky notes in the temple compound, and that they were searching for the printing house.

Khao Sot newspaper quoted *Luang Phor* Khoon as saying, 'I am worried, but people who do bad things will receive them in return. The public and my followers know what kind of man I am, and I have never allowed anyone to do this [producing the lucky notes].'

The paper said officials of the Bank of Thailand had informed Bank Governor Vijit Supinit of the lucky notes and that Vijit was also considering taking legal action against those who produced the notes.[13]

But no action was ever taken against the producers of the banknotes, whose identity remained obscure. The lucky banknotes had many differences from legal tender and there does not appear to have been any effort to produce counterfeit money. The lucky banknotes were produced solely for ritual purposes. Furthermore, any charge that replacing King Bhumibol's image with that of Khoon was disrespectful to the monarchy was countered after the king himself visited the monk's monastery of Wat Ban Rai only a couple of months after the notes first appeared for sale at street-side markets around the country. This visit was widely seen as conferring royal approval upon the cult of *Luang Phor* Khoon and all the images and paraphernalia associated with it.

The use of spiritually symbolic "money" in religious ritual is not unique to Thailand, with "hell banknotes" being burnt in Chinese rituals as offerings to the spirits of the deceased for them to use as "cash" in the supernatural realm. While Khoon's lucky banknotes may reflect this Chinese practice, his banknotes were not incinerated for the benefit of the dead but rather were kept and displayed for the benefit of the living owner. The Khoon lucky banknotes integrated spiritual and worldly symbolisms, with images of legal tender superimposed upon "spiritual tender" in a mutual intensification of meanings. In the lucky banknotes, the import of spiritual symbolisms was heightened by their association with images of wealth, while representations of cash were taken beyond their merely commercial significance as a medium of material exchange to signify ritual exchange and an accumulation of the immaterial quality of religious merit.

Large black lettering on the front of these lucky banknotes read, "Lucky banknote, *Luang Phor* Khoon, great fortune (*maha-lap*), receiving wealth", followed by a blessing from Khoon: "Blessings, I'll make

IMAGE 26. *Luang Phor* **Khoon Lucky Banknote**
Front (top) and reverse (bottom) of the *Luang Phor* Khoon ("Reverend Father Multiply") lucky banknotes based on the design of 1,000-baht Thai banknotes, demonstrating the incorporation of representations of multiple cults of wealth in ritual products. In addition to a photo of *Luang Phor* Khoon holding money and gold jewellery and incantations to call in wealth, these lucky banknotes include images of *Nang* Kwak, multiple *keji ajan* magic monks, King Chulalongkorn, King Bhumibol and the local heroine *Thao* Suranaree.

you rich" (*sirimongkhon ku hai ruay*). The front of the lucky banknotes also included a picture of King Chulalongkorn, plus an image of *Nang Kwak*, the "Beckoning Lady", who is at the centre of one of the oldest prosperity cults. The notes all bore the serial number, 9X9999999, which in addition to being the greatest possible numerical value also included associations with the "ninth reign" of King Bhumibol, Rama IX, and the numerologically auspicious properties of the number nine described above. The letter "X" in the serial number can be read both as a multiplication sign and an indexical symbol of the name "Khoon", which means "to multiply". Khoon himself was pictured holding wads of banknotes in the place where King Bhumibol's image usually appeared on Thai legal tender, with the words "Multiplying wealth a hundred thousand million times". On the area where a watermark was printed on real notes there appeared a mixed Pali-Thai verse called "the incantation to call in money" (*khatha riak ngoen*), which read: "The Buddha battles; The Dhamma battles; The Sangha overcomes the dangers that would destroy peace." The garuda, the official symbol of the Thai government and bureaucracy that appears on legal tender, was replaced by Khmer or Khom magic letters inside a mystic symbol. The reverse of the notes bore an image of *Thao* Suranaree, popularly called *Ya* Mo, a local heroine from the early nineteenth century who has become a supernatural patron of Khoon's home province of Nakhon Ratchasima. The following incantation was printed with this auspicious image: "Victory, Victory, Victory. *Ya* Mo goes out to battle. This is an incantation of victory over enemies and demons."

On later versions of the lucky banknotes produced in 1996, a photograph of King Bhumibol standing with *Luang Phor* Khoon at Wat Ban Rai appeared with the inscription, "Increase good fortune, increase happiness, long life, fortitude." In this second series of the lucky banknotes, an image of King Bhumibol's visit to Wat Ban Rai in 1995 was included as a symbolic legitimator of the *Luang Phor* Khoon cult. The visual message conveyed was that even King Bhumibol had become a *luk-sit* or follower of Khoon, becoming part of the circuit of merit making and money making for which *Luang Phor* Khoon was a focus.

Expansion of the Symbolic Complex in the Early 2000s

In the first decades of the twenty-first century, the commercial and enchanting influence of Thai supernaturalism continued to spread into still more domains that had previously been secular. Since the early 2000s, the field of Thai postage stamps has become yet another commercial space for the visual collocation and further auraticization of the many deities of the symbolic complex of prosperity cults. In recent years, designs representing all the major figures in the symbolic complex of Thai cults of wealth have appeared on special issues of Thai postage stamps. Indeed, in Thailand the previously secular field of postage stamps has been progressively sacralized. Postage stamps with images of the various deities of the prosperity cults are not only used to post letters and parcels but are also framed and displayed as ritual objects in their own right, in much the same way as amulets, icons and statues of the deities themselves.

Since 2004, the year when the Thai postal service was semi-privatized and restructured into the government enterprise Thailand Post, a significant number of special issue stamps have represented (1) famous *keji ajan* magic monks; (2) famous amulets reputed to possess supernatural protective powers; (3) Indian deities, including Brahma, Vishnu, Ganesh and Shiva; (4) Chinese Taoist deities such as the Eight Immortals (*poi sian*) and the bodhisattva Kuan Im; and (5) royal figures from Thai history such as King Chulalongkorn. Many of these special issues were released with the numerologically auspicious values of five baht and nine baht, when the price for mailing an ordinary domestic letter in Thailand in this period was only three baht. The representation of the major deities and figures at the centre of the prosperity cults in the state-sanctioned medium of official postage stamps points to a significant transition in these movements' status and prestige. It marks their relocation from the margins to the very centre of mainstream religious observance in the early twenty-first century. It would not be possible for the deities and spirits at the devotional heart of the cults of wealth to appear on nationally marketed official postage stamps if they had not already become mainstream forms of Thai religious observance. Furthermore, we can read the appearance of magical themes on Thai stamps, and of stamps' becoming sacralized objects in their own right, as reflections of a state project to harness the new religious movements. Space does not allow treatment of all the special issues in question, but selected examples indicate the scope and diversity of magical themes that appeared on stamp issues in the final years of the reign of King Bhumibol.

King Chulalongkorn and King Bhumibol on Stamps

Royal-themed stamps have also become increasingly common among Thai special issue stamps since the 1970s. Here I only note the subset of royal special issues whose design reflects the cult of King Chulalongkorn and the cult of the demi-divine monarchy surrounding

King Bhumibol (Jackson 2009). We can interpret the visual symbolism of stamp design for keys to understanding the significance of these designs in the cults of wealth. As noted, the collocation of images is one important indicator of cultic belief in the symbolic complex of Thai prosperity cults. A significant number of special issues have included images of both King Chulalongkorn and King Bhumibol on the same stamp. Furthermore, Thailand Post has also issued stamps in honour of King Bhumibol with pink-coloured design elements, in a reference to King Chulalongkorn and the astrologically auspicious colour associated with his birth day. These visual features directly associate King Bhumibol with the divine aura of King Chulalongkorn.

Chinese Deities and Religious Festivals on Stamps
The first Thai stamp to feature a Chinese religious theme—representing an image of the Mahayana bodhisattva Kuan Im—reflected the numerological significance of the number nine. The Kuan Im special issue stamp had a face value of nine baht and was issued on the numerologically auspicious date of 9 September 2009, with the date of issue "09 09 09" printed on the selvedge of the sheet of stamps.

Brahmanical Deities on Stamps
While Brahmanical beliefs and worship have been part of Thai court ritual and popular religious practice for centuries, Brahmanical deities did not appear on any Thais stamps until 2 June 2009, when Thailand Post issued a set of four stamps representing Ganesh, Brahma, Narayana (a name of Vishnu) and Shiva for the numerologically auspicious value of five baht each.

Magic Monks on Stamps
On 5 December 2005, Thailand Post issued a set of four five-baht stamps representing highly revered monks in honour of King Bhumibol's birthday that year. The monks on this special commemorative set hailed from each of the four main geographical regions of the country: *Somdet* To from the central region, *Luang Phor* Thuat from the South, *Than Ajan* Man from the Northeast and *Khruba* Sriwichai from the North. As Justin McDaniel observes, this set of stamps included "the most famous monks from each region of Thailand ... depicted under the seal of the king" (McDaniel 2011, p. 199). The appearance of *Somdet* To and *Luang Phor* Thuat on these stamps was especially significant as each is the centre of a cult of amulets grounded in reputed magical abilities.

Magical Amulets on Stamps

In 2011, Thailand Post issued five nine-baht stamps of the *benjaphakhi* or "league of five", regarded as "the five highest-ranking amulets of the nation" (McDaniel 2011, p. 189).[14] In announcing the release of these stamps to collectors, *Julasan Khao Sataem Thai* (Thai stamp bulletin), an official philatelic publication of Thailand Post, explicitly referred to the magical beliefs surrounding these five amulets by using terminologies and vocabularies of Thai magical ritual that are employed by devotees.[15] For example, the maker of one of the amulets represented in the *benjaphakhi* set, *Luang Phor* Klan of Wat Phrayatikaram in Ayutthaya province in Central Thailand, was described as a monk who "was interested in and became an expert in the art of Buddhist magic (*phutthakhom*)" (Thailand Post 2011a, pp. 8–9).

Thailand Post issued another numerologically significant set of stamps on 28 March 2008, with the release of twelve stamps showing

IMAGE 27. Stamp Set of the Benjaphakhi Amulets
Sheetlet of five stamps issued by Thailand Post in 2011 representing the Benjaphakhi set of magically empowered amulets, popularly regarded as the most important amulets in Thailand. Each of the five stamps is valued at nine baht, reflecting the numerological importance of the numbers five and nine in Thai magical belief. Gold leaf has been applied to the sheetlet, reflecting the ritual practice of honouring icons and images in Thai vernacular Buddhism.

different Jatukham-Ramathep amulets, each with a face value of nine baht and the total value of the complete set being the auspicious price of 108 baht (Somchai 2008, p. 186). The number 108 is another numerologically significant one in Theravada Buddhist belief. This Jatukham-Ramathep stamp set demonstrated Thailand Post's prompt responsiveness to the market for supernaturally themed special issues. As detailed in the previous chapter, this style of amulet had only become nationally popular in 2006 and 2007.

Stamps as Sacralized and Magically Empowered Objects

Thailand Post also followed magical practices in the production of the *benjaphakhi* set of stamps referred to above and noted the magicality of this special issue in *Thai Stamp Bulletin*: "A special invisible ink printing technique was used. The ink cannot be seen to the naked eye, but the cabalistic writing [*rup yan*; that is, *yantra*] on the back of each stamp will become visible under ultraviolet light" (Thailand Post 2011a, pp. 8–9). Furthermore, before their release for sale, the *benjaphakhi* stamps were ritually sacralized by eleven monks at Wat Nang Ratchaworawihan, the monastery of *Luang Pu* Iam, maker of one of the series of amulets in the Chom Thong district of Thonburi, at the numerologically auspicious (*suay*, "beautiful") time of 11:11 a.m. on 1 November 2011; that is, at 11:11 a.m. on 1/11/11. The manager of the Chom Thong branch of Thailand Post and a representative of the office of the Supreme Patriarch of the Thai sangha presided at the ceremony. Thailand Post's sponsoring of a ritual to sacralize and ritually empower stamps in this special issue series rendered representations of magical amulets on postage stamps into sacred objects in their own right. *Warasan Trapraisaniyakorn—Philatelic Magazine*, a magazine published by the marketing department of Thailand Post's stamps division, reported this sacralization and ritual empowerment in an article titled, "Ritual Chanting of Buddhist Mantras to Render Stamps Auspicious" (*Phithi jaroen phraphutthamon pheua pen sirimongkhon kae trapraisaniyakorn*) (Thailand Post 2011b, p. 34). Postage stamps have now become part of the commodified cult of amulets, and the aura of amulets reputed to have supernatural properties has been transferred to stamps whose designs include images of those amulets. The public ritual by Thailand Post to sacralize these stamp issues followed the same ritual of magical empowerment used to sacralize amulets themselves.

Chalong Soontravanich observes, "Thailand must rank alone, in this era of globalisation and high technology, as a country in which the cult of the amulet is so popular that it has become an industry in its own right" (Chalong 2013, p. 181). Further to Chalong's observation, even reproduced images of amulets on stamps have now become sacred objects, marketed by a Thai state enterprise as integral parts of the cults of wealth. Indeed, the emergence of Thai postage stamps as auspicious objects in their own right—not merely as a medium for representing images of amulets or the deities of the cults of wealth—further extends the cult of amulets. Stamps, like coins and amulets, are commodified collectible objects produced by modern printing and minting technologies; and communities of expert collectors, serviced by markets, collectors' magazines and catalogues, seek out all of these objects. And all these objects are now also regarded as having the potential to carry auspicious magical power. In Thailand the triumvirate of amulets, stamps and coins now collectively belong to the same complex of auspicious and ritually sacralized collectible items that symbolize prosperity and the acquisition of wealth.

The Symbolic Complex in Elite Settings

The symbolic complex of royal figures and Buddhist, Brahmanical and Chinese deities continues to find expression in some of the country's most upmarket shopping locations, being lavishly produced in expensive materials oriented to the luxury market. In September 2019, the Gold Master Company, producer of high-end gold jewellery and gold-plated religious images, held a sales promotion exhibition of its products on the ground floor events area of the flagship store of the Central Department Store chain at Chitlom in downtown Bangkok. Central is one of Thailand's oldest chains of upmarket department stores. Gold Master prominently displayed gold-plated images of the late King Bhumibol in the form of statuettes that reproduced a famous photograph of the king as a younger man with a camera around his neck and holding documents in one hand on one of his widely publicized national development visits to the Thai countryside in the 1960s and 1970s. These statuettes were displayed alongside similar-sized images of King Chulalongkorn and reproductions of the famous Phutthachinarat Buddha image in Phitsanulok in mid-Northern Thailand. These statuettes were placed on upper levels of the promotional display cases, with gold-plated images of Ganesh, Kuan Im and Buddhist naga serpent deities placed on lower shelves. The images were advertised for sale at 17,900 baht, approximately 600 US dollars, per item. Similar-sized images of Mary Mother of Jesus were also displayed, indicating that Gold Master markets its products to customers among Thai Catholics. Giuseppe Bolotta (2017) reports that household shrines of Thai Catholics often include images of King Bhumibol, reflecting the influence of the cult of the monarchy among this community of Thai Christians.

Alongside the display of gold-plated royal and religious images, a video was played continuously. This video showed the gold used in plating the images being ritually blessed by a monk, as well as gold-pouring rituals from different dates over the previous decade and a half presided over by different members of the royal family, including a visibly frail King Bhumibol in 2008, Princess Sirindhorn and then Crown Prince Vajiralongkorn. This video clearly demonstrated the connection of the company to the royal family and undoubtedly indicated that the company had received royal approval to reproduce and market images of King Bhumibol and King Chulalongkorn.

Prima Art, another company producing gold jewellery and gold-plated ritual images, also sells images of the symbolic complex of cults of wealth at the Central Chitlom Department Store. In September 2019, Prima Art displayed images of Kuan Im, Ganesh, *Luang Phor* Thuat, *Phra* Siwali, and the three Chinese star deities Hok Lok Siw, who symbolize fortune, prosperity and longevity, in addition to various Buddha images. But unlike Gold Master, Prima Art did not display images of King Bhumibol or King Chulalongkorn, suggesting that this company had not received royal approval to reproduce such images.

Gold Master's prominent promotional display of statuettes of figures from the cults of wealth, as well as Catholic Christian images of Mary, in one of the country's most high-class department stores and accompanied by a video of royal participation in producing the images demonstrates the extent to which the symbolic complex has become a mainstream religious phenomenon that is now supported by those at the highest levels of the Thai hierarchy of wealth, power and authority.

Summary

This chapter has outlined the national importance of the new magical cults of wealth in Thailand in recent decades. What has permitted the symbolic complex to emerge, and for originally unrelated cults to be represented together in the same mediatized and commercial spaces, is the polytropic approach to religious observance detailed in Chapter Three. The dynamically expanding Thai religious field is not held together by doctrinal or interpretative unity, but rather by a pervasive culture of ritually expressed respect. Devotion to the diverse deities and spirits represented together on the ritual objects and images of the symbolic complex is not manifested by expressions of faith in doctrines or cosmologies. Rather, it is demonstrated through prayerful incantation of *khatha* and by embodied expressions of respect shown by the gesture of the *wai*—bowing the head and bringing the palms of the hands together—in the presence of representations of the spiritual figures of the prosperity cults. And, as Michael Carrithers (2000) describes in the Greek etymology of the term "polytropy", Thai devotees can turn to all the spiritual figures in the cults of wealth with the same embodied attitude of respectful reverence and supplication. It is the dominance of ritual over doctrine that has enabled what Rosalind Morris (2000, p. 115) describes as the "baroque" representational "excess" of Thai popular religion to cohere in the lines of ritual products and the richly textured visual imagery of the symbolic complex. The symbolic complex of cults of wealth has come into being at the hands of decentralized networks of lay businesspeople and devotees who share the common experience of having been socialized in and acculturated to a polytropic ritual life, not as the outcome of the teachings or pronouncements of any single prophet or spiritual authority.

Notes

1. *Bangkok Post*, 7 January 2005, p. B10.
2. "Boe Suay 20 l. woe: 2 mai-lek khai mai ork, ching deuat khae 8 tua meuan" [20 million baht beautiful numbers overpriced, two numbers left unsold, hot bidding only for mobile phone numbers with 8 digits the same], *Matichon*, 29 November 2016, pp. 1, 11. Numbers in what the office termed the "platinum group" had all nine digits the same, with mobile phone numbers having eight digits the same being called the "gold group". Two phone numbers of nine numerals the same, 09 9999 9999 (offered through the True Network) and 08 8888 8888 (offered through the DTAC network) had opening bid set prices of 20 million baht but were not sold on the first day of the auction.
3. "Ching Boe Suay 09 8888 8888" [Hot competition for beautiful number 09 8888 8888], *Naew Na*, 28 November 2016, p. 1.
4. Chatrudee Theparat and Suphaphan Plengmanipun, "Government Spending: Token Budget Cut as Cabinet Opts for 'Lucky Nines'", *Bangkok Post*, 6 February 2002.
5. Amy Sawitta Lefevre, "New Thai PM Uses Holy Water, Feng Shui to Ward off Occult", Reuters, 8 September 2014 (news.yahoo.com accessed 10 September 2014).
6. Captions to photos published in *The Nation* (20 October 2016, p. 2A) stated: "A customer gets the phrase 'I was born in the reign of Rama IX' at Tattoo OD Studio in Bangkok. Tattoo parlours have reported a boom in art related to the King"; and "Two boys have the Thai number '9' shaved on the side of their heads as they queue to sign farewell messages for the late King".

7. "Mourners at Sanam Luang Mark Symbolic Significance of Seventh Day [after the King's death]", *The Nation*, 20 October 2016, p. 4A.

8. Richard C. Paddock, "Thais Throng the Capital to Bid Farewell to Their King", *New York Times International Edition*, 15–16 October 2016, p 5.

9. Queen Camadevi is regarded as the first ruler of the Kingdom of Haripunchai, modern Lamphun, in northern Thailand in the late seventh century CE.

10. The deities of the "leading mediums" detailed in the *Mahalap* special issues and the honorific titles accorded to them by each medium were as follows. **Mediums for Thai Royal Spirits:** *Sadet Phor R. 5* (Royal Father King Chulalongkorn)—three mediums; *Phra Jao* (Honoured Lord) Taksin, founder of Thonburi—one medium; *Krommaluang* (Prince) Chumphon, a brother of King Vajiravudh—one medium; *Phor Khun* (Father King) Ramkhamhaeng of Sukhothai—one medium; and *Phra Mae-jao* (Reverend Lord-Mother) Camadevi, legendary founder queen of Lamphun in northern Thailand—one medium. **Mediums for Chinese Spirits:** *Ong Phra Mae* (Reverend Mother) Kuan Im, *Phra Mae* (Reverend Mother) Kuan Im (in her form with a thousand eyes and a thousand arms), and *Phra Mae* (Honoured Mother) Kuan Im—three mediums. **Mediums for Brahmanical Deities:** *Phor Thao* Mahaphrom (Lord Father Brahma), *Thao* Mahaphrom (Lord Brahma), and *Sadet Phor Thao* Mahaphrom (Royal Lord Father Brahma)—three mediums; *Sadet Phor Phra* Phikkhanet (Royal Father the Blessed Ganesh)—one medium; *Ong Phra* Narai (Revered Lord Narayana, Vishnu), *Pu* Narai (Grandfather Narayana, Vishnu), *Phor* Narai (Father Narayana, Vishnu)—three mediums; *Jao Mae* (Lord Mother) Uma Parwati (Parvati, consort of Shiva)—one medium; *Sadet Phor Phaya* Khrut (Royal Lord Father Garuda, the vehicle of Vishnu and the state symbol of the Royal Thai Government)—one medium; *Sadet Mae* Umathewi (Royal Mother Umadevi)—one medium; *Sadet Phor Phra* Siwa (Royal Father Honoured Shiva)—one medium; *Pu Jao* Saming Phrai Siwabut (Lord Grandfather Saming Phra Shivaputra, a son of Shiva)—one medium; and *Sadet Mae* Laksami Thewi (Royal Mother Laksmi Devi)—one medium. **Mediums for Famous Buddhist Monks:** *Luang Pu* Thuat—one medium. **Mediums for Other Saints and Religious Figures:** *Sadet Pu Thao* Wetsuwan—one medium; *Mor* Chiwok Koman Jan—one medium; *Pu Reusi* Na-rort, *Pu* Na-rort Wipatsanakammathan—two mediums; Rom Pho—one medium; *Jao Mae Ong* Jan (a moon goddess?)—one medium; *Pu* Sam Worng Ya (Chinese deity)—one medium; Komin(?)—one medium; *Jao Phor* Lak Meuang (Nonthaburi), the protective spirit of Nonthaburi town installed in the city pillar shrine—one medium; *Pu Reusi* Nakha and Jukkuman—one medium; *Sadet Mae* Malai Thorng—one medium; *Pu* Saeng Athit (Grandfather Sunlight)—one medium; *Jao Phor* Song Chai—one medium; and *Sadet Phor Phra* Kan—one medium.

11. *Daily News*, 6 October 1995, p. 13.

12. It was not only on the lucky banknotes that Khoon's image replaced that of a monarch. One series of *Luang Phor* Khoon amulets (uncertain date) was produced in the form of nineteenth and early twentieth century

Siamese stamps with Khoon's image and name replacing that of King Chulalongkorn, who appeared on the original philatelic item (*Luang Phor Khoon Parisuttho* [1996?]).

13. "Monk's Reputation Damaged over Defamatory Lucky Notes", *The Nation*, 31 October 1994, p. A5.

14. Chalong Soontravanich notes that Army Major General Prachon Kittiprawat, writing under the nom-de-plume of Triyampawai, "was the first to propose in 1954 the idea of the 'League of Five' as the most sacred Buddhist amulets of the Thai nation" (Chalong 2013, p. 203). Craig Reynolds observes that the league of five are regarded "as the most sacred Buddhist amulets of the Thai nation" (Reynolds 2019, p. 128).

15. *Julasan Khao Sataem Thai* (Thai stamp bulletin) described this special issue set of images as being of "*benjaphakhi* amulets of revered magic monks" (*rian benjaphakhi phra keji ajan*) (Thailand Post 2011a, p. 8).

Part Three

How Modernity Makes Magic

Chapter Seven

Capitalism, Media and Ritual in the Enchantment of Thai Modernity

> Modernity not only constitutes magic as its counterpoint, it also produces its own forms of magic. (Volker Gottowik 2014, p. 21)

Introduction: Modernity and the Making and Remaking of Enchantment

The diverse and diverging trends of religious change across the globe in recent decades have taken many by surprise. In Southeast Asia many scholars of religion have been kept busy keeping up with the pace of change by detailing the empirical contours of the many new ritual-based magical and doctrinalist reform movements that have appeared with such rapidity. As Boike Rehbein and Guido Sprenger observe,

> We are witnessing a 'return of religions' (Reisebrodt 2000) that contradicts any interpretation based on Marx and Weber. This observation has led Talal Asad (2003, p. 1) to claim that there is only one certainty concerning the relation between modernisation and religion: The relevance of religion does not decrease. If this is true, we have to revisit the relation between rationalisation, capitalism and religion. (Rehbein and Sprenger 2016, p. 15)

Sections of this chapter draw on material presented in Jackson (1999a) and Jackson (2009).

Change in post–Cold War social reality has often outpaced our capacity to develop analyses that account for what is happening in the world's religious cultures. In Chapter One I noted that in some of his writings Weber described modernity as a complex of contradictory rationalizing and potentially enchanting processes. However, as a sociologist Weber only presented a theory of modernity as a force for disenchantment, and this theoretical exposition still dominates much contemporary social analysis. By and large it has been anthropologists who study non-Western societies who have presented theories of how modernity may be productive of new forms of enchantment. A range of anthropological studies have provided theoretical perspectives on the respective impacts of state power, capitalism, new media and the performative force of ritual on religious thought and practice. We now have enough reflective analyses based on detailed empirical work to begin to address broader comparative questions of what is taking place across the full spread of religious expression in Southeast Asia. As Jean Comaroff states in critically assessing the research now at hand, a key guiding principle is the need "to be cognizant of the complexity of the world, to be accountable to its paradoxes" (Comaroff and Kim 2011, p. 176).

In this chapter I return to the question posed at the outset of this study: what factors have supported the emergence of the Thai cults of wealth and their semiotic convergence into the symbolic complex that has become such a notable feature of religious life in Thailand today? More broadly, I engage the question of how it is that the further development of Thai capitalist modernity has been marked by an increasingly pervasive enchantment of the new social world that has emerged in that country in recent decades.

Understanding the processes underpinning the development of cults of wealth not only provides insights into these sociologically and politically important forms of ritual in Thailand. Analysis of the forces producing enchantment in modern Thailand are relevant beyond Thai area studies and the history of modern Thailand because they enhance understanding of the productive relationship between modernity and enchantment at the global level. The Thai cults of wealth are significant beyond studies of religion in Southeast Asia because they contribute to understanding the conditions under which twenty-first-century global modernity makes, and remakes, magic.

The Many Stories of Thailand's Cults of Wealth

> Personally, I do not believe in the possibility of any explanation of a complex reality with recourse to any one simple principle. (Georges Bataille, correspondence to Michel Leiris, 5 July 1939)

An initial general observation is that several processes have merged synergistically to incite new forms of magic in Thailand. The symbolic complex of Thai prosperity cults, and the enchantment of Thai capitalist modernity, are multiply determined phenomena that have not emanated from any single process or operation of power. Unlike some other religious trends or movements in modern Thai history, such as the royal-initiated Thammayut order of Buddhist monks (see Ishii 1986; Jackson 1989; Somboon 1982), the complex of cults of wealth did not develop as the result of any state-initiated policy or from the charismatic influence of any single religious figure. Rather, the amalgamated complex of cults developed within popular culture as devotional expressions that reflect a coalescence of a diverse range of ritual and symbolic forms.

Paralleling the decentralized form of the market, the symbolic complex of cults of wealth is a product of the actions of a multitude of players engaging in symbolic exchange within religious, commercial and mediatized spaces. The diverse cults of wealth have been produced by a mutually reinforcing series of decentralized processes involving large numbers of ritual specialists and devotees. Evers and Siddique (1993) have proposed a schematic chronology for the development of new religious movements in Thailand, with new spirit medium cults first appearing in the 1960s followed by a range of new reformist Buddhist movements in the 1970s. In both cases they argue that the impulse for religious revivalism began outside institutional Buddhism, and they see similar social bases for both new magical and reformist religious phenomena in the new, socially mobile urban middle classes.

The rise of the Thai prosperity cults and their convergence into a symbolic complex cannot be explained by any single historical narrative. Rather, this phenomenon recounts several interrelated stories from Thailand's recent history. The symbolically rich devotional movements surrounding King Chulalongkorn, Kuan Im, Indian deities and numerous *keji ajan* prosperity monks each emerged at the intersection of networks of economic, media, political, ethnic and religious influences. To tell the full story of all the prosperity cults would be to relate the broad history of Thailand's social, economic and political changes over recent decades, for the movements touched upon and drew from all the groups and influences involved in the country's multiple transformations. The rise of the marketized forms of religiosity considered in this study involves a series of interconnecting narratives that relate some of the most significant stories to be told of Thailand's economically roaring 1990s and the political crises that saw the entrenchment of military power and royal authority in the early twenty-first century.

The popularity of each of the movements, respectively focussed on King Chulalongkorn, Kuan Im, Brahma, Ganesh and magic monks, requires its own account that relates each cult's particular audiences or markets to the distinctive historical and cultural resonances of these different figures of devotion. In the rise of the worship of Kuan Im we can read the story of the further integration of Thailand's ethnic Chinese into the country's political and cultural mainstream. In the popularity of magic monks such as *Luang Phor* Khoon we can see the aspirations of the rural and urban poor to participate in the wealth of "globalizing" Thailand. And in the devotional movement centred on King Chulalongkorn we can detect anxieties about the future of the institution of the monarchy as well as state attempts to harness the prosperity movements for nationalist political purposes. In particular, a symbolic complex incorporating all these movements could only have come into being if cultural and sociological divides that historically separated Chinese and Thai religious symbologies had broken down. Pattana Kitiarsa observes that cults of Kuan Im and Ganesh have been able to gain popularity beyond their traditional ethnic boundaries and draw in ethnic Thai followers, as well as new generations of Sino- and Indo-Thais, "as a result of the ethno-cultural assimilation project under the modern nation-building scheme" (Pattana 2012, p. 194).

A distinctive regime of semiotic production capable of bringing together premodern and late-modern cultural trends was also required to bring about the integration of symbolic elements from diverse traditions. And while the state and the institution of the Buddhist sangha were not central to the creation of this religious phenomenon, they nonetheless increasingly engaged with the cults as the economic boom continued into the 1990s. The state and sangha lent tacit official and institutional support to a form of religious expression that incorporated Buddhism as one, albeit privileged, element in a larger symbolic framework dominated by the market and capitalist enterprise. Indeed, the rise of the movements and their symbolic amalgamation has required a certain degree of complicity by key political figures and the civilian and military bureaucracies. Nonetheless, the broad phenomenon of the prosperity cults also requires a more general explanation that relates all the movements to overall changes within the Thai religio-cultural and political domains.

Integrating Several Partial Theories of Modern Enchantment: Ritual as the Keystone of Modern Magic

In their accounts of post–Cold War religious change, different scholars of religion have focused on the roles of state authority, capitalism, media and the power of ritual as transformative forces. In detailing "millennial capitalism" Jean and John Comaroff (2000) argue that new forms of supernaturalism share a similar cultural logic with neoliberal capitalism, while in her study of resurgent Thai spirit mediumship Rosalind Morris argues that new visual media operate as "technologies of the uncanny" (Morris 2000, p. 195) that engender forms of cultural spectralization that have "incited a reformed magicality" (Morris 2000, p. 183). But these different accounts of processes of modern enchantment do not yet speak to one another. To date, we have only a series of partial perspectives that focus on one or other of the multiple processes at work. These analyses of the multiple impacts of changing forms of modernizing state power, the market, new media and ritual need to be brought together to understand the full panoply of processes underpinning the diversification of religious expression in Thailand, and across the world, today. In this chapter I summarize the findings of a range of studies to consider how state power, capitalism, media and ritual have worked together to influence the direction of religious change in Thailand. In summary, the retreat of the state, the commodification and mediatization of social and cultural life, the convergence of premodern and late-modern cultural trends and the productive power of ritual together set the overarching frame within which the Thai prosperity cults have each emerged and subsequently converged symbolically.

While the state has not played a direct role in bringing the cults of wealth into being, the retreat of Thai political actors from their historical role of attempting to manage and direct national religious life created an opening within which the extra-political forces of the market and media could be welded within ritual processes to become the dominant determinants of religious change and innovation. The enchantment of Thai modernity in the late twentieth century was predicated upon a certain depoliticization of the religious field, at least to the extent that commerce, media and ritual could come into play as independent forces of transformation.

Economically, the metamorphosis of capitalism from a system based on production to one that focuses on consumption, together with the rise of a mass culture of consumerism within a neoliberal setting that emphasizes the primacy of the market over government, was central to the incitement of new forms of magical enchantment. Before the mid-decades of the twentieth century, the social context of capitalism was indeed founded on processes of rationalized production that, as Weber observed in the 1920s, contributed to a broader disenchantment of culture, including religion. It is perhaps unfair to criticize Weber for failing to account for the workings and cultural impact of a form of capitalism that did not exist at the time he conducted his studies. But it is incumbent upon scholars today to recognize, as Robert Hefner (2010, 2017) observes, that things have changed since Weber's time. Our analyses therefore need to move beyond Weber, even as we acknowledge the debt owed to his seminal studies.

There have also been dramatic changes in the cultural impact of modern imaging technologies and media. The development of photography in the nineteenth century was often associated with a scientific outlook that emphasized the claimed capacity of this representational medium to accurately reflect reality and hence demystify the world. However, in the latter twentieth century, the proliferation of photographic images, mass produced by commercial technologies in a post-Fordist capitalist economy centred on consumption, severed any necessary link between images and external scientific "reality". In what Jean Baudrillard (1994) calls the mediatized society of the simulacrum, images come loose from objects that they may be presumed to represent and take on enchanting effects. This separation of images from reality and the enchanting force of mass visual representation has further intensified with the development of digital imaging technologies disseminated by new media of personal computers, smart phones and the internet.

At a broader level, our understanding of the cultural force and productive capacities of ritual practice have also been transformed by the application of John L. Austin's (1962) theory of the performative effects of language in the study of culture, including anthropology and studies of gender and sexuality. Performative accounts of ritual detail how the repetition of systematically ordered practices may engender cosmological schemas and enchanting effects. This perspective deepens our understanding of the primacy of ritual over doctrine in magical cults, revealing that ritual is no mere adjunct to magical "beliefs" but contributes to the very creation of enchanted outlooks. To some extent, performative accounts of ritual reverse the primacy of mind over body, and of belief over practice, that characterized dominant trends in Western thought after the Enlightenment, instead positing that embodied ritual actions induce enchanting effects that are associated with magical perspectives.

The processes of modern enchantment discussed below—consumerist neoliberal capitalism and mass mediatization—are widespread, indeed pervasive, influences across the contemporary world. But I suggest that it is in religious contexts and forms that emphasize ritual over belief that their enchanting influences are most pronounced. Consumer capitalism induces "occult economies" and mass media produce "auras" in most societies. In marketized and mediatized religious settings where practice dominates belief, however, the performative force of ritual accentuates and intensifies processes of modern enchantment. It is in the ritual-focussed dimensions of Thai religiosity that we find the most pronounced presence of modern enchantment. This is not a situation unique to Thailand. As Bruno Latour (1993) shows, all forms of modernity are marked by a cleavage between ideologies of rational purification and practices of hybridization. It will be in the fields of hybrid practice found in all modern societies that the enchanting influences of the market and media will be felt most forcefully, and where we can expect to find modern enchantments across the world today.

It is especially noteworthy that scholars of spirit cults—including Jean and John Comaroff (2000), Rosalind Morris (2000a, 2000b) and Stanley Tambiah (1981, 1985, 1990)—have not only been prominent critics of the thesis that modernity leads to the disenchantment of social worlds, but they have also been at the forefront of theorizing the processes by which modern technologies and forms of life produce new forms of magical ritual and enchanted imaginaries. The analyses of these authors of the enchanting effects of neoliberal capitalism, media and ritual are central to the arguments presented in this chapter.

From State-Sponsored to Market-Based: The Retreat of the State and the Rise of the Market in Thai Religiosity

The Thai prosperity movements could not have become so prominent without a significant shift in the relations between state and religion in Thailand in the 1980s and 1990s. As Tatsuki Kataoka (2012b) points out, forms of ritual expression have proliferated and diversified to the greatest degree in those fields of religious life beyond the Thai state's supervision and management of institutional Buddhism. Indeed, the rise of the prosperity movements as expressions of popular religiosity in the 1990s paralleled the Thai state's retreat from its historical role of harnessing Buddhism for state purposes. For much of the twentieth century, Thai governments attempted to link the institution of Buddhism to the task of nation-building and state-guided socio-economic development, instituting a centralized model of Thai Buddhist religiosity and at times suppressing regional varieties of Buddhism that were perceived as not conforming to state objectives (see Jackson 1988; Easum 2013; Bowie 2017). Across the first decades of the twentieth century, Thai absolute monarchs and authoritarian military rulers both sought to establish legitimatory relationships between Buddhism and the state by decree. Buddhism became a state-sponsored and state-controlled religion, with an arm of the civilian bureaucracy—the Department of Religious Affairs—dedicated to monitoring and enforcing the legally determined organizational structure of the monkhood and the form of state-sangha relations.

The organization of the sangha and forms of Buddhist ritual have been important in legitimating the exercise of state power in Thai kingdoms since at least the Sukhothai period in the thirteenth century. However, Somboon Suksamran (1982), Yoneo Ishii (1986) and myself (Jackson 1989) have argued that Buddhism's political importance as a system of legitimating practices and discourses underpinned an intensification of state control over the sangha in the twentieth century. This was exercised through a series of efforts to restructure the monkhood in the image of the secular political order. At three key junctures across the twentieth century, the state imposed new bureaucratic structures upon the sangha, showing the importance that political leaders placed on harnessing the Buddhist monkhood to state-defined projects. Sangha Acts in 1902, 1941 and 1962, initiated and enforced by the state, decreed that the national organization of the monkhood should have a form that mirrored the changing structures of secular power—from absolute monarchy, to popular democracy and, subsequently, to military dictatorship.

From the mid-1980s, however, the Thai state showed less interest in orchestrating the national structure of Buddhism. While state control over the sangha remains in the form of the Sangha Act administered by the Department of Religious Affairs, effective state control over religious expression declined markedly during the years of the economic boom. This decline in interest by politicians in controlling the forms of Buddhist religiosity—except to eradicate clerical corruption and counter immorality—created a space within which popular religious movements were able to flourish.

Several factors influenced this retreat of the Thai state from its former role in managing Buddhist religious organization. With the decline and eventual end of the communist insurgency in the country in the early 1980s, and the end of hostilities with communist regimes in neighbouring Laos and Cambodia, the Thai state under Prime Minister General Prem Tinsulanonda and the subsequent civilian prime minister Chatichai Choonhavan began to follow a less centralist cultural policy. After the end of the Cold War, affirmations of local religious culture that were often expressed in regional languages were no longer seen as politically threatening. In part, this was because of the success of earlier centrist policies that had entrenched the dominance of the Central Thai language and the Bangkok-based state apparatus throughout the country. Given the unchallenged strength of the central state based in Bangkok, resurgences of local linguistic-religious-cultural sentiment and expression were not perceived as a threat to the hegemony of the Central Thai language and state administration. Indeed, in sharp contrast to the Cold War period, since the 1980s the state has sought to affirm and harness aspects of local culture as a strategy of further integrating regional populations into the state apparatus. Local cultural differences are now celebrated as aspects to promote domestic and international tourism. In the 1990s, a weak form of internal multiculturalism came to supplant the imposed Bangkok-centred mono-culturalism of the middle decades of the century. This state-sponsored affirmation of local culture now goes by the name of *phumi-panya* or "local wisdom".

The retreat of the state from the field of religious expression has not been limited to Thailand. Robert Hefner notes that since the Doi Moi reforms of the late 1980s, Vietnam has also witnessed a major reorientation of the state's role that has been accompanied by a significant resurgence of ritual practice (Hefner 2010, p. 1032). He adds more generally that "Asia's religious resurgence is a response to the ostensible retreat of the state in the face of a globally ascendant neoliberalism" (p. 1033). It is indeed significant that the post–Cold War efflorescence of magical cults and spirit possession in mainland Southeast Asia has occurred with equal intensity in West-aligned capitalist societies such as Thailand and in ostensibly socialist countries such as Vietnam. In the twentieth century, competing political discourses of socialist and capitalist rational modernity in Vietnam and Thailand both critiqued spirit mediumship as a superstitious residue of premodern tradition that, it was argued, held each country back from achieving the desired transition to scientific (socialist or capitalist) modernity. The governments of both countries instituted similar anti-supernaturalism policies across the middle decades of the twentieth century. However, despite continuing political differences, spirit possession cults have been resurgent in both Thailand and Vietnam, as well as in neighbouring countries such as Burma and Cambodia, over the period of neoliberal globalization (see Bénédicte Brac de la Perrière and Peter A. Jackson 2022). The differing political complexions of post–Cold War societies in mainland Southeast Asia have proven to be irrelevant to the growth of supernatural belief and ritual, with spirit mediumship flourishing under twenty-first-century versions of both market-oriented socialism and neoliberal capitalism.[1] Since the 1980s, the Thai and Vietnamese governments have both relaxed central controls over religion and placed more emphasis on market-based, export-led economic growth. To some extent the same has been true of China, where some forms of folk religion have also been tolerated since the transition to market-based socialism (see Mayfair Yang 2008). This comparative perspective reveals the centrality of the highly productive role of neoliberal capitalism in the religious efflorescence across Asia.

Erick White (2014) argues that there have been two important consequences of the ideological and institutional decline of both establishment state and modernist reform varieties of Buddhism to shape Buddhist religiosity. First, it has become more culturally acceptable and socially viable for once marginal spirit mediums to publicly claim mainstream Buddhist legitimacy for their moral authority and charismatic authenticity or *barami*. And second, as the general public has increasingly come to perceive *barami* as legitimately residing outside the sangha in non-conformist Buddhist monks and religious movements, it has also become more common for non-monastic religious specialists such as spirit mediums to be identified as possessing charismatic authority (White 2014, p. 249). White contends that the decline of state influence and authority over religious expression has permitted an overall Buddhacization and upgrading of spirit possession and other forms of ritual, which have appropriated forms of discourse and charismatic authority once reserved only for monastic Buddhism and royal cults. As noted in Chapter Five, the spirits at the centre of the cults of wealth and related spirit possession rituals are no longer called *phi* ("spirits"), but rather are addressed as *thep* ("deities") and *jao* ("lords"), terms that were previously reserved for deities invoked in elite and royal rituals.

The growing popularity of non-monastic ritual specialists also appears to have been influenced by a seemingly continuous series of widely publicized sex scandals and cases of clerical fraud and corruption that have rocked institutional Buddhism over the past several decades (see Jackson 1997; Keyes 1995). In the 1990s, prominent monks such as *Phra* Nikorn in Chiang Mai and the internationally famous *Ajan* Yantra were exposed as having ongoing relationships with female followers and fathering children. In 1996, the formerly respected monk *Phra* Phawana Phuttho was defrocked after being charged with raping underage girls from ethnic minorities who were living at his Nakhon Pathom monastery west of Bangkok. The perceived inaction, even complicity, of senior echelons of the sangha administration in these and other highly publicized cases contributed to a decline in the moral standing of state-sponsored institutional Buddhism, creating a mood of disillusionment with establishment religion and undoubtedly contributing to the attractiveness of new movements that were seen as being untainted by the moral decline of the mainstream sangha.

In Thailand the decline of political control over religion occurred at the same time that the economic boom gathered pace, with economic forces rising at the historical moment when political influences over religion and other aspects of cultural production waned. The rise of the economy then created an expanded space of cultural production that went beyond the historical scope of state-based authority, with the withdrawal of state power and the emergence of a significantly expanded market together creating a domain within which economic forces became more important determinants of religious expression.

Marketization and the Cultural Logic of Neoliberalism

Hefner reminds us of the distinctive features of neoliberalism and that things have changed significantly since the time of Max Weber: "[C]apitalism has *itself* changed in the late-modern era, in a manner quite different from what Marx, Durkheim, Weber, or even the post-war Parsonians anticipated" (Hefner 2017, p. 269; emphasis in original). Most significant, Hefner argues, is the consumerist dynamic driving contemporary transnational capitalism. Different phases of capitalism have had distinctive impacts on the religious field in Thailand. David Ip observes that "[t]here are two types of capitalist spirit at work, one based on rational productivism and the other on gambling and specu-lation" (Ip 1999, p. 29). Indeed, in the middle decades of the twentieth century, the teachings of the reformist monk Buddhadasa that the good Buddhist is disciplined and hard-working, and that success in life is achieved through careful cultivation of Buddhist virtues (Jackson 2003), were prominent influences in Thailand. Buddhadasa was strongly critical of magical cults and undertook a systematic demythologization of Theravada Buddhist doctrine, imagining hard-working Thai Buddhists as inhabiting a coherent ethical universe. In contrast, the cults of wealth emerged in the context of neoliberal capitalism after the end of the Cold War, in which the successful person is more likely to be compared to a gambler who engages in speculative risk-taking ventures. This late-modern Thai Buddhist lives in a culture of luck. Reflecting views of neoliberalism as a form of "casino capitalism", Alan Klima sees Thailand's prosperity cults as emerging from a "fusion of Buddhism, spirit possession, gambling, public works, and irregular financial instruments" (Klima 2006, p. 56).

In the context of these different historical phases and modalities of capitalism, two sets of arguments have been presented for how we can understand the productive roles of the market, as well as new visual media, in the emergence of new forms of magical ritual. One set of analyses argues that capitalism and new media promote the dissemination of information about new religious movements and make them widely accessible through efficient marketing. These accounts detail the processes behind the proliferation of existing movements. While helping us understand how magical cults may be communicated and expand their influence among media-connected and commercially savvy consumers of ritual, they do not describe how new movements may emerge in the first place. A second set of analyses makes a stronger case, arguing that capitalism and new media are themselves productive sources of new forms of ritual and, in radical contrast to theories of modernity as a process of disenchantment, they contend that mediatized neoliberalism constitutes a set of productive forces that contribute to bringing new magical cults into being.

Modern Religion as a Market Place: Religious Expression as a Commodity

David Lyon summarizes accounts that view different religions as brands competing in a capitalist spiritual marketplace:

> [R]eligiously significant symbols are available in what is in effect a single marketplace, dominated by the cultural commodification practices of the media industries. At the same time, that marketplace is extremely deregulated, so that signs circulate freely, and personal

choice rather than traditional authority determines how they are appropriated. (Lyon 2000, p. 56)

In this setting, Lyon contends that it is those religious groups that are skilled in marketing that may succeed in the new commercial environment (Lyon 2000, p. 32). In this vein, Raymond Lee has presented an analysis to account for religious diversity in Malaysia in the 1990s and his findings are also relevant to Thailand. Lee proposes that religious diversification has occurred in capitalist Asian societies in recent decades because no single organization can offer all the religious services for which there is a demand in the spiritual marketplace. As a consequence, there will be many faiths, each specializing in meeting the requirements of a segment of the market:

> Religion in late capitalism may be conceptualised as an international salvationary market.... [T]he declining public power of religion frees individuals to privately select from a wide range of religious services without necessarily responding to institutional pressures.... [T]he buying and selling of religious ideologies must be examined within the context of competitive pluralism. In short, the religious market thrives on ideological variety. (Lee 1993, p. 35)

This market model provides an apt description of the diversification of religion in contemporary Thailand; in particular, the disintegration of a centrally organized, overarching religious system and its replacement by a mass market of segmented religious forms. Writing at the height of Thailand's economic boom, Apinya Feungfusakul (1993) was among the first to consider the religious efflorescence of the 1990s as a Thai "religious marketplace" in which ritual participation merged with consumption. Erick White argues that the expansion of new wealth beyond traditional elites has also been a factor in religious diversification:

> [T]he increased financial wealth now circulating outside of the direct control of the state and those bureaucratic and economic elites most closely affiliated with it means that these diverse movements ... outside, or on the periphery, of the Thai state's religious bureaucracy have a greater degree of relative social and institutional autonomy than was previously the case with non-conforming religious movements in earlier historical eras. (White 2014, p. 236)

Neoliberal Occult Economies and Magical Prosperity Religions

The account by Michael Carrithers (2000) of religious polytropy in India demonstrates the way in which patterns of ritual diversity parallel the operations of the market, providing insight into why popular religion has been so amenable to commodification. Carrithers argues that the sociology of ritual polytropy that he presents, in which worshippers turn "to one deity or another as need and inclination suggest", is reminiscent of models of a free market (Carrithers 2000, p. 839). That is, the pre-existing religious culture of polytropy, or what in Thailand Justin McDaniel (2011) terms repertoire religiosities, conforms in many ways to the patterns of mediatized consumer societies. Based on research conducted in Vietnam, Oscar Salemink similarly observes, "what is striking about spirit mediumship is its highly transactional nature, leading many observers to comment on the 'commercial' character of spirit mediumship" (Salemink 2010, p. 268). Salemink summarizes Philip Taylor's (2004) analyses of new forms of devotion and pilgrimage in a modern market context in southern Vietnam as offering a "quasi-Marxist interpretation that the transactional nature of people's dealings with deities and spirits is a way of 'embodying market relations' (Taylor 2004: 83–110)" (Salemink 2010, p. 269). Salemink contends that in Southeast Asia "[t]he market becomes a direct metaphor to articulate the transactional relationship between human beings and deities in the other world" (p. 275). The argument that there are structural parallels between popular religiosity and the marketplace provides a basis for understanding the ways in which some forms of capitalism may actively incite new modalities of magical ritual and enchantment. Pattana Kitiarsa sees Thailand's *phuttha phanit* cults of prosperity as reflecting a situation in which "conventional Theravada Buddhism, state and Sangha authorities, multi-original religious beliefs and the drive for material success in the capitalist market all come to coexist and produce a hybrid moment of religious change" (Pattana 2005, p. 468).

Thailand's prosperity cults are far from being unique. Jean and John Comaroff argue that religions in which a "messianic, millennial capitalism ... presents itself as a gospel of salvation" (Comaroff and Comaroff 2000, p. 292) are a worldwide phenomenon linked with the global triumph of neoliberal capitalism after the end of the Cold War. They point to "the exuberant spread of innovative occult practices and money magic, pyramid schemes, and prosperity gospels; the enchantments, that is, of a decidedly neoliberal economy" (p. 292). Comaroff and Comaroff argue that new forms of market-based enchantment, which they call "occult economies" (Comaroff and Comaroff 1999), have emerged under neoliberalism because "[o]nce legible processes—the workings of power, the distribution of wealth, the meaning of politics and national belonging—have become opaque, even spectral" (Comaroff and Comaroff 2000, p. 305). More recently, Jean and John Comaroff have defined occult economies as, "arcane modes of attempting to generate value, often by experimental means,... to access the hidden mechanisms held to operate behind conventional forms of accumulation" (Comaroff and Comaroff 2018, p. 290). They emphasize that occult economies are not limited to disenfranchized underclasses in economically emerging societies but include

> the wealthy and powerful everywhere who seek new, unconventional ways to become yet wealthier and more powerful. Mark also our stress on the fact that, at core, occult practices seek to produce knowledge by experimentation with means and ends. This is true of, and no more ir/rational than, most other techniques of knowledge production, which have their own enchantments—as do such 'hard' scholarly disciplines as economics. (Comaroff and Comaroff 2018, p. 292)[2]

In this context, "the occult becomes an ever more appropriate, semantically saturated metaphor for our times" (Comaroff and Comaroff 2000, p. 318). Indeed, the popular supernaturalism that emerged in tandem with 1990s neoliberalism was paralleled by a religion-like faith in the market amongst the ideologues of finance capital. Magical capitalism is not a mere persistence of premodern "superstition" but rather is a refraction through local cultural metaphors of the beliefs of capitalism's ruling elites, for whom neoliberalism was "a gospel of salvation" (p. 291).[3] As Jean Comaroff has noted more recently, "[t]he prosperity gospels that currently are so appealing in many parts of the world bear the impact of a cult of salvation through the market.... [I]f market futures often sound redemptive, faith-based language also bears the imprint of the market. Weber's interplay of Christianity and capitalism continues in our late-modern age" (Comaroff and Kim 2011, p. 172).[4]

In a similar vein, Beng-Lan Goh details what she terms "modern capitalist sacralisation" (Goh 2011, p. 147) and summarizes analyses that

> [overturn] assumptions about capitalism as merely a descralised, individualistic, and accumulative activity. Instead they provide us with a way to view capitalism as being ineluctably entwined with historical and socio-moral imperatives of social reproduction. It is the imbrications of capitalism and the historical and socio-moral forces of reproducing society that explain the forces of capitalist sacralisation. (Goh 2011, pp. 146–7)

In 1994, Charles Keyes et al. observed that many students of religion as well as political leaders were puzzled why "popular religion should continue to appeal to people in a world that has become increasingly rationalised" (Keyes et al. 1994, p. 10). However, the late-modern world of neoliberal capitalism is not in fact a highly rationalized social order. The hypercomplexities of the contemporary world are post-rational in the sense that they exceed the ability to be fully subjected to logical analysis. While Weber may have described industrial capitalism as presenting an iron cage of bureaucratic reason, the complexity of contemporary social orders built upon post-industrial capitalism has outstripped the predictive capacity of many established forms of rational analysis. White argues that because Buddhism has functioned as a repository of beliefs and practices designed to provide control over social insecurity and uncertainty, it is not surprising that popular Thai religiosity has flourished within a social environment characterized by capitalist development:

> Numerous scholars of Thai religion have noted, although sometimes only in passing, that those religious beliefs and practices which function to provide individuals with an increased sense of protection, control and success in the face of a hostile and unpredictable environment have thrived and even diversified during the final decades of the twentieth century (Irvine 1984, Mulder 1990: 39–40 … Jackson 1999a, 1999b). (White 2014, p. 232)

Marjorie Muecke notes that these views have been expressed by scholars of Theravada Buddhism since the 1960s:

> Both [Melford] Spiro (for Burma) and [Gananath] Obeyesekere (for Sri Lanka) use a functional argument: they see the shaman's practice of divination as providing an element of predictability that contravenes the change and luck that are characteristic of life in the modernising urban environments of post–World War Two Southeast Asia (Obeyesekere 1967; Spiro 1970: 208). (Muecke 1992, p. 97)

Jean Comaroff locates the distinctiveness of late-modern communities as lying in "their participation—to a greater or lesser extent—in a global order of commodity production, transaction, and consumption" (Comaroff 1994, p. 305). In this setting, she takes a post-rationalist stance in accounting for the rise of Asian prosperity religions:

> Like ritual movements all over the late capitalist world, these cults address the impact of radically diffused and individuated production, of the insecurities of life in a capricious market where greed and luck appear as effective as work and rational choice....

[T]hese practices also promise the possibility of getting in on the act, of redirecting some of the largesse to those previously denied it. (Comaroff 1994, p. 310)

Levels of complexity and uncertainty beyond the predictive power of the most powerful computer programs and analytical algorithms may encourage post-rational religious responses. Because of the limits of rational analysis to map what is happening in the contemporary world, there may be a convergence of outlooks that gives supernaturalism a continuing relevance in marketized neoliberal societies. There may then be a commonality between premodern and postmodern symbolic orders in that both see the world as being beyond human beings' rational capacity to fully comprehend and control. Keyes et al. note that the continuing relevance of the supernatural may emerge from the limits of reason:

> By insisting on the superiority of rational action over traditional practice, the modernisers have made the limits of rationality much more clear: the gap between the conclusions reached about the world through recourse to rational decision making and the practical reality of the world generates uncertainty and ambiguity that many seek to resolve through turning to religion. (Keyes et al. 1994, p. 15)

This is where ritual and magic return, albeit in highly modified, mediatized and commodified forms. Magical ritual is a practical response to living in a decentralized marketized and increasingly complex world that often defies predictability. This is not a premodern survival or an atavistic return to the past, although it may appear so to a rationally minded observer. Rather, it is the emergence of ritual and magic within the conditions of late-modern hypercomplexity. Modernization theory is not able to distinguish between, on the one hand, an older premodern cultural order that it disparages as superstitious, mystical and irrational and, on the other hand, a contemporary late-modern cultural order that is post-rational. The limitations of rationalist modernization theory prevent it from distinguishing premodern magic from late-modern ritual because it fails to acknowledge that the capitalist social order that was predicted to impose an iron cage of rationalized disenchantment is in fact productive of its own new enchantments.

Jean and John Comaroff propose that many of the enigmatic features of late-modern economy and society "are concrete, historically specific outworkings of millennial capitalism and the culture of neoliberalism" (Comaroff and Comaroff 2000, p. 334) and that prosperity religions need to be seen as "imaginative efforts to reclaim a runaway world" (Comaroff 1994, p. 310). Furthermore, the Comaroffs argue that occult economies were not a passing, ephemeral phenomenon of late twentieth-century neoliberalism but have indeed persisted and expanded over the first decades of the new century "as the millennial mood has given way to a new normal, a time of entrepreneurial governance" (Comaroff and Comaroff 2018, p. 293). Forms of commodity-based enchantment have proved "to be every bit as protean as modernity itself, thriving on its contradictions and its silences, usurping its media, puncturing its pretensions" (p. 303). In concluding their recent survey, they argue,

> [E]nchantment in its diverse manifestations, far from slipping away with the resolute march of modernity, seems virtually everywhere on the ascent.... The conditions that gave rise to the occult economy with which we were concerned almost 20 years ago, it seems, have not disappeared. If anything, that economy has become endemic, constantly reinventing itself in step with the contingencies of the historical present. (Comaroff and Comaroff 2018, p. 313)

In this light, we can regard Thailand's prosperity movements as pragmatic cultural forms in a society that has located the rationally intractable and theoretically recalcitrant globalized market at its heart. There is a reinforcing parallelism, rather than any contradiction, between efflorescing supernaturalism and a globalized economy. Thai money magic represents an attempt to clothe in symbolic order the hypercomplexity of the marketized social formation, with the cults of wealth imposing forms of meaningfulness upon the disorienting dynamism of economic and social transformations by spiritualizing the market and symbolically taming the unruly power of globalizing capitalism. In this marketized social formation it is "reason" that is often the stranger and the outsider, not the supernatural.

Mass Media and the Production of Devotional Cults

The Role of the Media in Popularizing New Cults

New mass media have also contributed to the nationwide popularity of the cults of wealth in Thailand by delocalizing cultic figures and making information about local deities and spirits available to national audiences. Chalong Soontravanich notes that before the twentieth century, magic monks or *keji ajan* were only known to their local communities. But with modern media the fame of monks, and their amulets, has spread beyond local communities, with many *keji ajan* becoming the focus of national cults. Chalong reports that *Luang Phor*

Ngoen of Wat Don Yaihom in Nakhon Pathom west of Bangkok, whose name means "Reverend Father Silver/Money",

> was one of the very first local Buddhist saints whose prestige during the postwar years grew well beyond the confines of his home province.... *Luang Phor* Ngoen became a popular and highly revered Buddhist saint among many police generals in Bangkok. During the 1950s and 1960s, they frequently invited him to take part in consecration ceremonies for the production of Buddhist amulets in Bangkok and other provinces. (Chalong 2013, p. 206)

IMAGE 28. CD of *Khatha* Magical Incantations
An audio CD of *khatha* magical incantations to request blessings from a diverse array of royal and Buddhist deities and spirits, sold for the numerologically auspicious price of ninety-nine baht by the 7-Eleven convenience store chain. Titled "Blessed *Khatha* to Worship Magical Entities (*sing saksit*) in Thailand", the CD contains incantations dedicated to King Chulalongkorn (centre); the image of the Emerald Buddha (top right); Siam Thewathirat (top left); King Naresuan (r. 1590–1605) (centre left); King Taksin (r. 1767–82) (centre right); and *Krommaluang* (Prince) Chumphon (lower right). (Collection of the author.)

Rosalind Morris similarly argues that

> People in northern Thailand are no longer beholden to the spirits of place.... [T]hey are now less likely to pay respects to local shrines, when they argue that place has given way to a more abstract spatial sense, they recognise that a new conceptual universe is operative. (Morris 2000, p. 245)

Lawrence Babb and Susan Wadley (1995) argue that in South Asia, print media, movies and television have created a shared national ritual field by standardizing and disseminating a limited number of religious symbols. National media have also contributed to a democratization of access to ritual technologies. In the past, *khatha* or magical formulae were kept private and not publicized. In 1985, Louis Golomb wrote,

> Were magical formulae to be printed or interpreted for the masses, traditional magical/medical practices would probably decline rapidly. Erwin Ackerknecht (1955: 106) has described a comparable medical revolution following the invention of the printing press in sixteenth-century Europe. Paracelsus brought about the collapse of the Galenic humoral theory when he attacked it in print using the vernacular language. (Golomb 1985, p. 87)

However, in contrast to the rationalist undermining of medieval magical practices in sixteenth-century Europe, the mass publication of *khatha* incantations in nationally marketed booklets and audio CDs has now become a thriving industry in early twenty-first-century Thailand, making magical incantations available to all. In late-capitalist Thailand, media are contributing to disseminating *saksit* formulae and ritual techniques rather than challenging the authority of these forms of magical expertise.

In this context, many in Thailand now pay respect to figures linked to the enveloping commercial space of the market that has become the common experience of all. The new spirits that are now the most popular, and which are at the centre of the cults of wealth at the national level, are those that sacralize the national-scale economic space, especially when that space of commercial enterprise is linked to figures regarded as symbols of national protection, such as King Chulalongkorn.

Devotional Movements and Waves of Religious Populism

Nevertheless, of the large number of personality-based devotional movements in Thailand, only a small number achieve prominence in terms of the number of their followers and the extent to which they are represented in the national press and media. In recent decades,

Thai popular religion has repeatedly produced new forms of mass religiosity focussed on a changing array of charismatic personalities and magically empowered *saksit* religious objects. The phenomenon of repeated waves of religious populism emerges from the impact of the mass media on the devotional focus of Thai religiosity, which emphasizes powerful personalities and objects. The personality- and object-focussed character of Thai popular religion, which is continually expanding as new *saksit* personalities and objects become focuses of veneration, provides a rich source of copy for Thailand's print and electronic media. Justin McDaniel argues that the great rise in followings of various religious figures "shows that modern communication and transportation technology and the mechanical reproduction of visual images has led to more diversity in Thai religiosity" (McDaniel 2011, p. 225). Pattana Kitiarsa also argues that the mass media have played important roles in fostering new religious phenomena in Thailand:

> [T]he mass media is the most decisive catalyst for religious hybridisation. The heavy religious content and coverage in the popular media have shaped the public's beliefs and practices in the direction of a more prosperity-oriented religion. (Pattana 2005a, p. 486).

The Thai language press in particular has been central to the production of religious populism in recent decades. Competition among national dailies such as *Thai Rath*, *Daily News*, *Khom Chat Leuk* and *Khao Sot* is intense, with each trying to secure sales by exclusive coverage of page-one stories. Sex scandals, political corruption, graphic photographs of motor accident victims, blood-chilling crimes and national sporting triumphs as well as tales of magical phenomena commonly fill the pages of these newspapers. Accounts of a particular figure's reputed prophetic, healing or protective powers are often reported as news items by these papers.[5] Rachelle Scott argues that discourses and practices aimed specifically at winning the lottery form a distinct subset within the field of Thai prosperity cults (Scott 2017, p. 242). She details how networks of "lottery spirits" have been facilitated by the mass media, which have "disseminated stories of the spirits and their lucky patrons throughout the kingdom and around the globe" (p. 232). In what can be regarded as an instance of the symbolic complex of cults of wealth, Scott proposes that Thai media have been instrumental in bringing into being a "media space" in which "disparate spirits from a wide variety of origins are linked together in a network of lottery lore and practice" (p. 232).

Media-Induced Charismatic Inflation: The Role of the Press in Making and Marketing Luang Phor *Khoon as a National Saint*

Reporting of the reputed magical powers of a religious figure or icon by the more sensationalist dailies can create a media-induced aura and contribute to establishing a circuit of charismatic inflation whereby the more that a particular figure is sought out and the more they are reported, the more their popularity increases. Once a focus of supernatural power or charisma is established then, under certain conditions, it can continue to attract more followers in an almost exponential process. Such charismatic appeal is not merely a sacral phenomenon but also derives from the power of the mass media to produce and circulate influential images and symbols. The mass media simultaneously facilitate and incite this process, becoming agents promoting the fame and reputation of a cultic figure.

For example, *Luang Phor* Khoon, the magic monk discussed in several of the preceding chapters, could only have become a national phenomenon in the era of a competitive, sensationalist national press. The popular press was a key factor in the creation of Khoon as a national cult figure, with reporting of his reputed supernatural power in saving disaster victims in the early 1990s catapulting him to national prominence. And as the press inflated his charisma by promoting his supernatural reputation, local and national politicians sought to be associated with him to promote their careers. *Luang Phor* Khoon's reputation in Northeast Thailand for miraculously empowered amulets dates from the 1970s. But it was a dramatic tragedy in the early 1990s that brought him to national attention. On 13 August 1993, in one of modern Thailand's worst disasters, the shoddily constructed Royal Plaza Hotel in Nakhon Ratchasima city northeast of Bangkok collapsed, killing 137 and injuring hundreds.[6] Three days after the collapse, rescuers located a hotel cleaner, Nartthaya Chimdee, still alive but with her legs trapped by a massive block of concrete. The rescuers found it impossible to remove the concrete block until, it is claimed, one worker dropped a *Luang Phor* Khoon amulet to the trapped woman. As Nartthaya held the amulet and prayed to Khoon for help, the rescuers managed to lift the block of concrete and save her life. As the *Bangkok Post* reported on the first anniversary of the disaster:

> The objects produced at *Luang Phor* Khoon's [monastery] Wat Ban Rai became more famous when the Royal Plaza Hotel in Nakhon Ratchasima collapsed last year and ... survivors were found to be wearing a '*Luang Phor* Khoon' amulet. People believe an amulet or object from [Wat Ban Rai] or even a touch on the head with the hand of *Luang Phor* Khoon will protect them from any danger.[7]

Khoon's reputation was further enhanced by a second disaster only a couple of months after the hotel collapse. According to one biography of the monk (*Luang Phor Khoon Parisuttho* [1996?]), in late 1993 a young female worker at the Kader doll factory on the outskirts of Bangkok survived a leap from the factory's third storey when escaping a fire in which more than 200 of her co-workers died. Twenty-one-year-old Phairat Jeemkhunthot, a native of Khoon's home district of Dan Khun Thot, survived the leap while other escaping workers who jumped with her died. She later told reporters that as she jumped she had held on to her *Luang Phor* Khoon amulet, which was struck in 1987 as part of the "Cooperatives Batch" (*run sahakorn*). Apparently Phairat's fall was cushioned by the bodies of colleagues who had leapt before her and on whom she landed. But the popular Thai language press attributed her survival to the miraculous power of the amulet. The 1987 Cooperatives Batch of amulets subsequently became highly prized and expensive, with a thriving market in forgeries.

The popular press reported these events as miracles, crediting Khoon with supernatural powers. Accounts of Khoon's reputed prophetic, healing and protective powers were often reported as news by *Thai Rath*, *Daily News* and *Khao Sot*, and in these populist Thai language dailies the monk was often referred to by epithets that reflected his supposed supernatural powers, often being called a *thepphajao* or "Divine Lord" (from Pali *deva*; Thai *jao*), an expression that can denote either a divine being or a human with a heightened level of spiritual authority. Another common epithet for Khoon in the popular press was "The Divine Lord of the Plateau [i.e., Isan]" (*thepphajao haeng thi-rap-sung*).

Throughout the mid-1990s, the sensationalist press regularly gave front-page coverage to a stream of miracles attributed to Khoon's protective power. In December 1996, *Thai Rath* published a page-one photo story of a Bangkok taxi driver whose vehicle had been crushed in an accident with a tour bus and who claimed he had been saved by a *Luang Phor* Khoon amulet hung around his cab's rear-view mirror.[8] Many prominent people, including politicians, attested to the magical power of *Luang Phor* Khoon amulets and told their stories to the press. In 1992, Suvat Liptapallop, former deputy-secretary-general of the Chart Pattana Party—led by former prime minister the late Chatichai Choonhavan—became a staunch believer in Khoon's powers when he credited his *Luang Phor* Khoon amulet with preventing a plane crash.[9] In that year, he and eighteen officials from the Thai Fine Arts Department were returning from a visit to the United States when their plane's landing gear malfunctioned. The pilot ditched fuel over the sea and returned to Los Angeles, where the plane landed safely. Suvat later told *The Nation*: "At that time, I thought the plane would crash and I would die—so I took the *Luang Phor* Koon amulet from my neck and began to pray 'May *Luang Phor* Koon save me'."[10] Suvat said that all of the eighteen officials on the plane were also wearing *Luang Phor* Khoon amulets, and explained that this was why a 170–member *khon* classical dance troupe from the Fine Arts Department subsequently performed at Wat Ban Rai to celebrate Khoon's seventy-second birthday in 1994, because the department's senior staff wished to show their appreciation to the abbot for having been saved.[11]

Continual reporting of Khoon's reputed powers through the mid-1990s and his association with prominent national political figures created a media-induced aura around him, establishing a circuit of charismatic inflation whereby the more he was sought out and the more his image was represented in the press and media, the more his popularity increased. Khoon's charismatic appeal was not merely a sacral Buddhist phenomenon but also flowed from the power of the mass media to manufacture influential images and symbols.

Print and Visual Media as Technologies of Enchantment

However, contemporary media may not only contribute to the popularity of one or other devotional movement by disseminating information about them. New media also create magic-like effects that can auraticize cult figures or objects, thereby contributing to the production of new forms of religiosity and magical ritual. In analysing popular culture in contemporary India, Bhaskar Mukhophadhyay argues that the mediatization of myth now constitutes a political force in that country:

> Mass-media have made the gods more real, not less.... The semiotic valences of objects are no longer functions of secular historical memory or social taxonomy ... but are determined by the serial logic of spectacular assemblages. It is not a matter of virtuality or 'spectacle'. It is myth sanctified by technology—a techno-mythologisation of the body politics. (Mukhophadhyay 2006, pp. 288–89)

In a study titled "Religion and/as Media", Jeremy Stolow observes that media have become central to "the imagined worlds that constitute the sacred in the global present" (Stolow 2005, p. 123), and he makes a similar argument to that presented by Mukhopadhyay, contending that "the transcendental, enchanting, thaumaturgical, uncanny, haunting—powers of media technologies themselves" (p. 124) induce a "reactivation of aura" (p. 127).

In words that echo Michael Taussig's (1997, pp. 250ff) reflections on "sympathetic magic in a post-colonial age" in his book *The Magic of the State*, Rosalind Morris describes how the proliferation of new forms of imaging technology has reincited a "primordial sacrality" rather than contributing to a decay of sacredness in Thailand. Morris links the resurgence of spirit mediumship in Thailand with the rise of capitalism and marketized lifestyles, on the one hand, and the explosive growth of technologies of image reproduction and mass communication, on the other. Morris argues that the efflorescence of mediumship in recent decades has its roots in the mass media (Morris 2000a, p. 53) and mediumship's growing popularity is linked to a radically new attitude to imaging technologies. She observes that until the 1970s it was uncommon for spirit mediums to permit themselves to be represented via the mass media (Morris 2000b, p. 458). In contrast, "[n]ow all mediums display photographs of themselves, and even media personalities have joined the ranks of the possessed" (p. 460), and indeed "[m]ediums now recognise themselves in technologies of mass mediatisation" (p. 465). Morris also observes,

> If, forty years ago, mediums were largely ignored by a media industry self-defined as an instrument of modernity and national integration, they are now the stars of a grand pageant in which ritual and tradition are the signifiers of an authenticity on which the nation grounds itself.... [N]either Weberian prophecies of modernity's inevitable secularisation nor Benjaminian anticipations of revolutionary materialism could have anticipated the full encompassment of mediumship by the technologies of mass reproduction.... Mass mediatisation seems not to have entailed de-auraticisation so much as it has incited a reformed magicality. Or rather, these two have been entwined in a dual and mutually productive trajectory. (Morris 2000a, p. 183)

John Clark (2011) similarly argues that in Thailand images have been resacralized through their increased availability. As "a culture of reception for the dissemination of reprographic images, photographic and electronic", expanded across the country in the twentieth century, "some of the new imagery acquired statuses that were previously those of religious icons" (Clark 2011, p. 3). In drawing on Clark, Clare Veal argues that there has been a reversal of Walter Benjamin's theory of the aura of the image in Thailand, where an image now "gains status with reproduction rather than loses it" (Veal 2013, n41). Writing in the first decades of the twentieth century, Benjamin (2008) argued that there had been a decline of the aura of images because of their reproduction by new visual technologies such as photography. This process has been

reversed in late modernity, however, with images now gaining in auratic status the more they are reproduced. As an example, Veal (2013)
cites "the charismatic power" and "iconic power and presence" that
is now inherent in photographs of the late King Bhumibol that are
widely displayed across Thailand. The ascribed spiritual status of King
Bhumibol is demonstrated in situations where photographic images
or statuettes of the late king, often displayed alongside images of the
Buddha, revered monks or other spiritual figures, are treated with gold
leaf. This is in line with ritual practices of consecration in which gold
leaf is applied to Buddha images as a sign of worship and respect:
"[T]he display of [photographic] images reinforced the hierarchical
structuring of Thai society based on the magical aspects of power and
associated with merit" (Veal 2013).

Morris argues that the massive scale of imaging technologies
produced within a market-centred consumerist culture distorts established patterns of representation and creates magic-like effects as
rational modes of analysis are swamped by waves of promiscuously
circulating images. It is here, Morris argues, that we find

> a reinvestment in the power of appearances. This is where the magic
> returns…. The logic of appearances has changed…. In the age of
> mechanical reproduction, every empiricist project, every attempt to
> render the world a mere object of representation, seems haunted by
> its opposite. (Morris 2000a, pp. 238–39)

Postmodern Mediums and the Symbolic Complex of Prosperity Cults

In considering new professional spirit possession cults, Pattana Kitiarsa
plays upon the double sense of the term "medium" as denoting both a
technological means of communication and the human being at the
centre of possession rituals. To emphasize the point that new forms of
ritual in Thailand have emerged from contemporary social conditions,
he describes both magic monks who sacralize amulets and spirit mediums as "postmodern mediums" (Pattana 2012, p. 104). He writes,
"The most compelling characteristic of postmodern mediums is their
ability to ignore existing sociopolitical hierarchies and to juxtapose a
religious message and symbolism with the capitalist desire for making
profit and material wealth" (p. 108). Pattana argues that Thailand's
phuttha phanit prosperity cults develop within "a regime of signification in which speech, objects, and appearance are more important than
written language" (p. 105). And, echoing Jean Baudrillard (1994), he
contends that the production and consumption of sacralized amulets

and other auspicious objects constitute a form of "religious hyperreality"; that is, a mode of representation dominated by "the image and its manipulation by the media" (Pattana 2012, p. 108).

Christine Gray argues that in Theravada Buddhism "visual experience is granted primacy over the verbal", and "the functions of persuasion and semantic transfer that are identified in metaphor, in linguistic forms in Western societies, can be found ... in monastic, architectural, and ritual traditions, in the exemplary behaviour of religious virtuoso" (Gray 1986, p. 793). This emphasis on the visual over the discursive in Thai Buddhist epistemologies has now been intensified by the image-based communicative regime of new visual and digital media. The old visual epistemology of Theravada Buddhism has been accentuated in the late-modern visually mediatized society. This situation is not unique to Thailand. In describing the mediatization of Hindu mythology in contemporary India, Mukhopadhyay observes,

> The aura of ritual has given way to ... *technologies of enchantment*....
> This enchantment is not predicated on what Marxists call the
> 'fetishism' of the commodity, it is rather a matter of commoditisation
> of the fetish. (Mukhopadhyay 2006, p. 288; emphasis in original).

Thailand's prosperity cults are one instance of global-level processes, whereby new media and the commodification of everyday life have transformed all cultures, both Western and non-Western. Couze Venn argues that in all image-based capitalist cultures there has been a movement away from "signification and meaning" towards "communication and affect" (Venn 2007, p. 51), where affect denotes a diffuse, often impersonal stratum characterized by the experience of intensity. While Venn only considers Western societies and does not discuss religion, his analysis nonetheless helps us understand the rise of ritual-based magic, such as spirit mediumship, in which intense experience has greater significance than doctrinal interpretation or expressions of belief. Indeed, it could be argued that contemporary popular culture in the West is just as focussed on intensity, experience and affect as the séances of Thai spirit mediums. The sea of commodified images that forms the visual environment of contemporary mediatized societies produces forms of enchantment in which quests for affect and intense experience may take precedence over a search for meaning or truth. In this cultural setting, ritual participation becomes more important than belief, and much of contemporary mass-mediatized popular culture follows a cultural logic more similar to that of magical religion than of text-based forms of orthodoxy.

The Mediatization of Royal Charisma

As noted above, the mediatized production of charisma is also evident in cults surrounding the Thai monarchy. As Irene Stengs notes,

> The worship of King Chulalongkorn draws upon Thai concepts of Buddhist kingship and popular beliefs in the power of sacred images. At the same time, the cult is shaped and carried by mass media promotion of the image of the king, commercial as well as governmental. With respect to mass-media involvement, the cult is as modern a phenomenon as the hype around the death of Princess Diana and the enduring popularity of modern icons like Elvis Presley ('the King'). (Stengs 2009, pp. 14–15)

Stengs contends that the modern imaging of Thailand's kings constitutes a "visual hagiography" (Stengs 2009, p. 223). Indeed, the auraticization of the Thai monarchy also emerges in the context of a highly visual culture flooded with print and electronic images. And in Thailand the market-driven, technologically based incitement of magic-like effects also has political implications because, as Morris argues, imaging technologies have "enhanced and extended the auratic power of the monarch" (Morris 2000, p. 246) and contributed to the rehabilitation of the symbolisms of "absolute theologico-political power" (Morris 1998, p. 370). She contends that

> the era of mass media in Thailand corresponds directly to that of a new monarchical visibility. Where once the King's power entailed his secrecy, his withdrawal from commoners' eyes, he is now the most visible of all Thai citizens. (Morris 1998, p. 358)

Morris describes the technologically induced change in the relations between forms of visual representation and political power:

> [T]he restoration of kingship is at least partly due to the power of images ... and one might even argue that it has been restored to prominence in direct proportion to its privileged place as the subject of photographic representation.... Far from ... de-auraticising the monarchy and ushering in an era of secular democracy, mechanically reproduced images of the king appear to have extended that ... transformation. (Morris 1998, pp. 358–59)

The resacralization of the monarchy is indeed part of the return of magic in Thailand, but in this instance conservative political regimes have also had a role, playing upon the supernatural charisma of the king to bolster authoritarianism. Since the regime of Sarit Thanarat in the late 1950s and early 1960s, a conservative and often authoritarian state-sponsored project of monarchical resacralization has been reinforced by the marketized technological return of magic in Thai popular culture. The intensity of the contemporary Thai regime of images emerges from its overdetermination by the impact of the market and new imaging and communication technologies as well as the political projects of the political regimes that have guided Siam's modernizing transformation into Thailand.

Premodern-Modern Convergences

Premodern Logic of Association and Modern Semiotic Logic of Advertising

As noted in the preceding discussion, consumerism and new communication technologies together produce cultural conditions that in many ways mimic, and accentuate, the conditions of Thai premodernity. This creates a sense of cultural continuity between Thailand's premodern past and its late-modern present. As Morris observes, the convergence of premodernity and late modernity steps over the forms of rationalized social order that were the basis of earlier theories of modernization. In the new forms of magical imagining produced out of intensely mediatized conditions, Morris contends that the desire for magic has become the end point of Thailand's journey to modernity in a situation in which "[t]he past comes back from the future" (Morris 2000, p. 79). Stanley Tambiah also noted the imbrication of modern technologies with the efflorescence of magic:

> Western technology and Western technological knowledge, which amplifies and extends traditional technological knowledge, does not necessarily drive out or displace ritual and magical acts which combine the purposive aims of better mechanical performance ... with the aims of a moral and prosperous social and religious life. (Tambiah 1990, p. 137)

Indeed, there is a convergence and mutual reinforcement between the premodern religious logic of association of Thai popular religion described in Chapter Three and the semiotics of contemporary advertising. Commercial design, advertising and marketing often follow principles very similar to the magical system of signification that defines the semiotic logic of Thai popular religion. Tambiah observes that accounts of the relation of modern media and advertising to the production of enchantment and magical worldviews dates to the work of Bronislaw Malinowski, where, in *Coral Gardens and their Magic*, Malinowski (1935) compared the language of advertising and "the beauty magic of Helena Rubinstein and Elizabeth Arden" (Tambiah 1990, p. 80) to magical thinking.

The symbolic principles of similarity and association of Thai popular religion are mirrored in the commercial imperatives of mass production and marketing, with a continuity between the principles that underpin magical symbolic production and those that now guide product design and retailing in the marketplace. The symbolic effect of images from all the different cults of wealth being represented in products manufactured in the same format, and then being displayed together on the same department store shelves or in sets of nationally distributed postage stamps, reproduces in commercial space the eclectic collocation of statues, amulets and portraits found in Thai spirit shrines. The production and marketing of these lines of images represent the operation of a logic of association, not only in the spatial collocation of elements of the cults of wealth on the same department store shelf, but also by their similar packaging. They are united by a similar commercial style in their production. At one and the same time, this phenomenon is a marketing strategy by entrepreneurs who are in the business of producing ritual objects as well as a re-highlighting of a pre-existing semiotic logic. Mediatized capitalism thus reinforces and intensifies the cultural patterns of Thai popular religion, and the existence of this common animist-capitalist symbolic order helps us further understand how magical cults of wealth became such prominent religious forms in the era of globalization and the neoliberal market economy.

Ritual and Performativity: Keys to the Production of Modern Enchantment

In addition to the contemporary forms of neoliberal capitalism and new print and digital media in societies in which the modern state has largely retreated from managing religion, the very character of ritual action is also a force productive of magicality. This is especially the case in settings, such as Thai popular religion, in which ritual practice is a more important dimension of religiosity than doctrine. In the conclusion to her 1994 study "Defying Disenchantment" and titled "The Relevance of Ritual", which in significant measure draws on sources from Thailand, Jean Comaroff argues that ritual "generates the very force it presupposes", and understanding this process must be central to our "assessment of religion in the modern world" (Comaroff 1994, p. 311). Referencing Stanley Tambiah and his studies of Thai and Sri Lankan religiosity, Comaroff presents a performative theory of popular religion as emerging within settings of ritualized action. She criticizes the sociology of religion for being overly concerned "with the referents of thought and action, rather than with the language in which they are expressed" (p. 311). Comaroff also contends that one of the "deeply rooted myths of modernity" that underpins social science is that ritual is only a distinctive feature of small-scale, "traditional" societies, while complex societies are "held to be radically deritualised" (p. 312). In contrast, she describes ritual as being "positively productive" in all societies:

> Its productivity lies in its capacity to create morally charged experience, to speak with and without words, in diverse sensory registers and through 'multiple channels' (Tambiah 1985, pp. 60ff).... [Ritual] is intensely pragmatic. It not only makes and remakes its actors, but can also call on them to make and remake worlds. Its modes are indispensable to the forging of 'culture' and 'society', in the modern world as in any other. Ritual, in the end, defies disenchantment. (Comaroff 1994, p. 314)

In bringing into being collective values beyond the mundane, Comaroff argues that the performative productivity of ritual is a powerful force that acts counter to the presumed bureaucratic rationality of modernity.

Based to a large degree on his comparative research on Theravada Buddhism in Sri Lanka and Thailand, Tambiah was a major figure in the development of a performative approach to ritual as well as the transcultural, and indeed transhistorical, importance of magic in human life. Tambiah (1977, 1981) was among the first anthropologists of ritual to draw on the linguistic philosophy of John L. Austin (1962), who argued that some uses of language, which he calls illocutionary utterances, function as forms of social action that effect change in the world. Also drawing on Austin, as well as Jacques Derrida's (1988, p. 12) notion of "iteration" and "citationality" and anthropological studies of ritual, Judith Butler describes performativity as the "iterative power of discourse to produce the phenomena that it regulates and constrains" (Butler 1993, p. xii).[12] For theorists of the performativity of ritual, the key to the enchanting effects of action and discourse is repetition: acts and statements must be performed consistently in a regulated manner to exert power.

Theorists of ritual were alerted to Austin's work in the philosophy of language because of his proposition that illocutionary utterances achieve performative force as a result of their ceremonial and ritual-like character. Amy Hollywood notes that anthropologists turned to

Austin's account of the performative character of illocutionary utterances to address limitations in earlier theories of ritual action:

> Given the bankruptcy of symbolic accounts of ritual, and under pressure to come to an understanding of how the parallel between language and action might operate, Tambiah and others argue that … rituals are not constative but performative…. [A]ny good theory of ritual must deal with its multimedia character. This is precisely what Tambiah [1985, pp. 132–34] attempts to do by playing on the multiple meanings of performance. (Hollywood 2002, p. 96n18)

Drawing on Austin, Tambiah argued that ritual constitutes

> conventionalised enactments (employing words and acts as an interlaced amalgam) [that] attain much of their 'illocutionary force' by their very performance. The enactment of the ritual is a 'doing' in itself and an instrumental attainment of a new state. (Tambiah 1977, p. 124)

The key point on which Austinean philosophers of language, theorists of ritual such as Tambiah and critical gender theorists such as Butler concur is that performative utterances *do* something rather than say something and can constitute the phenomenon to which they refer. As Hollywood observes, Austinean theorists of ritual posit that signification is not solely a linguistic phenomenon: "Performative actions, like linguistic performatives, constitute that to which they refer" (Hollywood 2002, p. 96). Tambiah described ritual as having the capacity to construct social reality, with the effect of "creating and bringing to life the cosmological scheme itself"[13] (Tambiah 1985, p. 129). For Tambiah, "[r]itual is symbolic action that has a telic or instrumental purpose—to effect a change of state" (Tambiah 1977, p. 112). He argued that in Thai spirit cults "ritual is seen as a translation of a cosmology, and the sign, symbols and other components of the ritual act as vehicles for expressing cosmological meanings" (p. 97), in the sense that cosmological constructs are embedded in rites, which "in turn enact and incarnate cosmological conceptions" (Tambiah 1985, p. 130).

Tambiah maintained that it is mistaken to judge rituals "solely against the perspective and truth canons of Western scientific rationality, for as constitutive and persuasive acts they cannot be 'falsified'" (Tambiah 1985, p. 136). In this, he followed Austin, who claimed that performative utterances can be judged as efficacious or not efficacious, felicitous or infelicitous, but cannot be assessed in epistemological terms of truth or falsity. As Michael Lambek observes, Austin shows "the limits of a distinction between representational truth and falsity, replacing 'truth' in certain contexts with what he terms 'felicity'. Unlike the absoluteness of truth, the criteria for felicity differ according to the kind of speech act being considered" (Lambek 2014, pp. 264–65). Ritual then is not a smokescreen that mystifies a "real world" of "brute facts", but rather is "an ideological and aesthetic social construction that is directly and recursively implicated in the expression, realization and exercise of power" (Tambiah 1985, p. 155). Ritual has a "duplex existence" in that it "symbolically represents the cosmos and at the same time indexically legitimates and realizes social hierarchies" (p. 155). From this foundation, Tambiah then argued that one of the most fruitful developments in anthropology, whose implications have "still to be completed and exhausted" (Tambiah 1990, p. 83), is the understanding that magic "is constituted of speech acts in a performative and persuasive mode, and that therefore they [are] pragmatically reasonable" (pp. 82–83).

This performative account of ritual and its formative role in the constitution of magic provides a key to understanding the significant extent of the production of modern magic across the Thai religious field in new cults of wealth, cults of amulets and professional spirit mediumship. In these novel forms of enchantment, it is not necessary for followers to agree on the meaning or interpretation of rituals for the cults to cohere as religious systems. As Edoardo Siani (2018) observes, practitioners may have diverging interpretations of the same ritual action. Rather, it is the common performance of an acknowledged set of formalized ritual actions, which in their most basic form in Thailand are embodied in the ritual obeisance of the *wai*, that constitutes the formative node of these cults as religious systems. Here we see a crucial source of the generation of enchantment through embodied ritual. When we combine the observation detailed throughout this study that Thai popular religion focuses more on ritual practice than on belief, with the understanding that ritual is performatively productive in bringing into being that which it invokes, then we begin to better understand why the emergence of new forms of magicality has been such a distinctive feature of modern religious life in Thailand.

Conclusion: The Enchanting Intensities of Ritual in Mediatized Neoliberal Thailand

In bringing together the several accounts of modern magic summarized above, I propose that the enchanting effects of capitalism and new media will be most intense and most elaborate in those societies in which religious ritual is prioritized over belief and doctrine. Furthermore, we can expect enchanted cosmologies to emerge in social settings wherever embodied ritual action is emphasized over belief, faith and reason, whether in polytropic Asian religions or in mediatized consumer societies. This finding is as relevant to the late-modern West as to neoliberalized Thailand. David Lyon emphasizes the importance of embodied ritual practice in all postmodern societies: "Modernity made a lot of the mind, especially as a means of controlling and regulating the body, but in a postmodernising world the body itself becomes a site of consumption, of controversy and conflict" (Lyon 2000, p. 47). In their account of James Foard's (n.d.) description of what he calls Japanese endemic religion, Charles Keyes et al. identify the synergistic operation of a similar range of forces to those detailed above. They describe Japanese endemic religion as being

> nurtured by mass media and an elaborate commercialisation of ritual goods and services.... [E]ndemic religion is also a postmodern phenomenon self-consciously acknowledged as 'tradition'. But this is not the frozen artifactual stuff of museum displays and cultural performances. Endemic religion is saturated with associative meanings that combine remembered personal experience with shared cultural imagery. (Keyes et al. p. 10)

And drawing implicitly on a notion of the performative productivity of ritual, Keyes et al. conclude: "Endemic religion derives its authority from its practice, which generates 'tradition' as an ongoing process" (Keyes at al. 1994, p. 10).

The performative force of ritual in constituting magical imaginaries operates in all societies and historical periods. Furthermore, consumer capitalism and mass mediatization are common conditions across the world today. However, the auraticizing and enchanting effects of all these influences are not uniform within global modernity. The fractured condition of modernity, divided between the contradictions of purificatory rationalist and practical hybridizing trends, leads to differential interactions with the enchantments of ritual, neoliberal capitalism and visual media. The magic of rituals embedded in the market and media is often trenchantly resisted by both secular scientific and fundamentalist religious varieties of purifying rationalism. Despite often representing each other as opposing binaries, religious doctrinalism and scientific rationality in fact share a foundational commonality of being equally opposed to all forms of magic, whether premodern or modern. In Thailand, both reformist Buddhists and secular rationalists denounce the cults of wealth as *phuttha phanit*, "commercialized Buddhism". The simple presence of enchanting trends within mediatized consumer societies does not mean that auraticizing processes will necessarily find expression or come to the fore. Similarly, while the performative force of ritual to engender cosmological schemas is a potentiality wherever actions are repeated in rigid regulatory frames, this capacity is not always realized within the nexus of oppositional forces that constitute modernity.

Where state-based rationalizing political power or the religious authority of doctrine is dominant, the multiple enchantments of modernity may be challenged, resisted or even actively expunged. It is only when rationalizing state power is withdrawn and the homogenizing influence of religious doctrine can be evaded that we witness dramatic efflorescences of modern enchantment, such as evidenced in Thailand in recent decades. These efflorescences will be most pronounced and most visible in modern social domains that Latour describes as being characterized by hybridizing practice and in religious cultures that reflect this non-rational underside of global modernity; that is, in religions marked by the primacy of ritual over doctrine. It will be in the modern religions of ritual that the performative force of ritual to generate magical enchantments will be most pronounced. As seen in Thailand's cults of wealth, amulets and professional spirit mediumship, when the state retreats and the purificatory intentions of religious doctrinalism are held at bay, then the ritual generation of magic can reinforce and accentuate the enchantments of neoliberalism and the auraticizing power of visual technologies. In an observation that remains as relevant today as when first published three decades ago, Tambiah concludes his account of the performative force of ritual by stating that the puzzling character of magic for moderns, whether in Asia or the West,

> will only disappear when we succeed in embedding magic in a more ample theory of human life in which the path of ritual action is seen as an indispensable mode for man anywhere and everywhere of relating to and participating in the life of the world (Tambiah 1990, p. 83).

Notes

1. For studies of the efflorescence of Vietnamese spirit mediumship, see Philip Taylor (2004), Kirsten Endres (2010), Karen Fjelstad and Nguyen Thi Hien (2011).
2. Jean and John Comaroff (2018) have defended their original formulation and analysis of occult economies under neoliberalism from criticisms by Bruce Kapferer (2002) and others.

3. For accounts of magical capitalism in contemporary Western societies, see Brian Moeran and Timothy de Waal Malefyt's 2018 edited collection.

4. These quotes, and others from the same article, are from an interview David Kyuman Kim conducted with Jean Comaroff. While the article citation is for "Comaroff and Kim", all the quotes here are Jean Comaroff's responses to David Kim's questions.

5. In contrast, more highbrow Thai language dailies such as *Siam Rath*, *Matichon* and *Phu-jat-kan* (Manager) and the English language *Bangkok Post* and *The Nation* rarely make reports of magical phenomena front-page news stories. As noted in Chapter Two, if forms of popular devotionalism are reported in these papers, it is likely to be in a critical or disbelieving tongue-in-cheek style and relegated to an inside page.

6. "Prayers for Victims of Korat Hotel Collapse", *Bangkok Post Weekly Review*, 26 August 1994, p. 4.

7. "Thousands in Korat for Celebrated Monk's Birthday", *Bangkok Post Weekly Review*, 14 October 1994, p. 6.

8. *Thai Rath*, 13 December 1996. The page-one photo story was captioned, "I'll save you from death" (*ku hai meung rort tai*). A Bangkok taxi driver in whose cab I rode in December 1997 insisted that he too had been saved from injury or death by *Luang Phor* Khoon. The driver recounted that once when he had fallen asleep at the wheel of his taxi he had been startled into wakefulness in time to avoid having an accident when he felt someone tapping him on the shoulder. At the time, however, he had no passengers and was alone in the cab. The driver insisted he had been saved by *Luang Phor* Khoon, one of whose amulets hung around his cab's rear-view mirror.

9. "Those Not-So-Magic Charms of *Luang Phor* Koon", *The Nation*, 21 September 1995, p. A5.

10. Ibid.

11. "Thousands in Korat".

12. Tambiah's (1977, 1981) development of Austin's theory of illocutionary utterances into a theory of the performative force of ritual predates by over a decade Judith Butler's (1988, 1990, 1993) use of the same philosophical model in her account of the performative generation of gender identity from repeated, ritualized acts of gendering.

13. By cosmology, Tambiah here means "the body of conceptions that enumerate and classify the phenomena that compose the universe as an ordered whole and the norms and processes that govern it" (Tambiah 1985, p. 130).

Conclusion

The Thai Cults of Wealth into the Twenty-first Century

In the early twenty-first century, the Thai cults of wealth have continued to proliferate and diversify, spreading into new forms and finding new followers in Thailand as well as in neighbouring East and Southeast Asian countries. One new figure in the Thai pantheon of wish-granting deities is *Thep* Than-jai, the "Deity [who grants wishes] immediately". *Thep* Than-jai is the Thai name given to the Burmese spirit being called a *bobogyi*, a generic spiritual figure that in Burma is believed to guard treasures buried beneath pagodas and whose name means "great-grandfather" (Brac de la Perrière and Munier-Gaillard 2019). In Thailand, *Thep* Than-jai is represented as a grandfatherly figure dressed in regal Burmese attire standing and pointing his index figure towards the faithful. In Burma, this figure is linked to the foundation of the Shwedagon Pagoda in Yangon, where he is believed to be pointing to the location where relics of past Buddhas are supposed to have been enshrined.

The cult of the Hindu deity Ganesh has also expanded rapidly since the turn of the new century and increasing numbers of white-robed lay ascetics called *reusi*, from the Sanskrit *rishi*, now offer spiritual advice for wealth and wellbeing (see McDaniel 2013). New digital media and social networks have quickly become central features of the expanding field of Thai popular ritual and belief across the region. In 2017, *The Nation* reported how a fortune teller *reusi* in Northeast Thailand named Toon used the internet to provide divinatory commercial advice to clients in several countries:

Using Facebook and [smartphone application] Line to advertise his services, he has tapped a deep well of overseas intrigue, especially among ethnic Chinese, for rituals and charms aimed at boosting business prospects.... He now has hundreds of followers in ... Hong Kong, Taiwan, China, Malaysia and Singapore, and travels far and wide to offer spiritual solace.... A lot of customers, especially business owners, now come to Thailand to seek auspicious power. It is undoubtedly a lucrative business for people like Toon, whose clients pay hundreds of dollars for ceremonies. Thanks to the power of the web, he now has more foreign customers than Thais.[1]

In 2019 and 2020 worship of the spirit of a young boy, *Ai* Khai, who in legend is said to have been a disciple of the famed Southern Thai magic monk *Luang Phor* Thuat (see Chapter Four) and who died protecting a treasure trove at Wat Chedi monastery in Sichon district of Nakhon Srithammarat, emerged as the devotional focus of Thailand's latest cult of wealth. *Ai* Khai, literally "Egg Boy", is a common southern Thai nickname for young boys. As the *Bangkok Post* reported in September 2020, "[i]nterest in the story of Ai Khai had been growing after word spread that visitors to the [Wat Chedi] temple had been granted their wishes—such as lottery wins, business success, and the recovery of lost or stolen items."[2] When travel restrictions were lifted in the second half of 2020 after Thailand was largely successful in suppressing the first wave of COVID-19 infections in the country, hundreds of thousands of pilgrim-tourists visited Wat Chedi to seek *Ai* Khai's blessing. Airlines more than doubled the number of weekly flights from Bangkok to Nakhon Srithammarat to meet demand, producing a tourism-led economic boom in the southern province. Vast numbers of *Ai* Khai amulets were produced and shrines to *Ai* Khai housing images of the young boy spirit were quickly added to monasteries around the country. *Ai* Khai now stands alongside images of other deities of wealth described in this book, becoming the most recent addition to the ever-expanding symbolic complex of Thai cults of wealth.

Thai Cults of Wealth in East and Southeast Asia

As noted above, Thai popular religion and Thai magic are now considered auspiciously powerful among many in ethnic Chinese populations of East and Southeast Asia. The Erawan shrine in central Bangkok dedicated to the deity Brahma has become a popular site of pilgrimage for tourists from China, Hong Kong, Taiwan, Singapore and Malaysia. Images of the four-faced Brahma at this shrine are especially popular among Chinese Singaporeans, appearing on the dashboards of taxis and in house shrines as icons of good luck, protection and prosperity in that country (see Shirley Yee 1996; Andrew Johnson 2016). However, while Thais recognize Brahma, or *Phra* Phrom or *Thao* Mahaphrom, as a Brahmanical deity, among Chinese in the region this deity is often Buddhacized by being called the "Thai four-faced Buddha". Amulets blessed by Thai *keji ajan* magic monks are also popular in Singapore, and several stores in the Bugis shopping precinct of the city close to the Guan Yin Chinese temple specialize in selling Thai ritual objects.

At the same time that the Thai have increasingly appropriated elements of Chinese religion into the heart of their religious amalgam, Buddhist, Taoist and Confucian Chinese from Southeast Asia, China, Taiwan and Hong Kong have also incorporated aspects of Thai religious practice and symbolism into their own complexly amalgamated religious systems. Thailand's economic development has not only seen an expansion of agricultural and manufacturing exports, but also a parallel growth in the export of Thai popular religious culture to the region. Nidhi Eeoseewong (1994) commented on the commercial origins of this phenomenon in the 1990s, noting that many southern Thai monasteries had installed Kuan Im images within their compounds in order to encourage visits and donations from Chinese tourists from nearby Malaysia and Singapore. Jovan Maud (2007) reports that Chinese devotees from Malaysia and Singapore are often the most important sponsors of ritual events in some Thai Buddhist monasteries and Taoist shrines in the south of the country. A shared Thai-Chinese religious cosmos is coming into being across the region, based on implicit narratives of Thailand's modern economic success that are conveyed by the cults of wealth. We now find the beginnings of a Sino-Thai religious complex of cults of wealth throughout mainland Southeast Asia and Southern China, with Thailand a focus of intersecting international religious pilgrimage and tourism shopping routes. The history of this fascinating transnational religious cross-fertilization is yet to be written. However, a number of factors seem to have been at play.

From the 1980s, the diaspora of overseas Thai labourers took their religious practices with them to work sites in Kuala Lumpur, Singapore and other cities in the region. Markets and stores dedicated to supplying Thai food, products and religious icons appeared in these cities, and over time also found customers among local populations. Another factor in the development of this transregional complex of Thai cults of wealth has been the renewing of connections among the Chinese populations in the region, with the Thai Chinese providing conduits for the communication of Thai beliefs and practices to relatives, clansmen and members of their language and regional Chinese associations throughout Southeast Asia and Southern China. The amalgamated Theravada-Mahayana form of some of the cults of prosperity has also meant that the Sinicized aspects of Thai popular religion have given them a Chinese aesthetic and sensibility that makes them amenable to being appropriated by Chinese outside Thailand. As noted, some of *Luang Phor* Khoon's ritual objects had a decidedly Chinese aesthetic in their design. The polytropic character of both Chinese and Thai popular religion also makes them open to mutual appropriation and symbolic and ritual interpenetration.

IMAGE 29. *Thep* Than-jai
An image of *Thep* Than-jai, described in the text as "bestowing good luck instantly", based on Burmese cults of *bobogyi* "grandfather" spirits. The addition of *Thep* Than-jai to the pantheon of wealth-bestowing deities and spirits since the early 2010s reflects the open-ended capacity of Thai popular religion to expand and appropriate diverse cultural influences. (Source: *Raeng Sattha* [Power of faith] magazine, special issue, 2019.)

IMAGE 30. Thailand's Erawan Brahma in Singapore
The Erawan Brahma statue on the cover of a booklet listing Thai ritual products sold by the Singaporean company Fordlane, which specializes in selling Thai amulets and religious images in the city state. Since the mid-1990s, the Thai cults of wealth have become international phenomena, finding followers in Hong Kong, Taiwan, China and across Southeast Asia.

The Symbolic Complex of Thai Cults of Wealth: Commercializing Thai Spirituality or Spiritualizing Thai Capitalism?

A number of studies of Thailand's economic expansion since the boom decade in the 1980s and 1990s detailed the social dislocation (Pasuk and Baker 1995, 1998), environmental degradation (Hirsch 1996; Rigg 1995), political corruption (Pasuk and Sungsidh 1994) and cultural and religious commercialization (Jackson 1997) of this era. But the prosperity cults that have now moved to the centre of national ritual life also integrated Thailand's new neoliberal social formation within religious symbolisms that provide an overarching frame within which both the past and the urban industrializing present can be understood. The complex of cults of wealth has provided sources of social and cultural cohesion both during and after the boom years, acting as symbolic reference points for an increasingly mobile populace. Seen in this light, the commodification of Thai religion that accompanied the boom years, and which has continued into this century, is not a symptom of cultural collapse but rather operates as the productive core of a new highly popular expression of Thai religio-cultural symbolism and ritual. While the 1990s boom disrupted the subsistence agrarian social formation and its older cultural and symbolic forms, it was simultaneously productive of a new marketized urban social formation and an associated new cultural and symbolic order.

The complex of cults of wealth represents an expansion of the Thai symbolic domain to the market, and the incorporation of the neoliberal capitalist economy within a religio-symbolic order. The cults of wealth not only reflect the enveloping power of the market to co-opt cultural forms, as argued by critics of *phuttha phanit* commercialized Buddhism, they also provide a means of accommodating the market to Thai religio-symbolic expectations. The cults demonstrate the plasticity of Thai cultural forms to incorporate and indigenize new ways of living and working, effectively constituting a Siamization of globalizing neoliberal capitalism. The success of this Asian localization of capitalism is indicated by the extent to which the Thai cults of wealth have become popular internationally across Southeast and East Asia in the past two decades. This spiritualizing of the market and capitalist risk taking can be seen as a symbolic taming of the unruly power of capitalism. By this, the novel and formerly alien capitalist forms of life have been resymbolized and indigenized by being integrated within Thai religio-symbolic expectations. Reformist Buddhist critics contend that the cults of wealth represent the all-enveloping power of the market to debase Thai culture. But this complex of cults also represents the converse situation; namely, the plasticity of Thai cultural forms and their capacity to incorporate new ways of living and working.

As a symbolic Siamization of neoliberalism, the cults facilitated socio-economic change by avoiding labelling the disruptive cultural and other consequences of the economic boom years as foreign or Western. In Thailand, the "foreign" economic-cultural form of globalizing capitalism was re-dressed in the images of saffron-robed grandfatherly magic monks, a Chinese bodhisattva, Indian deities and respected Thai kings from earlier eras, which both permitted and incited an active desire for national transformation rather than provoking resistance. A stunning feature of Thai cultural life in the 1980s and 1990s was that within a couple of decades pre-capitalist symbolisms were resignified in market terms and given new vitality in the process of their commodification. As noted in the previous chapter, the rapidity of this cultural transformation reflected a convergence between the forms of semiotic production in Thai popular religious culture and the commodified media-saturated urban cultures of globalization.

The introduction of a materialist consumer ideology in Thailand has not been accompanied by either an end to ritual or its sidelining. Rather, we have seen a progressive enchantment of Thai capitalism, where the market and consumer culture have become new domains for the expanded operation of Thai ritual. The cultural dominance of the market has not undermined Thai ritual, but it has radically transformed it and underpinned its proliferation into an expanding multitude of new forms. Late-modern Thailand represents the arrival of magical capitalism, a form of consumer capitalism in which access to supernatural knowledge is not a mere façade but rather is integral to life within a market-oriented social order.

The Political Conservatism of the Cults of Wealth and State Appropriation

Given that the cults of wealth are cultural forms that have facilitated mass participation in the neoliberal market, we can understand their generally conservative rather than subversive character and why business people as well members of the military, civilian bureaucratic and royal elites have also been active participants. For example, as a religious patron of Thailand's economic boom, *Luang Phor* Khoon was taken into the heart of the Thai state, providing business, the army, bureaucracy and monarchy with a Buddhacized symbolic link to the burgeoning economic activity of that era. Khoon linked the ethnic Thai populace, Sino-Thai business interests and the state under the symbolic roof of Buddhism and rustic ritual, becoming the symbol of a Thailand united in a common quest for national self-transformation through global enmeshment, productive activity and, above all, wealth creation.

The *Luang Phor* Khoon phenomenon, and the complex of prosperity cults as a whole, represents much more than quaint or eccentric religious oddities. The cults of wealth bring together popular aspirations for a better, richer life, with nationalist narratives of Thailand taking its place in the world as an economically developed country. At the height of the boom, the cults of wealth were symbols of national unity in which many sectors of the population—ethnic Thai rural and urban labourers, Sino-Thai businesspeople, politicians, military figures, bureaucrats and the monarchy—were represented as working to become rich together and proud of what, for a brief historical moment, was viewed as their country's march to globally recognized developed status.

In earlier decades of the twentieth century, reformist monks such as Buddhadasa and educated lay Buddhist social critics sought to reform Thai Buddhism and, in their eyes, make it more relevant to a modernizing society by excising Brahmanical and animist "accretions" and returning to the religion's scriptural and doctrinal roots. The views of these critics reflect mid-twentieth-century Western concerns about whether "traditional" cultures were capable of modernizing. As Douglas Pressman states,

> A good part of the drama of mid-century scholarly commentary on Thailand derived from its open wondering whether people who behave like Buddhists, and think like Thais, would ever be capable of running efficient factories and a substantively democratic state. Conversely, various scholars ... fretted in print over whether the seemingly unstoppable imposition of modern institutions on such a people might not throw their internal cultural compasses pathologically out of kilter, making them the inhabitants of a normless wasteland. (Pressman 1993, pp. 61–62)

The adaptable conservatism of the cults of wealth shows that an alternative, and definitely more widely popular, strategy for ensuring that Buddhism retains cultural and social relevance in the late-modern era has not been to institute doctrinal or fundamentalist reforms but rather to draw on religious ritual to bless and sacralize social change. Cult figures such as *Luang Phor* Khoon provided religious sanction for Thailand's socio-economic transformation while appearing to remain unchanged, remaining based in the symbolic forms of traditional life-styles and discourses even as they blessed and provided supernatural guidance for dramatic social and economic transformation. The cults of King Chulalongkorn, Kuan Im, Hindu deities and magic monks created an apparent image of remaining anchored in the past while in fact being intimately involved in the creation of a new capitalist society. The complex of prosperity cults were symbols of change with stability, of becoming something new while remaining attached to the old, and of blessing the disruptive and often disconcerting new market economy by drawing on comforting if innovative rituals. As Arif Dirlik states, contemporary religious trends in Asia "point not to the past but, taking a detour through the past, to an alternative future" (Dirlik 2005, p. 6). Indeed, the modernity of twenty-first-century magic cannot be emphasized too strongly. It was the great failure of twentieth-century social theory to mistakenly imagine the supernatural as being in opposition to modernity, rather than seeing the two as intimately imbricated phenomena.

However, understanding the continuing significance of the prosperity cults in Thailand in the early twenty-first century also requires an analysis that adds a political perspective to studies of the formative roles of the market, media and the cultural valorization of ritual undertaken in this book. Cultic practices retain an important political currency because they are intimately linked to notions of power. In Thailand today, there are several sources of elite power: the long-standing political and bureaucratic power of military and civilian elites, the economic power of the Sino-Thai business groups who have provided the wealth for the transformation of the country, and the charismatic authority of the monarchy as symbol of national unity. The new cultic complex can also be seen as a symbolic expression of politico-economic-administrative alliances among these various players. The symbolic interconnections among different Buddhist, Chinese, Indian and royal ritual forms in the complex of cults of wealth reproduce, at the level of religious culture, symbiotic relationships among the various elites that collectively dominate the Thai peasantry, as it has been refashioned into an agricultural and urban industrial labour force.

The field of religion, broadly conceived, remains as important to the twenty-first-century Thai state as was the case in earlier eras. But understanding this continuity in the state-religion nexus requires leaving behind modernist biases that privilege the role of institutional Buddhism over magical ritual. It requires an understanding of how the political relevance of different elements of Thailand's diverse Buddhist-Brahmanical-Chinese-spirit religious amalgam may rise and fall over time in response to changing socio-economic and geopolitical conditions. As Niels Mulder argues, power in Thailand is imagined as emerging from ritual practices fused from a complex polytropic amalgam of religious influences rather than from belief or professions of faith:

> Thai animism, as a religious practice, is essentially a system that deals with power.... Whether the religious complexes that deal with such power are classified as animistic, Brahmanic or Buddhist is irrelevant because the way in which they deal with power is inspired by the same animist mentality. In that mentality supernatural powers do not question intentions but react reflexively to a show of respect, to ritual prescriptions and to ceremonial form. (Mulder 1990, p. 24)

What the convergence of the cults of wealth into a symbolic complex shows is the continuing relationship of all forms of spiritual and symbolic authority in Thailand with notions of power. And in the era of neoliberalism, the domain over which that sacralized (*saksit*) and charismatic (*barami*) power operates expanded to include the economy. The comparative reluctance of the state to intervene in Buddhist affairs in recent decades (at least until King Maha Vajiralongkorn acceded to the throne in 2016) should not be mistaken for a secularization of Thai politics, or of Thai politics becoming institutionally separated from the field of religious ritual. Rather, it marks a distinctive new character of state-religion relations in which the Buddhist sangha is no longer the sole or necessarily the primary religious field of interest to the state. State actors now augment their relations to symbolic sources of authority to include ritual forms that, for much of the modern era, were classed as being antithetical to the project of modernity. This shift in the state-religion nexus is marked by the fact that the twentieth-century projects of repeatedly refashioning the administration of the Buddhist sangha in the symbolic image of the state (see Jackson 1989) effectively ceased by the 1970s.

Nonetheless, the increasingly public participation of Thailand's elites in magical ritual raises a number of questions. Why have criticisms, at times vocal, of *phuttha phanit* supernaturalism in Thailand failed to halt the rise of ritual practice in the general population? And why do many members of Thailand's bureaucratic and business elites blithely ignore these criticisms and number among the participants in the cults of wealth? I will explore the story of the continuing popularity of the cults of wealth after the Asian economic crisis of the late 1990s in a separate study where I will consider the state's progressive appropriation of these cults over the first decades of the new century. To prefigure that analysis, I contend that the wide range of prosperity movements that began as expressions of popular devotion during Thailand's economic boom years not only survived the economic downturn of the 1997 Asian economic crisis but also expanded their influence in part because they have increasingly enjoyed the implicit approval of sections of the state. Despite the often-vocal critiques of *phuttha phanit* by reformist Buddhists, some members of Thailand's social, economic and political elites have mobilized the new forms of magical expression. These new cults are no longer, if they ever were, a form of resistance to the ravages of the market among dispossessed underclasses. On the contrary, the cults of prosperity represent spirits of genuine power supported by many at the summit of the pyramid of authority in the country.

Two broad historical narratives are key to understanding the importance of new cults of wealth to Thai society and the national polity. In this study I have detailed the first story, of the emergence of the cults in the 1980s and 1990s in the context of Thailand's growing economy and their rapid expansion and movement from the margins to the centre of national religious life during the economic boom years in the decade leading up to the Asian economic crisis. The second story of the cults of wealth is how, despite becoming the focus of intense criticisms as deviations from true Thai Buddhism in the years of economic crisis in the late 1990s, they nonetheless assumed growing political importance in the early twenty-first century. The first narrative, broadly covering the period until 1997, is the story of the production of new forms of religious enchantment in societies that have been restructured under globalizing neoliberalism. The second story, from the turn of the new century, is how political factors have been central to the outcome of the conflict between the competing rationalizing reformist and enchanting magical moments of religious modernity in Thailand that were outlined in Chapter One.

The tensions between modern magic and modern religious reformism have had dramatically different outcomes in the predominantly Buddhist societies of mainland Southeast Asia, on the one hand, and the predominantly Islamic societies of peninsular and insular Southeast Asia, on the other. New magical and fundamentalist reform movements are found in both Buddhist and Muslim Southeast Asian societies, and the contradictions of religious modernity detailed in Chapter One are equally active in inciting diverse forms of religious change across the entire region. However, in predominantly Buddhist Thailand magic has achieved ascendancy over its reformist critics, while in Malaysia and Indonesia Islamic fundamentalists have become increasingly politically influential in challenging and demonizing the continuing practice of magical ritual. Socio-economic factors alone do not determine the relative strength of these competing rationalizing and enchanting tendencies within religious modernity. Political factors—the extent of support for either magical ritual or fundamentalist doctrine by power elites in governments and national bureaucracies— are central influences on the outcome of the contest between magical and reformist visions of Southeast Asian modernity. In the associated study, I will consider the ways that the symbolic association of the cults of wealth with figures from Thailand's royal history contributed to their continued expansion in the first decades of the twenty-first century. Enchantment emerges not only from the social, economic and cultural contexts of mediatized neoliberal modernity, but, in order to thrive in the twenty-first century, it also needs a political setting in which ritual and cultic practice play key roles in contests for wealth and influence. In the second part of this study, I will argue that Thailand's politicized forms of magic emerge from mutually reinforcing circuits between the socio-economic forces of mediatized neoliberalism and the exigencies, and contingencies, of contemporary Thai political conflicts. Supported by sections of the civilian and military bureaucracies as well as by politicians, the symbolic complex of cults of wealth have become part of a form of spiritualized politics in Thailand.

Notes

1. "Out of the Woods: Thai 'Hermits' Harness Web to Go Global", *The Nation Online Edition*, 17 July 2017, http://www.nationmultimedia.com/detail/national/30320938 (accessed 16 March 2019).

2. "'Egg boy' a Tourist Draw: Legend of Ai Khai has Given Welcome Boost to Nakhon Si Thammarat", *Bangkok Post*, 13 September 2020, https://www.bangkokpost.com/thailand/special-reports/1984271/egg-boy-a-tourist-draw (accessed 22 January 2021).

Glossary of Thai and Buddhist Terms

Ajan — A title for a respected Buddhist monk or lay specialist regarded to be a teacher, religious instructor or adept in ritual lore.

Arahant — A Buddhist saint, regarded to have attained enlightenment and to be close to attaining the ultimate salvation of *nibbana*.

Barami — Charismatic prestige, believed to accrue from religious merit acquired in either this life or previous lives as a result of the perfection of forms of Buddhist ethical conduct.

Bodhisattva (Sanskrit) — In Mahayana Buddhism, a person who is generally regarded as having attained enlightenment, or is a saint on the path to enlightenment, and who has taken a vow to help other sentient beings to also attain spiritual awakening.

Jao — "Lord", a common title in the names of honoured deities and spirits.

Jao Mae — "Lord Mother", a common title in the names of honoured female deities and spirits.

Kae bon — A ritual to repay a deity or spirit after a requested boon or blessing has been granted.

Kala-thesa — "Time and place", denoting the contextualized hierarchical separation of distinct bounded domains of social life and religious expression.

Kathin — Ceremony to offer new robes and other donations to Buddhist monks, regarded as an important opportunity for members of the laity to make merit.

Keji ajan — "Magic monks"; senior Buddhist monks revered for their expertise in meditation and ritual practice who are believed to possess the ability to magically empower (*pluk sek*) amulets, predict the future and provide protective blessings.

Khatha — An incantation or magical formula, often composed in a mix of Sanskrit, Pali and Thai, that is recited in prayers to seek the blessing of a deity or spiritual figure.

Khun — A noble title conferred by the Siamese king in the period of the absolute monarchy.

Khwam-cheua — "Belief", a term that often refers to rituals and religious practices conducted outside the scope of monastic Buddhism. Now often paired with *sattha*, "faith" and contrasted with *sasana*, "religion".

Lak meuang — "City pillar", a ritual pillar installed in a shrine believed to be the residence of the protective deity or deities of a town or city.

Latthi — "Cult", a belief viewed as inferior to an established religion (*sasana*).

Latthi-phithi — "Belief-ritual", an academic term for "cult" or "cultic ritual", a more formal synonym for *khwam-cheua*, "belief", and *sattha*, "belief", and contrasted with *sasana*, "religion".

Luang Phor — "Reverend Father", a title in the name of honoured Buddhist monks, often used for the abbots of Buddhist monasteries.

Luang Pu — "Reverend Grandfather", a title in the name of honoured Buddhist monks who have spent many decades in the monkhood.

Pha yan — "*Yantra* cloth", a rectangular piece of cloth inscribed with images of a deity or religious icon and *khatha* incantations. Like amulets, *pha yan* may be sacralized in *pluk sek* rituals of magical empowerment and kept as protective wealth-conferring talismans.

Phi — A spirit or ghost.

Phithi — Ritual.

Phra — An honorific for a Buddhist monk, Buddha image, deity or royal figure.

Phra Khreuang — A term for amulets that have been sacralized in a *pluk sek* ritual and are believed to possess magical powers of protection and wealth conferral.

Phuttha phanit — "Commerce in Buddhism", "Commercialized Buddhism"; a term used by reformist and doctrinal Buddhists to criticize the commodification of Buddhist ritual practice and the production and marketing of amulets and other "auspicious objects".

Pluk sek — The ritual of magically empowering amulets and other "auspicious objects" (*watthu mongkhon*) conducted by a Buddhist monk, Brahmin or other ritual specialist regarded to have skills in *saiyasat* magical practice.

Saiyasat — "Magic", the invocation of supernatural power in ritual practice, covering all dimensions of the instrumental knowledge and skills involved in ritual. *Saiyasat* is often used in a derogatory sense by secular and religious critics, who disparage it as "animism", "superstition", "mysticism" or "black magic".

Saksit — Magical power and authority of a person, deity, icon or image acquired from *saiyasat* ritual or from an exalted religious status.

San-jao — The shrine of a deity or spirit.

Sangha (Sanskrit) — The Buddhist monkhood.

Sasana — "Religion", denoting an institutionally established religion with recognized canonical texts, formalized doctrine and teachings and a specialist clergy, often used as a shorthand for "Buddhism" (*sasana phut*) and contrasted with *khwam-cheua*, "belief", and *sattha*, "faith".

Sattha — "Faith", a term that often refers to rituals and religious practices conducted outside the scope of monastic Buddhism. Now often paired with *khwam-cheua*, "belief", and contrasted with *sasana*, "religion".

Somdet — A royal-conferred title for senior monks in the administration of the Buddhist sangha or monkhood. Also a title for senior members of the royal family.

Talat phra — Amulet market.

Tamnak — "Palace", "abode"; a term often used to describe the shrine or temple of a spirit medium where possession rituals are conducted.

Thao — "Lord", a title in the name of some deities and spirits.

Thep — A deity, often used to refer to gods from the Hindu pantheon, from the Sanskrit *deva*.

Wai — To show respect and honour to a person, deity or religious image by placing the palms of the hands together and bringing them to the level of the chest or head, often accompanied with a bowing of the head.

Wai khru — "Honouring the teacher", a ritual to honour teachers of ritual traditions as well as instructors in Thai classical music and dance, in which the spirit of the original teacher, often regarded to be a Brahmanical deity or sage, is invoked.

Wat — A Buddhist monastery.

Watthu mongkhon — "Auspicious objects"; a generic term for amulets and other objects that have been sacralized in a *pluk sek* ritual and are believed to possess magical powers of protection and wealth conferral.

Bibliography

Ackerknecht, Erwin H. 1955. *A Short History of Medicine*. New York: The Ronald Press.

Agarwal, Ruchi, and William J. Jones. 2018. "Ganesa and His Cult in Contemporary Thailand". *International Journal of Asia Pacific Studies* 14, no. 2: 121–42.

Akira, Suehiro. 1996. *Capital Accumulation in Thailand: 1855–1985*. Chiang Mai: Silkworm Books.

Alexeiev, Basil M. 1928. *The Chinese Gods of Wealth*. London: School of Oriental Studies and the China Society.

Anan Senakhan. 1981 (BE 2524). *Phi Bun Haeng Hupphasawan* [The false prophet of Hupphasawan]. Bangkok: Anan Senakhan.

Anderson, Benedict R. 1972. "The Idea of Power in Javanese Culture". In *Culture and Politics in Indonesia*, edited by Claire Holt, pp. 1–69. Ithaca: Cornell University Press.

———. 2012. *The Fate of a Rural Hell: Asceticism and Desire in Buddhist Thailand*. London: Seagull Books.

(*Phya*) Anuman Rajadhon. 1968. *Essays on Thai Folklore*. Bangkok: Social Science Association Press of Thailand.

Apinya Fuengfusakul. 1993. "Empire of Crystal and Utopian Commune: Two Types of Contemporary Theravada Reform in Thailand". *SOJOURN: Journal of Social Issues in Southeast Asia* 8, no. 1: 153–83.

Århem, Kaj. 2016a. "Southeast Asian Animism in Context". In

Animism in Southeast Asia, edited by Kaj Århem and Guido Sprenger, pp. 3–30. New York: Routledge.

———. 2016b. "Southeast Asian Animism: A Dialogue with Amerindian Perspectivism". In *Animism in Southeast Asia*, edited by Kaj Århem and Guido Sprenger, pp. 279–301. New York: Routledge.

Arratee Ayuttacorn and Jane Ferguson. 2018. "The Sacred Elephant in the Room: Ganesha Cults in Chiang Mai, Thailand". *Anthropology Today* 34, no. 5: 5–9.

Assman, Jan. 2003. *Die Mosaische Unterscheidung. Oder des Preis des Monotheismus*. Munich: Hanser.

Austin, John L. 1962. *How to Do Things with Words*. Oxford: Clarendon Press.

Babb, Lawrence, and Susan Wadley, eds. 1995. *Media and the Transformation of Religion in South Asia*. Philadelphia: University of Pennsylvania Press.

Bakhtin, Mikhail M. 1981. *The Dialogic Imagination: Four Essays*, translated by Michael Holquist. Austin: University of Texas Press.

Barami phra Siam Thewathirat: bandan chat rom-yen [The charisma of Phra Siam Thewathirat: Bringing peace to the nation]. 1997. Bangkok: Liang Chiang Press.

Barmé, Geremie R. 1996. *Shades of Mao: The Posthumous Cult of the Great Leader*. New York: Sharpe.

Bataille, Georges, and Michel Leiris. 2008. *Correspondence: Georges Bataille, Michel Leiris, Edited with Notes by Louis Yvert, Afterword by Bernard Noël*, translated by Liz Heron. Calcutta: Seagull Books.

Baudrillard, Jean. 1975. *The Mirror of Production*, translated by Mark Poster. St Louis: Telos Press.

———. 1994. *Simulacra and Simulation*, translated by Sheila Glaser. Ann Arbor: University of Michigan Press.

Bauer, Thomas. 2011. *Die Kultur der Ambiguität: Eine andere Geschichte des Islam*. Berlin: Verlag der Weltreligionen im Insel Verlag.

Baumann, Benjamin Jens Ronald. 2017. *Ghosts of Belonging: Searching for Khmerness in Buriram*. PhD dissertation, Südostasien-Studien, Humboldt-Universität zu Berlin.

Bautista, Julius, ed. 2012. *The Spirit of Things: Materiality and Religious*

Diversity in Southeast Asia. Ithaca: Cornell Southeast Asia Program Publications.

Bechert, Heinz. 1994. "Buddhistic Modernism: Present Situation and Current Trends". In *Buddhism into the Year 2000: International Conference Proceedings*, pp. 251–62. Pathumthani, Thailand, Dhammakaya Foundation.

Bell, Catherine. 1992. *Ritual Theory, Ritual Practice*. Oxford: Oxford University Press.

Benjamin, Walter. 2008. *The Work of Art in the Age of Its Technological Reproducibility and Other Writings on Media*, edited by Michael Jennings, Brigid Dohert and Thomas Levin, and translated by Edmund Jephcott, Rodney Livingstone and Howard Eiland. Cambridge, MA: Harvard University Press.

Bhabha, Homi K. 1994. *The Location of Culture*. London: Routledge.

(*His Majesty King*) Bhumibol Adulyadej. 1999. *The Story of Mahajanaka* (*reuang phra mahachanok*). Bangkok: Chitrlada Villa (royal palace).

Bolotta, Giuseppe. 2017. "A Christmas Mourning: Catholicism in Post-Bhumibol Thailand". *Kyoto Review of Southeast Asia*, no. 22. Kyoto: Centre for Southeast Asian Studies, Kyoto University. https://kyotoreview.org/issue–22/thai-cosmic-politics-locating-power-in-a-diverse-kingdom/ (accessed 8 September 2017).

Bot-suat bucha jao mae Kuan Im lae phra owat khorng than arahan Ji Kong [Prayers to worship Lord Mother Kuan Im and the teachings of the Arahant Ji Kong]. [1997?] (BE 2540). Bangkok: Thammasapha.

Bouquet, Mathieu. 2010. "Vietnamese Party-State and Religious Pluralism Since 1986: Building the Fatherland". *SOJOURN: Journal of Social Issues in Southeast Asia* 25, no. 1: 90–108.

Bourdieu, Pierre. 1977. *Outline of a Theory of Practice*, translated by Richard Nice. Cambridge: Cambridge University Press.

———. 1991. "Genesis and Structure of the Religious Field", translated by Jenny B.N. Burnside, Craig Calhoun and Leah Florence. *Comparative Social Research: A Research Annual*, vol 13: 1–44. Greenwich, CT: JAI Press. Originally published as "Gènese et Structure du Champ Religieux", *Revue français de Sociologie* 12 (1971): 295–334.

Bowie, Katherine. 2017. "Khruba Siwichai: The Charismatic Saint and the Northern Thai Sangha". In *Charismatic Monks*

of Lanna Buddhism, edited by Paul Cohen, pp. 27–57.
Copenhagen: NIAS; Chiang Mai: Silkworm Books.

Brac de la Perrière, Bénédicte. 2007. "To Marry a Man or a Spirit?:
Women, the Spirit Possession Cult, and Domination in
Burma". In *Women and the Contested State: Religion, Violence
and Agency in South and Southeast Asia*, edited by M.
Skidmore and P. Lawrence, pp. 208–28. Notre Dame, IN:
University of Notre Dame Press.

———. 2009. "An Overview of the Field of Religion in Burmese
Studies". *Asian Ethnology* 68, no. 2: 185–210.

———. 2011. "Being a Spirit Medium in Contemporary Burma".
In *Engaging the Spirit World: Popular Beliefs and Practices
in Modern Southeast Asia*, edited by Kirsten W. Endres and
Andrea Lauser, pp. 164–83. New York: Berghahn.

———. 2016. "Spirit Possession: An Autonomous Field of Practice
in the Burmese Buddhist Culture". *Journal of Buddhist Studies*
20, no. 1: 1–29.

———. 2017. "Initiations in the Burmese Ritual Landscape". *Journal
of Ethnology and Folkloristics* 11, no. 1: 65–82.

Brac de la Perrière, Bénédicte, and Cristophe Munier Gaillard. 2019.
Bobogyi: A Burmese Spiritual Figure. Bangkok: River Books.

Brac de la Perrière, Bénédicte, and Peter A. Jackson, eds. 2022.
*Spirit Possession in Buddhist Southeast Asia: Worlds Ever More
Enchanted*. Copenhagen: NIAS Press.

Brac de la Perrière, Bénédicte, Guillaume Rozenberg and Alicia
Turner, eds. 2014. *Champions of Buddhism: Weikza Cults in
Contemporary Burma*. Singapore: NUS Press.

Butler, Judith. 1988. "Performative Acts and Gender Constitution:
An Essay in Phenomenology and Feminist Theory". *Theatre
Journal* 40, no. 4: 519–31.

———. 1993. *Bodies That Matter: On the Discursive Limits of "Sex"*.
New York: Routledge.

———. 1997. *Excitable Speech: A Politics of the Performative*. New
York: Routledge.

Carrithers, Michael. 2000. "On Polytropy: Or the Natural Condition
of Spiritual Cosmopolitanism in India, the Digambir Jain
Case". *Modern Asian Studies* 34, no. 4: 831–61.

Chakrabarty, Dipesh. 2000. *Provincializing Europe: Postcolonial*

Thought and Historical Difference. Princeton, NJ: Princeton University Press.

Chalong Soontravanich. 2013. "The Regionalisation of Local Buddhist Saints: Amulets, Crime and Violence in Post–World War II Thai Society". *SOJOURN: Journal of Social Issues in Southeast Asia* 28, no. 2: 179–215.

Chau, Adam Yuet. 2011. "Modalities of Doing Religion and Ritual Polytropy: Evaluating the Religious Market Model from the Perspective of Chinese Religious History". *Religion* 41, no. 4: 547–68.

Chiwa-prawat lae phra khatha jao mae Kuan Im phothisat [The biography and incantations of the Bodhisattva Lord Mother Kuan Im]. [1997?] (BE 2540). Bangkok: Samnak-phim Lan Asok Press Group.

Chua, Lawrence. 2018. "A Tale of Two Crematoria: Funeral Architecture and the Politics of Representation in Mid-Twentieth Century Bangkok". *Journal of the Society of Architectural Historians* 77, no. 3: 319–38.

Clammer, John. 2000. "In but Not Of the World? Japan, Globalisation and the 'End of History'". In *Demystifying Globalisation*, edited by Colin Hay and David Marsh, pp. 147–67. London: MacMillan.

Clark, John. 2011. "Icon and Image in Modern Thai Art: A Preliminary Exploration". Special issue, *Contemporary Aesthetics*, no. 3. http://hdl.handle.net/2027/spo.7523862. spec.306.

Cohen, Erik. 2001. *The Chinese Vegetarian Festival in Phuket: Religion, Ethnicity and Tourism on a Southern Thai Island*. Bangkok: White Lotus Press.

———. 2008. "Kuan To: The Vegetarian Festival in a Peripheral Southern Thai Shrine". In *Religious Commodifications in Asia: Marketing Gods*, edited by Pattana Kitiarsa, pp. 68–88. New York: Routledge.

Comaroff, Jean. 1994. "Epilogue: Defying Disenchantment: Reflections on Ritual, Power and History". In *Asian Visions of Authority: Religion and the Modern States of East and Southeast Asia*, edited by Charles F. Keyes, Lauren Kendall and Helen Hardacre, pp. 301–14, Honolulu: University of Hawai'i Press.

Comaroff, Jean, and John L. Comaroff. 1999. "Occult Economies and the Violence of Abstraction: Notes from the South African Postcolony". *American Ethnologist* 26: 279–301.

———. 2000. "Millennial Capitalism: First Thoughts on a Second Coming". *Public Culture* 12, no. 2: 291–343.

———. 2002. "Alien-Nation: Zombies, Immigrants, and Millennial Capitalism". *South Atlantic Quarterly* 101, no. 4: 779–805.

———. 2018. "Occult Economies, Revisited". In *Capitalism: Enchantment, Spells, and Occult Practices in Contemporary Economies*, edited by Brian Moeran and Timothy de Waal Malefyt, pp. 289–320. Cham, Switzerland: Palgrave Macmillan.

Comaroff, Jean, and David Kyuman Kim. 2011. "Anthropology, Theology, Critical Pedagogy: A Conversation with Jean Comaroff and David Kyuman Kim". *Cultural Anthropology* 26, no. 2: 158–78.

Condominas, Georges. 1976. "Quelques Aspects du Chamanisme et des Cultes de Possession en Asie du Sud-Est et dans le Monde Insulindien". In *L'autre et l'ailleurs: Homages à Roger Bastide*, edited by J. Poirier and F. Raveau, pp. 215–32. Nice: Institut d'études et de recherches interethniques et interculturelles.

Cook, Nerida. 1989. *Astrology in Thailand: The Future and the Recollection of the Past*. PhD dissertation, Australian National University.

———. 1992. "A Tale of Two City Pillars: Mongkut and Thai Astrology on the Eve of Modernisation". In *Patterns and Illusions: Thai History and Thought*, edited by Gehan Wijeyewardene and E.C. Chapman, pp. 279–312. Canberra: Australian National University; Singapore: Institute of Southeast Asian Studies.

Cornwel-Smith, Philip. 2013. *Very Thai: Everyday Popular Culture*, 2nd ed. Bangkok: River Books.

Crawford, T. Hugh. 1994. "Book Review: We Have Never Been Modern". *Configurations* 2, no. 3: 578–80.

Daston, Lorraine, and Katherine Park. 1998. *Wonders and the Order of Nature: 1150–1750*. New York: Zone Books.

De Heusch, Luc. 1962. "Cultes de Possession et Religions Initiatiques de Salut en Afrique". *Annales du Centre d'Études des Religions*, no. 2: 226–44.

Derrida, Jacques. 1988. "Signature Event Context", translated by Samuel Weber and Jeffrey Mehlman. In *Limited Inc.*, by Jacques Derrida, pp. 1–23. Evanston, IL: Northwestern University Press.

Descola, Philippe. 2005. *Par-delà nature et culture*. Paris: Gallimard.

(*Phra*) Dhammapitaka (*Prayuth Payuttho*). 1997 (BE 2540). *Tha yak phon wikrit torng loek tit saiyasat* [If we want to overcome the crisis we must abandon our attachment to *saiyasat*]. Bangkok: Korng-thun Wutthitham.

Dirlik, Arif. 2005. "The End of Colonialism? The Colonial Modern in the Making of Global Modernity". *boundary 2*, 32, no. 1: 1–31.

Easum, Taylor M. 2013. "A Thorn in Bangkok's Side: Khruba Sriwichai, Sacred Space and the Last Stand of the Pre-modern Chiang Mai State". *South East Asia Research* 21, no. 2: 211–36.

Eisenstadt, Shmuel Noah. 2000. "Multiple Modernities". *Daedalus* 129, no. 1: 1–29.

Ek Angsanon. 2011 (BE 2554). *Phra di tamruat dang* [Auspicious amulets of famous policemen]. Bangkok: Matichon.

Endres, Kirsten W. 2011. *Performing the Divine: Mediums, Markets and Modernity in Urban Vietnam*. Copenhagen: NIAS Press.

Endres, Kirsten, and Andrea Lauser, eds. 2011. *Engaging the Spirit World: Popular Beliefs and Practices in Modern Southeast Asia*. New York: Berghahn Books.

Evers, Hans-Dieter, and Sharon Siddique. 1993. "Religious Revivalism in Southeast Asia: An Introduction". *SOJOURN: Journal of Social Issues in Southeast Asia* 8, no. 1: 1–10.

Fjelstad, Karen, and Nguyen Thi Hien. 2011. *Spirits without Borders: Vietnamese Spirit Mediums in a Transnational Age*. New York: Palgrave Macmillan.

Foard, James H. n.d. "Position Paper Prepared for the Workshop 'States of Change: Religion in East and Southeast Asia'". Boston, April 1987. Cited by Keyes et al. 1994.

Formoso, Bernard. 2010. *De-Jiao – A Religious Movement in Contemporary China and Overseas: Purple Qi from the East*. Singapore: NUS Press.

———. 2016. "Thai Buddhism as the Promoter of Spirit Cults". *South East Asia Research* 24, no. 1: 119–33.

Foucault, Michel. 1994. *The Order of Things: An Archaeology of the Human Sciences*. New York: Vintage Books.

Freud, Sigmund. 1955. *The Uncanny in Art and Literature*, 2nd ed. London: Penguin Books.

Fuck Ghost (pseud.). 2016. *Fuck Ghost: Samakhom tor-tan sing ngom-ngai* [Fuck Ghost: The society against ignorant blind faith]. Bangkok: Mars Space.

Fuhrmann, Arnika. 2016. *Ghostly Desires, Queer Sexuality and Vernacular Buddhism in Contemporary Thai Cinema*. Durham, NC: Duke University Press.

Fukuura, Kazuo. 2011. "A Ritual Community: The Religious Practices of Spirit Mediums Who Worship the Spirit of the Chiang Mai City Pillar". *SOJOURN: Journal of Social Issues in Southeast Asia* 26, no. 1: 105–27.

Funahashi, Daena. 2017. "In the Name of the People: Magic and the Enigma of Health Governance in Thailand". *Kyoto Review of Southeast Asia*, no. 22. https://kyotoreview.org/issue–22/thai-cosmic-politics-locating-power-in-a-diverse-kingdom/ (accessed 8 September 2017).

Gane, Mike. 1991. *Baudrillard: Critical and Fatal Theory*. London: Routledge.

Gane, Nicholas. 2002. *Max Weber and Postmodern Theory: Rationalization versus Re-enchantment*. New York: Palgrave.

Geertz, Clifford. 1973. "'Internal Conversion' in Contemporary Bali". In *The Interpretation of Cultures: Selected Essays*, by Clifford Geertz, pp. 360–411. New York: Basic Books.

Gellner, David N. 2017. "Afterword: So What Is the Anthropology of Buddhism About?" *Religion and Society: Advances in Research* 8: 203–9.

Giddens, Anthony. 1990. *The Consequences of Modernity*. Cambridge: Polity Press.

Goh, Beng-Lan. 2011. "Spirit Cults and Construction Sites: Trans-Ethnic Popular Religion and Keramat Symbolism in Contemporary Malaysia". *Engaging the Spirit World: Popular Beliefs and Practices in Modern Southeast Asia*, edited by Kirsten W. Endres and Andrea Lauser, pp. 144–62. New York: Berghahn Books.

Golomb, Louis. 1985. *An Anthropology of Curing in Multiethnic Thailand*. Urbana: University of Illinois Press.

Gombrich, Richard F. 1971. *Precept and Practice: Traditional Buddhism in the Rural Highlands of Ceylon*. Oxford: Oxford University Press.

Gong, Gerrit W. 1984. *The Standard of 'Civilisation' in International Society*. Oxford: Clarendon Press.

Gottowik, Volker. 2014. "Preface & Introduction". In *Dynamics of Religion in Southeast Asia: Magic and Modernity*, edited by Volker Gottowik, pp. 7–29. Amsterdam: Amsterdam University Press.

Gray, Christine E. 1986. *Thailand: The Soteriological State in the 1970s*. PhD dissertation, Faculty of the Division of Social Sciences, University of Chicago.

———. 1991. "Hegemonic Images: Language and Silence in the Royal Thai Polity". *Man* 26, no. 1: 43–65.

———. 1992. "Royal Words and their Unroyal Consequences". *Cultural Anthropology* 7, no. 4: 448–63.

———. 1995. "Buddhism as a Language of Images: Transtextuality as a Language of Power". *Word and Image: A Journal of Verbal/ Visual Inquiry* 11, no. 3: 225–36.

Hamilton, Gary G., and Tony Waters. 1997. "Ethnicity and Capitalist Development: The Changing Role of the Chinese in Thailand". In *Essential Outsiders: Chinese and Jews in the Modern Transformations of Southeast Asia and Central Europe*, edited by Daniel Chirot and Anthony Reid, pp. 258–84. Seattle: University of Washington Press.

Hanegraaff, Wouter J. 2011. "How Magic Survived the Disenchantment of the World". *Religion* 33, no. 4: 357–80.

Harrison, Rachel V., and Peter A. Jackson, eds. 2010. *The Ambiguous Allure of the West: Traces of the Colonial in Thailand*. Hong Kong: Hong Kong University Press.

Harvey, David. 2005. *A Brief History of Neoliberalism*. New York: Oxford University Press.

Hefner, Robert W. 2010. "Religious Resurgence in Contemporary Asia: Southeast Asian Perspectives on Capitalism, the State, and the New Piety". *Journal of Asian Studies* 69, no. 4: 1031–47.

———. 2017. "Epilogue: Capitalist Rationalities and Religious Moralities – An Agonistic Plurality". In *New Religiosities, Modern Capitalism, and Moral Complexities in Southeast*

Asia, edited by Juliette Koning and Gwenaël Njoto-Feillard, pp. 265–85. Singapore: IRASEC/Palgrave Macmillan.

Heine-Geldern, Robert. 1942. "Conceptions of State and Kingship in Southeast Asia". *Far Eastern Quarterly* 2, no. 1: 15–30.

Heinze, Ruth-Inge. 1988. *Trance and Healing in Southeast Asia Today*. Bangkok: White Lotus.

Herzfeld, Michael. 2016. *Cultural Intimacy: Social Poetics in the Nation State*. New York: Routledge.

Hewison, Kevin. 1993. "Of Regimes, State and Pluralities: Thai Politics Enters the 1990s". *Southeast Asia in the 1990s: Authoritarianism, Democracy and Capitalism*, edited by Kevin Hewison, Richard Robison and Gary Rodan, pp. 161–89. St Leonards, Australia: Allen & Unwin.

Hirsch, Philip, ed. 1996. *Seeing Forests for Trees: Environment and Environmentalism in Thailand*. Chiang Mai: Silkworm Books.

Hollywood, Amy. 2002. "Performativity, Citationality, Ritualization". *History of Religions* 42, no. 2: 93–115.

Holt, John, 2011. *Spirits of the Place. Buddhism and Lao Religious Culture*. Chiang Mai: Silkworm Books.

Hughes-Freeland, Felicia, and Mary M.Crain, eds. 1998. *Recasting Ritual: Performance, Media, Identity*. London: Routledge.

Ip, David. 1999. "The Asian Financial Crisis: Responses of Chinese Diaspora Capitalism". *IIAS Newsletter*, no. 19 (June): 29.

Irvine, Walter. 1984. "Decline of Village Spirit Cults and Growth of Urban Spirit Mediumship: The Persistence of Spirit Beliefs and the Position of Women and Modernization". Special issue, "Spirit Cults and the Position of Women in Northern Thailand", *Mankind* 14, no. 4: 315–24.

Ishii, Yoneo. 1986. *Sangha, State and Society: Thai Buddhism in History*, translated by Peter Hawkes. Honolulu: University of Hawai'i Press.

Israeli, Noam. 2005. "Reflections on Freud's 'The Uncanny'". *Journal of the Society of Existential Analysis* 16, no. 2: 378–89.

Ito, Tomomi. 2012. *Modern Thai Buddhism and Buddhadāsa Bhikkhu: A Social History*. Singapore: NUS Press.

Jackson, Peter A. 1988. "The Hupphaasawan Movement: Millenarian Buddhism among the Thai Political Elite". *SOJOURN: Journal of Social Issues in Southeast Asia* 3, no. 2: 134–70.

———. 1989. *Buddhism, Legitimation and Conflict – The Political*

Functions of Urban Thai Buddhism. Singapore: Institute of Southeast Asian Studies.

————. 1997. "Withering Centre, Flourishing Margins: Buddhism's Changing Political Roles". In *Political Change in Thailand: Democracy and Participation*, edited by Kevin Hewison, pp. 75–93. London: Routledge.

————. 1999a. "The Enchanting Spirit of Thai Capitalism: The Cult of Luang Phor Khoon and the Postmodernisation of Thai Buddhism". *South East Asia Research* 7, no. 1: 5–60.

————. 1999b. "Royal Spirits, Chinese Gods and Magic Monks: Thailand's Boom Time Religions of Prosperity". *South East Asia Research* 7, no. 3: 245–320.

————. 1999c. "Thailand's Culture Wars: Economic Crisis, Resurgent Doctrinalist Buddhism and Critiques of Religions of Prosperity". Paper presented at the 7th International Conference on Thai Studies, Amsterdam, 4–8 July 1999.

————. 2003. *Buddhadasa: Theravada Buddhism and Modernist Reform in Thailand*. Silkworm Books, Chiang Mai.

————. 2004a. "The Thai Regime of Images". *SOJOURN: Journal of Social Issues in Southeast Asia* 19, no. 2: 181–218.

————. 2004b. "The Performative State: Semicoloniality and the Tyranny of Images in Modern Thailand". *SOJOURN: Journal of Social Issues in Southeast Asia* 19, no. 2: 40–74.

————. 2009. "Markets, Media, and Magic: Thailand's Monarch as a 'Virtual Deity'". *Inter-Asia Cultural Studies* 10, no. 3: 361–80.

————. 2016. "The Supernaturalisation of Thai Political Culture: Thailand's Magical Stamps of Approval at the Nexus of Media, Market and State". *SOJOURN: Journal of Social Issues in Southeast Asia* 31, no. 3: 826–79.

Jackson, Peter A., and Benjamin Baumann, eds. 2021. *Deities and Divas: Queer Ritual Specialists in Myanmar, Thailand and Beyond*. Copenhagen: NIAS Press.

Jenkins, Richard. 2000. "Disenchantment, Enchantment and Re-Enchantment: Max Weber at the Millennium". *Max Weber Studies* 1: 11–32.

Johnson, Andrew A. 2014. *Ghosts of the New City: Spirits, Urbanity and the Ruins of Progress in Chiang Mai*, Honolulu: University of Hawai'i Press.

————. 2015. "A Spirit Map of Bangkok: Spirit Shrines and the City in Thailand". *Journal for the Academic Study of Religion* 28, no. 3: 293–308.

———. 2016. "Dreaming about the Neighbours: Magic, Orientalism, and Entrepreneurship in the Consumption of Thai Religious Goods in Singapore". *South East Asia Research* 24, no. 4: 445–61.

———. 2017. "Land and Lordship: Royal Devotion, Spirit Cults and the Geobody". *Kyoto Review of Southeast Asia*, no. 22. https://kyotoreview.org/issue–22/thai-cosmic-politics-locating-power-in-a-diverse-kingdom/ (accessed 8 September 2017).

Johnson, Paul Christopher. 1997. "'Rationality' in the Biography of a Buddhist King: Mongkut, King of Siam (r. 1851–1868)". In *Sacred Biography in the Buddhist Traditions of South and Southeast Asia*, edited by Juliane Schober, pp. 232–55. Honolulu: University of Hawai'i Press.

Jones, David Martin. 1995. "Post-Modernity and Political Science: A Contradiction in Terms". Special issue, *SOJOURN: Journal of Social Issues in Southeast Asia* 10, no. 1: 7–32.

Jory, Patrick. 2016. *Thailand's Theory of Monarchy: The Vessantara Jātaka and the Idea of the Perfect Man*. Albany, NY: SUNY Press.

Kapferer, Bruce. 2002. "Outside all Reason: Magic, Sorcery and Epistemology in Anthropology". *Social Analysis: The International Journal of Social and Cultural Practice* 46, no. 3: 1–30.

Kasian Tejapira. 1997. "Imagined Uncommunity: The Lookjin Middle Class and Thai Official Nationalism". In *Essential Outsiders: Chinese and Jews in the Modern Transformation of Southeast Asia and Central Europe*, edited by Daniel Chirot and Anthony Reid, pp. 75–98. Seattle: University of Washington Press.

———. 2001. *Commodifying Marxism: The Formation of Modern Thai Radical Culture, 1927–1958*. Kyoto: Kyoto University Press.

Kataoka, Tatsuki. 2012a. "Introduction: De-institutionalising Religion in Southeast Asia". *Southeast Asian Studies* (Center for Southeast Asian Studies, Kyoto University) 1, no. 3: 361–63.

———. 2012b. "Religion as Non-Religion: The Place of Chinese Temples in Phuket, Southern Thailand". *Southeast Asian*

Studies (Center for Southeast Asian Studies, Kyoto University) 1, no. 3: 461–85.

Keyes, Charles F. 1995. "Moral Authority of the Sangha and Modernity in Thailand: Sexual Scandals, Sectarian Dissent, and Political Resistance". Paper presented at the conference on "Buddhism, Modernity and Politics in Southeast Asia", Arizona State University, 8 December 1995.

———. 2006. "The Destruction of a Shrine to Brahma in Bangkok and the Fall of Thaksin Shinawatra: The Occult and the Thai Coup in Thailand of September 2006". Asia Research Institute Working Paper Series no. 80. Singapore: Asia Research Institute

Keyes, Charles F., Lauren Kendall and Helen Hardacre. 1994. "Introduction: Contested Visions of Community in East and Southeast Asia". In *Asian Visions of Authority: Religion and the Modern States of East and Southeast Asia*, edited by Charles F. Keyes, Lauren Kendall and Helen Hardacre, pp. 1–16. Honolulu: University of Hawai'i Press.

Khao sot. 2010. *Phra di khon dang* [Auspicious amulets of famous people]. Bangkok: Matichon.

Kirsch, A. Thomas. 1977. "Complexity in the Thai Religious System: An Interpretation". *Journal of Asian Studies* 36, no. 2: 241–66.

Klima, Alan. 2002. *The Funeral Casino: Meditation, Massacre, and Exchange with the Dead in Thailand*. Princeton: Princeton University Press.

———. 2006. "Spirits of 'Dark Finance' in Thailand: A Local Hazard for the International Moral Fund". *Cultural Dynamics* 18, no. 1: 33–60.

Klum Bua Hima (pseud. "Snow Lotus Group"). 1993. *Kamnoet aphinihan jao mae Kuan Im* [The origins of the miracles of Lord Mother Kuan Im]. Bangkok: Samnak-phim MBA.

Knee, Adam. 2005. "Thailand Haunted: The Power of the Past in Contemporary Thai Horror Film". In *Horror International*, edited by Steven J. Schneider and Tony Williams, pp. 141–59. Detroit, MI: Wayne State University Press.

Krirkkiat Phiphatseritham and Kunio Yoshihara. 1983. *Business Groups in Thailand*. Singapore: Institute of Southeast Asian Studies.

Ladwig, Patrice, and Paul Williams. 2012. "Introduction: Buddhist Funeral Cultures". In *Buddhist Funeral Cultures of Southeast*

Asia and China, edited by Patrice Ladwig and Paul Williams, pp. 1–19. Cambridge: Cambridge University Press.

Latour, Bruno. 1993. *We Have Never Been Modern*, translated by Catherine Porter. Cambridge, MA: Harvard University Press.

Lauser, Andrea. 2018. *Staging the Spirits: Len Dong – Cult – Culture – Spectacle: Performative Contexts of a Vietnamese Ritual from Controlled Possession to Staged Performance*, Occasional Paper no. 20. Göttingen: Göttingen Institute for Social and Cultural Anthropology.

Lee, Raymond L.M. 1993. "The Globalisation of Religious Markets: International Innovations, Malaysian Consumption". *SOJOURN: Journal of Social Issues in Southeast Asia* 8, no. 1: 35–61.

———. 2010. "Weber, Re-enchantment and Social Futures". *Time Society* 19, no. 2: 180–92.

Lee, Raymond L.M., and Susan E. Ackerman. 2018. *The Challenge of Religion after Modernity: Beyond Disenchantment*. Abingdon, UK: Routledge Revivals.

Lehman, F.K. (F.K.L. Chit Hlaing). 2003. "The Relevance of the Founders' Cult for Understanding the Political Systems of the Peoples of Northern Southeast Asia and its Chinese Borderlands". In *Founders' Cults in Southeast Asia: Ancestors, Polity, and Identity*, edited by Nicola Tannenbaum and Cornelia Ann Kammerer, pp. 15–39. New Haven: Yale University Southeast Asian Studies.

Leithart, Peter J. 2014. "[Review of] *We Have Never Been Modern*". *First Things*, 19 December 2014. http://www.firstthings.com/web-exclusives/2014/12/we-have-never-been-modern (accessed 7 April 2017).

Luang Phor Khoon Parisuttho – 74 pi Khoon raksa [74 years of Luang Phor Khoon Parisuttho's Protection]. [1996?] (BE 2539). Bangkok.

Lyon, David. 2000. *Jesus in Disneyland: Religion in Postmodern Times*. Cambridge: Polity Press.

Mackenzie, Rory. 2007. *New Buddhist Movements in Thailand: Towards an Understanding of Wat Phra Dhammakaya and Santi Asoke*. New York: Routledge.

Malinowski, Bronislaw. 1935. *Coral Gardens and Their Magic: A Study of the Methods of Tilling the Soil and of Agricultural Rites in the Trobriand Islands*. London: Allen and Unwin.

Marty, Martin E., and R. Scott Appleby, eds. 1991. *Fundamentalisms Observed*. Chicago: Chicago University Press.

Maud, Jovan. 2007. *The Sacred Borderland: A Buddhist Saint, the State, and Transnational Religion in Southern Thailand*. PhD dissertation, Macquarie University, Sydney.

McCargo, Duncan. 1993. "The Three Paths of Major-General Chamlong Srimuang". *South East Asia Research* 1, no. 1: 27–67.

———. 1997. *Chamlong Srimuang and the New Thai Politics*. London: Hurst.

McDaniel, Justin Thomas. 2008. *Gathering Leaves and Lifting Words: Histories of Buddhist Monastic Education in Laos and Thailand*. Seattle: University of Washington Press.

———. 2011. *The Lovelorn Ghost and the Magical Monk: Practicing Buddhism in Modern Thailand*. New York: Columbia University Press.

———. 2013. "This Hindu Holy Man is a Thai Buddhist". *South East Asia Research* 21, no. 2: 191–209.

———. 2016. "SOJOURN Symposium, Review Essay II". *SOJOURN: Journal of Social Issues in Southeast Asia* 31, no. 3: 927–38.

McIntosh, Janet. 2019. "Polyontologism: When 'Syncretism' Does Not Suffice". *Journal of Africana Religions* 7, no. 1: 112–20.

Mérieau, Eugénie. 2018. "Buddhist Constitutionalism in Thailand: When Rājadhamma Supersedes the Constitution". *Asian Journal of Comparative Law* 16: 1–23.

Meyer, Birgit. 2003. "Ghanaian Popular Cinema and the Magic in and of Film". In *Magic and Modernity: Interfaces of Revelation and Concealment*, edited by Birgit Meyer and Peter Pels, pp. 200–222. Stanford: Stanford University Press.

Moeran, Brian, and Timothy de Waal Malefyt, eds. 2018. *Capitalism: Enchantment, Spells, and Occult Practices in Contemporary Economies*. Cham, Switzerland: Palgrave Macmillan.

Morris, Rosalind C. 1994. "Three Sexes and Four Sexualities: Redressing the Discourses on Gender and Sexuality in Thailand". *Positions* 2, no. 1: 15–43.

———. 1998. "Surviving Pleasure at the Periphery: Chiang Mai and the Photographies of Political Trauma in Thailand, 1976–1992". *Public Culture* 10, no. 2: 341–70.

———. 2000a. *In the Place of Origins: Modernity and its Mediums in Northern Thailand*. Durham, NC: Duke University Press.

———. 2000b. "Modernity's Media and the End of Mediumship? On the Aesthetic Economy of Transparency in Thailand". *Public Culture* 12, no. 2: 457–75.

———. 2002. "Failures of Domestication: Speculations on Globality, Economy, and the Sex of Excess in Thailand". *Differences: A Journal of Feminist Cultural Studies* 13, no. 1: 45–76.

Muecke, Marjorie A. 1992. "Monks and Mediums: Religious Syncretism in Northern Thailand". *Journal of the Siam Society* 80, no. 2: 97–104.

Mukhopadhyay, Bhaskar. 2006. "Cultural Studies and Politics in India Today". *Theory, Culture & Society* 23, nos. 7–8: 279–92.

Mulder, Niels. 1979. *Everyday Life in Thailand: An Interpretation*. Bangkok: Duang Kamol.

———. 1985. *Everyday Life in Thailand: An Interpretation*, 2nd ed. Bangkok: Editions Duang Kamol.

———. 1990. *Inside Thai Society – An Interpretation of Everyday Life*. Bangkok: Editions Duang Kamol.

———. 1996. *Inside Southeast Asia: Religion, Everyday Life, Cultural Change*. Amsterdam: The Pepin Press.

Nidhi Eeoseewong. 1991 (BE 2534). "Pheun-thi nai khati thai" [Space in Thai thought]. *Sinlapa-watthanatham* [Art and culture] 13, no. 2: 180–92.

———. 1993 (BE 2536). "Latthi-phithi sadet phor R. 5" [The cult of King Rama V]. Special issue, *Sinlapa-watthanatham* [Art and culture].

———. 1994 (BE 2537). "Latthi-phithi jao-mae Kuan Im" [The cult of Lord Mother Kuan Im (Guan Yin)]. *Sinlapa-watthanatham* [Art and culture] 15, no. 10: 79–106.

Obeyesekere, Gananath. 1967. "Social Change and the Deities: Rise of the Kataragama Cult in Modern Sri Lanka". *Man* 12: 377–96.

Ong, Aihwa. 1988. "The Production of Possession: Spirits and Multinational Corporations in Malaysia". *American Ethnologist* 15, no. 1: 28–42.

Ortner, Sherry B. 2016. "Dark Anthropology and its Others: Theory Since the Eighties". *HAU: Journal of Ethnographic Theory* 6, no. 1: 47–73.

Oughourlian, Jean-Michel. 1991. *The Puppet of Desire: The Psychology of Hysteria, Possession, and Hypnosis*, translated by Eugene Webb. Stanford: Stanford University Press.

P. Suwan. 1996. "Yak mi chok lap bucha Phra Siwali, phra arahan phu mi lap mak" [If you want good luck and fortune, worship Phra Siwali, the arahant who possessed great fortune]. Minburi: Samnak-phim Ban Mongkhon.

Pasuk Phongpaichit and Chris Baker. 1995. *Thailand: Economy and Politics*. Oxford: Oxford University Press.

———. 1998. *Thailand's Boom and Bust*. Chiang Mai: Silkworm Books.

Pasuk Phongpaichit and Sungsidh Piriyarangsan. 1994. *Corruption and Democracy in Thailand*. Bangkok: Chulalongkorn University Political Economy Centre, Faculty of Economics.

Pattana Kitiarsa. 2002. "'You May Not Believe, but Never Offend the Spirits': Spirit-Medium Cults and Popular Media in Modern Thailand". In *Global Goes Local: Popular Culture in Asia*, edited by Timothy J. Craig and Richard King, pp. 160–76. Vancouver: University of British Columbia Press.

———. 2005a. "Beyond Syncretism: Hybridisation of Popular Religion in Contemporary Thailand". *Journal of Southeast Asian Studies* 36, no. 3: 461–87.

———. 2005b. "Magic Monks and Spirit Mediums in the Politics of Thai Popular Religion". *Inter-Asia Cultural Studies* 6, no. 2: 209–26.

———. 2008a. "Introduction: Asia's Commodified Sacred Canopies". In *Religious Commodifications in Asia: Marketing Gods*, edited by Pattana Kitiarsa, pp. 1–12. London: Routledge.

———. 2008b. "Buddha Phanit: Thailand's Prosperity Religion and its Commodifying Practices". In *Religious Commodifications in Asia: Marketing Gods*, edited by Pattana Kitiarsa, pp. 120–44. London: Routledge.

———. 2011. "The Horror of the Modern: Violation, Violence, and Rampaging Urban Youths in Contemporary Thai Ghost Films". In *Engaging the Spirit World: Popular Beliefs and Practices in Modern Southeast Asia*, edited by Kirsten Endres and Andrea Lauser, pp. 200–220. New York: Berghahn Books.

———. 2012. *Mediums, Monks and Amulets: Thai Popular Buddhism Today*. Chiang Mai: Silkworm Books.

Peleggi, Maurizio. 2002. *Lords of Things: The Fashioning of the Siamese Monarchy's Modern Image*. Honolulu: University of Hawai'i Press.

Peltier, Anatole-Roger. 1977. *Introduction à la Connaissance des hlvñ ba1 [luang phor] de Thaïlande*. Paris: École Française d'Extrême-Orient.

(*Phra*) Phaisan Visalo. 1986 (BE 2529). *Phutthasasana Kap Khun-kha Ruam Samai* [Buddhism and contemporary values]. Bangkok: Munnithi Komon Khimthorng.

———. 2003 (BE 2546). *Phutthasasana Thai Nai Anakhot: Naeo-nom Lae Thang-ork Jak Wikrit* [Thai Buddhism in the future: Trends and the way out of the crisis]. Bangkok: Munnithi Sot-sri Saritwong.

Photjananukrom Khorng Than Phutthathat [Buddhadasa's Dictionary]. [2004?] (BE 2547). Bangkok: Thammasapha.

Pierucci, Antônio Flávio. 2000. "Secularisation in Max Weber: On the Current Usefulness of Re-assessing That Old Meaning". Special issue, *Brazilian Review of Social Sciences* 1: 129–58.

Poet Pratu Tamnak Song, Khu-meu Nae-nam Tamnak Song Radap Naeo-na Thua Meuang Thai No. 1 and No. 2 [Opening the door to spirit medium shrines, a handbook introducing leading spirit medium shrines from across Thailand, no. 1 and no. 2] [1998?] (BE 2541). Bangkok: Mahalap (prepared by the *Mahalap* "Special Project Team", *Mahalap thim ngan chaphor-kit*).

Pou, Saveros. 1991. "Sanskrit, Pāli and Khmero-Pāli in Cambodia". In *Panels of the VIIth World Sanskrit Conference*, edited by Johannes Bronkhorst, vol. 7, *Sanskrit Outside India*, edited by J.G. de Casparia, pp. 13–28. Leiden: Brill.

Preedee Hongsaton. 2018. "The Silver Guardian Demon of the Jungle: Modern Buddhism and the Suppression of the Shan Rebellion in Thailand, 1900s–1920s". *Warasan Prawattisat Thammasat* [Thammasat journal of history] 5, no. 2: 221–57.

Pressman, Douglas Harold. 1993. *Thai Modernity: A Study in the Sociology of Culture*. PhD dissertation, Department of Sociology, Brown University.

Rajagopal, Arvind. 2001. *Politics after Television: Hindu Nationalism and the Reshaping of the Public in India*. Cambridge: Cambridge University Press.

Ram Watcharapradit. 2007. (BE 2550) *Thepphajao haeng rattanakosin*

[The guardian angel of Rattanakosin]. *Khom Chat Leuk*, 9 April 2007, p. 31.

Rataporn Patamajorn. 2007. *Spirit Mediumship in Thailand: A Performance Theory Approach*. PhD dissertation, University of Heidelberg.

Rehbein, Boike, and Guido Sprenger. 2016. "Religion and Differentiation: Three Southeast Asian Configurations". In *Configurations of Religion, a Debate: A DORISEA Network Discussion Opened by Boike Rehbein and Guido Sprenger*, DORISEA Working Paper 24, edited by Peter J. Braünlein, Michael Dickhardt and Andrea Lauser, pp. 7–19. Georg-August-University Göttingen.

Reuter, Thomas, and Alexander Horstmann. 2013. "Religious and Cultural Revitalisation: A Post-modern Phenomenon?" In *Faith in the Future: Understanding the Revitalisation of Religions and Cultural Traditions in Asia*, edited by Thomas Reuter and Alexander Horstmann, pp. 1–14. Leiden: Brill.

Reynolds, Craig J. 1972. *The Buddhist Monkhood in Nineteenth Century Thailand*. PhD thesis, Cornell University.

———. 1976. "Buddhist Cosmography in Thai History — With Special Reference to Nineteenth Century Culture Change". *Journal of Asian Studies* 35, no. 2: 203–20.

———., ed. and trans. 1979. *Autobiography: The Life of Prince Patriarch Vajirañaṇa of Siam, 1860–1921*. Athens: Ohio University Press.

———. 1998. "Globalisation and Cultural Nationalism in Modern Thailand". In *Southeast Asian Identities: Culture and the Politics of Representation in Indonesia, Malaysia, Singapore and Thailand*, edited by Joel S. Kahn, pp. 115–45. Singapore: Institute of Southeast Asian Studies.

———. 2019. *Power, Protection and Magic in Thailand: The Cosmos of a Southern Policeman*. Canberra: Australian National University Press.

Reynolds, Frank. 1978. "Buddhism as Universal and Civic Religion in Laos and Burma". In *Religion and Legitimation of Power in Thailand, Laos and Burma*, edited by B. Smith, pp. 194–203. Chambersburg, PA: Anima Books.

Rigg, Jonathan, ed. 1995. *Counting the Costs: Economic Growth and Environmental Change in Thailand*. Singapore: Institute of Southeast Asian Studies.

Roberts, Richard H. 1995. "Introduction, Religion and Capitalism: A New Convergence?" In *Religion and the Transformations of Capitalism: Comparative Approaches*, edited by Richard H. Roberts, pp. 1–18. London: Routledge.

Rung-arun Kulthamrong. 2004 (BE 2547). "Phra Siam Thewathirat: Miti Watthanatham Thai" [Phra Siam Thewathirat: Dimensions of Thai culture]. *Nation Weekly*, 7 June 2004, *Phinit Thai* column, p. 78.

Ruth, Richard A. 2019. "Prince Abhakara's Experiences with Britain's Royal Navy: Education, Geopolitical Rivalries and the Role of a Cretan Adventure in Apotheosis". *SOJOURN: Journal of Social Issues in Southeast Asia* 34, no. 1: 1–47.

Saengphet [1994?] (BE 2537). *Itthipatihan watthu-mongkhon Luang Phor Khoon – thepphajao Dan Khun Thot* [The miraculous auspicious objects of Luang Phor Khoon – The Divine Lord of Dan Khun Thot]. Bangkok: Samnak-phim Trong Hua.

Sakserm Siriwong. [1998?] (BE 2541). *Thai Stamps 1998: Standard Catalogue of Thai Postage Stamps – Sataem thai 2541: khumeu kan-sasom sataem thai.* Bangkok: Siam Stamp Trading Company.

Salemink, Oscar. 2007. "The Emperor's New Clothes: Re-fashioning Ritual in the Hue Festival". *Journal of Southeast Asian Studies* 38, no. 3: 559–82.

———. 2008a. "Spirits of Consumption and the Capitalist Ethic in Vietnam". In *Religious Commodifications in Asia: Marketing Gods*, edited by Pattana Kitiarsa, pp. 147–68. London: Routledge

———. 2008b. "Embodying the Nation: Mediumship, Ritual, and the National Imagination". *Journal of Vietnamese Studies* 3, no. 3: 261–90.

———. 2010. "Ritual Efficacy, Spiritual Security". In *A World of Insecurity: Anthropological Perspectives on Human Security*, edited by Thomas Hyland Erikson, Ellen Bal and Oscar Salemink, pp. 262–89. London: Pluto Press.

Saler, Michael. 2006. "Modernity and Enchantment: A Historiographic Review". *American Historical Review* (June): 692–716.

Saowanee T. Alexander. 2018. "Red Bangkok? Exploring Political Struggles in the Thai Capital". *Critical Asian Studies* 50, no. 4: 647–53.

Saranyu Wongkrajang. 2011 (BE 2554). *Khon khon: tanha lae maya bon khwam-wijit haeng natakam, Saranyu Wongkrajang kamkap kan-sadaeng* [The Khon People: Lust and delusion amidst the beauty of classical dance drama, directed by Saranyu Wongkrajang]. Bangkok: Samnakphim Ban Athit.

Scott, Rachelle M. 2017. "Religion, Prosperity and Lottery Lore: The Linkage of New Religious Networks to Gambling Practices in Thailand". In *New Religiosities, Modern Capitalism, and Moral Complexities in Southeast Asia*, edited by Juliette Koning and Gwenaël Njoto-Feillard, pp. 223–45. Singapore: IRASEC/Palgrave Macmillan.

Seth, Sanjay. 2013. "'Once was Blind but Now Can See': Modernity and the Social Sciences. *International Political Sociology* 7: 136–51.

Siani, Edoardo. 2017. "Thai Cosmic Politics: Locating Power in a Diverse Kingdom". *Kyoto Review of Southeast Asia* 22. https://kyotoreview.org/issue–22/thai-cosmic-politics-locating-power-er-in-a-diverse-kingdom/ (accessed 8 September 2017).

———. 2018. "Stranger Diviners and their Stranger Clients: Popular Cosmology-Making and its Kingly Power in Buddhist Thailand". *South East Asia Research* 26, no. 4: 416–31.

Skilling, Peter. 2009. "King, Sangha and Brahmans: Ideology, Ritual and Power in Pre-modern Siam". In *Buddhism, Power and Political Order*, edited by Ian Harris, pp. 182–215. London: Routledge.

Smith, Pamela H. 2000. "Review of *Wonders and the Order of Nature: 1150–1750*, Lorraine Daston and Katherine Park. New York, Zone Books, 1998". *Configurations* 8, no. 3: 419–23.

Somboon Suksamran. 1982. *Buddhism and Politics in Thailand: A Study of Sociopolitical Change and Political Activism in the Thai Sangha*. Singapore: Institute of Southeast Asian Studies.

Somchai Saeng-ngern. 2008 (BE 2551). *Khu-meu sataem thai chabap sombun 2551 – Thai Stamps Catalogue 2008, Completed Edition*. Bangkok: Hobby International.

Somphong Amuay-ngerntra. 2007. "King Mongkut's Political and Religious Ideologies through Architecture at Phra Nakhon Kiri". *Manusya: Journal of Humanities* 10, no. 1: 72–88.

Soraj Hongladarom. 1996. "How is Thai Philosophy Possible?" Paper presented at the International Conference on Thai Studies, Chiang Mai University, 14–17 October 1996.

Sorrentino, Paul. 2022. "Whose Religion is the Cult of the Four Palaces? Genealogies of a Vietnamese Pantheon". In *Spirit Possession in Buddhist Southeast Asia: Worlds Ever More Enchanted*, edited by Bénédicte Brac de la Perrière and Peter A. Jackson. Copenhagen: NIAS Press.

Spiro, Melford E. 1970. *Burmese Supernaturalism: A Study in the Explanation and Reduction of Suffering*. Philadelphia: Institute for the Study of Human Issues.

———. 1978. *Burmese Supernaturalism: Expanded Edition*. Philadelphia: Institute for the Study of Human Issues.

Stengs, Irene. 1999. "A Cult between Patronage and Civil Society: King Chulalongkorn as an Imagination of the Ideal State". Paper presented to the 7th International Conference of Thai Studies, July 1999, Amsterdam.

———. 2009. *Worshipping the Great Moderniser: King Chulalongkorn, Patron Saint of the Thai Middle Class*. Singapore: NUS Press.

Stolow, Jeremy. 2005. "Religion and/as Media". *Theory, Culture & Society* 22, no. 4: 119–45.

Suchit Wongthet. 1987 (BE 2530). *Jek Pon Lao (Jor Por Lor)*. Bangkok: Samnak-phim Sinlapa Watthanatham.

Suntaree Komin and Snit Smuckarn. 1979 (BE 2522). *Kha-niyom lae rabop kha-niyom Thai: Khreuang-meu nai kan-samruat-wat* [Thai value systems: A measurement instrument]. Bangkok: National Institute of Development Administration (NIDA).

Tambiah, Stanley J. 1968. "The Ideology of Merit and the Social Correlates of Buddhism in a Thai Village". In *Dialectics in Practical Religion*, edited by Edmund Leach, pp. 41–121. Cambridge: Cambridge University Press.

———. 1970. *Buddhism and the Spirit Cults in North-east Thailand*. Cambridge: Cambridge University Press.

———. 1973. "Buddhism and This-worldly Activity". *Modern Asian Studies* 7, no. 1: 1–20.

———. 1976. *World Conqueror and World Renouncer: A Study of Buddhism and Polity in Thailand against a Historical Background*. Cambridge: Cambridge University Press.

———. 1977. "The Cosmological and Performative Significance of a Thai Cult of Healing through Meditation". *Culture, Medicine and Psychiatry* 1: 97–132.

———. 1978. "*Sangha* and Polity in Modern Thailand: An

Overview". In *Religion and Legitimation of Power in Thailand, Laos and Burma*, edited by Bardwell L. Smith, pp. 111–33. Chambersburg: Anima Books.

————. 1981. "A Performative Approach to Ritual: Radcliffe-Brown Lecture, 1979". *Proceedings of the British Academy* 65: 113–69.

————. 1984. *The Buddhist Saints of the Forest and the Cult of Amulets: A Study in Charisma, Hagiography, Sectarianism, and Millennial Buddhism*. Cambridge: Cambridge University Press.

————. 1985. *Culture, Thought and Social Action: An Anthropological Perspective*. Cambridge, MA: Harvard University Press.

————. 1990. *Magic, Science, Religion and the Scope of Rationality*. Cambridge: Cambridge University Press.

————. 2013. "The Galactic Polity in Southeast Asia". *HAU: Journal of Ethnographic Theory* 3, no. 3: 503–34.

Tanabe, Shigeharu. 2002. "The Person in Transformation: Body, Mind and Cultural Appropriation". In *Cultural Crisis and Social Memory: Modernity and Identity in Thailand and Laos*, edited by Shigeharu Tanabe and Charles F. Keyes, pp. 43–67. Honolulu: University of Hawai'i Press.

Taussig, Michael T. 1997. *The Magic of the State*. New York: Routledge.

Taylor, Philip. 2004. *Goddess on the Rise: Pilgrimage and Popular Religion in Vietnam*. Honolulu: University of Hawai'i Press.

Terwiel, Barend Jan. 1976. "A Model for the Study of Thai Buddhism". *Journal of Studies* 35, no. 3: 391–403.

————. 1979. *Monks and Magic: An Analysis of Religious Ceremonies in Central Thailand*. London: Curzon Press.

————. 2012. *Monks and Magic: Revisiting a Classic Study of Religious Ceremonies in Thailand*. Copenhagen: Nordic Institute of Asian Studies.

Thai Royal Institute. 2003 (BE 2546). *Photjananukrom Chabap Ratchabandittayasathan Phor. Sor. 2542* [Thai Royal Institute dictionary, BE 2542 edition]. Bangkok: Borisat Nanmi Books.

Thailand Post. (October–December) 2011a. "Trapraisaniyakorn chut phra benjaphakhi rian keji ajan – Miti mai sataem rian benjaphahki" [Set of five venerated monks amulets postage stamps: New dimension in stamps]. *Julasan Khao Sataem Thai* [Thai stamp bulletin] 4: 8–9.

Thailand Post. 2011b. "Phithi jaroen phraphutthamon pheua pen sirimongkhon kae trapraisaniyakorn" [Ritual chanting of Buddhist mantras to render stamps auspicious]. *Warasan trapraisaniyakorn* [Philatelic magazine] 45, no. 2: 34.

Thongchai Winichakul. 1994. *Siam Mapped: A History of the Geo-Body of a Nation*. Honolulu: University of Hawai'i Press.

———. 2000a. "The Quest for 'Siwilai': A Geographical Discourse of Civilisation Thinking in Late Nineteenth and Early Twentieth Century Siam". *Journal of Asian Studies* 59, no. 3: 528–49.

———. 2000b. "The Others Within: Travel and Ethno-spatial Differentiation of Siamese Subjects 1885–1910". In *Civility and Savagery: Social Identity in the Tai States*, edited by Andrew Turton, pp. 38–62. Richmond, Surrey: Curzon Press.

———. 2015. "Buddhist Apologetics and a Genealogy of Comparative Religion in Siam". *Numen* 62: 75–98.

Treitel, Corinna. 2004. *A Science for the Soul: Occultism and the Genesis of the German Modern*. Baltimore, MD: Johns Hopkins University Press.

Turner, Victor. 1967. *The Ritual Process: Structure and Anti-structure*. Chicago: Aldine.

Ünaldi, Serhat. 2014. "Politics and the City: Protest, Memory and Contested Space in Bangkok". In *Contemporary Socio-cultural and Political Perspectives on Thailand*, edited by Pranee Liamputtong, pp. 209–22. Dordrecht: Springer.

———. 2016. *Working Towards the Monarchy: The Politics of Space in Downtown Bangkok*. Honolulu: University of Hawai'i Press.

Van den Akker, Robin, Alison Gibbons and Timotheus Vermeulen, eds. 2017. *Metamodernism: Historicity, Affect and Depth after Postmodernism*. London: Rowman & Littlefield.

Vandergeest, Peter. 1993. "Hierarchy and Power in Pre-national Buddhist States". *Modern Asian Studies* 27, no. 4: 843–70.

Van Esterik, Penny. 1999. "Repositioning Gender, Sexuality, and Power in Thai Studies". In *Genders and Sexualities in Modern Thailand*, edited by Peter A. Jackson and Nerida M. Cook, pp. 275–89. Chiang Mai: Silkworm Books.

———. 2000. *Materializing Thailand*. Oxford: Berg.

Veal, Clare. 2013. "The Charismatic Index: Photographic Representations of Power and Status in the Thai Social

Order". *Trans Asia Photography Review* 3, no. 2. http://hdl.
handle.net/2027/spo.7977573.0003.207.

Vella, Walter F. 1978. *Chaiyo! King Vajiravudh and the Development of
Thai Nationalism.* Honolulu: University Press of Hawai'i.

Venn, Couze. 2007. "Cultural Theory and its Futures: Introduction".
Theory, Culture & Society 24, no. 3: 49–54.

Verellen, Franciscus. 2003. "The Twenty-four Dioceses and Zhang
Daoling: The Spatio-Liturgical Oranization of Early
Heavenly Master Taoism". In *Pilgrims, Patrons, and Place.
Localizing Sanctity in Asian Religions*, edited by Phyllis
Emily Granoff and Koichi Shinohara, pp. 15–61. Vancouver:
University of British Columbia Press.

Visisya Pinthongvijayakul. 2015. *Performing the Isan Subject: Spirit
Mediums and Ritual Embodiment in a Transitional Agrarian
Society.* PhD dissertation, Australian National University.

———. 2018. "Personhood and Political Subjectivity through Ritual
Enactment in Isan (Northeast Thailand)". *Journal of Southeast
Asian Studies* 49, no. 1: 63–83.

"Walk of Faith: Ratchaprasong Square Trade Association Invites You
to Visit 8 Gods in One Walk". *Thai Smile Inflight Magazine*,
July 2017, pp. 32–35.

Weller, Robert P. 1994. "Capitalism, Community and the Rise of
Amoral Cults". In *Asian Visions of Authority: Religion and the
Modern States of Southeast Asia*, edited by Charles F. Keyes,
Laurel Kendall and Helen Hardacre, pp. 141–64, Honolulu:
University of Hawai'i Press.

———. 2008. "Asia and the Global Economies of Charisma". In
Religious Commodifications in Asia: Marketing Gods, edited by
Pattana Kitiarsa, pp. 15–30. London: Routledge.

Wet Worawit. 1997 (BE 2540). *Phra aphinyajan mongkhon nam ngoen
sot* [The auspiciously named spiritual teachers, Ngoen and
Sot]. Bangkok: Samnak-phim Worawit.

White, Erick. 2014. *Possession, Professional Spirit Mediums, and the
Religious Fields of Late-Twentieth Century Thailand.* PhD
dissertation, Cornell University.

———. 2016. "Contemporary Buddhism and Magic". In
The Oxford Handbook of Contemporary Buddhism,
edited by Michael Jerryson. https://doi.org/10.1093/
oxfordhb/9780199362387.013.34.

————. 2017. "Rethinking Anthropological Models of Spirit Possession and Theravada Buddhism". *Religion and Society: Advances in Research* 8: 189–202.

————. 2022. "Rethinking Vernacular Religion across Mainland Southeast Asia". In *Spirit Possession in Buddhist Southeast Asia: Worlds Ever More Enchanted*, edited by Bénédicte Brac de la Perrière and Peter A. Jackson. Copenhagen: NIAS Press.

Winkel, Heidemarie. 2017. "Multiple Religiosities, Entangled Modernities and Gender: What is Different about Gender across Religious Cultures?" *Zeitschrift für Religion, Gesellschaft und Politik* 1: 89–109.

Wipha Jiraphaisan. 2007 (BE 2550). "Jatukham-Ramathep: sang-khom sattha lae mun-kha kan-talat" [Jatukham-Ramathep: Society, faith and market value]. *Sinlapa-watthanatham* [Art and culture] 28, no. 8: 81–99.

(*Phreutajan*) Wiphutthayokha Rattanarangsi. [1997?] (BE 2540). *Kret prawattisat lae khatha kiaw-kap rup mae nang kwak* [Historical notes and incantations of the image of Mother Nang Kwak]. Bangkok: Samnak-phim Lan Asok Press Group.

Wisan Thaosungnern. [2016?] (BE 2559). *Rian Yort Niyom Ngoen Lan To Ngoen To Thorng, Phoem x Khun x Ruay, khu-meu Sian* [The most popular million baht amulets, big silver big gold, increase x multiply x rich, amulet specialists handbook]. Nonthaburi: Samnakphim But-Boss Book Centre.

Wong, Deborah. 2001. *Sounding the Centre: History and Aesthetics in Thai Buddhist Performance*. Chicago: University of Chicago Press.

Wright, Michael. 2007 (BE 2550). *Tam ha thi ma khorng Jatukham-ramathep* [In search of the origins of Catu-gama-rama-deva]. *Sinlapa-watthanatham* [Art and culture] 28, no. 8: 101–5.

Yang, Mayfair Mei-hui. 2000. "Putting Global Capitalism in its Place: Economic Hybridity, Bataille and Ritual Expenditure". *Current Anthropology* 41, no. 4: 477–509.

Yee, Shirley. 1996. "Material Interests and Morality in the Trade of Thai Talismans". *Southeast Asian Journal of Social Science* 24, no. 2: 1–21.

Zehner, Edwin. 1990. "Reform Symbolism of a Thai Middle-Class Sect: The Growth and Appeal of the Thammakai Movement". *Journal of Southeast Asian Studies* 21, no. 2: 402–26.

Index

Honorifics have been placed in parentheses and ignored in listing names, so (*Luang Phor*) Khoon Parisuttho and (*Jao Mae*) Kuan Im, for example, will both be found under **K**. Page references in bold refer to figures. References in italics refer to a definition of the term. Numbers prefixed by "n" refer to notes.

About the Author

Peter A. Jackson is Emeritus Professor in Thai cultural history in the Australian National University's College of Asia and the Pacific. Over the past four decades, he has written extensively on religion, gender and sexuality in modern Thailand as well as critical approaches to Asian area studies. Peter's most recent books are *Deities and Divas: Queer Ritual Specialists in Myanmar, Thailand and Beyond* with Benjamin Baumann and *Spirit Possession in Buddhist Southeast Asia: Worlds Ever More Enchanted* with Bénédicte Brac de la Perrière. His ongoing research collaborations include studies of media and masculinity in Thai gay cultures and the significance of religion and ritual in Thai communities affected by HIV.

Milton Keynes UK
Ingram Content Group UK Ltd.
UKHW051833070224
437430UK00010B/1127